DISCIPLESHIP
—— *of* ——
EQUALS

Elisabeth Schüssler Fiorenza is the Krister Stendahl Professor of Divinity at the Harvard Divinity School. The first woman president of the Society of Biblical Literature (1987), she is best known for her book *In Memory of Her: A Feminist Reconstruction of Christian Origins* (1983). Among her other books are *The Book of Revelation: Justice and Judgment* (1984), *Bread Not Stone: The Challenge of Feminist Biblical Interpretation* (1986), *Revelation: Vision of a Just World* (1991), and *But She Said: The Rhetoric of Feminist Interpretation for Liberation* (1992). She is co-editor of the *Journal of Feminist Studies in Religion* and an editor of *Concilium*. Among the *Concilium* volumes she has edited are *Holocaust as Interruption: Concilium* 175 (with David Tracy), *Women: Invisible in Church and Theology: Concilium* 182 (with Mary Collins), and *Motherhood: Experience, Institution, Theology: Concilium* 206 (with Anne Carr).

DISCIPLESHIP

—— *of* ——

EQUALS

A Critical Feminist *Ekklēsia*-logy of Liberation

Elisabeth Schüssler Fiorenza

CROSSROAD · NEW YORK

1993

The Crossroad Publishing Company
370 Lexington Avenue, New York, NY 10017

Printed in the United States of America

Library of Congress Cataloging-in-Publication Data
Schüssler Fiorenza, Elisabeth, 1938–
    Discipleship of equals : a critical feminist ekklēsia-logy of
liberation / Elisabeth Schüssler Fiorenza.
      p. cm.
    ISBN 0-8245-1244-8 (pbk.)
    1. Feminist theology. 2. Feminism—Religious aspects—
Christianity.   I. Title.
BT83.55.S38 1993
261.8'344–dc20   92-31264
                                                          CIP

The lines from "Heroines" are reprinted from *A Wild Patience Has Taken Me
This Far, Poems 1978–1981,* by Adrienne Rich, by permission of the author
and W. W. Norton & Company, Inc. Copyright © 1981 by Adrienne Rich.

WISDOM HAS BUILT HERSELF A HOUSE
SHE HAS ERECTED HER SEVEN PILLARS.
SHE HAS SLAUGHTERED HER BEASTS, PREPARED HER WINE,
SHE HAS LAID HER TABLE.
SHE HAS DISPATCHED HER MAIDSERVANTS
AND PROCLAIMED FROM THE CITY'S HEIGHTS: . . .
"COME AND EAT MY BREAD,
DRINK THE WINE I HAVE PREPARED!
LEAVE YOUR FOLLY AND YOU WILL LIVE
WALK IN THE WAYS OF PERCEPTION."

Proverbs 9:1-4, 6

IN CELEBRATION AND GRATITUDE

TO THE WOMEN

OF THE FEMINIST MOVEMENT

IN THEOLOGY AND CHURCH

WRITE THE VISION DOWN
INSCRIBE IT ON TABLETS
TO BE EASILY READ.
FOR THERE IS STILL A VISION
FOR ITS OWN APPOINTED TIME,
EAGER FOR ITS OWN FULFILLMENT.
IT DOES NOT DECEIVE!
IF IT SEEMS TO TARRY, WAIT FOR IT;
IT WILL SURELY COME,
IT WILL NOT DELAY.

Habakkuk 2:2-3

Contents

ACKNOWLEDGMENTS

This book is dedicated to the strong, creative, and inspiring women of the feminist movements in theology and church whom I have had the privilege to meet and work with in the last twenty years or so. I want to thank especially the organizers and participants in my workshops, lectures, and conferences, and many more.

Periodically the mass media announce the "demise" of the women's movement in society and religion. Yet like Mary of Magdala, my sisters in Spirit and struggle testify to the movement's life-powers of resurrection. Such a witness would not be possible without the support, energy, solidarity, and friendship of so many women around the globe. I hope that this cartography of struggle and vision will inspire especially young women to join us in dreaming the dream of a world free of patriarchal oppression.

As always, I am very much indebted and grateful to Dr. Margaret Studier for her tireless work, unfailing support, and consummate care in preparing the manuscript. I am very privileged to have the backing of such a superb secretary and dedicated co-worker. I am indebted to Ann Millin and Katherine Messina for sorting through my published and unpublished essays identifying those that they found most interesting. I am grateful to Michelle Lelwica and Renee Fall for their stylistic and editorial assistance and Solveig Nielsen-Goodin for her proofreading assistance.

Thanks are also due to my editors at the Crossroad Publishing Company, George Lawler, who encouraged the proposal, and Frank Oveis, who has patiently waited for its incarnation through several years of delay. Frank's editorial suggestions and unflagging support have been invaluable.

I cannot adequately express my appreciation for Francis and

Chris Schüssler Fiorenza, who have staunchly supported me through the ups and downs of these struggles. They have not only left me the space and freedom necessary for doing my work but also spent their "quality time" with me when I most needed it. I am deeply grateful for their love, care, and friendship in the discipleship of equals.

CREDITS

Most of the chapters in this book have appeared in earlier versions. They have all been revised for publication here.

Chapter 1: Selections in translation from *Der vergessene Partner: Grundlagen, Tatsachen und Möglichkeiten der beruflichen Mitarbeit der Frau in der Heilssorge der Kirche*. Düsseldorf: Patmos Verlag, 1964.

Chapter 3: "Saints Alive Yesterday and Today," *Brooklyn Tablet*, December 7, 1972.

Chapter 5: "Feminist Theology as a Critical Theology of Liberation," *Theological Studies* 36 (1975): 606-26.

Chapter 6: "Women Apostles: The Testament of Scripture," in *Women and Catholic Priesthood: An Expanded Vision*. Ed. A. M. Gardiner. New York: Paulist Press, 1976, 94-102.

Chapter 7: "Feminist Spirituality, Christian Identity and the Catholic Vision," *National Institute for Campus Ministries Journal* 1 (1976): 29-34.

Chapter 9: "Toward a Liberating and Liberated Theology: Women Theologians and Feminist Theology in the United States" ("Für eine befreite und befreiende Theologie: Theologinnen und Feministische Theologie in den USA," *Konzilium* 8 [1978]: 287-94); Eng. version in *Concilium* 15 (1979): 22-32.

Chapter 10: "To Comfort or to Challenge: Theological Reflections," in *New Woman, New Church, New Priestly Ministry*. Ed. M. Dwyer. Rochester, N.Y.: Women's Ordination Conference, 1981.

Chapter 11: "You Are Not to Be Called Father: Early Christian History in a Feminist Perspective" *Cross Currents* 29 (1979): 301-19.

Chapter 12: "We Are Still Invisible: A Theological Analysis of the Study of Women and Ministry," in *Women and Ministry: Personal Experience and Future Hopes.* Ed. Doris Gottemoeller and Rita Hofbauer. Washington, D.C.: LCWR, 1981, 29–43.

Chapter 13: "Gather Together in My Name: Toward a Christian Feminist Spirituality," in *Women Moving Church.* Ed. Diann Neu and Maria Riley. Washington, D.C.: Center of Concern, 1982.

Chapter 14: Invocations in *Was Meinst du dazu, Gott? Gebete von Frauen.* Ed. Susanne Kahl-Passoth. GBT Sibenstern 485. Gütersloh: Gerd Mohn, 1984.

Chapter 15: "Patriarchal Structures and the Discipleship of Equals," *Probe* (NAWR tabloid) 10 (1983).

Chapter 17: "Claiming Our Authority and Power," in *The Teaching Authority of Believers, Concilium* 180 Ed. J. B. Metz and Edward Schillebeeckx. Edinburgh: T. & T. Clark, 1985, 45–53.

Chapter 18: "Breaking the Silence – Becoming Visible," in *Women: Invisible in Church and Theology. Concilium* 182. Ed. Elisabeth Schüssler Fiorenza and Mary Collins. Edinburgh: T. & T. Clark, 1985, 3–16.

Chapter 19: "Theology after the Synod: So Far So Bad." *Commonweal* (January 31, 1986): 144–46.

Chapter 20: "Commitment and Critical Inquiry," *Harvard Theological Review* 82 (1989): 1–11.

Chapter 22: "Daughters of Vision," in *Towards a Feminist Theology: Papers and Proceedings from a National Conference Called Together by MOW, National WATAC, Women-Church, August 18–20, 1989, Calaroy Centre, Sydney.* Ed. Elaine Lindsay. Helensburgh, Australia: The Conference Committee, 1990, 15–21.

Chapter 23: "The Ethics and Politics of Liberation" has appeared in Dutch as "Patricarchale mach schept verdeeldheden, Feministische verschilen geven ons kracht: De ethiek en politiek van bevrijding," in *Overhoeren, taarten en vrouwen die voorbijgaan.* Ed. Hedwig Meyer Wilmes and Lieve Troch. Kampen: J. H. Kok, 1992.

Chapter 24: "A Democratic Feminist Vision for a Different Society and Church" has appeared in Spanish as "Visión feminista para una sociedad o iglesia diferentes," in *La función de la teología en el futuro de América Latina: Simposio Internacional.* Ed. Armando J. Bravo. Mexico City: Universidad Iberoamericana, 1991, 216–37.

Introduction ————————

CARTOGRAPHY OF STRUGGLE

Your old shall dream dreams
and your young shall see visions
                                    —Joel 2:28

If someone dreams alone,
then it remains only a dream.
If many dream together
then this is the beginning,
the beginning of a new reality.
Dream our Dream.
                              —Author unknown[1]

Everything I write is for the sake of women.
                    —Hedwig Dohm

This book represents the cartography of my feminist theological struggles, the mapping of my attempts over the years to reclaim and rename women's spiritual powers in very concrete particular situations. It took a long time to realize my promise to publish these feminist theological essays. Again and again, I postponed the work because I was doubtful whether it was possible to frame this

---

1. Wenn eine alleine träumt,
   ist es nur ein Traum.
   Wenn viele gemeinsam träumen,
   so ist das der Begin,
   der Beginn einer neuen Wirklichkeit
   Träumt unsern Traum.

See Helga Kohler-Spiegel and Ursula Schachl-Raber, eds., *Wut und Mut: Feministisches Materialbuch für Religionsunterricht und Gemeindearbeit* (Munich: Kösel Verlag, 1991), 125.

1

collection of essays in a way that could move beyond their primary specific location within a Roman Catholic context so that these essays might also inspire women in other churches and religious communities in their particular struggles. Many of my students, for instance, who are members of "liberal" Protestant churches do not understand why I have spent so much time and energy in a church that is as blatantly patriarchal as the Roman Catholic denomination. Nevertheless, working in the past eight years in "liberal" Protestant institutions has not only taught me that patriarchal discrimination is ubiquitous, although it assumes different forms and shades. But it has also driven home that overt misogynism is sometimes easier to combat than its more implicit liberal versions.

This book is not meant to be a systematic topical discussion. Rather, it seeks to map chronologically the cartography of a particular feminist's struggles in church and theology. As such, it invites readers to reflect on their own history of struggle and vision. Such a chronological mapping of particular feminist struggles and voices seems especially pressing today in light of the growing societal and religious suppression of feminist thought and vision. Not only Roman Catholic women, but also women in high-church and low-church Protestant denominations, as well as women in the biblical religions of Judaism and Islam, are experiencing this religious repression of feminist ideas and the feminist movement. While the road maps of struggle must be charted differently in these three biblical religions, they nevertheless converge in showing an increase in the patriarchal powers of oppression. Meanwhile, the infiltration of "Goddess-religion" and of feminist spirituality movements by "new age" psychologism and spiritual consumerism indicates that like traditional biblical religions these forms of feminist religion are also not immune to the virus of capitalist patriarchy and its uses of religion for its own interests.

More than ever before, the women's movements in society and religion need a critical feminist analysis of patriarchal religious structures and a critical feminist theological articulation of liberation. By tracing my own unfolding journey of vision and struggle and by relating it to the collective struggle of women in theology and biblical religions, I seek to intervene in the contest over who has the right and authority to define and claim biblical religions. Without question, fundamentalist right-wing patriarchal elements often have the financial and institutional hegemony to do so. Moreover, while some feminists relinquish religion as hopelessly patriarchal, the Right claims the power to name and to define the "true" nature of biblical religions over and against liberation theologies. These well-financed and well-organized reactionary religious groups are often linked with right-wing financial and political institutions. They collaborate in the religious defense of capitalist patriarchy by bad-mouthing emancipatory movements and theologies in general and feminist theology and the feminist movement in particular, declaring them to be un-Christian and antichurch.

In such a context of struggle over the power of naming, the question is often asked of me: "Why don't you leave the church if you don't agree with the church's [i.e., the speaker's] opinion and teaching?" In the past years, I have encountered this challenge again and again from right-wing Catholics and feminists alike. However, to seriously entertain this question already concedes the power of naming to the reactionary forces insofar as it recognizes their ownership of biblical religions. I do not want to be misunderstood. I do not argue that feminists must remain members of biblical religions and churches that they experience as oppressive and dehumanizing. Rather, I argue that those of us who have experienced the liberating power of religion must claim this power as our own estate and inheritance.

Certainly, religious feminists must decide where they best spend their energy and talents in the struggle against religious patriarchy. Nonetheless, whether we decide to move into another religious denomination or choose not to belong to any religious institution at all, we can never surrender our claim to spiritual authority. Thus Christian feminists may not give up their religious authority to define biblical religion and the Christian church. We must never abandon our religious power to articulate a feminist religious vision of justice and liberation. Hence in this cartography of struggle, I seek to assert the power of feminist theological naming to transform patriarchal religions, a power that for centuries has been stolen from us and today is threatened again in various ways.

One way of stealing our religious power of self-naming involves the loss of historical memory. For instance, I am often asked by young students how I came to take up feminist studies in religion and from whom I have learned my brand of feminist liberation theology. They are surprised to learn that feminist theology did not exist during the time of my theological training. They are even more surprised to learn that white women have gained ground in theology only during the past thirty years, while women of color have become visible in theology only in the last fifteen years or so. Since many of my students have encountered feminist theology among the available curricular offerings in their college or seminary, they assume that such an opportunity has always existed and is available to everyone studying theology today. While such an assumption testifies to the institutional progress feminist studies in religion and theology have made, it also attests to the kind of historical forgetfulness that threatens to undermine this very progress.

In her book *Women of Ideas (And What Men Have Done to Them)*, Dale Spender, an Australian feminist scholar, argues that the absence of women's voices and their invisibility in intellectual history — as well as the experience that every feminist work has been received as if it emerged from nowhere — is fundamental to the perpetuation and hegemony of patriarchal power in the academy.[2] Feminist thinkers and artists disappear from historical records and consciousness because the continuation of patriarchy requires that feminist challenges to elite male power remain invisible and nonexistent. Generation after generation feminists again and again must reinvent the "wheel," so to speak, and with hard intellectual labor discover and re-create a critical feminist systemic analysis of patriarchy. Needless to say, the emancipatory intellectual history and creative vision of women in biblical religions have also suffered from historical forgetfulness. By constructing this cartography of the struggles for my own theological voice, I seek to prevent such a loss of theological consciousness and history.

This seems especially necessary when one realizes that the women's movement itself has sometimes contributed to the erasure of women's intellectual work when such work was deemed too "radical" or "unfitting" given the prevailing articulations of the movement's interests. Two examples of how the intellectual work of women has been "written out of history" by feminists themselves come to mind. Until 1980 the work of Matilda Joslyn Gage (1826–98) had been almost completely erased from feminist historical consciousness since it did not fit into the dominant framework for telling the history of the nineteenth-century women's suffrage movement. Such a standard framework for recounting the

---

2. Dale Spender, *Women of Ideas (And What Men Have Done to Them)* (London: ARK Paperbacks, 1983).

nineteenth-century women's suffrage movement was probably intentionally established by Susan B. Anthony and her biographer Ida Husted Harper. It conceptualizes and narrates the women's suffrage movement as a linear, unified struggle for the vote beginning with the Seneca Falls Convention in 1848 and ending in the victorious passage of the suffrage amendment in 1920.

> Following this line of reasoning it makes sense that the woman's movement would virtually end with the achievement of suffrage; there was no more work to do. . . . A woman like Gage does not fit into this standard historical analysis. She might be viewed as an interesting scholar who, unfortunately, put her primary energy into the side issue of the church. Or she could emerge as a malcontent who tried to block progress by opposing the merger [of the National Woman's Suffrage Association (NWSA) with the American Woman's Suffrage Association (AWSA) and the Woman's Christian Temperance Union (WCTU)] and is never heard from again after the union in 1890.[3]

Another example of how feminists write other feminist ideas and theories out of history is found in the evaluation of the intellectual work of the German feminist Hedwig Dohm (1833-1919), whose critical writings in many ways anticipate the feminist theoretical work of the past twenty years. Already in the last quarter of the nineteenth century, Dohm published critical analyses of Christian doctrinal positions on women, the oppression of women in the family, women's nature and privilege, the scientific emancipation of women, and antifeminist attacks on women. She also published a very comprehensive discussion of educational issues and ageism, entitled "The Mothers," which is devoted especially to older women.[4] One of her articles in *Sozialistische Monatshefte* has the title "The Rights of the Unborn Child," which is not an essay on birth control or abortion, but an argument for the rights of both unborn children and their mothers — their rights to a decent,

---

3. Sally Roesch Wagner, "Introduction," to Matilda Joslyn Gage, *Woman, Church & State: The Original Exposé of Male Collaboration against the Female Sex* (1893; reprinted Watertown, Mass.: Persephone Press, 1980), 38.
4. See works by Hedwig Dohm: *Was die Pastoren von den Frauen denken* (Berlin: Schlingmann, 1872; reprinted Zürich: Alta, 1977); *Der Jesuitismus im Hausstande: Ein Beitrag zur Frauenfrage* (Berlin: Wedekind & Schwieger, 1873); *Die wissenschaftliche Emanzipation der Frau* (Berlin: Wedekind & Schwieger, 1874; reprinted Zürich: Alta, 1977); *Der Frauen Natur und Recht: Eigenschaften und Stimmrecht der Frauen* (Berlin: Wedekind & Schwieger, 1876); *Die Antifeministen: Ein Buch der Verteidigung* (Berlin: F. Dümmler Verlag, 1902; reprinted Frankfurt: Verlag Arndstr., 1976); *Die Mütter: Beitrag zur Erziehungsfrage* (Berlin: S. Fischer Verlag, 1903); and several novels and a novella.

humane, and materially secure life, which must be guaranteed by the state.[5]

Unlike Matilda Joslyn Gage, Hedwig Dohm never belonged to a women's suffrage association; nor did she ever speak publicly at women's conventions or organize resistance to movement leadership. Instead, Dohm "fought with her pen." Nevertheless, her impressive intellectual work has been pushed aside even by feminists. It has been belittled as polemical, anecdotal, pamphleteering, apolitical, or individualist and has not been recognized as having the status of "theory." Renate Duelli-Klein sums up her case:

> In my view, one of the contributing causes to Dohm's erasure from history was the fact that she did not conveniently fit any one category: there was no group that aspired to claim her for itself, and thus continue to discuss her ideas after her death: the socialist wing of the women's movement found her suspiciously bourgeois; the radical wing was not at ease with her solitary life style and the liberal wing found her too radical for their reformist ideals.[6]

A second way in which patriarchal institutions control feminist intellectual work — work that can no longer be passed over in silence — is by redefining it and evaluating such work in terms of the dominant scale of patriarchal values. Numerous instances could be cited here, ranging from the media's identification of early feminism with "bra-burning," to their declaration every few years of the "demise" of the women's movement. Such a redefinition and patriarchal appropriation of feminism for public consumption serves to frighten women away from identifying themselves as feminists. Surveys have shown how successful such a strategy is: more than 69 percent of those polled will still not identify themselves explicitly as "feminists," although a high percentage of Americans identify with feminist values and policies.

The accusation of "reverse discrimination" is another instance of such scare tactics. After lectures I am often asked whether as a Christian I do not worry about injustice and domination that will be inflicted upon men by the ongoing cultural and ecclesial "matriarchal revolution." My response, that I will start to worry when women begin to control all the power in the world and in the

5. Hedwig Dohm, "Das Recht des Ungeborenen," *Sozialistische Monatshefte* 2 (1912): 746–49.
6. Renate Duelli-Klein, "Hedwig Dohm: Passionate Theorist," in *Feminist Theorists: Three Centuries of Key Women Thinkers,* ed. Dale Spender (New York: Pantheon Books, 1983), 178.

church, usually takes the audience off guard since the facile slogan of "reverse" sexism or racism conceals such power inequalities and suggests that the sexes or races share equal power and influence in modern society.

To be sure, to brush someone with the label of "radical feminism" has become a powerful weapon of patriarchal mind control in Christian circles. Whereas biblicist fundamentalist circles equate feminism with secular humanism, Roman Catholic reactionary discourses often equate it with "Gnosticism." Taking their cue from the pope and Cardinal Joseph Ratzinger, some of the American cardinals and bishops, and especially the right-wing Catholic press, have made "radical feminism" a scare word for many church women. However, many bishops who label "radical feminism" as *the* evil infecting the church today are not aware that the expression "radical feminism" usually has connotations in feminist literature quite different from those they generally associate with it. Theoretically, the "radical feminism" of the women's spirituality movements, for instance, has arguably more in common with the patriarchal "eternal woman" theology promulgated by the Vatican than it does with a feminist liberation theology: both the "radical" feminists and the Vatican appeal to a female nature – an appeal that assumes a metaphysical essence of woman. I do hope that the following essays will persuade readers that such a slanderous defamation and labeling of feminist theology resorts to the age-old method of vilifying those who, in the power of the Spirit, call the patriarchal church to conversion.

A third way of "stealing the power of naming from us" is to maintain patriarchal control over feminist theology and the feminist movement by defining feminism. The procedure of typecasting and "classifying" feminisms is often used in the interest of a "divide and conquer" strategy. Insofar as such a strategy seeks to position the different types of feminist theology (as it has defined them) vis-à-vis the bishops and the hierarchy, it not only ignores that some members of the hierarchy might be feminists, but it also arrogates to itself the position of judging feminist theologians as well as bishops. Indeed, precisely this strategy is illustrated in an article published in the influential Jesuit journal *America* by a relatively unknown diocesan theologian. The article's headline, "The Church and the Voices of Feminism," already suggests a "divide and conquer" tactic insofar as it assumes that the voices of feminism are not voices of the church.[7] The author defines feminism as "a movement dedicated to advancing and securing the appropriate roles (however understood) of women in church and society"[8] — a definition that declares patriarchal structures to be feminist, even those that engender exploitative "appropriate" roles for women. Although the author is well aware that neither "radical feminists" to the left nor conservative women to the right would agree with his definition, he nevertheless employs this method because it not only allows him to construe a scale of values for assessing the different types of feminism, but it also allows him to include antifeminist movements among them.

According to this article, "affirmative" feminism is represented by Phyllis Schlafly; Donna Steichen, author of *Ungodly Rage;* Ronda Chervin, consultant for the bishops' ill-fated letter on women; the Catholic Daughters of America; *Consortium Perfectae Caritatis;* and "Women for Faith and Family" under the leadership of Helen Hull Hitchcock. Next comes "corrective" feminism, which is less conservative than affirmative feminism but shares the same values. Besides Pope John XXIII, Jean Bethke Elshtain and the League of Women Voters are said to belong to this type. The National Council of Catholic Women and the National Conference of Catholic Bishops are said to tend toward corrective feminism.

The center of this feminist spectrum is taken by "reformist" feminism, which is a product of mainstream "equity" or liberal feminism represented by Betty Friedan and Gloria Steinem, among others, as well as the National Organization of Women, the National Women's Political Caucus, and the National Abortion Rights Action League. Mentioned among those who are advocating the "institutional advancement of women in the church but have been cautious about women's ordination"[9] are sisters Agnes Cunningham and Sara Butler, as well as German bishops Karl Lehmann and Walter Kasper.[10] Most U.S. Catholics are said to sympathize with this brand of feminism.

Whereas the author does not label the first three types of fem-

---

7. Rev. M. Francis Mannion, "The Church and the Voices of Feminism," *America* (October 5, 1991): 1–6.

8. Ibid., 2.

9. Ibid., 3.

10. Bishop Kasper has recently refused the *nihil obstat* to biblical scholar Sylvia Schroer, because of her feminist work. She is the first Roman Catholic woman to have been nominated to a chair in theology at a distinguished Roman Catholic faculty in Germany.

inism as radical, he does so for the next two types. By classifying
the first two antifeminist perspectives as feminist, the author man-
ages to displace the fourth type, "reconstructive" feminism from
the center and to brand it as radical. Reconstructive feminism is
not only shown to include almost all directions in Catholic feminist theology and the Catholic feminist movement, but it is also
said to incorporate Matthew Fox's Creation spirituality, Native
American spirituality, and New Age phenomena. Moreover, reconstructive feminism is said to have its intellectual roots in such
diverse persuasions as Marxism, socialism, utopianism, psychoanalysis, and modern liberation movements. Finally, the author
argues that reconstructive feminism is "uncompromisingly critical
of the inherited shape of human societies," identifying "patriarchy,
sexism, and racism as systemic to traditional cultures and the institutions of Judaism and Christianity." Unlike reformist feminism,
reconstructive feminism is supposedly not so much concerned
with "short term gains" for women. Rather, it is believed to seek a
radical reconstruction of society and church according to a model
of human interaction that is nonhierarchical, noncompetitive, and
ecologically sensitive.

The author's last type of feminism — "separatist" feminism — is
in feminist discourses generally understood as "radical" feminism.
In distinction to reformist feminism, separatist feminism, according to Mannion, no longer believes that existing social or religious
structures can be reformed.[11] In addition to its supposedly Marxist
and Socialist leanings, separatist feminism is said to be committed
to utopianism, deconstructionism, and cultural relativism. Its most
prominent advocates in the author's opinion include ex-Catholic
Mary Daly, ex-Protestants Carol Christ and Daphne Hampson, ex-
Mormon Sonia Johnson, and ex-Jew Starhawk among others. Often
such separatist feminists, who are said to have an enormous influence on reconstructive feminists, advocate ancient goddess
religions and the European tradition of witchcraft. Therefore, according to the author, a dialogue between separatist feminists and
bishops is not an option. One wonders why since official church
dialogues exist with atheists, Marxists, and other world religions.

That the purpose of this exercise is to indict reformist femi-

---

11. For a reconsideration of the split between reformist and radical feminism, cate-
gories that Judith Plaskow and Carol P. Christ used in *Womanspirit Rising*, see Judith
Plaskow and Carol P. Christ, eds., *Weaving the Visions: New Patterns in Feminist
Spirituality* (San Francisco: Harper & Row, 1989), 6–7.

nism becomes obvious when the author states that "reconstructive feminism, no doubt, provides the most troublesome challenge for episcopal leadership, since there is less in common between the participants than in the case of the first three groups."[12] He insists that the U.S. bishops must challenge reformist feminism's acceptance of secular models of autonomy, self-realization, success, power, personhood, and reproductive freedom, as well as its down-playing of the differences between the sexes, motherhood, and traditional family values. Moreover, the bishops are instructed to caution reformist feminism not to subject the long tradition of the church against women's ordination to the "relatively untested" values of the modern women's movement.

My own work charted in this book obviously is of the "reconstructive reformist" type — a type that draws its theological power, however, not from "secular" (whatever that means) feminism but from the Christian tradition of the *basileia,* the vision of G-d's[13] alternative world, a vision of justice, human dignity, equality, and salvation for all. My hope is that not only women but also bishops share this vision.

Finally, I need to say something about the title "Discipleship of Equals," which I have chosen for this cartography of struggle, since feminist discourses have challenged both the terms "equality" and "discipleship." Equal rights and equality are usually associated with liberal feminism, which is said to fight for the right of women to become like men. Consequently, combining this term with discipleship is considered by some to be an argument for women's equal opportunity with men, to follow as disciples in the footsteps of Jesus, the man, and to imitate his example.

For instance, in a critical review of the French edition of my book *In Memory of Her,* the psychoanalyst Luce Irigaray, whose work is indebted to two male thinkers, Jacques Derrida and Jacques Lacan, asks "Equal to Whom?"[14] Since she has very little appreciation for a critical sociohistorical method of reconstruction, she speculates that I share the opinion of those European femi-

---

12. Mannion, "The Church and the Voices of Feminism," 6.

13. Since our language is not capable of adequately expressing the Divine, making all our names and titles for G-d insufficient, I seek to indicate this theological insight by writing the standard designation of the Divine in a "broken" form rather than to adopt the lengthy "Goddess/God" or the unpronounceable "God/ess" spelling advocated by Rosemary Radford Ruether.

14. Luce Irigaray, "Egales à qui?" *Critique* 43 (1987): 420–37, which has appeared in English translation as "Equal to Whom?" *Differences* 1 (1989): 59–76.

nists who believe that equality in the workplace and in science will grant them sufficient status as subjects. These feminists, she believes, seek to bring about their own neutralization by identification with the generic masculine. The wish to become men or man, she suspects, both prevents me from articulating a feminine identity and leads me to give short shrift to the divinization of sex.

"What does equal mean," Irigaray asks, "as far as religion goes? Does it mean being equal to the other disciples or to God? And how can woman be equal to the other when he is another sex?"[15] A theology of women's liberation, she argues, must therefore establish

> as its priority not equal access to the priesthood but rather equal share in the divine. This means that what I see as a manifestation of sexual liberation is God made a couple: man and woman and not simply God made man.[16]

Irigaray argues on the one hand that (hetero)sexuality should be the locus of the divine and on the other that feminine difference should be divinized. She juxtaposes the demand for women's equality with the call for women's divinity, positioning them as exclusive alternatives.

It is obvious that Irigaray and I use two different types of discourse and intellectual frameworks: Irigaray's discourse seeks to "divinize" sexual difference, albeit one of "radical otherness that would function on its own terms beyond the world of the phallus;"[17] whereas my own discourse seeks to demystify the cultural and theological constructs of femininity and masculinity that are dualistic, heterosexist, and essentialist as ideological obfuscations of the multiplicative structures of patriarchal domination.[18]

When I speak of the discipleship of equals I do not mean to argue for women's access to and integration into patriarchal structures. Nor am I interested in theologically reinscribing (white, heterosexist) feminine identity as divine equality. Neither do I maintain the equality of female with male disciples in following the man Jesus. Finally, I am not interested in retrieving an essential

---

15. Ibid., 73.
16. Ibid., 69.
17. Morny Joy, "Equality or Divinity — A False Dichotomy," *Journal of Feminist Studies in Religion* 6 (1990): 15.
18. For a fuller development of my own theoretical framework in dialogue with postmodern feminist theory see my book *But She Said: Feminist Practices of Biblical Interpretation* (Boston: Beacon Press, 1992).

feminine identity. Rather, I want to articulate *ekklēsia* as a *disciple-ship of equals* that can make present the *basileia*, the alternative world of justice and well-being intended by the life-giving power of G–d as reality and vision in the midst of the death-dealing pow-ers of patriarchal oppression and dehumanization. Like Jesus, the disciples of the *basileia* are called to proclaim the "good news" of G–d's alternative world of justice and love and to make it present by gathering people around the table and inviting everyone without exception to it, by feeding the hungry, healing the sick, and liber-ating the oppressed. The discipleship of equals must be *basileia* discipleship.

In short, like my other theological work this cartography of struggle insists on women's spiritual power of naming and shaping religious vision and community. As a Catholic Christian femi-nist theologian, I argue that the Jewish *basileia* vision of the gospels, which constitutes the mission and reason for any eccle-sial existence, cannot be adequately proclaimed and realized in a patriarchal church. Rather, such a vision can be actualized and af-firmed only in a space where women attain full spiritual autonomy, power, self-determination, and liberation. Consequently, Christian feminists must first reclaim the *ekklēsia* as our own community, heritage, theology, and spirituality before we are able to name the divine differently. The vision of a different world of justice makes us dreamers. I recall a short song of the women's movement that I learned on my last visit to Germany: "If someone dreams alone, then it remains only a dream. If many dream together, then this is the beginning, the beginning of a new reality. Dream our Dream."

I would like to think that this cartography of struggle can serve to recall the dream that we dream together. On the window of my study hangs a Native American "dream catcher," which Chris made. It is fashioned from twigs, strands of fiber, pearls, and feath-ers bent into a circle of webs. The woven dream catcher is found in variations among several indigenous nations. "The web in the cen-ter is said to catch bad dreams in the web, releasing the dreamer of fears. Good dreams slip down the beads and feather, remaining with the dreamer."[19] The symbol of the dream catcher is a sign of healing and spiritual power for the gathering of women. It is a blessing.

---

19. From "Dream Catcher," *Common Ground* 6 (1992): 69.

1 ——————————————

THE FORGOTTEN PARTNER:
THE PROFESSIONAL MINISTRY
OF WOMEN IN THE CHURCH

CONTEXTUALIZATION

My first book on the ministries of women in the church appeared in 1964.[1] It was written in 1962 and submitted as a licentiate thesis in pastoral theology in 1963. In that book, I anticipated, though in a rather unsophisticated way, several methodological issues that would later become decisive in the development of feminist and liberation theologies.

The first of these issues (which appears as a seed in my earlier thought and as fruit in more recent feminist liberation theology) has to do with the starting point of theological reflection: just as most feminist liberation theology today argues that theologizing must start with a systemic reflection on experience, so my thesis sought to reflect theologically on my own experience. Although so-called lay theology as a selective study of theology was well established, I was the first woman in Würzburg to enroll for the full course in theology that students for the priesthood were required to take. However, my choice to study as a lay-woman for

---

1. Elisabeth Schüssler, *Der vergessene Partner: Grundlagen, Tatsachen und Möglichkeiten der beruflichen Mitarbeit der Frau in der Heilssorge der Kirche* (Düsseldorf: Patmos, 1964). Although the publisher was responsible for the main title, I did not object at the time to its grammatically masculine form. The contradiction between the title and the subtitle illustrates the irony of androcentric language.

the equivalent of the M.Div. degree was severely challenged by the progressive theology that found its way into the documents of the Second Vatican Council. Catholic theologians such as Rahner, Auer, Congar, Comblin, Suenens, and many more argued that whereas the mission of the clergy, nuns, and brothers was to the church, the calling of the laity was to the world. Therefore, in this thesis I sought to clarify theologically whether I had missed my calling as a member of the laity when I decided to become a professional theologian.

The second methodological issue that connects my earlier work to contemporary feminist liberation theology has to do with hermeneutical questions: just as liberation theologies begin with the praxis of the people of G–d, scrutinizing, evaluating, and re-articulating theology in light of this praxis, so my thesis attempted to show that the new progressive ecclesiology, to which I otherwise subscribed, did not correspond to the actual pastoral praxis of the Roman Catholic Church. This discrepancy between theory and praxis that I wanted to highlight was that women who were not members of orders and who certainly did not belong to the clergy were working full-time as professional ministers within the institutional church. Although my book adopted the traditional framework that begins by discussing theory and then seeks to "apply" it to pastoral practice, its aim was quite the opposite. I argued for a reformulation of ecclesiology so that it could do justice to the actual practice of the churches.

The third issue that my earlier work and feminist liberation theology share has to do with questions about the structural character of oppression. At the outset I was not so much interested in women's special role as in articulating a theology of church and ministry in which the ecclesial rights and responsibility of all the people of G–d were foundational. At this point, however, I still worked with a hierarchal model of church. For instance, although I was well aware of the negative connotation that the word "lay" assumed in contrast to the designation "cleric," I nevertheless argued that the word should be understood positively, referring to the people of G–d and Christian "brotherhood" rather than to the uneducated, uncouth, vulgar masses.[2]

Ironically, I sought to argue for a participatory model of church by pointing to the de facto clerical status of professional women

---

2. Ibid., 102–8.

ministers in the churches. Not surprisingly, when the book was published, it read more like an argument for women's ordination although I was not interested in the clericalization of women but in the declericalization of the church as the people of G–d. Believing that women's ordination would amount to a clerical co-optation of women, I argued that Roman Catholic women must demand to be ordained first to the fullness of priesthood and jurisdictional power of bishops before accepting ordination to the lower ranks of the hierarchy. Only in this way, I contended, would women's gifts be able to engender structural change in the church. A similar contradictory strategy has been pursued by the Women's Ordination Conference (WOC) in the United States. From its beginnings WOC has insisted on the ordination of women but into a *different* church and priestly ministry.

A fourth issue that runs through both my early work and that of feminist liberation theology today has to do with gaining a more critical understanding of gender. In writing and researching the book I came to focus more and more on the dominant theology of woman and its significance for the ministry of women in the church. In the process I became aware that the theology of the "eternal feminine," which had replaced the theological assumption of women's inferiority and sinfulness, was buttressed by the all-pervasive cultural ideology of woman's nature and biological/ essential difference from man. This ideology had been advocated by scholars in biology, philosophy, sociology, and psychology. Although I rejected this cultural ideology of the feminine and argued that the scientific understanding of the world and of women would change when looked at from the perspective of women, I lacked a comprehensive theoretical framework to articulate such a different perspective. Though I knew and partially accepted Simone de Beauvoir's existentialist analysis, which Mary Daly subsequently used as a theoretical foundation for her book *The Church and the Second Sex,* I was groping for a more sociopolitical framework, one that would be more compatible with my vision of church and its mission to the world. The following translation of excerpts might indicate the flavor of my nascent argument "from a woman's point of view."

—— ✤ ——

QUESTIONS SURROUNDING WOMEN in the ministry of the
church are not just a modern phenomenon; already Paul had to deal
with the question of women's active participation in the church.
Moreover, again and again throughout church history great and exceptional women have emerged. The church's calendar of saints
eloquently testifies to this. Frederic Ozanam (1813–53) sums up
this insight: "Nothing great could happen in the church unless a
woman had a share in it."[3] Generally man had public, outward-
directed leadership, whereas woman's contribution was hidden
and private. Woman's historical contribution was made under the
sign of the "veil." Therefore, throughout the centuries primarily
women in canonical orders[4] had the vocation to work full-time in
the church.

This situation changed at the beginning of this century. The
change was occasioned by both the new status of woman in society
and by the rediscovery of the laity in the church. The women's
movement struggled for woman's access to all levels of education
and for her full participation in all professions. Gradually, woman
moved from the private sphere into public light. Because of her
capabilities and hard work, woman conquered all areas of public
life to the point that it has become commonplace that education
seeks to prepare girls not just for marriage or religious life, but
also for professional life.

In modern times the church, stripped of its political and temporal power, confronted a more and more secularized world.
"Catholic Action" was engendered by the insight that the clergy no
longer can satisfy the needs of our times either because there are
not sufficient numbers of clergymen around or because the clergy
can no longer reach certain groups of people. In this situation, it
became necessary for all the members of the church to become
apostles, for the laity to move out of its inactivity. Indeed lay-men
and lay-women were encouraged to participate in close cooperation with and obedience to the hierarchy "in the holy struggles":
They should with "full personal dedication, through prayer and
freely given cooperation seek to revive the faith and to renew
church morals."[5]

---

3. Quoted by Linus Bopp, *Unsere Seelsorge in geschichtlicher Sendung* (Freiburg:
Herder Verlag, 1952), 46–52.
4. This is my translation of the German word *Ordensfrau,* which is a synonym for
Klosterfrau, i.e., nun-woman.
5. Pope Pius XI in a letter of November 6, 1929, to Cardinal Seguray Saens, as quoted

However, it soon became evident that the mere haphazard help of the laity, which was limited with regard to time and resources, could not solve the problems facing the church in the modern world. Therefore, in the first three decades of this century, full-time ministries for women were created in the areas of pastoral care, catechetics, and Catholic Action. Although these positions were for the most part filled by lay-women, the traditional feminine image of woman and the spirituality of nun-women served as the guiding and inspiring idea and model. Only "under the veil" could woman contribute significantly.

In addition, these lay ministries were shaped and limited by the theological arguments for their creation. It was not the appreciation of the capabilities and gifts that the laity could bring to ministry but rather the shortage of priests that motivated their creation. Consequently, the laity could gain no access to those ministries where the lack of priests was not apparent or where hierarchical control was deemed necessary. At the same time, the ministry of the laity could not develop its full potential for the church because its importance was still not recognized and appreciated....

In the past decades a deeper theological self-understanding of the laity and its responsibilities in the church has been developed. Few, however, have attempted to apply this positive theological understanding of the laity to the ecclesial understanding of woman and her importance for the church and her apostolate. And yet it is precisely this positive theological basis that facilitates and energizes the collaboration between priests and women. Only such a positive theological understanding of lay ministry can provide the basis for the professional ministry of women. More than ever before, the church needs the gifts and energy of all its members, since the pastoral work that is needed far surpasses the capabilities of the clergy. Therefore, it should not be up to the clergy to allow women to collaborate in the ministry of the church, merely tolerating their participation. Rather, the leadership of the church must recognize the positive implications of the shortage of priests.

In order to fulfill all the demands and needs in the life of the church, all members of the church must work together in solidarity. In such solidarity, the ordained must not restrict themselves to

---

by Hans Urs von Balthasar, *Der Laie und der Ordenstand* (Freiburg: Herder Verlag, 1949), 5.

their sacramental functions, and the nonordained members of the church must, on the basis of their baptism and confirmation, contribute to the "building up" of the body of Christ and its Christian mission to the world. The future of the church would be endangered if, because of clerical misunderstanding or false authority, the hierarchy should miss this historic mandate of God. In this century, which is characterized by the "awakening of the church" in the hearts and souls of the people (Romano Guardini), the hierarchy and the clergy must do everything possible to make sure that not a single Christian is forced to repeat the judgment that Florence Nightingale pronounced against the church: "I wanted to give her my head, my hands, my heart. She didn't want them; she did not know what to do with them."[6]

However, mere toleration of the ministry of the faithful does not suffice. The official church must also create the preconditions for a self-determining, responsible ministry of the laity. Such a ministry does not require pious, otherworldly girls and women, but women who have sufficient theological knowledge, self-affirmation, and independence to "complement" the male ministry of priests.

This book does not start with a systematic theological question but with an issue of ecclesial praxis. The discipline of practical theology has the task both of analyzing sociotheologically "the present practices of the church and of working out principles and imperatives for their actualization. The formal and specific perspective under which practical theology articulates ecclesial praxis is nothing but the present situation intended by God."[7] In this light, Christian mission is not partial to the past; "it lives neither from the anger about the vanishing of the old order, nor with the sterile desire for the so-called good old days or for a future change" (Pius XII).[8] Rather it knows of the challenge of our times — a challenge that God makes through our time.

Confronting this challenge the theoretical part of this book seeks to elaborate the theological basis for the professional ministry of woman in the church. It seeks to show how woman in the professional ministry of the church has to understand herself if she wants to fulfill her God-given mission for our times. However,

6. Quoted by Kathleen Bliss, *Frauen in den Kirchen der Welt* (Nürnberg, 1954), 14.

7. Heinz Schuster, "Die Aufgabe der Pastoraltheologie," *Zeitschrift für katholische Theologie* 85 (1963): 40.

8. *Herder Korrespondenz* 18 (1963): 161.

the book also seeks to bring to our attention that the church must scrutinize and revise her theological teachings about woman to be able to mine the possibilities and resources that God has given to her in the ministry of women.[9]

. . .

Werner Heisenberg has argued that a system founded on a certain basic conceptual notion allows only those kinds of questions that are adequate to its conceptual basis.[10] In terms of my discussion, this means that society looks different from the standpoint of woman from the way it does from the dominant male perspective. Almost all works that discuss the nature and calling of woman highlight an essential gender difference and view woman within the perspective of the dominant human-man-male framework that has been prevalent in classic Christian cultures for centuries. For thousands of years man/male has exercised cultural, scientific, and institutional domination. It is not surprising that state, public, and economic institutions clearly have masculine characteristics, since they are a part of a world that is constructed and controlled by males; they stem from a society that is patriarchally stigmatized. In such a world woman's nature can be understood only in relation to that of man.

Consequently, those women who want to participate actively in this male-determined world must adapt themselves to men. Initially, the women's emancipation movement strove for equal rights of women with men, which resulted in the ability of women to be and act "like a man." It is important to note, however, that in the past decades not only have the lives of women been transformed in and through the confrontation with a male-defined world, but so have the lives of a great number of men. Ironically, most men find themselves being controlled in the workplace in the same ways that they have always controlled women in the home. The sharp contrasts between the work of men and that of women have become blurred and often cancel each other out.[11] The question, then, is not simply how much women's participation in work outside the home will change notions about the so-called nature or essence

---

9. Schüssler, *Der vergessene Partner,* 11–14.
10. Werner Heisenberg, *Philosophic Problems of Nuclear Science* (New York: Pantheon Books, 1952), 24.
11. See L. Preller, "Bemerkungen zum Problem der Frau in der Gesellschaft," in *Krisis und Zukunft der Frau,* ed. Wilhelm Bitter (Stuttgart: E. Klett, 1962), 300.

of woman, but also how much it will transform male-oriented society. . . .

At stake here is the integration of the traditional male consciousness and the emerging female consciousness into a personal human consciousness. Today women must learn to understand themselves first of all as human persons.[12] Like men they must realize their human personhood in autonomy, partnership, and self-determination; they must come of age and no longer tolerate any tutelage. . . . Only when woman is acknowledged as an equal partner in societal discourses will our one-sidedly male-structured society be transformed. In short, the women's movement is still not finished today. [39–41]

A short review of church teaching about woman in the ancient, the medieval, and the modern church can raise consciousness about how difficult the struggle for the personhood of woman and her equality with man has been not just in society but even more so in the church. It must not be overlooked, however, that throughout the history of the church exceptional and creative women leaders have emerged who have decisively influenced church life and spirituality. Names such as Helena, Olympas, Pulcheria, Domitilla, Lioba, Thecla, Hildegard of Bingen, Elisabeth of Hungary, Catherine of Siena, Bridget of Sweden, Teresa of Avila, Mary Ward of England, and Thérèse of Lisieux prove this. . . .

It is understandable that both the Church Fathers and Thomas Aquinas, because of their misinformation about genetics and biology as well as because of the patriarchal image and status of woman in their times, fell into such grave errors. It is less understandable, however, when Catholic women seek to justify such errors in the twentieth century:

> Yet it appears as if this portentous error was not just allowed for by Divine Providence, as sins are allowed to happen, but actively intended, as salvific measures are willed. And this apparently did not happen for the sake of St. Thomas but for the sake of womankind. A tree, which is to be shaped by a higher will into a form that its nature does not want to take, must be bent for a time with violence. . . . Fallen nature carries with it the inclination to insurrection, always prepared to revolt. Since the habit of service must be required from woman with great urgency, not for the sake of herself but for that of all of humankind, it was apparently better after the constitution of her supernatural freedom to keep her

---

12. Dietrich von Oppen, *Das personale Zeitalter* (Stuttgart: Verlagsgemeinschaft Burckhardthaus–Kreuz-Verlag, 1960), 183.

bent because of her nature until she became mature enough for the liberation from this handicap.[13]

That this "process of maturation" took very long is not surprising, considering the influence of Thomas on medieval and modern theology. The equality of women has been in doubt until today. Even an independent thinker such as Hermann Schell interprets the teaching of Paul as follows:

> The woman represents the nature-side of humanity that is expressed in the potential and fate of sexuality. Therefore, woman is created for the sake of man and can find her complement, support, and perfection only in him. Man to the contrary represents the nature-free personality, which should control the pitfalls of nature and use it. Thus woman stands in the service of nature, but man in the immediate service of humanity's personal destination for God.[14]

The Thomistic devaluation of woman continues to influence Catholic thought insofar as the necessity to be made whole through the other gender is postulated only for women but not for men — even though the Bible teaches that it was man who needed a helpmate. Such a devaluation of woman also informs exegetical work, for instance, that of Peter Ketter, who argues that the curse of original sin is more grave for Eve and her daughters than for Adam and his sons. Woman is therefore doubly saved by the Lord, both from sin and guilt and also from sinful womanhood.[15]

How little theologians have scrutinized and corrected the traditional Catholic image of woman comes to the fore in the new edition of the *Lexikon für Theologie und Kirche*. Here one finds the following statement under the entry "nature of woman": God has called woman to be the "mother of life" (Gen. 3:20) and placed on her the main burden of propagation (Gen. 3:16). Her essential nature is therefore motherhood. Motherhood is rooted in receptivity and reproductivity; it matures into joyful sacrifice and never-ending surrender.

> Woman's mode of activity is person-related more than object-related: emotionality over rationality, heart over mind, goodness over truth, custom over right. The concrete and imaginable has greater appeal for

---

13. Oda Schneider, *Vom Priestertum der Frau* (Vienna, 1934), 15.
14. Hermann Schell, *Katholische Dogmatic* (Paderborn, 1893), 3:667.
15. Peter Ketter, *Christus und die Frauen* (Düsseldorf, 1933), 225.

woman than the abstract idea; she feels more at ease with intuitive
perception than with logical thought.[16]

The contemporary, almost canonical Catholic image of woman
is that of motherhood, of surrender, of service and of care, of the
silent rather than visible contribution of woman to the creative vocation of man in the world."[17] Gertrud von Le Fort has crystallized
in poetic language this traditional image of woman.[18] ...

Le Fort begins with the assumption that man and his work constitute the content of historical life. Woman must always work in
concealment and under the symbol of the veil. She is focused on
man but not on great works. Since only "occasional helping out" –
but not independent activity – corresponds to the essential nature
of woman, woman's ministry in the church must have a pneumatic-
charismatic character. However, in both society as well as in the
church, she is called to such public charismatic action only in very
rare and desperate circumstances.

Today women work in public and are not oriented just toward personal matters, but also toward sociopolitical affairs. These
sociopolitical aspects of women's activities are, however, completely missing in Gertrud von Le Fort's theology and image of
woman. Le Fort confirms this when she writes: "Contemporary
woman is for the most part no longer the one about whom this
book speaks."[19] ... Therefore, I agree with Elisabeth Gössmann,
who asserts: "Woman herself may under no circumstances derive
her existence from the notion of the 'eternal feminine.' Rather she
must live out of that humanity which is rooted in the very human
mysteries of Christian faith. One may not for the sake of symbolism
leap over the actual life of woman."[20]

16. Michael Buchberger, *Lexikon für Theologie und Kirche* (Freiburg: Herder Verlag,
1960), 4:298 (my translation).

17. Elisabeth Gössmann, "Frauenbild und Frauenbildung heute," *Erwachsenen-
bildung* 1 (1962): 1.

18. Gertrud von Le Fort, *Die ewige Frau,* 19th ed. (Munich, 1960); see also Alfred
Rosenberg, *Die Erhebung des Weiblichen* (Freiburg, 1959).

19. Le Fort, *Die ewige Frau,* 92.

20. Elisabeth Gössmann, *Das Bild der Frau Heute* (Düsseldorf, 1962), 21.

2

SHOULD WOMEN AIM
FOR ORDINATION
TO THE LOWEST RUNG
OF THE HIERARCHICAL LADDER?

In the long run history will not be changed by those who give new
answers but by those who make new ways of questioning possible.
                                                    —J. A. T. Robinson

CONTEXTUALIZATION

In 1967 I was invited by a local chapter of St. Joan's International
Alliance to address their assembly. Although I knew that as an international Catholic women's organization St. Joan's International
Alliance strongly supported the ordination of women to the diaconate and priesthood, I was also aware that the organization had
its roots in the women's suffrage movement. St. Joan's International
Alliance was founded in 1911 as the Catholic Women's Suffrage Society and began working for women's rights within the church in
1959.[1] Nevertheless, I hoped to persuade the audience that Catholic women needed to define their self-understanding and aims in
terms of the church as the people of G-d, rather than struggle for

---

1. See Rosemary Radford Ruether, "The Roman Catholic Story," in *Women of the
Spirit,* ed. Eleanor McLaughlin and Rosemary Radford Ruether (New York: Simon and
Schuster, 1979), 373–83.

inclusion in the clerical hierarchy in its Constantinian form. Further, I argued that Catholic women should organize women who already exercised professional ministries in the church, a task that they themselves could accomplish today. It seemed to me especially imperative to support positions and research in theology for women, since theology was crucial for the renewal of the church.

Although the lecture was to be published subsequently, the local chapter of St. Joan's International Alliance declined its publication. No reasons were given, but I surmised that they did not agree with my analysis and proposals. In their resolution of August 26–28, 1966, their annual assembly had just asked for all theological courses to be opened to women, for girls and women to be admitted as "altar servers," and for competent women to be appointed to all postconciliar committees. At the same time the delegates had confirmed their "fidelity and daughterly submission" and expressed their conviction "that women would be willing and eager to serve in the priesthood, if the church in her wisdom should decide to extend this dignity to them," a resolution that was first approved in 1963.[2] It seemed obvious that my proposals went either too far or not far enough. Two years later I submitted the paper to a liberal American journal. Its publication was denied again, this time because its content was not relevant to the U.S. situation.

ARTICLE 29 of the Dogmatic Constitution on the Church of Vatican II allows for national bishops conferences to renew the permanent diaconate as an ordained ministry. However, the "fathers" of the council expressly state that only males may be ordained to the diaconate. Teachers of religion, catechists, acolytes, missionaries, sacristans, organists, social workers, and youth leaders are to become deacons. Since almost all of these professions were originally founded to include women in ministry and today are mostly held by them, it is rather difficult to understand why the permanent diaconate remains restricted to men. If the growing shortage of priests is the reason for instituting the diaconate, one wonders how the church can do without the service of women in this field.[3]

2. For documentation see Gertrud Heinzelmann, *Die getrennten Schwestern: Frauen nach dem Konzil* (Zürich: Interfeminas-Verlag, 1967), 101.

3. For documentation of women's professional ministries see Elisabeth Schüssler,

Why is ordination to the permanent diaconate to be withheld from women when the functions of the permanent diaconate are now exercised by women as well as men?

Those who favor the renewal of the diaconate argue that de facto this office already exists and therefore should be acknowledged through ordination. However, they do not question its proposed restriction to men, even though women are its main practitioners. Is it, one may be tempted to ask, that a woman is less in need of the grace of ordination than a man? If the permanent diaconate were introduced without being open to women, its renewal would constitute another instance of injustice toward women in the church. Such a discrimination would be all the more aggravating as the church can no longer excuse its attitude by appealing to the inferior social status of women. One would think that these reasons would be grounds enough either to admit women to the permanent diaconate or to question its revival. It seems that Catholic women have no other choice but to support the revival of the permanent diaconate and to fight for admission to it.

Nevertheless, I will argue here that women in professional ministries should oppose the renewal of the permanent diaconate in their dioceses rather than seek to be incorporated into it. For its renewal neither helps women to get equal rights within the church, nor does it further a postconciliar understanding of church. If we want to argue at all for incorporation into hierarchical structures, then we must insist that women be first admitted to the office of bishop. Since appointment of women as bishops, cardinals, or even popes is not very likely to happen, women in professional ministry must ask why this is the case and whether established hierarchical structures by definition must exclude women.

Indeed, it is interesting to observe that theological discussions during and after the council have not raised this question, but have made only practical-ecclesiastical objections. The significance of the "woman's question" for ecclesiastical structures and for the theological understanding of the hierarchical office itself have not been touched upon. However, it is not enough simply to repeat women's demand for ordination on grounds of female emancipation. Nor can we simply consider the historical side of the problem or merely look for practical opportunities.

Der vergessene Partner: Grundlagen, Tatsachen und Möglichkeiten der beruflichen Mitarbeit der Frau in der Heilssorge der Kirche (Düsseldorf: Patmos Verlag, 1964).

The question of women's ordination to the diaconate, therefore, must be articulated primarily in terms of its significance for
the theological self-understanding of the church. In this light, the
following critical analysis of the theological arguments in favor of
the renewal of the permanent diaconate will have to examine the
specific understandings of church that these arguments imply and
presume. Furthermore we shall have to ask whether the demand
for the admission of women to the diaconate in its present form
will in any way foster women's equality in the church.

THEOLOGICAL ARGUMENTS
FOR THE REVIVAL OF THE DIACONATE

In giving the reasons for the revival of the diaconate the council
accepted Karl Rahner's arguments. Rahner argues that the office
of deacon already exists in fact, albeit without ordination:

> The office of deacon exists in the church and even (if not always) out-
> side the circle of ordained deacons. For there are full-time professional
> catechists, there are full-time and professional social workers (in the
> fuller sense of the word). They have chosen as a permanent profession
> to fulfill the social mission of the church by working all their lives in
> the service of the hierarchy. Commissioned by the hierarchy, they con-
> sider their work as the fulfillment of a task essential to the church. But
> this is not just the task of the church in general, which could also be
> fulfilled by the laity; it is, rather, in a special way the responsibility of
> the office-holders of the church, the hierarchy as such.

According to Rahner, these professional ministries should be acknowledged through ordination "at least where such functions are
to a great extent explicitly commissioned and directly supervised
by the hierarchy and done as an immediate aid to the task of the
hierarchy."[4]

Rahner points out, however, that the deacon needs no ordination to perform liturgical functions. By contrast, the Second
Vatican Council's texts understand the ordination to the permanent diaconate primarily in relation to the eucharistic celebration.
Consequently, they place a greater stress on the deacon's liturgical
functions.

---

4. Karl Rahner, "Die Theologie der Erneuerung des Diakonats," in *Diakonia in Christo*, Quaestiones Disputatae 15/16 (Freiburg: Herder, 1963), 298.

The diverse theological arguments for the reinstitution of the permanent diaconate are based on the following two theological assumptions:

1. Every office and service in the church is hierarchical. Active functions in the church are the responsibility and duty solely of the hierarchy, whose "lowest rank" is the diaconate. All professional activities within the social sphere of the church receive their legitimacy not by virtue of belonging to the responsibility of the whole church, but only through their relation to the hierarchy. Therefore, the arguments for reintroducing the permanent diaconate exhibit the theological tendency to understand all active participation in church ministry as hierarchical and clerical functions. A great number of professional ecclesial functions and ministries are thereby reduced to the mission and office of the hierarchy insofar as ordination would incorporate all others into the lowest rank of the hierarchy. In addition, ordination to the permanent diaconate would not only institutionalize the hierarchical subordination of the diverse professional lay ministries, but would also establish a sacramental-spiritual foundation for such a move.[5]

2. The arguments also imply that only the ministry of the "consecrated" or ordained person can be recognized as a legitimate ministry in the church. Indeed these arguments admit that professional ministers need not be ordained to those functions that they already exercise – not even the liturgical functions. Rather, ordination is considered to be desirable because it associates the deacon with the "altar" and strengthens his status among the faithful.[6] As a *consecrated* or *ordained* person, the married deacon would be uniquely capable of mediating between priest and people in the parish[7] since on the one hand he belongs to the lowest rank of the ordained hierarchy, and yet on the other hand he is related to the worldly sphere of the laity through marriage and professional (i.e., nonclerical) status.[8]

In short, the theological arguments for the renewal of the permanent diaconate sustain the ecclesial status dualism between clergy and laity, the dichotomy between sacred and profane, and

---

5. Heinz Fleckenstein, "Seelsorgliche Möglichkeiten des Diakonats in deutsch-sprachigen Länderns," in *Diakonia in Christo*, 416f.

6. Ibid., 421.

7. A. Kervoorde, "Die Theologie des Diakonates," in *Diakonia in Christo*, 271 n. 167.

8. P. Winninger, "Diakon und Laie," in *Diakonia in Christo*, 381.

the gap between the church and the world. Thus the theological basis for the renewal of the diaconate as a rung on the hierarchical ladder safeguards a Constantinian, medieval, pre-Vatican II conception of the church. The main aspects and structures of this theological understanding of church can be sketched as follows.

PRE-VATICAN II UNDERSTANDINGS OF THE CHURCH

When the Roman empire officially acknowledged and adopted Christianity as its state religion,[9] an epoch began that was characterized by a gigantic symbiosis of church and world. In this process all worldly spheres were sacralized and incorporated into the church. The church was now no longer a community of believers in a differently structured world, but it was the *populus christianus,* an entity that can be defined culturally, politically, and geographically.[10] According to this ecclesiology, one no longer becomes a Christian through a personal option for the Christian faith, but by being born into a certain culture and society. Salvation is obtained by attending church, receiving the sacraments, listening to sermons, etc., i.e., by taking part in the liturgical rites that assure individual sanctification and salvation mediated by the ordained hierarchy.[11] Ultimately, such a stress on ritual religiosity and priestly mediation rather than on ecclesial participation leads to an absolutizing of the ecclesiastical hierarchy, because it controls not only ecclesial salvation but also societal welfare.

The theological reinterpretation of the notion of "the people of God" can illustrate this development. Early Christian theology transfers Israel's honorary title of election to the ecclesia, the church as the "new" people of God. Patristic theology in turn interpreted the notion of "the people of God" in terms of salvation history: The Israel in the flesh is followed by the spiritual Israel, the church. In the eleventh and twelfth centuries, this antithesis is applied to the church itself. The patristic anti-Jewish Israel-church antithesis is now turned into the dualistic contrast between the

---

9. See the critical comments of H. Kühner, *Tabus der Kirchengeschichte,* 2d ed. (Nürnberg, 1965), 101ff.

10. See Joseph Ratzinger, "Wesen und Grenzen der Kirche," in *Das 2. Vatikanische Konzil,* ed. K. Forster (Würzburg: Echter Verlag, 1962), 49–68.

11. For the whole argument see Osmund Schreuder, *Gestaltwandel der Kirche,* Theologia Publica 5 (Olten: Walter, 1967), 42ff.

ordained and the laity, between the "sacred" or "religious" and the secular or "worldly" members of the church. Thus according to this reinterpretation the laity represents that part of the church which still lives, so to speak, in the sphere of "Israel according to the flesh." Those members of the church who are ordained or who live in "religious" orders take the place of the "new people of God." In this way the notion of the church as the people of God is transferred to a certain class of people within the church. The laity become the "world" who remain in the sphere of the "flesh" and have no "spiritual vocation."[12] The sphere of the "Spirit" thus no longer includes all the baptized, the church as a whole, but only the sacred in contrast to the profane sphere of the church. According to this theology of the church, only its ordained members can determine church life, teaching, and mission.[13]

During the Reformation and the period of European secularization that followed, ecclesiastical structures came under fire. In response to various challenges, the hierarchical church reacted with rejection, condemnation, and defense, on the one hand, and by consolidating its autocratic structures as divinely instituted on the other. In other words, in reaction to the Reformation and the Enlightenment the post-Constantinian medieval structures of the church, which were founded on the symbiosis of church and world, hardened. The Roman Catholic Church, with its emphasis on monarchical structures and absolute ecclesiastical power, became anachronistic in a democratic pluralistic society. It was not able to serve its ecclesial mission and to persuade and change the "world" with its gospel of justice, love, and equality.[14]

In line with the medieval church and in conflict with the values of the European Reformation and secularization, the Roman Catholic Church today has become more and more synonymous with the hierarchy; the forms of church government remain feudalistic and absolutist; ecclesiology becomes hierarchology. When we say, for instance, "the church" teaches or "the church" is involved in politics, we always have the hierarchy in mind. It is the clerical hierarchy who represent the church in the public sphere. A rigidly

---

12. Joseph Ratzinger, *Die christliche Brüderlichkeit* (Munich, 1960), has pointed to a similar reductionist process with respect to the notion of Christian brotherhood.

13. See Yves Congar, "Kirche und Welt," in *Weltverständnis im Glauben,* ed. Johann Baptist Metz (Mainz: Grünewald Verlag, 1965), 117.

14. Reinhold Niebuhr, *Essays in Applied Christianity* (New York: Meridian Books, 1959), 201–12.

structured and centralized authoritarian hierarchy demands absolute obedience and rigid discipline, organizational control, and uniform behavior on the part of lower clergy and laity. Since the theology and organization of the "lay apostolate" was conceived of as assistance to the mission and subject to the control of the clergy, the Catholic Action movement did not bring about a genuine change in the status of the laity. Nor did it alter its ecclesiological influence. Rather this movement was placed under clerical control, which supervised the so-called lay ministries. Similarly, the revival of the permanent diaconate would mean the further masculinization and incorporation of the professional ministry of the laity into the hierarchical structures of clerical office.[15]

Therefore, Rahner is correct in observing that the laity's professional employment in the church makes them totally dependent upon and subordinate to the hierarchy. One must ask, however, whether it is appropriate today to strengthen hierarchical ecclesiastical structures even further instead of democratizing the church as a community of "brothers" and as the people of God. Rahner himself acknowledges this when he asserts that the thousand-year-old misunderstanding of the church as solely a hierarchical institution, consisting of the clergy alone with the Christian laity as the object of its pastoral care, will cease to exist only when the church really becomes the people of God.

In short, one can say that the post-Constantinian church has all the characteristics of an (imperial) state-church,[16] into which one is born. When baptism has become a mere coincidence to citizenship, ordination or religious vows become necessary for all those who are determined to follow Christ radically and to dedicate themselves completely to the mission of the church. If priestly ordination becomes the mark of the true Christian and if only the clerical hierarchy has decision-making powers – in other words, if the church becomes identical with its clergy – if the clergy becomes identical with church, then women cannot but fight to become ordained. The demand of women to be admitted as altar girls, deacons, or priests, however, also betrays a clerical viewpoint insofar as it subscribes to a post-Constantinian understanding of church. Consequently, women's ordination to hi-

15. Joseph Comblin, *Versagt die katholische Aktion* (Graz, 1962), 79ff.
16. Rudolf Hernegger, *Macht ohne Auftrag – Die Entstehung der Staats- und Volkskirche* (Olten, 1963).

erarchical offices cannot but strengthen the monarchist structures of the post-Constantinian church. Women's ministries are robbed of their power to bring about fundamental change in the church.

STRATEGIES FOR EQUAL RIGHTS IN THE POST–VATICAN II CHURCH

Such a diagnosis, however, does not mean that women should give up the fight for active cooperation in all the ministries of the church. It is very important, not only for women, but also for the whole church and the authority of the gospel, that the clerical line dividing the sexes together with women's status as "second-class" Christians be abolished.[17] However, the history of the women's emancipation movement indicates that equality of the sexes is to be reached neither through women's conformity to patriarchal-authoritarian structures, nor through their incorporation into the lowest rank of the hierarchy.[18] Equality can be reached only in and through a change and transformation of the Constantinian form of church.

This assertion calls for further explication. Chesterton's quip is well known: "Millions of women arose and shouted, 'no one will ever dictate to us again' — and they became typists!" Chesterton has been proven right again by the most recent report of the German federal government on the status of women. In spite of a century of struggle for equality, women have not succeeded in getting important leading positions in our society. On the contrary, women have been incorporated into the economic-political system of patriarchical industrialized society, which merely organized their working capabilities for itself and which admitted women only to subordinate, low-paid positions. The "angel in the house" (Virginia Woolf) has become the "angel" at the conveyor belt or at the typewriter — an angel who has hardly any chance of rising to leading positions within the masculine authoritarian structures of our economy and society.

The movement for women's emancipation failed primarily because its moderate wing did not seek to change society, but sought

---

17. John A. T. Robinson, *Eine neue Reformation?* (Munich, 1965), 69.
18. For a critical assessment of the women's emancipation movement see Hermann Ringeling, "Die Frau in der heutigen Familie," *Zeitschrift für Evangelische Ethik* 8 (1964): 129–43, esp. 132.

instead to "humanize" work according to the principle of femininity and the family. In any case, it was an illusory hope to assume
that women could "feminize" industrial society, since the modern
world is not a product of the "masculine" mind, but obeys material
laws that determine the life of men and women alike. Insofar as the
conservative wing of the women's movement argued that the social status of women must be seen as complementing men's work
rather than having integrity of its own, it did not challenge the
notion that women worked for "pin" money but fostered women's
"dual role." Both sexes still believe the cliché that work in the home
is a woman's affair, whereas work in the public sphere remains the
responsibility of men who are paid a "family wage" as "heads of
households." In short, women's capabilities and role were adapted
to the economic needs of industrialized society rather than society
being transformed in the interest of women.

The contemporary movement for women's ordination seems to
take its cue from the moderate women's movement at the turn of
the century when it argues for the admission of women to subordinate, liturgical positions, without demanding the full authority
and sacramental power of the episcopal office for women.[19] In
contrast, I argue here, women have real "liberty" to serve in subordinate positions only after they are able to enter the highest church
offices. Insofar as it does not demand access to the highest echelons, the women's movement in the church will make it possible for
the hierarchal church to use women's gifts and work for strength-
ening its own exclusive clerical structures. An incorporation of
some celibate women as deaconesses into the lowest rank of the
hierarchy will not achieve the equality of all women. To achieve
women's emancipation in particular and that of all the laity in general nothing short of a reconceptualization of church and ministry
is necessary.

The theological foundation for such a transformation of the
monarchic form of church is initially laid in the Dogmatic Constitution on the Church of Vatican II, although the theological
discussion of its consequences for the institutional structures of
the church has hardly begun.[20] In line with the New Testament the

19. This can be illustrated with reference to the profession of "pastoral assistant,"
which in its structure and theological self-understanding approximates the theological proposals for the permanent diaconate. See my book *Der vergessene Partner* for
analysis and documentation of this ecclesial profession for women.

20. See Johannes Baptist Metz, "Versuch einer positiven Deutung der bleibenden

council emphasizes, first, the priesthood of all believers; second, service as the essence of church ministry; and third, the church as existing not for its own sake but for the world.

Thus the Second Vatican Council has made important theological corrections with respect to the Constantinian understanding of church as hierarchy. The Tridentine teaching on the ecclesiastical offices is corrected in three crucial points:[21]

First, where Trent uses the word "hierarchy" when speaking of ecclesiastical office, the Constitution on the Church prefers the expression "ecclesiastical ministry" (*ministerium ecclesiasticum;* see art. 28).

Second, whereas Trent uses *divina ordinatio* with reference to the threefold division of office (bishop, priest, and deacon), Vatican II understands ecclesial ministry as "divinely instituted" (*divinitus institutum*).

Third, according to Tridentine teaching the ecclesiastical hierarchy consists (*constat*) of bishops, priests, and deacons, whereas according to Vatican II ecclesiastical ministry is *exercised* in these different orders.

In line with such an understanding of ecclesial ministry, chapter 3 of the Constitution on the Church gives only a pastoral-theological description of the ecclesiastical offices, which are understood in light of the present situation. The council does not make any statement on the metaphysical essence and "indelible" character of these ecclesiastical offices, but paraphrases their contemporary and time-conditioned form. This correction of the Tridentine interpretation of "office" makes it possible for democratic changes in the hierarchical structure of the church to occur.[22] For "service" as the definition of ecclesiastical office will cease to be a cliché only when the autocratic, monarchic understanding and institutionalization of church office is abolished.

Such a transformation requires a desacralization and a declericalization of ecclesial ministry. In this sense, the ecclesiology of Vatican II has reaffirmed the New Testament teaching on the election, sanctity, and priesthood of all the faithful.[23] In the New

Weltlichkeit der Welt," in *Handbuch der Pastoraltheologie* 2/2, ed. Franz Zaver Arnold (Freiburg: Herder, 1966), 230–67.

21. The following points are taken over from Hans Küng, *Die Kirche* (Freiburg: Herder, 1967).

22. Harry Hoefnagels, *Kirche in veränderter Welt* (Essen, 1964), 104ff.

23. See my exegetical dissertation on the priesthood of the faithful in Christian Scripture, *Priester für Gott* (Münster: Aschendorff Verlag, 1972).

Testament the title "priest" refers to all the believers and to Christ, but not to any church "office." According to the Epistle to the Hebrews, the Israelite cultic priesthood is superseded once and for all through Christ, the high priest. The emphasis on the "once and for all" of Christ's "high priestly" action does not allow for a special caste of priests in the early Christian communities. Rather, it allows for the use of the title "priest" for all believers.[24] All Christians — women and men — have become cultically purified, sanctified, and elect through Christ's expiatory death. Thus the notion of priesthood in the New Testament does not yet know of the ecclesiastical dualism of sacred and profane. Rather, it proclaims sanctification and authorization of all Christians to approach God without any cultic mediation.

Not cultic priesthood but the "gifts" of the Spirit are decisive for ministry in the church. All members of the Christian community are called to exercise their "spiritual gifts" for the building up of the "body of Christ," the Christian community. Since the gifts of the Spirit are not restricted to a certain group within the community, everyone is able and authorized in the power of the Spirit to preach, to prophesy, to forgive sins, and to participate actively in the celebration of the Lord's Supper. Thus all members of the people of God, by virtue of their baptismal "priesthood," have the capability and right to exercise liturgical and ecclesial leadership functions. The arguments against the ordination of women are theologically invalid insofar as they are founded on the misconception of church as "cultically" divided into hierarchical classes. At the same time it becomes equally clear that women's demand for cultic ordination could repeat the same misconception if it is not accompanied by a radical critique of present church structures.[25] Again, the ordination of a few women into a sacralized cultic class must lead to the further exclusion of most women as "cultically" inferior. Instead, women must insist on the desacralization of ministry if "the priesthood of all the baptized" is not to remain an empty cliché. All the privileges and distinguishing characteristics of clerical rank must cease. Such a "demythologization" and relativization of the clerical hierarchy[26] will also make superfluous the

---

24. See H. Vorgrimmler, "Das allgemeine Priestertum," *Lebendiges Zeugnis* 2/3 (1964): 92–113.

25. Gertrud Heinzelmann, *Wir schweigen nicht länger* (Zürich, 1964).

26. One must not overlook that the official title for ordination to the priesthood is not *consecratio* but *ordinatio*.

theological arguments for the requirement of celibacy and clerical lifestyle.

The New Testament writings do not know of a fixed and exclusive catalogue of ministry. Instead, a great number of ecclesial leadership functions are mentioned, such as preaching, prophesying and speaking in tongues, healing and exorcism, community building, pastoral care, and administrative facilitation.[27] Theologically and practically, the distinction between the sexes is insignificant in such a multiform exercise of ministry. The apostolic and prophetic ministry has always been exercised in the church by women. Historically, the spiritual emancipation of women was acknowledged primarily by those churches that knew themselves to be governed by the Holy Spirit.[28] A close connection seems to exist between a Spirit ecclesiology and women's equal participation in the ministries of the church. Women ministers in the church must therefore be especially concerned with teaching, preaching, spiritual counseling, and theology. It will be an important step toward the ecclesial emancipation of women if the clergy's spiritual control is broken.

In short, I argue, if the further clericalization and hierarchical monopolization of ecclesial ministries is to be avoided, women must insist that as baptized and confirmed members of the church they are entitled to hold responsible leading positions in the church. Women and men, professors, directors of seminaries, college teachers, catechists, missionaries, liturgical ministers, church administrators, pastoral assistants, journalists, social workers, lawyers, or organists do not need ordination for exercising their ecclesial ministry. Vocation, spiritual giftedness, and commitment suffice.

However, women have no intrinsic right to ecclesial ministry just because they are women or because of their "feminine" qualities. Constitutive for any church ministry are the "gifts" of the Holy Spirit,[29] which are present and manifest in the ministries that women already perform in the church. True vocation to ministry must be recognized whenever and wherever it is exercised in the

---

27. Eduard Schweizer, *Gemeinde und Gemeindeordnung im Neuen Testament* Abhandlungen zur Theologie des Alten und Neuen Testaments 35 (Zürich: Zwingli Verlag, 1959); Rudolf Schnackenburg, *Die Kirche im Neuen Testament,* Quaestiones Disputatae 14 (Freiburg: Herder, 1961).
28. Ernst Käsemann, *Jesu letzter Wille nach Joh. 17* (Tübingen: Mohr, 1966), 60.
29. Küng, *Die Kirche,* 473ff.

church. Petitions or resolutions to the Holy See will not lead to the ecclesial emancipation of women. Such emancipation depends on effective and "gifted" ministerial engagement.

STRATEGIES FOR WOMEN IN MINISTRY TODAY

In closing I would like to make a practical suggestion for the strategic engagement of women concerned with ecclesial ministry today. I urge St. Joan's International Alliance to organize – perhaps together with other women's groups in the church – women in professional church ministry. To engender such an emancipatory movement of women in ecclesial ministry, I recommend the following:

First, St. Joan's International Alliance should create a public forum or committee consisting not only of theologians, but also of sociologists, ethnologists, psychologists, historians, anthropologists, etc., that could investigate and debate new forms of being church. Issues such as ordination, priesthood, church, world, ministerial structures, mission, the theology and image of the "eternal Woman," the contributions of women in the history of the church, and religious status differences among women should not be left to ecclesiastical pronouncements and male theologians.

Second, rather than fight for admission to the lowest ranks of the hierarchy, this proposed International Women's Forum should encourage all women to strive for a solid education and for leading positions in society and church. It must encourage women to become role models for younger women, while it seeks ways to support those women who are already working in such leading positions. In addition, it must reject the requirement of celibacy for ministry and discuss the questions of marriage and birth control. In collaboration with the autonomous women's movement in society it should seek to discuss traditional women's roles and the "double and triple" burden of women. Church history shows that structural changes in the church always presuppose changes in its surrounding societies and vice versa.

Third, such a forum could explore ways to facilitate the theological education of women, not only in theory but also in practice, e.g., with scholarships for talented women who are willing to study theology. Students need role models, introduction to academic life, spiritual encouragement, and financial support. In my view, the most important task and goal for the women's movement in Germany today should be to find every conceivable means for making it possible for women not only to study "lay" theology but also to complete the full course of theology concluding with the M.Div., licentiate, doctorate, or habilitation. We need to work for university positions for women assistants, lecturers, and ordinary professors on theological faculties.

Fourth, those professional ministries that are already exercised by women within the church must be examined with respect to their self-understanding. They should be reformed according to the new conciliar understanding of the church and its mission. At the same time it must be brought to public consciousness and discussion that in reality women already hold a great number and variety of ecclesial ministries. Therefore, ordination is *not* a question of the admission of women to ecclesial ministry. Rather, it is a question of recognition and confirmation of such ministries. Simultaneously, we have to stress women's right to be admitted to all ministerial functions in the church, including the episcopal and papal offices.

Finally, such a women's forum should discuss and explicitly advocate the abolition of mandatory celibacy, for the clerical mentality and lifestyle engender and continue negative attitudes toward and fear of women. Such clerical celibacy can, however, not simply be replaced with patriarchal marriage, as was the case in the Reformation. Rather ministerial spirituality, lifestyle, and education must be transformed in light of the theology and spirituality of church as the people of God.

And here I come to the end of my analysis and lecture, which because of time constraints remains sketchy and therefore may lead to misunderstandings. I have sought here to investigate the question of women's ministry within the Catholic Church. In light of the efforts to revive the permanent diaconate for men, I have argued that St. Joan's International Alliance and other women's groups in the church should not strive to incorporate women into the lowest ranks of the hierarchical structure of the post-Constantinian church. On the contrary, we have to assert women's right to be fully responsible members of the church. We have to strengthen the "lay," that is, baptismal ministries and to reconstruct all forms of hierarchalized, clericalized, and sacralized church ministries so that they can be put again into the hands and responsibility of the whole church. According to Vatican II it is the task of the postconciliar church to transform its authoritarian structure toward a dynamic ministry in the church and for the world. For the success of such an ecclesial transformation, the question of women's ministry and ordination has an essential hermeneutic and practical function. Only such an ecclesial transformation in the power of the Holy Spirit will bring about the full Christian emancipation of women and of the church in service to the well-being of the world.

3 ——————————————

SAINTS ALIVE
YESTERDAY AND TODAY

———————————————————————

CONTEXTUALIZATION

In 1972 I was invited by an editor of the Brooklyn *Tablet,* a Roman
Catholic diocesan newspaper, to contribute to their first issue on
women in the church. I had just returned from a workshop on
"Women Exploring Theology," sponsored by the Grail and Church
Women United. It was the first time that I had participated in
the discussions of an interconfessional and interreligious group of
women. Although I had taken courses at the Protestant faculty of
Münster, my ecumenical experience had been very limited, largely
restricted to some Lutheran friends. Since I grew up in Franco-
nia, an area of Germany that is almost completely Catholic, this
encounter with women of different faith communities was new, in-
vigorating, and challenging to me. It taught me that the women's
movement in theology shared a common ecumenical vision and
impetus. At the same time I realized that our discussions were,
consciously or not, also determined by our Christian or Jewish confessional differences. The following reflection sought to follow the
imperative of the workshop that women's theologizing must begin with experience, while it also strove to recognize that Catholic
women's experience was shaped differently.

———————————————

"Saints Alive Yesterday and Today," *Brooklyn Tablet,* December 7, 1972.

AS A CHILD I loved to read the stories of the saints. A significant number were women, and I identified with them. They were
teachers, mystics, missionaries, abbesses, soldiers, queens, and
peasants. Many of these stories did not limit women to the roles
of wife and mother within the nuclear family; rather they told of
women's outstanding contributions in the history of the church
and the Western world. These women were creative, independent,
and influential.

When I grew up, however, I lost interest in the "lives of the
saints." Perhaps many of those readers who have grown up in the
Roman Catholic tradition share this experience with me. The more
priests and nuns promoted devotion to the Virgin Mary, the humble handmaiden of God, or preached about Maria Goretti, who
preferred death over being raped, the more I started to lose interest in — or even reject — the saints who were women. After a retreat
in high school that concluded with the fervent sermon of a young
priest on the purity and chastity of Our Lady, I found out that I was
not alone with my resentment. The twenty young women in the
room shared the same observation: Maybe devotion to the Virgin
and to the saints gave something to the male psyche, but we could
not identify with the image of women presented by them. Our
images of ourselves, our problems as young women, and our goals
for life were totally different from the images of the female saints
that were preached to us. The lives of the saints presented more of a
hindrance than a help in finding our own self-identity. These stories
stressed suffering, sexual purity, submission, outmoded piety, and
total obedience. They were anti-intellectual and antierotic; they
told about many nuns and widows and some queens, but rarely
did they speak about ordinary women. While we desired our own
independence and love, the glorification of the saints demanded
humble feminine submission and fostered sexual neuroses.

At a recent workshop at Grailville, women from different Christian and Jewish communities came together to discuss theology
and ministry. There I realized in conversation with women from
other Christian churches that despite discrepancies between the
images of female saints and my own experience as a teenager, the
feasts and lives of the saints were part of my own religious history
and experience. I recognized that Catholic women cannot simply
turn away from the images and cult of the saints without paying the
price of alienation from ourselves and from our particular Christian
tradition and community. By withdrawing from our own experi-

ence and by repressing the images and rituals of the saints that have formed us, we are in danger of leaving these religious images of women in command and control of Catholic women's psyche, not to mention in the command and control of the male hierarchy, which interprets their meaning for women.

The struggle to liberate women and men from the sexist mind-sets and misogynist attitudes of schools, churches, and society at large calls for a new critical re-visioning of ourselves as well as of Christian tradition and community. It calls also for the historical rediscovery of the lives and contributions of women who have struggled with similar problems, albeit in quite different religious and cultural circumstances. It calls for the "liberation" of the women saints from the false and distorted images projected onto them by patriarchal culture and theology. The religious struggle against sexism also calls for the recognition of the suffering, maiming, and victimization of the female saints in this struggle. In short, such a demythologization and reshaping of the images and stories of women in Catholic Christian tradition is essential to the self-understanding and liberation struggles of women today, for we may not cut ourselves off from the religious images and historical memory that have shaped our experience.

Catholic women must also search for images and stories of women in the church's past and present with which we can identify. They will help us to build a new sisterhood that bridges not only the gaps between nuns, married women, and single women, but also those between our present experience and that of the women of the past. Our search for a new identity and a new Christian community of women will hopefully recover and reinterpret the images and stories of sainted women of the past since such images may help to illuminate and enhance our self-image as women, enabling us to articulate a religious identity of our own. Only when Catholic women get in touch with our own lived experience, while simultaneously confronting our own historical and dogmatic traditions, will we be able to reconstruct and create new and liberating images of women saints – images that will correct the traditional ideal of woman and femininity that church and society have inculcated. While these newly liberated and liberating images of women saints need to resonate with our personal experiences, feelings, and histories, they must also provide counterimages to the dominant image of woman in contemporary culture and religion. Such liberating images for women can serve both as corrective guide and paradigm for women.

Indeed, the traditional images and legends of the saints express the conviction that women like men have to follow their vocation from God. Like men, women are called to follow Jesus, even if this entails taking a stand or course of action frontally opposed to the ingrained cultural mores of their times. Granted, from both a theological and hagiographical point of view, the life-choices of the women saints were often limited, conforming to male stereotypes. Nevertheless, these choices also contradict the "total woman" image propagated by the feminine cultural mystique and by the Catholic "theology of woman" — both of which recognize the true vocation of woman to be motherhood alone, whether spiritual or physical in kind. The traditional biographies and images of the saints do not define women primarily by their family status or their biological or reproductive capacities. Rather, they understand women, like men, to be called to discipleship and sainthood. The early Christians considered themselves to be those who were called and elected by God; they believed themselves to be the saints of God. Such a call broke through all limitations of religion, culture, race, class, and sex. The gospels affirm in various ways that Jesus' call to discipleship had precedence over all other obligations, religious duties, and family ties. Jesus did not respect the patriarchal family and its claims but replaced it with the new community of disciples.

Throughout the centuries this vision of discipleship and community has evoked life-responses not only by men but also by women. Elisabeth of Hungary, my patron saint, was one of these women.[1] Her all too short life (1207–31) was spent in the pursuit of this vision of discipleship. Her life-story illustrates how difficult it was and still is for women to live the early Christian vision of discipleship in a patriarchal religion and culture. Inspired by the

---

1. Since I am not a medieval expert, I relied here on my own extensive readings on my patron saint, which at this point have mostly been in German. The following come to mind: Elisabeth Busse-Wilson, *Das Leben der heiligen Elisabeth von Thüringen* (Munich, 1931); A. Huysken, ed., *Die Schriften des Caesarius von Heisterbach über die heilige Elisabeth von Thüringen*, Publikationen der Gesellschaft für rheinische Geschichtskunde 43 (Bonn, 1937); W. Maurer, "Zum Verständnis der heiligen Elisabeth von Thüringen," *Zeitschrift für Kirchengeschichte* 65 (1953/54); Herbert Grundmann, *Religiöse Bewegungen im Mittelalter,* 3d ed. (Darmstadt, 1970); Philipps Universität Marburg, ed., *Sankt Elisabeth: Fürstin, Dienerin, Heilige. Aufsätze, Dokumentation, Katalog* (Sigmaringen: Thorbecke, 1981); Ernest W. McDonell, *The Beguines and Beghards in Medieval Culture* (New Brunswick, N.J.: Rutgers University Press, 1954).

gospels, Elisabeth, like other women of the twelfth and thirteenth centuries, sought a "religious" way of life, following her call to radical discipleship. Like Clare and Francis of Assisi she wanted to follow Jesus by living as a poor and itinerant beggar woman. Yet such an evangelical lifestyle for women was inconceivable to medieval men, even to St. Francis, who collaborated in restricting Clare and her women followers to the traditional cloistered way of life. Unlike Clare, however, Elisabeth succeeded at least partially in fulfilling her dream of following Jesus in his poverty. According to her words she understood herself as sharing the lifestyle of the "sisters in the world" (*vita sororum in saeculo*). Elisabeth thus participated in a widespread movement of medieval women and men who sought to live in the discipleship of equals, a movement that included not only the Beguines, but also the Albigensian and Waldensian "sisters."

Legend and theology have distorted Elisabeth's image and story as a radical follower of Jesus. Instead, they have made her into an idealistic but unrealistic charitable lady. The legend of the "rose miracle" illustrates this distortion of her image and vocation to radical discipleship. This legend portrays Elisabeth as hiding her activity of almsgiving and as fearful of a husband who opposed her charitable works. When detected she asks for and is granted a miracle that protects her from her husband's anger. The image and the message conveyed is clear: Elisabeth is seen as an extravagant wife, who excessively spends her husband's estate. She lives more in fear of than in love with him. Her biographical data appear to support this image that the legend conveys. Born as a child of the king of Hungary, Elisabeth was engaged at the age of four and married at age fourteen to the Landgrave of Thuringia, Ludwig IV. She had three children with him, was widowed at eighteen, and died at twenty-four. To be sure, her life appears to be very much a part of medieval culture and seems completely remote from the visions and goals of contemporary Christian women. Her marriage is seen as one of political convenience and her sainthood as an achievement of her widowhood.

Yet beneath the surface of her medieval legend, features of an outstandingly independent personality emerge. Characteristic elements of her life story, such as her soul-partnership with her husband, her independence from the roles prescribed by marriage and motherhood, her dedication to the pursuit of her own personal vocation, and her social awareness and sense of justice, whether despite or because of their medieval flavor, provide a quite different image.

First, although Elisabeth's marriage with Ludwig was arranged for political reasons, it was nevertheless a love-match. True, she offended her husband's family and the local nobility because she often went against the established etiquette for highborn women and the usual conventions of social intercourse. Her husband nevertheless treasured her love, supported her religious dedication, and shielded her against attacks. Contrary to commonly held expectations their marriage was not limited to a politically expedient arrangement. Having grown up together, they learned to cherish, respect, and love each other. Within their medieval cultural context, they lived a marriage of genuine companionship and friendship — not one of patriarchal domination and submission.

Contrary to the legend Ludwig not only supported Elisabeth's dedication to the poor, but he also defended her against accusations and slander from inside and outside his family. Their love and need for each other was so great that they could not bear to be separated for a long time. Elisabeth offended others because she did not hesitate to express her love freely and publicly. An early biographer found her expressions of love so remarkable (or scandalous?) that he explicitly states that Elisabeth publicly hugged Ludwig "and kissed him on his mouth more than a thousand times."

Second, although Elisabeth freely expressed her emotional attachment and passionate love for Ludwig, she also saw the danger of becoming totally absorbed and overwhelmed by this love. She once reported to her maid-friends that she needed to get up and pray throughout the night in order not to succumb to her overpowering desire and love for Ludwig. One ought not to construe her statement as ascetic contempt and pious repression of erotic love, but rather as a religious means of protecting her vocation from being obliterated and absorbed in such a marriage relationship. Elisabeth appears to have been aware of the danger for women of losing their own independence, self-identity, and call to discipleship because of their love of a man. Her reaction to Ludwig's death indicates that this danger was very real for her. She became so desperate that people feared she would lose her mind.

Third, the independent spirit of Elisabeth's personality, which feared losing itself in her privileged status of aristocratic courtship and motherhood, becomes manifest in her single-minded dedication to live the "option for the poor." Her desire to live as the poor must not be mistaken as conventional almsgiving, which was the duty of a noble lady. Very much influenced in her spirituality by Francis of Assisi, Elisabeth was not content to be the generous benefactor of the poor; instead, she wanted to live as one who is poor among the poor. Although Francis allowed only his brothers to beg in the streets, his example and preaching inspired Elisabeth to transgress all gender limitations and to follow Jesus as a woman by living among the poor and by begging in the streets. Forbidden to do so by her spiritual director, Konrad of Marburg, who deemed such a lifestyle of discipleship to be improper for a woman of her rank, she founded and administered a hospital in Marburg. Since clerics or nuns were usually the directors of such houses for the poor and sick, even this action was new for her time.

What makes Elisabeth's life most outstanding, however, is her sense of social justice. Elisabeth's contribution consisted in seeing poverty not as willed by God but as closely linked with the lifestyle of the rich and noble classes. She recognized that many consumer goods were unjustly taken away from the poor peasants who were her subjects. Peasants and petty workers paid for the luxurious living of the princes and lords. Not wanting to participate any more than necessary in such brutal exploitation, she vowed to eat only the food that had been justly acquired – a protest that anticipates by centuries our modern form of boycotting consumer goods in order to bring about change.

Elisabeth's vow was a decisive step forward in the medieval theology and praxis of almsgiving. She not only shared her and her husband's goods with the poor; she also publicly protested against the injustices done to them. Her contemporaries recognized the revolutionary potential of her action. Ludwig's family attacked her; the surrounding gentility ridiculed her. They claimed she was stupid and crazy. After Ludwig's death her brother-in-law tried to force her to eat all the food served at the table if she wanted to stay at the Wartburg. In so doing, he sought to prevent her from following her practice of discriminating between food that had been justly earned and food that had been unjustly earned. Resisting this coercion, Elisabeth left her home and lived in utmost poverty herself. Her maid-companion is quoted as giving the following reason for her predicament: "Since she did not want to live from the exploitation of the poor . . . , she chose banishment and the earning of her living by the work of her hands." Elisabeth felt that she came closest to this vision of discipleship when she had to live homeless and penniless for months after she fled with her children from the Wartburg.

Fourth, at this point in her life it becomes clear that her own vision of radical discipleship was fundamentally different from that of her confessor, Konrad of Marburg, who was renowned for his rigorous asceticism and zealousness against heretics. After the demise of Ludwig, Konrad appealed to the pope and was appointed Elisabeth's legal representative to decide how her vast fortunes should be utilized. When Elisabeth begged him to allow her to relinquish her elite status and wealth in order to live in total poverty as a beggar woman, he categorically denied her wish.

Although it is true that Elisabeth freely and with Ludwig's approval had chosen Konrad as her spiritual director, promising obedience to him while her husband was still alive, such a decision stemmed from her vocation to radical discipleship, which she desired to live in equality with the poor. Since Konrad wanted her to live an ascetic life in total obedience to him, he attempted to force her into a mold of religious lifestyle that he deemed appropriate for a noble widow. In order to break Elisabeth's will, Konrad brutally battered and in the name of God physically and emotionally abused her. He not only hit her if she deviated from his injunctions in the slightest way, but he also sought to isolate and deprive her of all human warmth and friendship. When he became the head of the hospital that Elisabeth founded, he moved into the patriarchal role of both worldly and spiritual head of household, who was entitled to control and chastise all members of the household.

Although hagiography seeks to persuade us that Konrad in this way sought to support Elisabeth's own quest for perfection, her women companions testify – after his death – that Elisabeth feared him greatly. By ostentatiously obeying him, yet astutely circumventing his injunctions in light of her own vocation and judgment, she sought to fulfill her desire for radical discipleship. The brutal violence that Konrad inflicted upon Elisabeth in the name of God provides a historical paradigm of spiritual male brutality directed toward women who do not conform and obey. Elisabeth, who was spared the battering and brutality of a patriarchal marriage, was not spared that of the patriarchal church. Elisabeth compares her strategy of spiritual survival to that of a reed bent by the impact of a torrential flood without being broken: "After the flood subsides such a reed raises up again in full power, serene and beautiful. In the same way, we must bend and humble ourselves occasionally and afterwards stand again erect, serene and beautiful." Konrad's savage attempt to extinguish Elisabeth's will and independence of vision could make her bend, but it could not detract from her own vision of radical discipleship. After she became a hospital sister, she finally managed to abandon all her possessions and to live the lowly life of the "sisters in the world." She sought to perform the most menial domestic tasks and to be one with the hospital sisters who generally came from the lower classes. Nevertheless, their awareness of her high status never allowed her to become one of them.

To conclude: The actual life story and image of Elisabeth differs from that of the legend. Elisabeth was a woman with her own vocation and vision of discipleship. She experienced love and marriage as supportive, rather than destructive, of her own mission. After Ludwig's death she left her home because of her vision of a discipleship dedicated to justice. She separated from her children so that she could live as a poor woman in solidarity with the poor. She did not make the poor objects of her piety and charitable works but sought to live with them as her equals.

Elisabeth also sought to live in solidarity with her women servants who were not of her own class. She never let herself be called "mistress" or be addressed with the formal "thou," but insisted that her companions should use the familiar "you" because they were her friends. Elisabeth suffered tremendously when Konrad cut off this bond of friendship between her and her companions. Yet she never gave up her vision to live as one of "the sisters in the world."

Despite its medieval flavor Elisabeth's vision of radical discipleship resonates with Catholic women today who understand themselves as fully committed and responsible Christians. The historical image of Elisabeth, freed from its legendary trappings and rescued from its medieval limitations, does not restrict women's vision and self-understanding to family, children, and feminine behavior appropriate to the "white lady." Instead, this image encourages women to break out of the cultural and religious limitations of femininity to a self-image and identity of full personhood and radical discipleship. Moreover, such an ideal suggests that women's struggles for liberation must not be limited to the values and interests of middle-class women. Rather, these struggles must work to build a new sisterhood of discipleship — one that transcends sex-stereotyped roles, social class, and religious caste as well as our separation in time and space.

Elisabeth's message to us, her sisters, today is: Women are not to be confined to cultural lifestyles of femininity, but they are called to live out their radical discipleship over and against these culturally and theologically sanctioned feminine middle-class sex roles. Just as Elisabeth experienced brutal violence because she sought to follow her vocation, defining the way to do so by overstepping the boundaries of her social class and historical horizon, so also Catholic women today have to be prepared to experience social and religious violence if they follow the gospel's call to radical discipleship. The women's movement in the church must never forget Elisabeth's wise counsel: bend like a reed in the storm in order to be able to survive and live upright in the power and beauty of the Spirit.

4 _____

HEAVY BURDENS, HARD TO BEAR

CONTEXTUALIZATION

In 1973 when the Supreme Court's *Roe vs. Wade* decision made abortion legal, the provost of the University of Notre Dame organized a series of liturgies and sermons denouncing this decision. When students asked him to invite a speaker who would be in favor of the Court's decision, he asked me to one of his nightly hall liturgies, just three hours before the service.

His call put me in a serious quandary: Should I go and speak on such a complex topic although I did not have much time for preparation? If I did not accept, however, I would let the students down and the provost would be justified in boasting that no one of the "Notre Dame family" would support such a barbarous ruling on abortion, which he likened to the Holocaust. A friend whom I called for advice counseled against giving such a sermon because as a biblical scholar I should not meddle in such an emotionally charged and controversial moral issue. Another friend advised that I should forget about delivering such a homily if I wanted to have a professional future at Notre Dame. In spite of these well-intentioned warnings, however, I decided to support those students who had the courage to insist that a dissenting voice must be heard.

——— ✤ ———

SISTERS AND BROTHERS,

I have chosen Matthew 23:1-4, 13-16, 23-24 as the Scripture text on which I want to meditate with you tonight:

> Then Jesus said to the crowds and to his disciples: "The theologians and clergymen [scribes and Pharisees] sit on Peter's [Moses'] seat; therefore do whatever they teach you and follow it; but do not do as they do, for they do not practice what they teach. They tie up heavy burdens, hard to bear, and lay them on the shoulders of others; but they themselves are unwilling to lift a finger to move them.
>
> Woe to you theologians and clergymen, hypocrites! For you lock people out of the kingdom of heaven. For you do not go in yourselves, and when others are going in, you stop them. Woe to you, theologians and clergymen, hypocrites! For you devour widow's houses. . . . Woe to you, theologians and clergymen, hypocrites! For you cross sea and land to make a single convert, and you make the new convert twice as much a child of hell as yourselves. Woe to you, blind guides. . . .
>
> Woe to you, theologians and clergymen, hypocrites! For you tithe mint, dill, and cumin, and have neglected the weightier matters of the law: justice, mercy, and faith. It is these you ought to have practiced without neglecting the others. You blind guides! You strain out a gnat but swallow a camel!

Those of you who know me are well aware that I was invited to this liturgy because I am one of those who approve of the Supreme Court's decision. Today I give thanks to God that women no longer have to bleed to death and die in back alleys from botched abortions. When my friend Maria did her hospital internship on a gynecological ward, she would come home and relate story after story of poor, young women who had been raped, of mothers with too many children already, of women for whom birth control had failed. The women tried to hide that they had attempted or suffered an abortion, since at the time such a procedure was not legal in Germany. Those women who survived often ended up with lifelong health problems. The Supreme Court's decision means freedom for women not only from threats to their health and well-being, but also from fear of criminalization and incarceration. Reason to give thanks!

Does this mean that I advocate abortion and think it is right in any circumstance? Such a rhetorical question misconstrues the legalization of abortion to be a prescriptive law that *demands* abortion. Far from it! The justices do not say to women you *should* have an abortion; rather, their decision states that women will not incur punitive sanctions if they decide to terminate a first trimester pregnancy. The law does not take away the moral responsibility of women: it calls for it. The American institution of the separation of church and state is envied by many German Catholics. It means that the state cannot meddle in religious ethics and *moral* theology. Rather than bemoan the Supreme Court's ruling, Catholics should welcome the law as creating the space of freedom for seriously discussing termination of pregnancy as a *moral* decision.

Since I am neither a philosopher nor a moral theologian, I do not want to discuss here the difficult question of when personal human life begins. Instead, I invite you to contemplate the warnings of the reading from Scripture that we have just heard. The woe pronouncements of Matthew's Gospel bemoan the gap between teaching and doing, between preaching and praxis. The text opens with the injunction "Do whatever they teach you and follow it; but do not do as they do." At the end the reading asserts that the central matters of this teaching are "justice, mercy, and faith." Any *moral* teaching on abortion must be shaped by the concern for "justice, mercy, and faith" not only for the fetus but also for the mother, her life, and her other children. It must seek to create a social situation where the interests of the mother and those of the fetus do not compete with each other. It must protect women's civil right to self-determination.

If Notre Dame as a Catholic university subscribes to the teaching that abortion is morally wrong, it must at the same time seek to safeguard the "weightier matters of the law" — justice, mercy, and faith. Its preaching and praxis must not contradict each other. What must the university do in order to avoid the charge of hypocrisy? Let us imagine a campus that would practice what it preaches. Such a moral imagination helps us to see that we need to change our policy and praxis at least in the following four areas.

First, the university must make information about and access to birth control readily available. Campus ministry should advocate — rather than oppose — the dissemination of birth-control information and counseling through student medical services on campus. We must realize that many of our students are sexually active instead of closing our eyes to it. Availability of birth control does not foster premarital sex. Its absence increases the number of Notre Dame and St. Mary's students who end up in downtown abortion clinics.

Second, we must reconsider our policy that expels pregnant unmarried women students but not their male partners from campus housing. Instead, we should provide nursery and day care facilities that would allow student mothers to finish their studies while their babies are cared for on campus. We must create housing on campus and scholarships that would allow unmarried women students — if they wish to do so — to bring up their children with dignity. We have the theological, moral, and economic resources to foster a communal vision that understands children to be the responsibility of the whole Notre Dame "family."

Third, we must stop advocating adoption as the moral solution to the problem of abortion. The adoption business of bartering "white babies" is morally more offensive than the termination of pregnancy in the first weeks after conception. In many cases, the trauma of adoption is as great as, if not greater than, that of early abortion. As long as adoption is shrouded in secrecy, as long as young white women are pressured to give up their babies for adoption, as long as mothers are not allowed to keep in touch with their adopted children, or at least to receive information about their development and circumstances, if they so desire, for just so long the morality of adoption must be questioned.

Finally, since Notre Dame has been traditionally a male, clerical institution, the administration and academic leadership of the university needs to communicate to women students and faculty that their intellectual gifts are treasured and their university contributions are respected. Women students are not like "flowers" whose presence beautifies the campus. Moreover, the very low number and status of women faculty must be increased. A moral antiabortion stance requires that the university adopt for staff and faculty a paid-pregnancy and family-leave policy, establish a child care center on campus, develop an affirmative action program, institutionalize a job-share policy, and make possible tenurable part-time positions with all fringe benefits.

As long as we do not practice what we preach, the woes and indictments that Jesus pronounced against the leaders of his own time are addressed also to us at Notre Dame: "Woe to you hypocrites, woe to you blind guides: You tie up heavy burdens, hard to bear, and lay them on the shoulders of others; but you yourselves are unwilling to lift a finger to move them."

5 _____

FEMINIST THEOLOGY
AS A CRITICAL THEOLOGY
OF LIBERATION

"Mother, what is a feminist?"
"A feminist, my daughter,
Is any woman now who cares
To think about her own affairs
As men don't think she oughter."

CONTEXTUALIZATION

When I used this ditty, written by Alice Duer Miller in 1915,[1] as
the epigraph for the following article, the editor of *Theological
Studies* cut it because, in his opinion, it was too flip for a scholarly
article in a scholarly journal. Since this issue was the first attempt
of an established journal to introduce women's "new" theologizing to a wider Roman Catholic audience, I accepted his censure. I
still think, however, that this ditty captures some of the assertive-
ness and opposition this new way of doing theology from women's
perspective was bound to encounter.

It is not known who was the first to use the expression "feminist
theology" to characterize this new way for women to do theology from women's perspective. However, I distinctly remember

1. Alice Duer Miller, *Are Women People? A Book of Rhymes for Suffrage Times*
(New York: George H. Doran, 1915).

choosing this designation to name my own "brand" of doing theology as a feminist liberation theology. In order to distinguish my approach from hermeneutic-liberal, Latin American, and black liberation theologies, I added the word "critical," which signals my indebtedness to the critical theory of Jürgen Habermas.

The argument of this essay emerged from the discussions of the New York Feminist Scholars in Religion group, which Carol Christ had initiated. Members of this group, which included among others Beverly Wildung Harrison, Judith Plaskow, Sheila Collins, Nelle Morton, Letty Russell, Anne Barstow, and Carol Christ herself, have decisively shaped feminist studies in religion. I was fortunate to be able to join them during a sabbatical year at Union Theological Seminary.

When this article appeared after I returned to my position at Notre Dame, however, my chairman was so upset by it that he tried to persuade me to retract it. He was especially distressed by my analysis of the "Mary myth" and its impact on Catholic women. When I refused to concede his point, he furiously told me that someone who had authored such an article was not fit to teach at a Catholic university. Since I had just received tenure I facetiously asked him whether he would appoint me to a research chair so that I would no longer teach Notre Dame students. In spite of my critical analysis I still found it hard to imagine the forms of institutional violence that could be unleashed against women "who think about their own affairs as men don't think they oughter."

———— ❖ ————

WRITING AN ARTICLE on feminist theology for an established theological journal is as dangerous as navigating between Scylla and Charbydis. Radical feminists might consider such an endeavor as collaboration with the "enemy" or at best as "tokenism." Professional theologians might refuse to take the issue seriously or might emotionally react against it. Even though the women's movement has been with us almost a decade, it is still surrounded by confusion, derision, and outright refusal to listen to its arguments. Yet since I consider myself a feminist as well as a Christian theologian, I am vitally interested in a mediation between feminism and theology. And good theology has always been a risky enterprise.

In the first part of the article I intend to circumscribe the concrete situation in which feminist theology is situated, insofar as I summarize some of the main tenets of the feminist critique of culture and religion and its reception by church men and theologians. The second part will present feminist theology as a critical theology. First, I will attempt to point out the feminist critique of the practice of theology by professional theologians and institutions. Then I intend to show how in the tradition androcentric theology functions to justify the discriminatory praxis of the church toward women. A final part will deal critically with myths and images of women. Even though the Mary-myth has emancipatory elements, it has not served to promote the liberation of women. Therefore, it has to be balanced and replaced by a new myth and images that evolve from a feminist Christian consciousness and praxis. The article concludes with such an example of the feminist search for new liberating myths and images.

FEMINISM AND THEOLOGY

The analyses of the women's liberation movement have uncovered the sexist structures and myths of our culture and society.[2] As racism defines and oppresses black people because of their color, so sexism stereotypes and limits people because of their gender. That women are culturally oppressed people becomes evident when we apply Paulo Freire's definition of oppression to the situation of women:

> Any situation in which "A" objectively exploits "B" or hinders his [*sic*] pursuit of self-affirmation as a responsible person is one of oppression. Such a situation in itself constitutes violence, even when sweetened by false generosity, because it interferes with man's [*sic*] ontological and historical vocation to be more fully human.[3]

---

2. The literature on the women's liberation movement is so extensive that it is impossible here to mention all the works from which I have learned. Especially helpful were Vivian Gornick and Barbara K. Moran, eds., *Woman in Sexist Society: Studies in Power and Powerlessness* (New York: Basic Books, 1971); Judith Hole and Ellen Levine, *Rebirth of Feminism* (New York: Quadrangle Books, 1971); Elizabeth Janeway, *Man's World, Woman's Place: Studies in Social Mythology* (New York: Morrow, 1971); Anica Vesel Mander and Anne Kent Rush, *Feminism as Therapy* (New York: Random House, 1974); Betty Roszak and Theodore Roszak, eds., *Masculine/Feminine: Readings in Sexual Mythology and the Liberation of Women* (New York: Harper & Row, 1969); Sheila Rowbotham, *Woman's Consciousness, Man's World* (Harmondsworth: Penguin, 1973).

3. Paulo Freire, *Pedagogy of the Oppressed* (New York: Continuum, 1970), 40–41.

In a sexist society a woman's predominant role in life is to be man's helpmate, to cook and work for him without being paid, to bear and rear his children, and to guarantee him psychological and sexual satisfaction. Woman's place is in the home, whereas man's place is in the world earning money, running the state, schools, and churches. If woman ventures into the man's world, then her task is subsidiary, as in the home; she holds the lowest-paid jobs, because she supposedly works for pocket money; she remains confined to women's professions and is kept out of high-ranking positions. G. K. Chesterton's ironical quip sums up the struggles and results of the suffrage movement: "Millions of women arose and shouted: No one will ever dictate to us again – and they became typists." In spite of a century of struggle for equality, women have not yet succeeded in obtaining leading positions and equal opportunity in the public and societal realm. On the contrary, they were incorporated into the economic system and moral values of our sexist culture, which merely organized women's capabilities for its own purposes.[4]

FEMINIST CRITIQUE OF CULTURE AND RELIGION

Whereas the suffrage movement did not so much attempt to change society as mainly to integrate women into it, in the conviction that women would humanize politics and work by virtue of their feminine qualities,[5] the new feminist movement radically criticizes the myth and structures of a society and culture that keep women down. The women's liberation movement demands a restructuring of societal institutions and a redefinition of cultural images and

---

4. See the various analyses in Deborah Babcox and Madeline Belkin, compilers, *Liberation Now! Writings from the Women's Liberation Movement* (New York: Dell Publishing Co., 1971); Caroline Bird, *Born Female: The High Cost of Keeping Women Down* (New York: D. McKay Co., 1968); Joan Huber, ed., *Changing Women in a Changing Society* (Chicago: University of Chicago Press, 1973).

5. Beverly Wildung Harrison, "Sexism in the Contemporary Church: When Evasion Becomes Complicity," in *Sexist Religion and Women in the Church*, ed. Alice L. Hageman (New York: Association Press, 1974), 195–216, makes the very helpful distinction between "radical" or "hard" feminism and "soft" feminism. See also her article "The Early Feminists and the Clergy: A Case Study in the Dynamics of Secularization," *Review and Expositor* 72 (1975): 41–52. For the documentation and analysis of the first women's movement, see Eleanor Flexner, *Century of Struggle: The Woman's Rights Movement in the United States* (Cambridge, Mass.: Belknap Press of Harvard University Press, 1959); Aileen S. Kraditor, ed., *Up from the Pedestal: Selected Writings in the History of American Feminism* (Chicago: Quadrangle Books, 1968).

roles of women *and* men, if women are to become autonomous human persons and achieve economic and political equality.

The feminist critique of culture has pointed out that not nature and biology but rather sexist culture and socialization are the "destiny" of women. Women are denied the full range of human potentiality; we are socialized to view ourselves as dependent on, less intelligent than, and derivative from men. From earliest childhood we learn our roles as subservient beings and value ourselves through the eyes of a male culture.[6] We are the "other," socialized into helpmates of men or sex objects for their desire. Journals, advertisements, television, and movies represent us either as dependent little girls (e.g., addressed as "baby"), as sexy and seductive women, or as self-sacrificing wives and mothers. Teachers, psychologists, philosophers, writers, and preachers define us as derivative, inferior, and subordinate beings who lack the intelligence, courage, and genius of men.

Women in our culture are either denigrated and infantilized or idealized and put on a pedestal, but they are not allowed to be independent and free human persons. They do not live their own lives, but are taught to live vicariously through those of husband and children. They do not exercise their own power, but manipulate men's power. They usually are not supposed to express their own opinion, but are expected to be silent or to voice only the opinions of their fathers, husbands, bosses, or sons. Not only men but women themselves have interiorized this image and understanding of woman as inferior and derivative. Often they themselves most strongly believe and defend the "feminine mystique."[7] Since women have learned to feel inferior and to despise themselves, they do not respect, in fact they even hate, other women. Thus women evidence the typical personality traits of oppressed people who have internalized the images and notions of the oppressor.

In the face of this cultural image and self-understanding of women, feminism first maintains that women are human persons, and it therefore demands free development of full personhood for all, women and men. Second, feminism maintains that human rights and talents or weaknesses are not divided by sex. Feminism has pointed out that it is necessary for women to become indepen-

---

6. This is elucidated from a linguistic point of view by Robin Lakoff, *Language and Woman's Place* (New York: Harper & Row, 1975).

7. See the now classic analysis of Betty Friedan, *The Feminine Mystique* (New York: Norton, 1963).

dent economically and socially in order to be able to understand and value themselves as free, autonomous, and responsible subjects of their own lives. If women's role in society is to change, then women's and men's perceptions and attitudes toward women have to change at the same time.

Feminism has therefore vigorously criticized all institutions that exploit women, stereotype them, and keep them in inferior positions. In this context, feminist analysis points out not only that Christianity had a major influence in the making of Western culture and sexist ideology,[8] but also that the Christian churches and theologies still perpetuate the "feminine mystique" and women's inferiority through their institutional inequalities and theological justifications of women's innate difference from men. Christian ethics has intensified the internalization of the feminine, of passive attitudes, such as meekness, humility, submission, self-sacrifice, self-denying love, which impede the development of self-assertion and autonomy by women. "The alleged 'voluntarism' of the imposed submission in Christian patriarchy has turned women against themselves more deeply than ever, disguising and reinforcing the internalization process."[9]

RESPONSES TO FEMINIST CRITIQUE

As society and culture often respond to the feminist analysis and critique with denial, co-optation, or rejection, so do the Christian churches and theologians in order to neutralize the feminist critics so that the social and ecclesial order remains unchanged.

1. They deny the accuracy and validity of the feminist analysis and critique. They point out that women are in no way inferior and oppressed but superior and privileged; e.g., Pope Paul's various statements on the superior qualities of women thus serve to support the "feminine mystique." Since women have most thoroughly

---

8. Simone de Beauvoir's analysis is still paradigmatic: *The Second Sex* (New York: Knopf, 1971); see also the discussion of her position by Mary Daly, *The Church and the Second Sex* (New York: Harper & Row, 1968), 11–31.

9. Mary Daly, *Beyond God the Father: Toward a Philosophy of Women's Liberation* (Boston: Beacon Press, 1973), 140 and 98–106. See also Gwen Kennedy Neville, "Religious Socialization of Women within U.S. Subcultures," in *Sexist Religion*, 77–91; Nancy van Vuuren, *The Subversion of Women as Practiced by Churches, Witch-Hunters, and Other Sexists* (Philadelphia: Westminster, 1973), deals with the "traits due to victimization" from a historical perspective.

internalized the ideals and values of this mystique, this repudiation is most effectively carried out by women themselves. Middle-class and middle-aged women who have learned to suppress their own interests, abilities, and wishes in order to support their husbands' egos and careers feel that the feminist critique makes them obsolete. They sense that the abolition of gender stereotypes and traditional roles threatens the value and security of their lives. As the Beecher sisters glorified domesticity and sang the praises of motherhood in the nineteenth century,[10] so today some women's groups behind the anti-ERA campaign idolize women's security in marriage and their protection by law. They support their claim by theological references to the divinely ordained order of creation.[11] Theological arguments justify the privileged status of middle-class women. These women do not realize that they are only one man away from public welfare and that even middle-class women's economic status and self-identity are very precarious indeed.

2. Another way of dealing with the feminist critique is to co-opt it by acknowledging some minor points of its analysis. The establishment can adopt those elements of the feminist critique that do not radically question present structures and ideologies. For instance, Paul VI maintains that the church has already recognized "the contemporary effort to promote 'the advancement of women'" as "a sign of the times" and he demands legislation to protect women's equal rights "to participate in cultural, economic, social, and political life."[12] Yet he maintains that women have to be excluded from hierarchical orders on the grounds of an antiquated and simply false historical exegesis.[13] Similarly, "liberal" Protestant theologians and churches pay lip service to the equal rights of women; for, even though they ordain women, they erect "qualifying standards" and "academic quotas" that effectively keep women out of influential parish or seminary positions.[14] Some theologians

---

10. See Gayle Kimball, "A Counter Ideology," in *Women and Religion*, ed. Judith Plaskow and Joan Arnold Romero (Missoula, Mont.: Scholars Press, 1974), 177–87; D. Bass Fraser, "The Feminine Mystique: 1890–1910," *Union Seminary Quarterly Review* 27 (1972): 225–39.

11. Marianne H. Micks, "Exodus or Eden? A Battle of Images," *Anglican Theological Review* 55 (1973): 126–39.

12. See E. Carroll, "Testimony at the Bicentennial Hearings of the Catholic Church, February 4, 1975, on Woman."

13. See *National Catholic Reporter*, May 2, 1975, 17.

14. Anonymous, "How to Quench the Spirit without Really Trying: An Essay in Institutional Sexism," *Church and Society* (September–October 1972): 25–37; N. Ramsay Jones, "Women in the Ministry," in *Women's Liberation and the Church: The New De-*

participate in this process of co-optation after the feminist movement has become "acceptable" in intellectual circles and in the
publishing industry. In writing articles and books on women in
the New Testament or in the Christian tradition, in filling church
commissions on "the role of women in the church," they not only
demonstrate they are still in charge but also enhance their professional status. Another way of co-opting the feminist critique is
to turn women against women — "religious" women against "lay"
women, moderate theologians against radical ones — or to endow
certain women with "token status" in order to turn them against
their not so "well-educated" or so "well-balanced" sisters.

3. Where co-optation of the feminist critique is not possible, outright rejection and condemnation often takes its place.
The reaction is often very violent, because the feminist demand
for institutional and theological change is always a demand for
far-reaching personal change and the giving up of centuries-old
privileges. Whereas the "liberal" Christian press and "liberal"
Christian theologians in general pay lip service to the goals of the
women's movement, they often label it "anti-Christian," because
the feminist critique holds, to a great part, Christianity responsible
for the "rationalization" of women's inferior status in our culture.
In other words, male theologians are accountable for the ideologization of women's image and role in Christian theology. Being
male and being male theologians, they no longer can uphold their
"liberal" attitude toward the feminist cause, since they are already
personally involved. They declare Christian feminism as "antimale"
and "anti-Christian" in order to avoid radical conversion and radical
change.

> Those of us who are men cannot escape the crisis of conscience
> embodied in that moment [the ordination of Episcopal women] be-
> cause whatever our politics on the issue, we are as men associates
> in the systematic violence done to women by the structures of male
> supremacy. . . .
>
> As men we must support the movement for equality by women, even
> as it becomes more radical. And as men, we must examine and repent
> of our own parts in the sexist mindset that dehumanizes us.[15]

---

mand for Freedom in the Life of the Christian Church, ed. Sarah Bentley Doely (New
York: Association Press, 1970), 60–69.
   15. J. Carroll, "The Philadelphia Ordination," *National Catholic Reporter,* August 16,
1974, 14.

The unwillingness for radical repentance and fundamental change is the Achilles' heel of the liberal male theologian and churchman.

Christian feminists respond to the systematic violence done to women by ecclesial institutions and their male representatives basically in two different ways. They do not differ so much in their analysis and critique of the cultural and ecclesial establishment and its ideologies, but more in their politics and strategies. Those who advocate an exodus and separation from all institutional religion for the sake of the gospel and the experience of transcendence point, as justification, to the history of Christianity and their own personal histories, proving that the submission of women is absolutely essential to the church's functioning. In the present structures and theologies of Christianity women can never be more than marginal beings.[16] Those Christian feminists who hope for the repentance and radical change of the Christian churches affirm their own prophetic roles and critical mission within organized Christianity. They attempt to bring to bear their feminist analysis and critique in order to set free the traditions of emancipation, equality, and genuine human personhood that they have experienced in their Christian heritage. They do not overlook or cover up the oppression and sin that they have experienced in Christian institutions and traditions, but brand them in order to change them. Aware that not only Christian institutions but also Christian theology operate in a sexist framework and language, they attempt to reconceptualize and to transform Christian theology from a feminist perspective.

FEMINIST THEOLOGY AS A CRITICAL THEOLOGY

Historical studies and hermeneutical discussions have amply demonstrated that theology is a culturally and historically conditioned endeavor. Moreover, historical-critical studies and hermeneutical-theological reflection have shown that not only theology but also the revelation of God in Scripture is expressed in human language and shares culturally conditioned concepts and problems. Revelation and theology are so intertwined that they no longer

---

16. See Mary Daly's "autobiographical preface" and her "feminist postchristian introduction" to the paperback edition of *The Church and the Second Sex* (New York: Harper & Row, 1975). See also Sally Gearhart, "The Lesbian and God-the-Father," *Radical Religion* 1 (1974): 19–25.

can be adequately distinguished. This hermeneutical insight is far-reaching when we consider that Scripture as well as theology are rooted in a patriarchal-sexist culture and share its biases and prejudices. Scripture and theology express truth in sexist language and images and participate in the myth of their patriarchal-sexist society and culture.

The feminist critique of theology and tradition is best summarized by the statement of Simone Weil: "History, therefore, is nothing but a compilation of the depositions made by assassins with respect to their victims and themselves."[17] This hermeneutical discussion has underlined that a value-free, objectivistic historiography is a scholarly fiction. All interpretations of texts depend upon the presuppositions, intellectual concepts, politics, or prejudices of the interpreter and historian. Feminist scholars, therefore, rightly point out that for all too long the Christian tradition was recorded and studied by theologians who consciously or unconsciously understood them from a patriarchal perspective of male dominance. Since this androcentric cultural perspective has determined all writing of theology and of history, their endeavor is correctly called his-story. If women, therefore, want to get in touch with their own roots and tradition, they have to rewrite the Christian tradition and theology in such a way that it becomes not only his-story but her-story as well, recorded and analyzed from a feminist point of view.

Yet a hermeneutical revision of Christian theology and tradition is only a partial solution to the problem. Radical Christian feminists, therefore, point out that the Christian past and present, and not only its records, have victimized women. A hermeneutics that merely attempts to *understand* the Christian tradition and texts in their historical settings, or a Christian theology that defines itself as "the actualizing continuation of the Christian history of interpretation," does not suffice,[18] since it does not sufficiently take into account that tradition is a source not only of truth but also of untruth, repression, and domination. Critical theory as developed in the Frankfurt school[19] provides a key for a hermeneutic

17. Simone Weil, *The Need for Roots* (New York, 1971), 225.
18. Against Edward Schillebeeckx, *The Understanding of Faith* (London: Sheed & Ward, 1974).
19. Jürgen Habermas, "Der Universalitätsanspruch der Hermeneutik 1970," in *Kultur and Kritik* (Frankfurt, 1973), 264–301; and his "Stichworte zu einer Theorie der Sozialisation 1968," in *Kultur und Kritik*, 118–94. For a discussion of Habermas and

understanding that is directed not just toward an actualizing continuation and perceptive understanding of history but toward a criticism of history and tradition to the extent that they participate in the repression and domination that are experienced as alienation. Analogously, in order to liberate Christian theologies, symbols, and institutions, critical theology uncovers and criticizes Christian traditions and theologies that have stimulated and perpetuated violence, alienation, and oppression. Critical theology thus has as its methodological presupposition the Christian community's constant need for renewal. Christian faith and life are caught in the middle of history and are therefore in constant need of prophetic criticism in order not to lose sight of their eschatological vision. The Christian community finds itself on the way to a greater and more perfect freedom that was initiated in Jesus Christ. Christian theology as a scholarly discipline, in turn, has to serve and support the Christian community on its way to such eschatological freedom and love.

TOWARD A LIBERATED AND LIBERATING THEOLOGY

Feminist theology presupposes as well as has for its goal an emancipatory ecclesial and theological praxis. Hence feminists today no longer demand merely admission and marginal integration into the traditionally male-dominated hierarchical institutions of the churches and theology; they demand a radical change of these institutions and structures. They do this not only for the sake of "equal rights" within the churches, but because they are convinced that theology and church have to be liberated and humanized if they are to serve people and not to oppress them.

Although we find numerous critical analyses of hierarchical church structures,[20] we do not find many critical evaluations of

the critical theory, see the Spring–Summer 1970 issue of *Continuum*, which was prepared by Francis P. Fiorenza. See also Albrecht Wellmer, *Critical Theory of Society* (New York: Continuum, 1971), esp. 41–51.

20. See, e.g., Emily C. Hewitt and Suzanne R. Hiatt, *Women Priests: Yes or No?* (New York: Seabury Press, 1973); C. H. Donnelly, "Women-Priests: Does Philadelphia Have a Message for Rome?" *Commonweal* 102 (1975): 206–10. C. M. Henning, "Canon Law and the Battle of Sexes," in *Religion and Sexism: Images of Woman in the Jewish and Christian Traditions*, ed. Rosemary Radford Ruether (New York: Simon and Schuster, 1974), 267–91; Letty M. Russell, "Women and Ministry," in *Sexist Religions*, 47–62; see the various contributions on ministry in Clare Benedicks Fischer, Betsy Brenneman, and Anne McGrew Bennett, *Women in a Strange Land* (Philadelphia: Fortress Press,

the theological profession as such. Most recently, however, liberation theologians have pointed out that theology in an American and European context is "white" theology and, as such, shares in the cultural imperialism of Europe and America.[21] Theology as a discipline is the domain of white clerics and academicians and thus excludes, because of its constituency, many different theological problems and styles within Christian communities. Whereas in the Middle Ages theology had its home in cloisters and was thus combined with an ascetic lifestyle, today its place is in seminaries, colleges, and universities. This *Sitz im Leben* decisively determines the style and content of theology. Since theology is mainly done in an academic context, its questions and investigations reflect that of the white, middle-class academic community. Competition, prestige, promotion, quantity of publications, and acceptance in professional societies are often primary motivations for the members of the theological guild.

Feminist theology maintains that this analysis of the life-setting of theology does not probe far enough. Christian theology is not only white-middle-class but white-middle-class-male, and shares as such in cultural sexism and patriarchalism. The "maleness" and "sexism" of theology is much more pervasive than the race and class issue. The writers of the Hebrew Bible lived in Palestine, and Augustine in North Africa, but their theology is no less male than Barth's or Rahner's. Today established theologians often feel free to tackle the social, class, and race issue, precisely because they belong as males to the "old boys club," and they themselves are neither poor nor oppressed. They generally do not, however, discuss the challenges of feminist theology, precisely because they refuse to begin "at home" and to analyze their own praxis as men in a sexist profession and culture. Therefore, the much-invoked unity between theory and praxis has to remain an ideology.

Since early Christian beginnings and the subsequent history of Christianity were immersed in cultural and ecclesial patriarchy, women — whether white or black or brown, whether rich or poor — never could play a significant rather than marginal role in

1975), and the NAWR publication *Women in Ministry* (Chicago, 1972). I find most helpful the collection of articles by Robert J. Heyer, *Women and Orders* (New York: Paulist Press, 1974).

21. See Frederick Herzog, "Liberation Theology Begins at Home," *Christianity and Crisis,* May 13, 1974, and "Liberation Hermeneutics as Ideology Critique?" *Interpretation* 28 (1974): 387–403.

Christian theology. When women enter the theological profession today, they function mostly as "tokens" who do not disturb the male consciousness and structures, or they are often relegated to the status of "junior colleagues" dependent on the authority of their teachers, to research assistants and secretaries, to mother figures and erotic or sex partners; but they are very rarely taken as theological authorities in their own right. If they demand to be treated as equals, they are often labeled "aggressive," "crazy," or "unscholarly."

How women feel in a sexist profession is vividly illustrated in an experiment that Professor Nelle Morton devised. In a lecture on "Preaching the Word,"[22] she asked her audience to imagine how they would feel and understand themselves and theology if the male-female roles were reversed. Imagine Harvard Divinity School, she proposed, as a school with a long female theological tradition. All the professors except one are women, most of the students are women, and all the secretaries are men. All language in such an institution has a distinctly feminine character. "Womankind" means all humanity; "women" as a generic word includes men (Jesus came to save all women). If a professor announces a course on "the doctrine of women" or speaks about the "motherhood of God," she of course does not want to exclude men. In her course on Christian anthropology, Professor Martha maintains that the Creator herself made the male organs external and exposed, so that man would demand sheltering and protection in the home, whereas she made the female reproductive organs compact and internal so that woman is biologically capable of taking her leadership position in the public domain of womankind.

> Once in a while a man gets nerve enough to protest her use of Mother God, saying that it does something to his sense of dignity and integrity. Professor Martha hastens to explain that no one really believes that God is female in a sexual sense. She makes it quite clear that in a matriarchal society the wording of Scripture, of liturgy and theology, could only come out in matriarchal imagery.[23]

This experiment in imagination can be extended to all theological schools or professional societies. Imagine that you are one of

---

22. Nelle Morton, "Preaching the Word," in *Sexist Religion*, 29–46, and "The Rising Women Consciousness in a Male Language Structure," in Jude Michaels, *Women and the Word: Toward a Whole Theology* (Berkeley: Office of Women's Affairs, 1972): 43–52.
23. Morton, "Preaching the Word," 30.

the few men at a theological convention, where the female bishop praises the scholarly accomplishments of all the women theologians without noticing that there are some men on the boards of this theological society. Or imagine that one of the Roman Catholic seminarians tells you, who cannot be ordained because you are a man, that (after her ordination) she will be essentially different from you. If your consciousness is raised and you complain that you are not considered a full human being in your church, then a liberal colleague might answer that you should protest yourself, since after all it is not her problem but yours. And all this is done to you in the name of Christian sisterhood!

Such an experiment in imagination can demonstrate better than any abstract analysis how damaging the masculine language and patterns of theology are to women. Therefore, feminist theology correctly maintains that it is not enough to include some token women in male-dominated theological and ecclesial structures. What is necessary is the humanization of these structures themselves. In order to move toward a "whole theology," women and men, black and white, privileged and exploited persons, as well as people from all nations and countries, have to be actively involved in the formulation of this new theology, as well as in the institutions devoted to such a "catholic" theologizing.

What, then, could feminists contribute to such a new understanding and doing of theology? Naturally, no definite answer can be given, since feminist theology is an ongoing process that has just begun.[24] I do not think that women will contribute specifically feminine modes to the process of theology.[25] However, I do think that feminist theologians can contribute to the development of a humanized theology, insofar as they can insist that the so-called feminine values,[26] e.g., concreteness, compassion, sensitivity, love,

---

24. See Peggy A. Way, "An Authority of Possibility for Women in the Church," in *Women's Liberation,* 77–94; also M. A. Doherty and M. Earley, "Women Theologize: Notes from a June 7-18, 1971 Conference," in *Women in Ministry,* 135–59. For a comprehensive statement of what Christian feminist theology is all about, see the working paper of Nelle Morton, "Toward a Whole Theology," which she gave at the Consultation of the World Council of Churches on Sexism, May 15–22, 1974, in Berlin.

25. Here I clearly distance myself from those Christian feminists and authors leaning in the direction of Jungian psychology. The "equal or better but different" slogan is too easily misused to keep women in their traditional place. Nevertheless I appreciate the attempt to arrive at a distinct self-identity and contribution of women based on female experience. For such an attempt, see Sheila D. Collins, *A Different Heaven and Earth* (Valley Forge, Pa.: Judson Press, 1974).

26. For philosophical analyses of how these "feminine" values contribute to women's

relating to others, and nurturing or community are human and especially central Christian values, which have to define the whole of Christian existence and the practice of the Christian churches. Feminist theology can thus integrate the traditionally separate areas of male/female, public/personal, and intellectual/emotional. Insofar as it understands the personal plight of women in a sexist society and church through an analysis of cultural, societal, and ecclesial stereotypes and structures, its scope is personal and political at the same time.

Against the so-called objectivity and neutrality of academic theology, feminist theology maintains that theology always serves certain interests and therefore has to reflect and critically evaluate its primary motives and allegiance. Consequently, theology has to abandon its so-called objectivity and has to become partisan. Only when theology is on the side of the outcast and oppressed, as was Jesus, can it become incarnational and Christian. Christian theology, therefore, has to be rooted in emancipatory praxis and solidarity. The means by which feminist theology grounds its theologizing in emancipatory praxis is consciousness-raising and sisterhood. Consciousness-raising makes theologians aware of their own oppression and the oppression of others. Sisterhood provides a community of emancipatory solidarity of those who are oppressed and on the way to liberation. Consciousness-raising not only makes women and men aware of their own situation in a sexist society and church, but also leads them to a new praxis insofar as it reveals to us our possibilities and resources. Expressed in traditional theological language, feminist theology is rooted in conversion and a new vision; it names the realities of sin and grace and it leads to a new mission and community.[27]

As theology rooted in community, feminist theology finds its expression in celebration and liturgy.[28] Feminist theologians maintain that theology has to become communal and holistic again.

---

oppression see J. Farr Tormey, "Exploitation, Oppression and Self-Sacrifice," *Philosophical Forum* 5 (1975): 206–21, and L. Blum, M. Homiak, J. Housman, and N. Scheman, "Altruism and Women's Oppression," ibid., 222–47.

27. See *Women Exploring Theology at Grailville*, a packet prepared by Church Women United, 1972, and S. Bentley and C. Randall, "The Spirit Moving: A New Approach to Theologizing," *Christianity and Crisis* (February 4, 1974): 3–7.

28. See the excellent collection of feminist liturgies by Arlene Swidler, *Sistercelebrations: Nine Worship Experiences* (Philadelphia: Fortress Press, 1974), and Sharon Neufer Emswiler and Thomas Neufer Emswiler, *Women and Worship: A Guide to Non-Sexist Hymns, Prayers, and Liturgies* (New York: Harper & Row, 1974).

Feminist theology expresses itself not only in abstract analysis and intellectual discussion, but it employs the whole range of human expression, e.g., ritual, symbol, drama, music, movement, or pictures. Thus feminist celebrations do not separate the sacral and the profane, the religious and the daily life. On the contrary, the stuff of feminist liturgies is women's experience and women's life. In such liturgies women express their anger, their frustrations, and their experience of oppression, but also their new vision, their hopes for the coming of a "new heaven and earth," and their possibilities for the creation of new persons and new structures.

In conclusion: Since feminist theology deals with theological, ecclesial, and cultural criticism and concerns itself with theological analysis of the myths, mechanisms, systems, and institutions that keep women down, it shares in the concerns of and expands critical theology. Insofar as it positively brings to word the new freedom of women and men, insofar as it promotes new symbols, myths, and lifestyles, insofar as it raises new questions and opens up different horizons, feminist theology shares in the concerns and goals of liberation theology.[29] But because Christian symbols and thought are deeply embedded in patriarchal traditions and sexist structures, and because women belong to all races, classes, and cultures, its scope is more radical and universal than that of critical and liberation theology. Feminist theology derives its legitimation from the eschatological vision of freedom and salvation and its radicalism from the realization that the Christian church is not identical with the kingdom of God.

TENSION BETWEEN CHRISTIAN VISION AND PRAXIS

Christian feminism is fascinated by the vision of equality, wholeness, and freedom expressed in Galatians 3:27–29: in Christ Jesus "there is neither Jew nor Greek, neither slave nor free, neither male and female." This Magna Carta of Christian feminism was officially affirmed by Vatican II in the Constitution on the Church (no. 32): "Hence there is in Christ and in the Church no inequality on the basis of race and nationality, social condition or sex, because there is neither Jew nor Greek . . . (Gal. 3:28)." Yet this vision was never

---

29. Letty M. Russell, *Human Liberation in a Feminist Perspective: A Theology* (Philadelphia: Westminster Press, 1974); J. O'Connor, "Liberation Theologies and the Women's Movement: Points of Comparison and Contrast," *Horizons* 2 (1975): 103–13.

completely realized by the Christian church throughout its history. The context of the conciliar statement reflects this discriminatory praxis of the church, insofar as it maintains equality for all Christians only with respect to salvation, hope, and charity, but not with respect to church structures and ecclesial office. The failure of the church to realize the vision of Galatians 3:28-29 in its own institutions and praxis had as its consequence a long sexist theology of the church, which attempted to justify the ecclesial praxis of inequality and to suppress the Christian vision and call of freedom and equality within the church.

A feminist history of the first centuries could demonstrate how difficult it was for the ecclesial establishment to suppress the call and spirit of freedom among Christian women.[30] Against a widespread theological apologetics that argues that the church could not liberate women because of the culturally inferior position of women in antiquity, it has to be pointed out that the cultural and societal emancipation of women had gained considerable ground in the Greco-Roman world. Paul, the post-Paul tradition, and the Church Fathers, therefore, not only attempted to limit or to eliminate the consequences of the actions of Jesus and of the Spirit expressed in Galatians 3:28, but also reversed the emancipatory processes of their society.[31] They achieved the elimination of women from ecclesial leadership and theology through women's domestication under male authority in the home or in the monasteries. Those women who did not comply but were active and leading in various Christian movements were eliminated from mainstream Christianity. Hand in hand with the repression and elimination of the emancipatory elements within the church went a theological justification for such an oppression of women. The androcentric statements of the Fathers and later church theologians are not so much due to a faulty anthropology as they are an ideological justification for the inequality of women in the Christian community. Due to feminist analysis, the androcen-

---

30. See my "The Role of Women in the Early Christian Movement," *Concilium* 7 (January 1976).

31. See the excellent article by K. Thraede, "Frau," in *Reallexikon für Antike und Christentum* 8 (Stuttgart, 1973), 197-269, with extensive bibliographical references. See also C. Schneider, *Kulturgeschichte des Hellenismus* (Munich: Beck, 1967), 1:87-117; and Wayne A. Meeks, "The Image of the Androgyne: Some Uses of a Symbol in Earliest Christianity," *History of Religion* 13 (1974): 167-80, who also point out that the emancipation of women in Hellenism provoked misogynist reactions in some groups.

tric traits of patristic and scholastic theology are by now well known.[32]

Less known, however, is how strong the women's movement for emancipation was in various Christian groups. For instance, in Marcionism, Montanism, Gnosticism, Manicheism, Donatism, Priscillianism, Messalianism, and Pelagianism, women had authority and leading positions. They were found among the bishops and priests of the Quintillians (see Epiphanius, *Haer.* 49, 2, 3, 5) and were partners in the theological discourses of some church theologians. In the Middle Ages women had considerable powers as abbesses, and they ruled monasteries and church districts that included both men and women.[33] Women flocked to the medieval reform movements and were leaders among the Waldensians, the Anabaptists, the Brethren of the Free Spirit, and especially the Beguines. The threat of these movements to the church establishment is mirrored in the statement of a German bishop who "complained that these women [the Beguines] were idle, gossiping vagabonds who refused obedience to men under the pretext that God was best served in freedom."[34] Such an emancipatory her-story is surfacing in the story of the mystics of the twelfth to fourteenth centuries[35] or in that of the witches; in figures like Catherine of Siena, Elizabeth I of England, and Teresa of Avila; in groups like the Sisters of the Visitation and the "English Ladies" of Mary Ward; in Quakerism and Christian Scientism.

Feminist theology as critical theology is driven by the impetus to make the vision of Galatians 3:28 real within the Christian community. It is based on the conviction that Christian theology and Christian faith are capable of transcending their own ideological sexist forms. Christian feminists still often hope against hope that the church will become an all-inclusive, truly catholic community. A critical analysis of Christian tradition and history, however, in-

---

32. Representative is the work of Rosemary Radford Ruether; see especially her article "Misogynism and Virginal Feminism in the Fathers of the Church," in *Religion and Sexism*, 150–83.

33. See my book *Der vergessene Partner: Grundlagen, Tatsachen und Möglichkeiten der beruflichen Mitarbeit der Frau in der Heilssorge der Kirche* (Düsseldorf: Patmos Verlag, 1964), 87–91, and Joan Morris, *The Lady Was a Bishop: The Hidden History of Women within Clerical Ordination and the Jurisdiction of Bishops* (New York: Macmillan, 1973).

34. Norman Cohn, *The Pursuit of the Millennium* (London: Secker and Warburg, 1957), 167.

35. Eleanor L. McLaughlin, "The Christian Past: Does It Hold a Future for Women?" *Anglican Theological Review* 57 (1975): 36–56.

dicates that this hope can be realized only if women are granted not only spiritual but also ecclesial equality. Twelve years ago, in my book on ministries of women in the church, I maintained that women have to demand ordination as bishops,[36] and only after they have attained it can they afford to be ordained deacons and priests. Today I would add that the very character of the hierarchical-patriarchal church structure has to be changed if women are to attain their place and full authority within the church and theology. The Christian churches will overcome their patriarchal and oppressive past traditions and present theologies only if the very base and function of these traditions and theologies are changed.[37] If there is no longer a need to suppress the Spirit who moves Christian women to participate fully in theology and church, then Christian theology and community can become fully liberated and liberating. Church Fathers and theologians who do not respect this Spirit of liberty and freedom deny the Christian community its full catholicity and wholeness. Feminist theologians and Christian feminists will obey this call of the Spirit, be it within or outside established church structures. They do it because of their vision of a Christian and human community where all oppression and sin is overcome by the grace and love of God.

Christian feminists are well aware that this vision cannot be embodied in "old wineskins" but has to be realized in new theological and ecclesial structures. If change should occur, a circular move is necessary.[38] Efforts concentrated on bringing women's experience and presence into theology and church, into theological language and imagery, will not succeed unless the ecclesial and theological institutions are changed to support and reinforce the new feminist theological understanding and imagery. On the other hand, efforts to change the ecclesial and theological institutions cannot be far-reaching enough if theological language, imagery, and myth serve to maintain women's status as a derivative being

---

36. Schüssler, *Partner,* 93–97.

37. This is not sufficiently perceived or adequately stressed by George H. Tavard, *Woman in Christian Tradition* (Notre Dame, Ind.: University of Notre Dame Press, 1973). See also his statement in his article "Women in the Church: A Theological Problem?" in *Ecumenical Theology No. 2,* ed. Gregory Baum (New York, 1967), 39: "Once a Christian woman knows – not only in her intellect, but in her heart and in her life – that in her mankind is fulfilled, it makes no more difference to her that, in the present circumstances, she cannot be ordained."

38. This is also pointed out by Sherry B. Ortner, "Is Female to Male as Nature Is to Culture?" in *Woman, Culture, and Society,* ed. Michelle Zimbalist Rosaldo and Louise Lamphere (Stanford: Stanford University Press, 1974), 67–87.

in church and theology. Structural change and the evolution of a feminist theology, and nonsexist language, imagery, and myth have to go hand in hand.

TOWARD NEW SYMBOLS, IMAGES, AND MYTHS

Whereas theology appeals to our rational faculties and intellectual understanding, images and myths provide a worldview and give meaning to our lives. They do not uphold abstract ideals and doctrines but rather offer a vision of the basic structure of reality and present a model or prototype to be imitated. They encourage particular forms of behavior and implicitly embody goals and value judgments. Insofar as a myth is a story that provides a common vision, feminists have to find new myths and stories in order to embody their goals and value judgments. In this search for new feminist myths integrating the personal and political, the societal and religious, women are rediscovering the myth of the mother goddess,[39] which was partially absorbed by the Christian myth of Mary, the mother of God.

Yet feminist theologians are aware that myths have also a stabilizing, retarding function insofar as they sanction the existing social order and justify its power structure by providing communal identity and rationale for societal and ecclesial institutions. Therefore, precisely because feminist theologians value myths and images, they first have to analyze and to "demythologize" the myths of sexist society and patriarchal religion in order to liberate them.

FEMINIST CRITIQUE OF THE MARY-MYTH

Since the "myth of Mary" is still a living myth today and functions as such in the personal and communal life of many Christian women and men,[40] it is possible to critically analyze its psychological and ecclesial functions. From the outset it can be questioned whether the myth can give to women a new vision of equality and

---

39. See, e.g., B. Bruteau, "The Image of the Virgin Mother," in *Women and Religion*, 93–104; Collins, *A Different Heaven*, 97–136.

40. Andrew M. Greeley, "Hail Mary," *New York Times Magazine*, December 15, 1974, 14, 98–100, 104, 108.

wholeness, since the myth has almost never functioned as symbol or justification of women's equality and leadership in church
and society, even though the myth contains elements that could
have done so. As the "queen of heaven" and the "mother of God,"
Mary clearly resembles and integrates aspects of the ancient goddess mythologies, e.g., of Isis or the Magna Mater.[41] Therefore, the
myth has the tendency to portray Mary as divine and to place her
on an equal level with God and Christ. For instance, Epiphanius,
bishop of Salamis, demonstrates this tendency in the sect of the
Collyridians, which consisted mostly of women and flourished in
Thracia and upper Scythia: "Certain women adorn a chair or a
square throne, spread a linen cloth over it, and on a certain day
of the year place bread on it and offer it in the name of Mary,
and all partake of this bread."[42] Epiphanius refutes this practice
on the ground that no women can exercise priestly functions and
makes a very clear distinction between the worship of God and the
veneration of Mary. Through the centuries church teachers maintained this distinction, but popular piety did not quite understand
it. The countless legends and devotions to Mary prove that people
preferred to go to her instead of going to a majestic-authoritarian
God.

Yet although this powerful aspect of the Mary-myth affected the
souls and lives of the people, it never had any influence upon the
structures and power relationships in the church. That the Mary-
myth could be used to support the leadership function of women
is shown by the example of Bridget of Sweden,[43] who was the
foundress of the Order of the Most Holy Savior, a monastery that
consisted of nuns and monks. She justified the leadership and the
ruling power of the abbess over women and men with reference
to Acts 2, where Mary is portrayed in the midst of the apostles.
This instance of a woman shaping the Mary-myth for the sake of
the leadership and authority of women is, however, the exception
in the history of Mariology.

On the whole, the Mary-myth has its roots and development in a
male, clerical, and ascetic culture and theology. It has very little to

---

41. For a wealth of historical material, see Hilda Graef, *Mary: A History of Doctrine
and Devotion*, 2 vols. (London: Sheed and Ward, 1963), and C. Miegge, *The Virgin
Mary* (Philadelphia, 1955).

42. Epiphanius, *Panarion*, 79. See F. J. Dölger, "Die eigenartige Marienverehrung,"
Antike und Christentum 1 (1929): 107–42.

43. Schüssler, *Partner*, 91.

do with the historical woman Mary of Nazareth. Even though the New Testament writings say very little about Mary and even appear to be critical of her praise as the natural mother of Jesus (Mark 3:31-35),[44] the story of Mary was developed and mythologized very early in the Christian tradition. Although some aspects of this myth, e.g., the doctrine of Mary's immaculate conception or her bodily assumption into heaven, were only slowly accepted by parts of the Christian church, we find one element of the image of Mary throughout the centuries: Mary is the *virginal* mother. She is seen as the humble "handmaiden" of God who, because of her submissive obedience and her unquestioning acceptance of the will of God, became the "mother of God."[45] In contrast to Eve, she was, and remained, the "pure virgin" who was conceived free from original sin and remained all her life free from sin. She remained virgin before, during, and after the birth of Jesus. This myth of Mary sanctions a double dichotomy in the self-understanding of Catholic women.

First, the myth of the virginal mother justifies the body-soul dualism of the Christian tradition. Whereas man in this tradition is defined by his mind and reason, woman is defined by her "nature," i.e., by her physical capacity to bear children. Motherhood, therefore, is the vocation of every woman regardless of whether or not she is a natural mother.[46] However, since in the ascetic Christian tradition nature and body have to be subordinated to the mind and the spirit, woman because of her nature has to be subordinated to man.[47] This subordination is, in addition, sanctioned with reference to Scripture. The body-spirit dualism of the Christian tradition is thus projected on women and men and contributes to the

---

44. The interpretation that points out the fact that the Fourth Gospel conceives of Mary as the prototype of a disciple overlooks the fact that the scene under the cross defines her as "mother" in relationship to the "Beloved Disciple."

45. This image of Mary led in Roman Catholic thought to the ideologization of womanhood and to the myth of the "eternal woman." See Gertrud von Le Fort, *The Eternal Woman* (Milwaukee: Bruce Publishing Co., 1954), and my critique in *Partner*, 79-83; see also Pierre Teilhard de Chardin, "L'Eternel féminin," in his *Ecrits du temps de la guerre (1916-1919)* (Paris: Edition du Seuil, 1965), 253-62; Henri de Lubac, *L'Eternel féminin: Etude sur un texte du Pierre Teilhard de Chardin* (Paris, 1968).

46. Tavard, *Woman,* 136: "Pope Paul clearly asserts one basic notion about woman: all her tasks, all her achievements, all her virtues, all her dreams are derived from her call to motherhood. Everything that woman can do is affected by this fundamental orientation of her being and can best be expressed in terms of, and in relation to, motherhood."

47. Vern L. Bullough, *The Subordinate Sex: A History of Attitudes toward Women* (Urbana: University of Illinois Press, 1973), 97-120.

man-woman polarity, which in modern times has been supported not only by theology but also by philosophy and psychology.[48] Moreover, the official stance of the Roman Catholic Church on birth control and abortion demonstrates that woman in distinction from man has to remain dependent on her nature and is not allowed to be in control of her biological processes.[49] According to the present church "fathers," as long as woman enjoys the sexual pleasures of Eve, she has to bear the consequences. Finally, all psychological qualities that are associated with mothering, e.g., love, nurture, intuition, compassion, patience, sensitivity, emotionality, etc., are now regarded as "feminine" qualities and, as such, privatized. The stereotyping of these *human* qualities led not only to their elimination from public life but also to a privatization of Christian values,[50] which are, according to the New Testament, concentrated and climaxed in the command to love.

Second, the myth of the virginal mother functions to separate women within the Roman Catholic community from one another. Since historically woman cannot be both virgin and mother, she has either to fulfil her nature in motherhood or to transcend her nature in virginity. Consequently, traditional Roman Catholic theology has a place for woman only as mother or nun. The Mary-myth thus sanctions a deep psychological and institutional split between Catholic women. Since the genuine Christian and human vocation is to transcend one's nature and biology, the true Christian ideal is represented by the actual biological virgin who lives in concrete ecclesial obedience. Only among those who represent the humble handmaiden and ever-virgin Mary is true Christian sisterhood possible. Distinct from women who are still bound to earthly desires and earthly dependencies, the biological virgins in the church, bound to ecclesial authority, are the true "religious women." As the conflicts of women congregations with Rome about the renewal of religious life indicate, dependency on ecclesial authority is as important as biological virginity.

The most pressing issue for women in the Catholic Church is,

---

48. Numerous analyses of the treatment of women in psychoanalysis and psychotherapy exist; see e.g., Phyllis Chesler, *Women and Madness* (Garden City, N.Y.: Doubleday, 1972).

49. See the analyses of phallic morality by Daly, *Beyond God*, 106–31; Janice Raymond, "Beyond Male Morality," in *Women and Religion*, 115–25; J. MacRae, "A Feminist View of Abortion," in *Women and Religion*, 139–49.

50. E. Hambrick-Stove, "Liberation: The Gifts and the Fruits of the Spirit," in *Women Exploring Theology at Grailville.*

therefore, to create a "new sisterhood" that is not based on sexual stratification. Such a new sisterhood is the *sine qua non* of the
movement for ordination within the Roman Catholic community.[51]
Otherwise the ordination of some women, who are biological virgins and evidence a great dependency on church authority, not
only will lead to a further clericalization and hierarchalization of
the church, but also to an unbridgeable metaphysical split between
woman and woman.[52]

Traditional Mariology thus demonstrates that the myth of a
woman preached to women by men can serve to deter women
from becoming fully independent and whole human persons. This
observation has consequences for our present attempts to emphasize feminine imagery and myth in feminist theology. As long as
we do not know the relationship between the myth and its societal functions, we cannot expect, for example, that the myth of the
mother goddess in itself will be liberating for women. The myth
of the "Mother God"[53] could define woman, as the myth of the
"mother of God" did, primarily in her capacity for motherhood
and thus reduce woman's possibilities to her biological capacity
for motherhood.

We have to remain aware that the new evolving myths and
images of feminist theology necessarily share the cultural presuppositions and stereotypes of our sexist society and tradition, into
which women as much as men are socialized. The absolute precondition of new liberating Christian myths and images is not only the
change of individual consciousness but that of societal, ecclesial,
and theological structures as well.

Yet, at the same time, feminist theologians have to search for
new images[54] and myths that could incarnate the new vision of
Christian women and function as prototypes to be imitated. Such

---

51. The issue is correctly perceived by Gabriel Moran, "The Future of Brotherhood
in the Catholic Church," *National Catholic Reporter,* July 5, 1974, 7, and G. B. Kelly,
"Brothers Won't Be Priests Because Priests Won't Be Brothers," *National Catholic
Reporter,* July 18, 1975, 9 and 14.

52. For an exegetical and theological discussion of the notion of priesthood in early
Christianity, see my book *Priester für Gott* (Münster: Aschendorff, 1972), 4–60.

53. This does not mean that we ought not to revise our sexist terminology and imagery in our language about God. It is absolutely necessary, in my opinion, that in a time
of transition our vision and understanding of God be expressed in female categories
and images. However, I do think we have to be careful not to *equate* God with female
imagery, in order that Christian women remain free to transcend the "feminine" images
and roles of our culture and be able to move to full personhood.

54. On the relationship of the image to the self, see Elizabeth Janeway, "Images of
Women," *Women and the Arts: Arts in Society* 2 (1974): 9–18.

a search ought not to single out and absolutize one image and myth but rather put forward a variety of images and stories,[55] which should be critical and liberating at the same time. If I propose in the following to contemplate the image of Mary Magdalene, I do not want to exclude that of Mary of Nazareth, but I intend to open up new traditions and images for Christian women. At the same time, the following meditation on Mary Magdalene might elucidate the task of feminist theology as a critical theology of liberation.

IMAGE OF MARY MAGDALENE, APOSTLE TO THE APOSTLES

Mary of Magdala was indeed a liberated woman. Her encounter with Jesus freed her from a sevenfold bondage to destructive powers (Luke 8:3). It transformed her life radically. She followed Jesus.

According to all four gospels, Mary Magdalene is the primary witness to the fundamental data of the early Christian faith: she witnessed the life and death of Jesus, his burial and his resurrection. She was sent to the disciples to proclaim the Easter kerygma. Therefore, Bernard of Clairvaux correctly calls her "apostle to the apostles."[56] Christian faith is based upon the witness and proclamation of women. As Mary Magdalene was sent to the disciples to proclaim the basic tenets of Christian faith, so women today may rediscover by contemplating her image the important function and role that they have for the Christian faith and community.

Yet when we think of Mary Magdalene, we do not think of her first as a Christian apostle and evangelist; rather we have before our eyes the image of Mary as the sinner and penitent woman. Modern novelists and theological interpreters picture her as having abandoned sexual pleasure and whoring for the pure and romantic love of Jesus the man. This distortion of her image signals a deep distortion in the self-understanding of Christian women. If as women we should not be forced to reject Christian faith and tradition, we have to reclaim women's contribution and role in it. We must free

---

55. A creative and brilliant retelling of the biblical etiological story of the origin of sin is given by Judith Plaskow Goldenberg, "The Coming of Lilith," in *Religion and Sexism,* 341–43.

56. *Sermones in Cantica, Serm.* 75, 8 (PL 183, 1148).

the image of Mary Magdalene from all distortions and recover her role as apostle.

In her book *A Different Heaven and Earth*, Sheila Collins likens this exorcising of traditions to the process of psychoanalysis: "Just as the neurotic who has internalized the oppressive parent within himself (herself) must go back to the origin of the trouble in his (her) childhood, so the oppressed group, if it is to move from a condition of oppression to one of liberation, or from self-contempt to self-actualization, must go back to its origins in order to free itself from its psychic chain."[57] Just as black people search history for models of identification that indicate the contributions of blacks to culture and history, just as they strive to eliminate racist interpretations of history and culture, so too women and men in the church must attempt to rewrite Christian history and theology in order to recover aspects that have been neglected or distorted by patriarchal historians and theologians.[58]

A close examination of the gospel traditions discloses already in the beginning of the tradition a tendency to play down the role of Mary Magdalene and the other women as witnesses and proclaimers of the Easter faith. This tendency is apparent in the Markan tradition, which stresses that the women "said nothing to anyone, for they were afraid" (16:8). It is also evident in the comment of Luke that the words of the women seemed to the Eleven and those with them "an idle tale and they did not believe them" but instead checked them out (24:11). It is, moreover, reflected in the Lukan confessional statement, "The Lord has risen indeed and appeared to Simon" (24:34). This Lukan confession corresponds to the pre-Pauline creedal tradition quoted in 1 Corinthians 15:3ff, which mentions Cephas and the Eleven as the principal Resurrection witnesses, but does not refer to any of the women. This tendency to play down the witness of Mary Magdalene is also apparent in the redaction of the Fourth Gospel that takes pains to ensure that the Beloved Disciple, but not Mary Magdalene, is the first believer in the Resurrection (20:1–18).

The apocryphal traditions acknowledge the spiritual authority of Mary Magdalene, but can express her superiority only in analogy to men. They have Jesus saying: "I will make her male that she too

---

57. Collins, *A Different Heaven and Earth*, 93.
58. For the justification of such a comparison, see. H. Mayer Hacker, "Women as a Minority Group," in *Masculine/Feminine*, 130–48, esp. the comparative chart on pp. 140f.

may become a living spirit resembling you males. For every woman who makes herself male will enter the kingdom of heaven."[59]

The liturgy and the legend of the Western church have identified Mary Magdalene with both the sinner in the house of Simon and the woman who anointed Jesus' feet before his death. Modern piety stresses the intimacy and love of the woman Mary for the man Jesus.

In looking at these various interpretations of Mary Magdalene and of ourselves, we are discouraged and tempted to avoid suffering. Thus we tend to fall back into the bondage of the "seven evil spirits" of our culture. Let us therefore recall the statement of Bernard: Mary and the other women were chosen to be the "apostle[s] to the apostles." The first witness of women to the Resurrection – to new life – is, according to all exegetical criteria of authenticity, a historical fact, for it could not have been derived from Judaism nor invented by the primitive church. Christian faith and community have their foundation in the message of the "new life" proclaimed first by women.[60]

59. *The Gospel of Thomas*, Logion 114. See also the apocryphal writings *Pistis Sophia, The Gospel of Mary* [Magdalene], and *The Great Questions of Mary* [Magdalene] in Edgar Hennecke and Wilhelm Schneemelcher, eds., *New Testament Apocrypha* (Philadelphia: Westminster Press, 1963), 1:256ff, 339, and 342f.

60. This meditation on Mary Magdalene was first published in the *UTS Journal* (April 1975): 22f. It formed part of a liturgy that was led by women of Union Theological Seminary. I am grateful to the women at Union for the experience of sisterhood. They and the Feminist Scholars in Religion group of the New York area helped me to sharpen my thinking on some issues of feminist theology.

6 _____

WOMEN APOSTLES:
THE FIRST WOMEN'S
ORDINATION CONFERENCE

CONTEXTUALIZATION

During the summer of 1975 I received a call from one of the organizers of the conference on women's ordination that was scheduled to take place that November in Chicago, inviting me to become a stand-in for one of the scheduled respondents to Sister Anne Carr's keynote address. After the voice on the phone had assured me that the meeting would not argue for the ordination of women into present hierarchical structures, I accepted without hesitation. I had expressed my concern about the direction of the conference because I had heard contradictory reports about the meeting that Mary Lynch had called together in Chicago in December 1974.

In my response I decided to take a feminist approach, one that would place women in the center of attention, instead of critically weighing and evaluating professor Carr's analysis of established theology. Since Anne's paper, "The Church in Process: Engendering the Future," had exhaustively discussed the prevailing theological arguments, I chose to focus on the apostolic roots of women's leadership in the church. I ended with an appeal to build a Christian Catholic sisterhood as the feminist precondition for women's ordination. Such an appeal has been criticized by Mary

Jo Weaver as using a mythic and "hopelessly idealistic" emotional familial term "that does not lend itself to critical examination."[1]

However, her objection overlooks that the address "sister" is used, for instance, in the black church for all women and has its roots in early Christian discourses. Moreover, in a Roman Catholic context the word "alliance" as a feminist replacement for the title "sister" obscures the structural patriarchal division that restricts the name "sister" to one group of women in the Catholic Church. Precisely in order to mark this canonical ecclesiastical division and to raise women's awareness of it, I began to speak in the 1980s of "nun-women" [in German *Klosterfrauen* or *Ordensfrauen*] and "lay-women." I introduced these terms as a consciousness-raising device for enabling Catholic women to retrieve "sister" as a common name for the baptized. Although I made it quite clear that lay-women and nun-women are not suggested as positive feminist self-designations, these words provoked a storm of emotion, negative debates, and vilifications. Such highly charged emotional reactions and tortured arguments against my suggestion, even on the part of leading Catholic feminists, not only surprised me, to say the least, but they also suggested that I had touched a "raw nerve" — one that was too painful to be treated. However, neglecting this patriarchal institutional division between Catholic women or declaring it to be a positive difference and a healthy diversity that ought to be celebrated seemed to me to intensify the problem. Ordination of women into clerical structures would only compound it.

———— ❖ ————

ST. BERNARD IS REPORTED to have been praying before the altar of the Madonna. Suddenly Mary opened her mouth and began to speak. "Be silent, be silent!" St. Bernard cried in desperation: "Women are not allowed to speak in church!"[2] Despite papal and episcopal warnings, we have today broken the silence. Our speaking is compelled by the vision of church expressed in Galatians 3:28. It is strengthened by a new experience of sisterhood. Since I am by trade a historian, theologian, and teacher of the Bible,

---

1. Mary Jo Weaver, *New Catholic Women: A Contemporary Challenge to Traditional Religious Authority* (San Francisco: Harper & Row, 1985), 137.

2. See Letha Scanzoni and Nancy Hardesty, *All We're Meant to Be* (Waco, Tex.: Word Books, 1974), 60.

my response to Anne Carr's paper is decisively determined by my professional involvement in the study of early Christianity. Insofar as I have experienced myself as a "sister among sisters," it is also inspired by the vision of sisterhood or brotherhood that the New Testament calls *ekklēsia*. The fundamental condition of this ecclesial community is pronounced in Matthew 23:8–10:

> But you are not to be called rabbi,
> for you have one teacher,
> and you all are brothers (and sisters).
> And call no one of you on earth "father,"
> for you have one father who is in heaven.
> Neither are you to be called leaders,
> for you have one leader, the Christ.

We can safely assume that the author of the Gospel of Matthew would have extended the list of forbidden titles if he had known monsignors, bishops, cardinals, or popes.

In order to ask what a new understanding of the history of primitive Christianity could contribute to the theological quest for women's leadership in the church, I would like first to look at women's role in the early churches and then to point out some conclusions that further corroborate the theological ramifications and ecclesial consequences of Professor Anne Carr's presentation.[3]

NASCENT CHRISTIAN COMMUNITY

Studies of the sociocultural conditions of the nascent Christian movement have shown that sociologically speaking it represented a socially and religiously deviant group similar to other sectarian groups in the Judaism of the first century.[4] In distinction to the sect of Qumran and the Pharisees, the Jesus movement in Palestine was not a cultic-exclusive but an inclusive group.[5] It questioned the

---

3. For a discussion of a feminist hermeneutic see my article "Feminist Theology as a Critical Theology of Liberation," *Theological Studies* 36 (December 1975): 605–26 (included as chapter 5 in the present volume).

4. For the most recent analyses see John G. Gager, *Kingdom and Community: The Social World of Early Christianity* (Englewood Cliffs, N.J.: Prentice-Hall, 1975); Gerd Theissen, "Legitimität and Lebensunterhalt: Ein Beitrag zur Soziologie urchristlicher Missionare," *New Testament Studies* 21 (1975): 192–221.

5. For a comparison of the Qumran and the early Christian community see my article "Cultic Language in Qumran and in the New Testament," *Catholic Biblical Quarterly* 37 (April 1976): 159–77.

cultic regulations of its religion and attracted the outcasts of its society. Jesus' followers were not the righteous, pious, or powerful of the time, but tax collectors, sinners, and women, all of whom were considered to be cultically unclean in light of the priestly code and did not belong to the religious establishment or the pious associations of the day. The inclusive character of Jesus' message and fellowship made it possible later to broaden the Christian group and to invite Gentiles of all nations into the Christian community, which transcended Jewish as well as Hellenistic societal and religious boundaries.

The theological self-understanding of this early Christian movement is best expressed in the baptismal confession Galatians 3:27–29.[6] In reciting this formula the newly initiated Christians proclaimed their vision of an inclusive community. Over and against the cultural-religious pattern shared by Hellenists and Jews alike, early Christians affirmed that all social, political, and religious status differences were abolished in the body of Christ, the church. This self-understanding of the Christian community rejected all distinctions of religion, race, class, and caste and thereby allowed not only Gentiles and slaves to assume full leadership in the Christian community but also women. Women were not marginal figures in this movement but exercised leadership as apostles, prophets, evangelists, and missionaries, offices similar to those of Barnabas, Apollos, or Paul.[7]

The controversies of Paul with his opponents prove that the leadership of *apostles* was most significant for the nascent Christian movement. According to Paul, apostleship is not limited to the twelve. All those Christians are apostles who were eyewitnesses to the resurrection and who were commissioned by the Resurrected One to missionary work (1 Cor. 9:4). According to Luke, however, only those Christians were eligible to replace Judas who accompanied Jesus in his Galilean ministry and were also eyewitnesses to his resurrection (Acts 1:21). According to all four gospels women fulfilled these criteria of apostleship enumerated

---

6. See Robin A. Scroggs, "Paul and the Eschatological Woman," *Journal of the American Academy of Religion* 40 (1972): 5–17; Wayne A. Meeks, "The Image of Androgyne," *History of Religion* 13 (1974): 165–208; Hans D. Betz, "Spirit Freedom and Law: Paul's Message to the Galatian Churches," *Svensk Exegetic Arsbok* 39 (1974): 145–60.

7. For a more detailed analysis see my article "Die Rolle der Frau in der urchristlichen Bewegung," *Concilium* 12 (1976): 3–9.

by Paul and Luke. Women accompanied Jesus from Galilee to Jerusalem and witnessed his death (Mark 14:40 par.). Moreover, women were according to all criteria of historical authenticity the first witnesses of the resurrection, for – to use the standard of historical criticism – this fact could not have been derived from Judaism nor invented by the primitive church.[8]

That these women were not left anonymous but identified by name suggests that they played an important role in the Christian movement in Palestine. Their leader appears to have been Mary Magdalene since all four gospels transmit her name, whereas the names of the other women vary.[9] Thus, according to the gospel traditions women were the primary apostolic witnesses for the fundamental data of the early Christian faith: They were eyewitnesses of Jesus' ministry, his death, his burial, and his resurrection.

An unbiased reading of Romans 16:7 provides us with one instance in the New Testament where a woman is called apostle. There is no reason to understand the accusative Junian as a short form of the male name Junianus, since Junia was a well-known name for women at the time. Marie-Joseph Lagrange, therefore, suggests that Andronicus and Junia were a missionary couple like Aquila and Prisca.[10] Both were fellow prisoners of Paul. They were Christians before Paul and outstanding figures among the "apostles."

From the very beginning prophets played an eminent role within the early Christian movement. Since they functioned as inspired spokespersons for the Resurrected One, their authority is based on divine revelations. Paul repeatedly mentions prophets directly after the apostles. He values the gift of prophecy higher than that of glossolalia. Despite the appearance of false prophets, prophets still had great authority at the end of the first century, as the Revelation of John and the Didache indicate. According to Didache 13:1-7 prophets have the prerogative in the leadership functions at the celebration of the Eucharist. Paul as well as

---

8. This is obvious when we observe that already the writers of the gospels attempt to downplay the importance of the women's witness. Moreover, the traditional formula in 1 Corinthians 15:3–5 does not even mention women as witnesses of the resurrection.

9. The apocryphal gospel literature presents Mary Magdalene's leadership role as equal if not superior to that of Peter. See Edgar Hennecke and Wilhelm Schneemelcher, eds., *New Testament Apocrypha*, vol. 1 (Philadelphia: Westminster Press, 1963).

10. Marie-Joseph Lagrange, *Saint Paul: Epître aux Romains* (Paris: Librairie Lecoffre, 1916), 366.

Luke and Revelation document that women exercised leadership as prophets in early Christianity.[11]

Finally, the references to women's leadership in the nascent Christian movement do not limit their activity to the circle of women, nor do they evidence ascetical tendencies (as later practiced by Encratite groups, which encouraged celibacy and the renunciation of marriage). We know that Prisca was probably married, whereas we do not know the marital status of women like Mary, Phoebe, Euodia, or Tryphena. These women were not yet defined by their societal gender roles as wives and mothers nor by their relationship to men. Indeed, women's leadership in early Christian communities was exceptional not only by the standards of Judaism or the Greco-Roman world, but also by those of the later Christian church.

GRADUAL CULTURAL COMPROMISE

The process of cultural adaptation and ecclesial institutionalization however, progressively limited women's role and influence. Since Jesus did not leave his followers a blueprint for the organization of his community, the early Christians assimilated structures and institutions of Judaism and Hellenism. Whereas in Paul's time leadership roles were still diversified and based on charismatic authority, the process of institutionalization set in gradually toward the end of the first century. In the second and third centuries church leadership shifted from itinerant missionaries to hierarchical offices, from apostles and prophets to local bishops and ruling elders, from charismatic leadership to traditional forms of authority. Whereas the various New Testament authors do not understand Christian leadership in a cultic sense and therefore apply the title "priest" only to Christ and to all Christians, the second and third century documents begin at first to liken Christian ministry to that of the Old Testament or Hellenistic priesthood and then to gradually identify Christian leadership with the hierarchical priesthood and cultic sacrifices of Jewish and Greco-Roman religion.[12]

---

11. The attack and slander of the author of Revelation against "Jezebel" demonstrates that this woman had a considerable authority in the community of Thyatira.

12. For an exegetical and theological discussion of the notion of priesthood in early Christianity see my book *Priester für Gott*, Neutestamentliche Abhandlungen 7 (Münster: Aschendorff, 1972), 4–60; A. Lemaire, "The Ministries in the New Testa-

This structural solidification and cultic hierarchization of church offices meant at the same time, however, a patriarchalization of Christian ministry and church. This process was bound to eliminate more and more women from ecclesial leadership roles and had to relegate them to subordinate "feminine" tasks. The more Christianity adapted to the societal and religious institutions of the time and, thus, became a genuine segment of its patriarchal Greco-Roman culture and religion, the more it had to relegate women's leadership to fringe groups or to limit it to roles defined by gender. The orders of deaconesses and widows for example no longer served the whole community but mainly ministered to women.[13] Moreover, not all women could exercise leadership functions but only those who, as virgins and widows, transcended sex roles.

PATRIARCHY DEFINED WOMEN'S "PLACE"

A feminist history of the following centuries could demonstrate how difficult it was for the ecclesiastical establishment to suppress the call and spirit of freedom and responsibility among Christian women.[14] The elimination of women from ecclesial leadership and theology was achieved through woman's domestication under male authority either in the home or in celibate communities. Those women who did not comply but rather were active and leading in various Christian communities were soon labeled "heretics" and pushed out of mainstream Christianity. Hand in hand with this elimination and repression of the emancipatory elements within the church went the theological justification for such a suppression of women's leadership and for the patriarchalization of church office. The trajectory of the Pauline tradition, which demands the submission of women on theologi-

---

ment, Recent Research," *Theological Bulletin* 3 (1973): 133–66; M. Houdijk, "A Recent Discussion about the New Testament Basis of the Priest's Office," *Concilium* 80 (1972): 137–47; J. L. Mohler, *The Origin and Evolution of the Priesthood* (New York, 1970).

13. See A. Kahlsbach, *Die altchristiche Einrichtung der Diakonissen bis zu ihrem Erlöschen* (Freiburg, 1926); G. J. Davies, "Deacons, Deaconesses and the Minor Orders in the Patristic Period," *Journal of Ecclesiastical History* 14 (1963): 1–15; Jean Danielou, *The Ministry of Women in the Early Church* (Buzzard, Engl.: Faith Press, 1961), Roger Gryson, *Le ministere des femmes dans l'Eglise ancienne* (Gembloux: Duculot, 1972).

14. For bibliographical references see K. Thraede, "Frau," in *Reallexikon für Antike und Christentum* (Stuttgart, 1973), 197–269.

cal grounds, reflects this reactionary, patriarchal evolution of the Christian church. Whether or not Paul himself initiated this patriarchal reaction is debated by scholars.[15] Certainly, however, the theological justification of the elimination of Christian women from the leadership of the church was able to claim the authority of Paul without being challenged. Further, the misogynist statements of the Church Fathers and later theologians are not so much due to a faulty anthropology as they are an ideological justification for the discrimination against women in the Christian community.

Even though my review of the early Christian development has had to be rather sweeping, it nevertheless demonstrates that it is invalid to deny ordination to women on scriptural grounds. Jesus called women to full discipleship and the Spirit empowered them as apostles, prophets, and leaders in the early church. If the church is indeed built on women apostles and prophets, then it must also acknowledge women as the successors of the apostles and prophets. Such an acknowledgement would mean a radical transformation of the present hierarchical male structures of the church. In my conclusion, I would therefore like to point out three steps that need to be taken if the full apostolicity and catholicity of the church are to be recovered.

CALL TO CONVERSION

The admission of women to the full leadership of the church requires the official recognition and confession of the hierarchy that the church has wronged women and has to undergo, therefore, a radical conversion. As the church has officially rejected all national and racial exploitation and publicly renounced all anti-Semitic theology, so it is now called to abandon all forms of sexism by rejecting a theological and institutional framework that perpetuates discrimination and prejudice against women. In its document on the church, the Vatican Council has affirmed the vision of church pronounced in Galatians 3:28: "Hence there is in Christ and in the

---

15. See Winsom Munro, "Patriarchy and Charismatic Community in Paul," in *Women and Religion,* ed. Judith Plaskow and Joan Romero, 2d ed. (Missoula, Mont.: Scholars Press, 1974), 189-98; W. O. Walker, "1 Cor. 11:2-16 and Paul's Views Regarding Woman," *Journal of Biblical Literature* 94 (1975): 94-110.

Church no inequality on the basis of race or nationality, social conditions or sex."[16]

Yet the context of this statement in the Dogmatic Constitution on the Church reflects the discriminatory mentality and praxis of the hierarchical church insofar as it maintains the equality of all Christians only with respect to salvation, hope, and charity, but not with respect to ecclesial office and power. An analysis of Christian tradition and history, however, indicates that church and theology will be able to transcend their own ideological sexist forms only when women are granted not just full spiritual, but also full ecclesial equality. The Christian churches will overcome their discriminatory and oppressive past and present praxis only if the very base and functions of this tradition and praxis are changed. If women would be admitted to full leadership in the churches, the need would no longer exist to suppress the Spirit who moves Christian women to participate fully in theology and ministry. Church leaders and theologians who do not respect this spirit of liberty and responsibility among Christian women deny the church its full catholicity and wholeness.

TRANSFORMATION OF THE HIERARCHICAL CHURCH

In my book on ministries of women in the church, which appeared [almost thirty] years ago, I maintained that women have to demand ordination as bishops first, and only after they have obtained it can they afford to be ordained deacons and priests.[17] Women have to become visible on all levels of the church; they have to be priests, bishops, cardinals, and popes; they have to be involved in formulating theology and church law, in issuing encyclicals and celebrating the liturgy, if the church is truly to become a community of equals before God and the world. Moreover, those women who as teachers, theologians, assistant pastors, religious educators, counselors, or administrators already actively exercise leadership in the church have to insist that their ministry be publicly acknowledged as "ordained ministry," if women's leadership is not to fall prey to the

---

16. Dogmatic Constitution on the Church, IV, 32; see Walter M. Abbott, ed., *The Documents of Vatican II* (New York: Herder & Herder, Association Press, 1966), 58.

17. Elisabeth Schüssler, *Der vergessene Partner: Grundlagen, Tatsachen und Möglichkeiten der beruflichen Mitarbeit der Frau in der Heilssorge der Kirche* (Düsseldorf: Patmos Verlag, 1964), 87–94.

pitfalls of the present clerical, celibate, and hierarchical form of the Catholic priesthood.[18] The ordination of women cannot simply mean their addition and integration into the male clergy but implies a psychological, structural, and theological transformation of the church. The Christian community no longer should be split into an active leadership of male dominance and a passive membership of female submission, but should be a community of persons who are all called by God and entitled to active participation and leadership in the mission of the church. Equal ordination is the test case, but the transformation of a celibate priesthood, a hierarchical church, and a male-clerical theology is its unconditional prerequisite and consequence.

NEW CHRISTIAN SISTERHOOD

The demand of women for ordination also has to be rooted in a theology and praxis of sisterhood that is not based on sexual stratification. Even though women were never ordained, traditional Roman Catholic theology and structure divide women into two classes: nuns and lay-women. The true Christian perfection and ideal is represented by the consecrated virgin, the nun. Only those who are the "brides" of Christ can lay claim to the name of sister in the Roman Catholic Church. In contrast to women who are still bound by sexual desire and marital dependency, those vowed virgins in the church who are subject to ecclesiastical authority are the true "religious women." As the emerging conflicts of women's congregations with Rome indicate, material dependency on and unquestioning obedience to ecclesiastical authority are as important as biological virginity.

Only when the deep psychological, theological, and institutional split between Roman Catholic lay-women and nun-women is healed and overcome will ordination be open to all women and bring about a new wholeness and catholicity of the church. Otherwise the ordination of some nuns who evidence a great dependency on church authority will lead not only to a further clericalization and hierarchization of the church but also to an unbridgeable theological and metaphysical split between women

---

18. See the various articles in Robert J. Heyer, ed., *Women and Orders* (New York: Paulist Press, 1974).

and women. Our most pressing task is therefore, in my opinion, to build a feminist Catholic sisterhood, which can close the institutional gap between women and women in the Roman Church. Women who wish to be ordained should be rooted in and must be accountable to such a new Catholic sisterhood if women's ordination is not to function as tokenism, but rather is to engender the transformation of the church toward the vision expressed in Galatians 3:28.

7

FEMINIST SPIRITUALITY, CHRISTIAN IDENTITY, AND CATHOLIC VISION

CONTEXTUALIZATION

When I was invited to contribute from a Roman Catholic point of view to the discussion of "the" or of "a" feminine religious identity, I was both very excited about the possibility of dialogue among leading women of different religious traditions and very hesitant to participate in such an enterprise. As a biblical scholar I have ceased to think of theology in "confessional" terms. My experience of feminist liturgies and theological dialogue, moreover, has taught me that feminist theology is truly *ecumenical* since the diverse Christian as well as Jewish religious traditions and symbols have their roots in the same patriarchal cultures and androcentric Scriptures. If I therefore speak of a Catholic vision, I do not intend to imply that such a vision is restricted to Roman Catholicism and is not shared by other Christian churches or expressed by other religions; I only want to say that my particular approach to the topic is strongly colored by my own experience as a Catholic woman and theologian. As a feminist liberation theologian I am continually challenged to explore the relationship among feminism, Christian faith, and the Catholic community, tradition, and spirituality. While I strongly hold that confessional divisions are literally "man-made," nevertheless I believe that it is important for feminist Christians to explore their particular experiences and differences.

When our daughter Christina was baptized, one of my college students asked me: "In light of your feminist consciousness how can you allow a girl-child to be initiated into such a patriarchal and sexist community as the Roman Catholic Church appears to be?" The former Roman Catholic theologian Mary Daly spells out this question in the most radical way when she insists that the myth and symbols of Christianity are *inherently and essentially sexist.* "Since 'God' is male, the male is God. God the Father legitimates all earthly God-fathers.... The idea of a unique divine incarnation in a male, the God-man of the 'hypostatic union,' is inherently sexist and oppressive. Christolatry is idolatry."[1] The assertion of some theologians that Christ was male and that women, therefore, cannot be ordained as priests and represent Christ before the community appears to substantiate Dr. Daly's contention. Yet if maleness is the essence of God and maleness but not humanness the goal of incarnation, how could women have been saved and in baptism made full members of the people of God?

FEMINIST SPIRITUALITY

My own experience as a woman who grew up in the Catholic tradition compels me to question the assertion that maleness is the essence of Christian faith and theology. In spite of the masculine terminology of prayers, catechism, and liturgy and in spite of blatant patriarchal male spiritual guidance, my commitment to Christian faith and love first led me to question the feminine cultural role that parents, school, and church had taught me to accept and to internalize. My vision of Christian life, responsibility, and community compelled me to reject the culturally imposed role of women and not vice versa. What was this liberating vision that came through to me despite all the patriarchal pious packaging and sexist theological systematization? What was the driving force

---

1. Mary Daly, "The Qualitative Leap beyond Patriarchal Religion," *Quest* (Women and Spirituality) 1 (1974): 21.

or spirituality that led me to question and to reject the cultural myth of femininity?

A comparison between a radical feminist spirituality and a Christian spirituality that understands the Spirit, not in a Platonic sense, but in the biblical sense of divine power and dynamic energy that enables us to live as Christians can show that both forms of spirituality are inspired by a similar vision, even though a radical feminist spirituality is often formulated over and against the patriarchal theology and sexist praxis of Christian churches. A radical feminist spirituality proclaims wholeness, healing love, and spiritual power not as hierarchical, as *power over,* but as *power for,* as enabling power. It proclaims *the Goddess* as the source of this power, as the enabling context of human lives and of a non-hierarchical, nonauthoritarian, and noncompetitive community. The Goddess is the giver and nurturer of life, the dispenser of love and happiness. Woman as her image is therefore not "the other" of the divine. She is not body and carnality in opposition to spirit and soul, not the perpetrator of evil and rebellion. Being a woman, living in sisterhood under the aegis of the Goddess, brings us in touch with the creative, healing, life-giving power at the heart of the world.

In my opinion, the Goddess of radical feminist spirituality is not so very different from the God whom Jesus preached and whom he called "Father." In ever new images of life, love, light, compassion, mercy, care, peace, service, and community, the writings of the New Testament attempt to speak of the God of Jesus Christ, and of this God's life-giving power, the Holy Spirit. All the New Testament authors agree that Christian faith has to be lived in the very concrete praxis of *agapē.* In various ways they spell out that Jesus rejected all hierarchical forms of power in his community of followers and explicitly warned that Christian leadership should not be exercised as the "power to lord over others" but in serving. The Second Vatican Council follows this New Testament spirituality when it attempts to speak of the church in terms of enabling love, inclusive community, and service to all humankind.

The traditions about the Goddess and those of the New Testament are conflated in the Catholic community's cult of Mary. The more the Christian understanding of God was patriarchalized and the more God became the majestic ruler and the stern judge, the more people turned to the figure and cult of Mary. The more Jesus Christ became divinized, the more it was necessary to have a mediator between the Christian community and the transcendent God and his majestic Son. One could almost say that through the gradual patriarchalization of the image of God and Christ, Mary became the "other face," the Christian "face" and image, of God. All the New Testament images and attributes that characterize God as loving, life-giving, compassionate, and caring, as being with the people of God, are now transferred to the "mother of God," who is as accessible to people as the nonpatriarchal God whom Jesus preached had been. Even though any Catholic school child can on an *intellectual-theological* level explain the difference between the worship of God and Christ and the veneration of Mary, on an *emotional, imaginative, experiential* level a Catholic child experiences the love of God in the figure of a woman. When Jesus Christ becomes so transcendentalized and divinized that his incarnation and humanity are almost totally absorbed into his divinity, in Catholic piety the "human face" of God is almost solely experienced in the image of a woman. The cult of Mary thus grew in proportion to the gradual repatriarchalization of the Christian God and of Jesus Christ. The Catholic tradition thereby still provides the opportunity to *experience* divine reality in the figure of a woman.

The Catholic cult of Mary also preserves a tradition of *female language* and imagery for speaking of the divine. Christian theology has always maintained that we can speak of God only in an "analogical way" and has never identified any human concept or image of God with the divine reality itself. God transcends all our human perceptions and language capabilities. Yet Jewish and Christian traditions have spoken of God predominantly in patriarchal language and imagery. We all are used to hearing: "God the Father loves you, and if you join the brotherhood and fellowship of all Christians you will become sons of God and brothers of Christ, who died for all men." For centuries such masculinized God-language has communicated to women that they are nonentities, a subspecies of men, subordinated and inferior to men not only on a cultural but also on a religious plane. The combination of male-language for God together with the stress on the sovereignty and absolute authority of this patriarchal God has sanctioned men's drive for power and domination in the church as well as in society.

If Christianity preaches a God of love who liberates every person for new possibilities and for discipleship, then we have to learn how to speak of this God in nonpatriarchal, nonsexist terms. Language about God, if it is rooted in a living faith and a living community, can and does change. The cult of Mary in the Catholic Church provides us with a tradition of theological language that speaks of divine reality in female terms and symbols. This tradition encompasses the myth and symbols of Goddess religions and demonstrates that female language and symbols have a transparency toward God. Only if Christians name God with male and female images and terms will language about God truly become "analogical" and no longer idolize man.

Yet such female-matriarchal language also ought not to be absolutized if we do not want to fall prey to a reverse sexist understanding of God in terms of cultural femininity. Christian language about God must transcend patriarchal as well as matriarchal language and symbols, while at the same time employing a variety of human symbols and images that reflect the pluriformity of human experiences. A truly Christian God-language has to affirm mutuality, fulfillment, maturity, and human potentiality not only in terms of gender, but also in terms of class, culture, race, and religion if it is to become catholic and universal. Christian faith would then enable all kinds of people to affirm themselves as whole human persons chosen and loved by God and as partaking in divine reality. Moreover, such a truly Catholic Christian spirituality would empower all of us to take on responsibilities both for eliminating discrimination, oppression, and the sin of sexism and for building a new community of mutuality and plurality that could mirror the universality of God's redeeming presence and show us her power of life and love.

CHRISTIAN IDENTITY

A second liberating experience that the Catholic tradition provided for me as a woman is the teaching that everyone is called to *sainthood.* Even the vocation to the priesthood is superseded by the call to become a saint. Any Catholic girl who grows up reading the "lives of the saints" has probably internalized all kinds of sexual hang-ups, but she could not believe that her only vocation and her genuine Christian calling consist in getting married and having children. Granted, from a theological and hagiographical point of view the life-choices of the women saints were often limited and conformed to male stereotypes. Nevertheless they still contradicted the middle-class cultural message that women's true vocation is the sacrifice of her life for the career of her husband and the total devotion of her time to diapering babies or decorating her living room. The biographies of the saints are indeed different from the image of the "total woman" propagated by the cultural-religious feminine mystique.

The "lives of the saints" provide a variety of role-models for Christian women. More importantly they teach that women, like men, have to follow their vocation from God, even if this means that they have to go up against the ingrained cultural mores and images of woman. Women, as well as men, are not defined by their biology and reproductive capabilities but by the call to discipleship and sainthood. The early Christians considered themselves as those who were called and elected by God, as the saints of God. This call broke through all limitations of religion, class, race, and gender. The gospels affirm in various ways that Jesus' call to discipleship has precedence over all other obligations, religious duties, and family ties. Jesus did not respect the patriarchal family and its claims, but replaced it with the new community of disciples. When his mother and brothers asked for him, he replied, according to Mark:

> Who is my mother? Who are my brothers? And looking round at those who were sitting in the circle about him he said: "Here are my mother and my brothers. Whoever does the will of God is my brother, my sister, my mother." (Mark 3:31-35)

This theological self-understanding of the Christian community is best expressed in the baptismal formula of Galatians 3:27-29. In reciting this confession, the newly initiated Christians proclaimed their vision of discipleship and inclusive community. Over and against the cultural-religious patterns shared by Hellenists and Jews alike, the Christians affirmed at their baptism that the Christian calling eliminates all status distinctions of religion, race, class, and caste and leads into a truly universal and catholic community of disciples. Early Christian self-identity is defined by the call to become disciples of Jesus and members of the Christian community. Unfortunately, this early Christian self-understanding did not continue to determine the definitions of Christian self-identity and Christian community proposed by later theology. Instead, theology often derived the understanding of Christian identity from cultural anthropology and patterned the structures of the Christian community after the patriarchal societal orders. Instead of formulating a new Christian anthropology in accordance with the call to discipleship and sainthood, it spelled out Christian vocation and discipleship in terms of a cultural anthropology embedded in patriarchy.

DUALISTIC ANTHROPOLOGY

Catholic theology and anthropology have operated for a long time with the concept of the "two natures" of humanity, according to which women and men are by nature essentially different from each other. This way of seeing human nature and Christian discipleship expressed in two essentially different modes of being human led in Christian tradition and theology to the denigration of women and to the glorification and mythologization of the feminine. Women are not only different from men but also inferior to them.

Traditional theology combined such a male/female dualism with a body/spirit dualism. Women then represented sexuality, carnality, and evil. Whereas this tradition defines man by his mind and reason, it sees woman as determined by her "nature" and sexuality. Motherhood, therefore, is the true Catholic vocation of every woman, regardless of whether or not she becomes a natural mother. Since in ascetic Christian traditions nature and body must be subordinated to mind and spirit, because of her nature woman must be subordinated to man. This subordination of woman is sanctioned by Scripture. The official stance of the Roman Catholic Church on birth control is based on this dualism. Women are not allowed through effective means of control to integrate their reproductive capabilities into a life plan of discipleship and vocation, but they have to remain subject to "natural" biological reproductive processes.

Catholic women have either to fulfill their nature and Christian calling in and through motherhood and procreation, or they have to renounce their female nature and sexuality in virginity. Consequently, this traditional theology offers Catholic women only a choice between two roles, that of mother or that of virgin. Since "the genuine" Christian and human vocation consists in transcending one's biological limitations, the ideal Catholic woman is represented by the actual biological virgin who lives in poverty and obedience. Therefore, Roman Catholic sisterhood is not open to all women but is based on sexual stratification and patriarchal anthropology. In my opinion, the most pressing task for Roman Catholic women today is to create a new, inclusive sisterhood based on the Christian commitment to discipleship and call to sainthood.

One of the more contemporary theological aspects of the "two natures" concept of humanity is expressed in the assertion that women and men are equal but different. This form of "dual nature" theology emphasizes the polarity and complementarity of women and men. Only women and men *together* achieve human wholeness. Such a concept is mistakenly derived from Genesis 1:27, insofar as this passage is taken as an explicative, dogmatic statement and not as an etiological explanation.

This form of theological anthropology corresponds with Jungian depth psychology, according to which the masculine and the feminine represent archetypes or principles embedded in a collective unconscious. In the opinion of Jungian theologians, the archetypes manifest not only the given structure of human reality, but also the structure of divine reality. The term archetype expresses

> the presence of a divine force within the human soul which manifests itself in all the typically human patterns of thought, feeling, imagery and behavior.... So, when we say women are stuck in archetypal feminine roles, we must recognize that these roles are not simply human creations but that they also express an aspect of the divine.[2]

Many Christian feminists have found in the Jungian myth of archetypes a "feminine religious identity." This form of Christian feminism tends to glorify feminine qualities associated with the emotions, the body, the unconscious, the tribal-communal, and magic. Such a feminism rejects the predominant masculine principle, associated generally with rationality, intellect, linear and hierarchical thinking, technology, and competitiveness. Whereas in traditional theological anthropology woman represented evil and temptation, in this new version of the "dual nature" concept of humanity, woman is the source of wholeness, life, and salvation. Consequently, the Father-God of patriarchal religion has to be replaced with the Mother-Goddess of matriarchy. In my opinion, this form of feminist theology is in danger of reintroducing into Christian faith and self-understanding a kind of cultural dualism that maintains two ultimate principles and creative powers.

---

2. R. M. Stein, "Liberating the Feminine," in *Male and Female: Christian Approaches to Sexuality,* ed. Ruth Tiffany Barnhouse and Urban T. Holmes, III (New York: Seabury Press, 1976), 77.

THE MYTH OF FEMALE POWER

The "two natures" concept of humanity, in its negative as well as in its positive forms, reflects the myth of female power. Both the fear and demonization of women and the mythic exaltation and praise of feminine qualities presuppose the myth of the magic-life-power of the female. This myth has decisively influenced the Catholic understanding of the sacraments and the priesthood of the ordained.

In cultures and periods when the mother was the only known parent and her pregnancy was easily attributed to the wild or to ancestral spirits, the power of women to create life must have been awesome indeed. In his study *The Masks of God,* Joseph Campbell suggests that the power of the female to create life was understood as a magical force that gave to women prodigious powers. The very earliest figurines of women, like that of the Venus of Willendorf, emphasize the swollen breasts, bellies, and huge buttocks of the female. Campbell believes that these earliest examples of the "graven image" were the first objects of worship and religion. In recent times anthropologists have, moreover, found numerous indigenous peoples who are unaware that the male seed is as necessary for procreation as the female ovum and womb. They are awed by women's life-creating power.

This awe for the magical female power to give life is not only a characteristic of early people but is also deeply ingrained in the psyche of modern persons. For instance, a few weeks after I had given birth we had a faculty retreat at which I had to make a presentation on the relationship of Lonergan's method in theology to the historical-critical method in biblical studies. To my great surprise, the chairman of the department summed up my contributions at the end of the meeting: "Elisabeth did something that none of you men could have done. She gave birth to a child, while at the same time working at theological methodology." Yet my ability to give birth had nothing to do with my intellectual ability to present a theological argument.

Scholars of religion suggest that the myth of female power may have led to the celebration of religious rituals and to the existence of religion as such. They interpret initiation ceremonies, at which one of the elders of the tribe confers adult status on young boys, as efforts by men to act out the rite of birth that nature denies them. Even though women give birth to children in the ordinary course of

events, by enacting the sacred rites of passage men turn the unfinished creatures who are born of women into adult human beings.
In token of this rebirth, the initiates often take on new names and
are granted new privileges and dignities. The ceremonial-religious
act of initiation becomes as significant for the process of human
maturation as pregnancy and birth.

In the light of cultural anthropology, it seems no accident that
those churches that have a sacramental priesthood most strongly
resist the ordination of women to the priesthood, since Christian
sacraments are all rites that convey life. Baptism is the rebirth to a
new everlasting life, the Eucharist is the "bread of life," catechesis
and proclamation are compared to "mother's milk and solid food."
The sacrament of reconciliation restores life to its fullness. The
sacrament of marriage protects and sanctifies the source of natural
life. Since the sacraments, as rituals of birthing and nurturing,
appear to imitate female powers of giving birth and of nurturing
the growth of life, one would think that women would be the
ideal administrators of the sacraments.

Yet a deep fear appears to exist in men that women's powers would become so overwhelming if they were admitted to the
priesthood and the sacramental ritual that men would be relegated
to insignificance. The demand of women to be admitted to the
sacramental priesthood is, therefore, often not perceived as a genuine desire of women to live their Christian vocation and to serve
the people of God, but as an attempt to "take over" the church completely. What men are often afraid of is that the change in role and
position will not mean a mere shift in the relationship between
men and women but a complete destruction of any relationship or
a fatal reversal of patriarchal relationships.

As long as the theology of church and ministry is based on
a Christian anthropology rooted in the myth of female power,
women will not be accepted into the sacramental ordained priesthood. On the other hand, as long as women are not accepted as
ordained priests, the sacraments will not completely lose their
magical character in the eyes of many people. Yet as long as the
sacraments and the priesthood are understood in magical terms,
they cannot become nurturing, enabling, and serving institutions,
but will continue to represent male power and control over the
spiritual life of Christians. The male/female dualism of traditional
Christian anthropology both engenders and is sustained by the
clergy/lay dualism of Catholic ecclesiology. This dualism is, how-

ever, not inherent to the Christian church, but was only gradually introduced into theology and church.

THE PILGRIM CHURCH

To affirm that Christian faith and theology are not inherently patriarchal and sexist and to maintain, at the same time, that Christian theology and the Christian churches are guilty of the sin of sexism is the task of a Catholic Christian feminist theology. Christian feminists respond to the ideology and praxis of sexism in the church basically in two different ways. We do not differ so much in our analyses and critique of the cultural and theological establishment as in our spirituality and strategies. Those who advocate an exodus from all the institutions of Christianity for the sake of the gospel and the genuine experience of transcendence point to the history of Christianity and to their own personal histories as justification for this exodus. They argue that the submission of women is absolutely essential to the churches' functioning. Women can never be more than marginal beings in the present Christian structures and theologies.

Christian feminists who hope for the repentance and radical change of the Christian churches and biblical religion affirm on the other hand our own prophetic roles and critical mission within organized Christianity. We attempt to bring our feminist analysis and critique to bear upon theology and the Christian church in order to set free the traditions of emancipation, equality, and genuine human community that we have experienced in our Christian heritage. We do not overlook or cover up the oppression and sin that we have suffered at the hands of Christian institutions and traditions, but we point them out in order to change them.

Catholic feminists who identify with the Christian tradition and remain within the institutional structures of the church can do so because we take seriously the Roman Catholic Church's self-understanding expressed in Vatican II. The Constitution on Divine Revelation, for instance, asserts that only those statements of the Bible are the revealed Word of God that pertain to "our salvation." Cultural and anthropological frameworks are not the content of divine revelation, just as scientific and cosmological statements are only expressions of the human perception and knowledge of the sacred authors. The council takes seriously the principle of incarnation when it asserts that divine revelation is only given in human, cultural, and societally conditioned language. This principle of incarnation is also employed by various other council documents that describe the reality of the church.

> Until there is a new heaven and a new earth where justice dwells (2 Peter 3:13), the Pilgrim Church in her sacraments and institutions which pertain to this present time takes on the appearance of this passing world. (*Lumen Gentium* 48)

This incarnational principle demands a feminist hermeneutic understanding that is directed not simply toward the actualizing continuation and perceptive understanding of Christian tradition and church, but rather toward a critique of Bible, tradition, and church to the extent that they contribute to the oppression and domination of women in a patriarchal and sexist culture and religion. Feminist spirituality must grow out of feminist theology understood as a critical theology of liberation. Such a spirituality has the task to uncover Christian theological traditions and myths that perpetuate sexist ideologies, violence, and alienation. A Christian feminist spirituality thus is based on the theological presupposition that Christian women as well as the Christian community are in constant need for renewal and conversion. Christian life, church, and theology are caught in the middle of history and, therefore, are in constant need of prophetic critique.

A positive formulation of a feminist Christian spirituality and identity can, in my opinion, never prescind from theological and cultural critique. It must not demand of women that they forget their own anger and hurt and overlook the violence done to their sisters. In Christian terms: no cheap grace is possible. At the beginning of Christian life and discipleship stands *metanoia,* a new orientation in the life-power of the Spirit. Christian theology and the Christian community will only be able to speak in an authentic way to the quest for feminist spirituality and for the religious identity of women when the whole church, as well as its individual members, has renounced all forms of sexist ideology and oppressive praxis that are manifested in church structures, theologies, and liturgies. The Roman Catholic Church must publicly and officially confess that it has wronged women. As it has officially rejected national and racial exploitation and publicly repented of its tradition of anti-Semitic theology, so the Catholic Church is still called to abandon all forms of sexism.

An analysis of Catholic Christian traditions and history, however, indicates that church and theology will transcend their own sexist ideologies only when women are granted full spiritual, theological, and ecclesial equality. The Christian churches will overcome their oppressive patriarchal traditions and their present sexist theologies and practices only if the very basis of these theologies and practices is changed. If women were admitted to full leadership in church and theology, the need would no longer exist to affirm theologically the maleness of God and Christ and to suppress the Spirit who moves women to full participation in the Catholic Church and its ministry. Church leaders and theologians who do not respect the Spirit of liberty and responsibility among Catholic Christian women deny full catholicity to church and theology. Only if we, women and men, are able to live in nonsexist Catholic communities, celebrate nonsexist Christian liturgies, think in nonsexist theological terms, and call on God with many names and images will we be able to formulate a genuine Christian feminist spirituality.

8 ─────────────────

THE TWELVE AND
THE DISCIPLESHIP OF EQUALS

CONTEXTUALIZATION

In January 1977 the Vatican issued the *Declaration on the Question of the Admission of Women to the Ministerial Priesthood* probably in response to both the ordination of women priests in the Episcopal Church and the high visibility of the ordination movement in the U.S. Catholic Church. However, the Sacred Congregation for the Doctrine of the Faith (CDF) probably issued its statement against the ordination of women in response to two Vatican commission reports, that of the Congregation for the Evangelization of Peoples on "The Role of Women in Evangelization," and that of the Biblical Commission, "On the Ordination of Women," which concluded that Scripture leaves the question open.

Immediately after the publication of the Vatican declaration and commentary, Arlene and Leonard Swidler invited forty-four Catholic activists, Scripture scholars, and theologians to respond to and assess its arguments.[1] The original form of this article was written

For Dr. Patricia Brennan in deep appreciation for her vision and work toward a discipleship of equals in the Australian Movement for the Ordination of Women (MOW) and in gratitude to the Group d'Orsay and especially Frances Beydon for their critical support of my work.

1. See Leonard and Arlene Swidler, eds., *Women Priests: A Catholic Commentary on the Vatican Declaration* (New York: Paulist Press, 1977) for text, commentary, and responses to the Vatican declaration against the ordination of women.

for this collection of essays. It has also been published in France and Australia in a revised and expanded form, since the reference to the "twelve apostles" is still used as a scriptural argument against the ordination of women not only by Roman Catholic but also by Anglican ecclesiastics. Although critical biblical scholarship has moved beyond such an anachronistic proof-texting approach, it is still being used in dogmatic discussions. For the declarations and debates on women's ordination and ecclesial self-understanding frame historical questions in such a way that they serve doctrinal interests.

—————— ✤ ——————

THE PROBLEM

A THEOLOGICAL RECONSTRUCTION of the early Christian movement as a discipleship of equals[2] often meets with the objection that Jesus chose and commissioned twelve men to be the apostolic leaders of the early church. The institution of the twelve apostles — so the argument goes — proves that the hierarchically ordered apostolic ministry stood above the equality of all believers in the very beginnings of the church.[3] Since the twelve apostles were according to the gospels without exception men, it is concluded that women could not have had equal access to leadership functions either in the Jesus movements or in the early Christian missionary movements. Therefore, the notion of a "discipleship of equals" is declared to be a feminist projection back into the first century, which has no support in our source texts.

Such an argument rests, however, on several faulty assumptions. It overlooks that the understandings of the early Christian movement as a "discipleship of equals," as "equality in the spirit," as "equality from below," or as *ekklēsia*, i.e., the democratic decision-making assembly of equals, are conceptualized as counter-

---

2. For this expression see my book *In Memory of Her: A Feminist Theological Reconstruction of Christian Origins* (New York: Crossroad, 1983); see also R. L. Sider, "Toward a Biblical Perspective on Equality," *Interpretation* 43 (1989): 156–69.

3. For such an argument see Louis William Countryman, "Christian Equality and the Early Catholic Episcopate," *Anglican Theological Review* 63 (1981): 115.

terms to the structures of domination and exclusion that are institutionalized in Greco-Roman patriarchy.[4]

Moreover, the argument against the reconstruction of early Christianity as a "discipleship of equals" seems to imply that social equality expressed in decentralized horizontal social structures does not admit of leadership functions. However, studies of Hellenistic and Jewish as well as early Christian missionary propaganda have shown that although the vast majority of religions in the Greco-Roman world "did not develop centralized hierarchical structures," they were not without missionary leadership.[5]

In addition, this objection presupposes not only that the maleness of the twelve is constitutive for their early Christian function but also that this function was that of apostolic leadership in the early Christian churches. Thus this objection seems to assume that the circle of the twelve was identical with the wider circle of apostles as well as with the wider circle of disciples.

Finally, this objection to the understanding of the Early Christian movements as a "discipleship of equals" reads the gospels in a positivist fashion as an accurate description of the events and agents in early Christian beginnings. However, on methodological grounds such an assumption must be judged as outdated and ideological.[6] It overlooks the rhetorical character of the gospels as theological responses to particular historical-ecclesial situations.

THE TWELVE AND THE APOSTLES

Popular and ecclesiastical understandings generally assume that the terms "apostles" and "the twelve" are coextensive categories as though both terms connote the very same historical circle with

---

4. See my article "Die Anfänge von Kirche, Amt, und Priestertum in feministisch-theologischer Sicht," in *Priesterkirche,* ed. Paul Hoffmann, Theologie der Zeit 3 (Düsseldorf: Patmos, 1987), 62–95.

5. See the epilogue in Dieter Georgi, *The Opponents of Paul in Second Corinthians* (Philadelphia: Fortress Press, 1986), 362, and Elisabeth Schüssler Fiorenza, ed., *Aspects of Religious Propaganda in Judaism and Early Christianity* (Notre Dame, Ind.: Notre Dame University Press, 1976).

6. For a discussion of such a positivist approach see my "Text and Reality – Reality as Text: The Problem of a Feminist Historical and Social Reconstruction Based on Texts," *Studia Theologica* 43 (1989): 19–34, and my Society of Biblical Literature presidential address "The Ethics of Interpretation," *Journal of Biblical Literature* 107 (1988): 3–17.

the same disciples' functions.[7] Yet this assumption goes against the technical evidence and the scholarly consensus that the apostles and the twelve were different circles in early Christianity, which only in the course of time were identified with each other.[8] Originally the word "apostle" described the function of a commissioned messenger. In the Pauline correspondence it designates a missionary sent by the Resurrected One. Clearly, the title is not restricted to the group of the twelve, since then Paul would not qualify as an apostle. Insofar as not every apostle was a member of the twelve, the term "apostle" seems to connote originally an independent and more comprehensive circle of leadership in the early church.

Only at a later stage of the tradition are the twelve identified with the apostles (see Mark 6:30; Matt. 10:2; Rev. 21:14), an identification that is especially characteristic of the Lukan work. However, it remains debated at what point of the tradition the twelve were also understood as apostles. Paul and Barnabas, for instance, are known as apostles in early Christianity (see Acts 14:4, 14), but they definitely did not belong to the circle of the twelve.

Moreover, our sources indicate that the circle of the twelve as a circle independent of the apostles is firmly rooted in the tradition. They are already traditional figures of the past toward the end of the first century (see Rev. 21:14).[9] The terms used are "the twelve," "the twelve disciples," the "twelve apostles," and "the eleven." It is astonishing that direct references to the twelve are rare in the Pauline writings (one in a traditional formula) and the Johannine

---

7. See my articles "The Twelve" and "The Apostleship of Women in Early Christianity," in *Women Priests,* 114–22 and 135–40; J. A. Kirk, "Apostleship since Rengstorf," *New Testament Studies* 21 (1974–75): 260ff; Andrew C. Clark, "Apostleship: Evidence from the New Testament and Early Christian Literature," *Vox Evangelica* 29 (1989): 49–82.

8. For a general discussion of the problem see also Beda Rigaux, "The Twelve Apostles," *Concilium* 34 (1968): 5–15; his "Die 'Zwölf' in Geschichte und Kerygma," in *Der historische Jesus und der kerygmatische Christus,* ed. Helmut Ristow and Karl Matthiae, 2d ed. (Berlin: Evangelische Verlagsanstalt, 1961), 468–86; Günter Klein, *Die Zwölf Apostel: Ursprung und Gehalt einer Idee,* Forschungen zur Religion und Literatur des Alten und Neuen Testaments 59 (Göttingen: Vandenhoeck & Ruprecht, 1961); Jürgen Roloff, *Apostolat — Verkündigung — Kirche* (Gütersloh: Mohn, 1965); Rudolf Schnackenburg, "Apostolicity: The Present Position of Studies," *One in Christ* 6 (1970): 243–73; Vincent Taylor, *The Gospel according to St. Mark,* 2d ed. (London: Macmillan, 1966), 619–27; Anton Vögtle in *Lexikon für Theologie und Kirche,* vol. 9, ed. Michael Buchberger, 2d ed. (Freiburg: Herder Verlag, 1966), 1443ff; Hans Dieter Betz, *Galatians,* Hermeneia (Philadelphia: Fortress Press, 1979), 74f, Excursus: Apostle.

9. See my book *Priester für Gott: Studien zum Herrschafts- und Priestermotiv in der Apokalypse* (Münster: Aschendorff, 1972).

literature (four) and completely absent in the Catholic and Pastoral Epistles. In the Pastorals it is Paul who has become the apostle par excellence.

Finally, although the four gospel accounts about the twelve (Mark 3:16–19; Matt. 10:2–4; Luke 6:12–16; Acts 1:13) differ,[10] they agree in listing only male names. Therefore, popular understanding assumes that the maleness of the twelve is essential for their function and mission. One must therefore ask whether it is essential for the twelve's mission and historical significance that they are males and whether masculinity is integral to their function. Do the early traditions about the twelve elaborate the male gender of the twelve and do they reflect on it? Moreover, is the function and mission of the twelve according to our sources continued in the structure and leadership of the early church? Did the twelve have successors, and if so did they have to be male? In other words, do we find any evidence in early Christian sources for the assumption that biological maleness and masculine gender were intrinsic to the function and mission of the twelve and therefore must remain intrinsic to the apostolic office of the church?

THE EARLIEST TRADITIONS ABOUT THE TWELVE

1 Corinthians 15:5 and the Jesus-Saying in Matthew 19:28 (cf. Luke 22:30) are the two oldest source-texts that refer to the twelve. In 1 Corinthians 15:3–5 Paul quotes a tradition that he has already received.[11] This pre-Pauline tradition maintains that the Resurrected One appeared first to Cephas and then to the twelve. The text refers to the twelve as a fixed and well-known group. Since it does not speak of Peter and the eleven, the text does not reflect the defection of Judas as the resurrection narratives of the gospels do when they consistently refer to the eleven. Furthermore, the traditional formula in 1 Corinthians 15:3–5 does not indicate whether the group of the twelve existed already before Easter as a definite circle of disciples in the ministry of Jesus or whether it was con-

---

10. For a discussion of the text and of the secondary literature see Joseph A. Fitzmyer, *The Gospel according to Luke,* Anchor Bible 28A, 28B (Garden City, N.Y.: Doubleday, 1985), 613–21.

11. For extensive bibliographic information see Hans Conzelmann, *I Corinthians,* Hermeneia (Philadelphia: Fortress Press, 1975), 251–54.

stituted by the resurrection appearances and commission of the
Risen One.

Paul's account parallels the statement in 1 Corinthians 15:5
with the statement in 15:7, which refers to the appearance of
the Risen One to James and then to "all the apostles." It is not
clear whether it was Paul who articulated the parallel statements
of 1 Corinthians 15:5 and 15:7 or whether he had already found
this parallel in his tradition.[12] In any case, the present text appears
to combine two different traditions and to speak of two different
groups, namely, the twelve and the apostles. As Peter stands out
among the twelve, so does James among the apostles. However,
neither the pre-Pauline tradition nor the Pauline text reflects upon
the gender of the twelve nor on that of the apostles.

The very old saying Matthew 19:28 (par. Luke 22:30) has a quite
different form and setting in Matthew and Luke. Even though the
Matthean and Lukan form of the saying are redactional,[13] the contrast between present sufferings and future glory is common to
both. In its original form the saying is an eschatological promise
to the disciples who have followed Jesus. This Q-logion[14] in its
Matthean form explicitly interprets the number twelve. When in
the new world the Human One (*huios tou anthrōpou*) will be revealed in all splendor and glory, the followers of Jesus also will sit
"on twelve thrones and judge [or rule] the twelve tribes of Israel"
(Matt. 19:28). The text clearly does not underline the historical
existence of a group of twelve men but the function that the disciples of Jesus would have for Israel in the eschatological future. The
faithful disciples will share with Jesus in the exercise of authority
and power when the *basileia* (the reign of God) is established.
Since at the time of Jesus only two and a half tribes still existed,
the number twelve is clearly symbolic. The circle of the twelve has
thus an eschatological symbolic function.

The number twelve refers back to the ancient constitution of
Israel consisting of twelve tribes and points forward to the eschatological restitution of Israel. The "maleness" of the twelve disciples
is not explicitly mentioned in this Q-logion. It could be inferred

---

12. For an extensive discussion and literature see Helmut Merklein, *Das kirchliche
Amt nach dem Epheserbrief*, Studia Antoniana (Munich: Kösel, 1973), 273–78.

13. For a discussion of the original Q-form and the Matthean and Lukan redaction see
Fitzmyer, *Gospel according to Luke*, 1413ff.

14. Q is used to designate the source of the material that is common to Matthew and
Luke but is not found in Mark. Since the material is almost wholly teaching material, Q
is often called the Sayings Source or Logia Source.

that the twelve must be male since the text seems to refer to and to symbolize the ancient tribal constitution of Israel, which in its religious and political leadership was patriarchal.[15] Yet the logion does not refer to the historical constitution of Israel but rather points to Israel's eschatological future. It does not refer to the church in the interim time but to the eschatological restitution of the people of Israel. This Q-saying does not postulate a historical continuum between Jesus, the twelve, and the church, but establishes a symbolic coherence between Jesus, the twelve, and the eschatological reconstitution of the twelve tribes of Israel.

Revelation 21:14 also indicates that the signifying function of the twelve is eschatological-symbolical rather than historical-masculine. According to this text the eschatological city, the New Jerusalem, is patterned after the twelve tribes of Israel. "And the wall of the city had twelve foundations and on them the twelve names of the twelve apostles of the Lamb." Here the twelve apostles are not said to be the foundation of the church but that of the New Jerusalem, which clearly is an eschatological reality.[16]

Finally, it cannot be argued, that this Q-saying was formulated only late in the ministry of Jesus and therefore did not have a great impact on the mission and the function of the twelve. Since the present position of the saying in Matthew and Luke is editorial, we no longer know when this saying was formulated. From a tradition-historical point of view, it could have been spoken by the historical Jesus, since it reflects the heart of his preaching to and concern for the renewal of his own people (Matt. 10:5–6). Thus it seems justified to conclude:

> The twelve exemplified the awakening of Israel and its gathering in the eschatological salvific community, something beginning then through Jesus. They exemplified this gathering simply through the fact that they were created as *twelve,* but they also exemplified it through being sent out to all of Israel.[17]

---

15. However, Christian feminists must learn to read such information in an anti-patriarchal fashion rather than perpetrate scholarly anti-Jewish readings. See Judith Plaskow, *Standing Again at Sinai: Judaism from a Feminist Perspective* (New York: Harper & Row, 1990).

16. For a comprehensive interpretation of Revelation see my book *Revelation: Vision of a Just World* (Minneapolis: Fortress Press, 1991).

17. Gerhard Lohfink, *Jesus and Community: The Social Dimension of Christian Faith* (Philadelphia: Fortress Press, 1984), 10. See also Ulrich Luz, *Das Evangelium nach Matthäus,* Evangelisch-katholischer Kommentar zum Neuen Testament 2 (Zürich: Benzinger/Neukirchener Verlag, 1990), 74–161.

THE MARKAN UNDERSTANDING OF THE TWELVE

According to the Gospel of Mark the twelve are likewise sent to the messianic people of God, Israel, in order to carry on Jesus' ministry and work. The two main passages cited for the historical mission of the twelve are Mark 3:13–19 and 6:6b–13. Most scholars suggest that these texts were formulated by the Markan redaction.[18] They therefore do not reflect the earliest tradition but spell out Mark's theological understanding of the twelve. These Markan texts stress that the specific power and authority given to the twelve is that of exorcism.[19] Mark 3:14 mentions their mission to preach but underlines that power is given to them to cast out demons. According to the commissioning scene in Mark 6:6b–13 they are neither explicitly authorized (v. 7b) nor commissioned (vv. 8–10) to preach. Their preaching is only mentioned in the concluding statement of v. 12. But the following v. 13 stresses again the power of the twelve to heal and to cast out demons. A careful reading of the text indicates that in Mark's view the twelve are primarily sent and have received the power of exorcism and healing, while Jesus is the one who proclaims the gospel of the *basileia* (1:14f).[20]

It should be noted that Mark's theological emphasis on the empowerment of the twelve to cast out demons and to heal is completely neglected by the theological articulation of "apostolic succession." Moreover, according to Mark not only the twelve apostles preach (*keryssein*), but also John the Baptist (1:4, 7), those who are healed (1:45; 5:20) or who are witnesses of healing (7:36), as well as the post-Easter community as a whole (13:10; 14:9). Further, the preaching activity of the twelve addresses Israel. Since in distinction to Matthew (Matt. 28:16–20) Mark does not know of a post-Easter commissioning of the twelve to universal mission,

18. See John Coutts, "The Authority of Jesus and the Twelve in St. Mark's Gospel," *Journal of Theological Studies* 8 (1957): 111–18; Karl-Georg Reploh, *Markus – Lehrer der Gemeinde,* Stuttgarter biblische Monographien 9 (Stuttgart: Katholisches Bibelwerk, 1969), 43–58; Klemens Stock, *Boten aus dem Mit-Ihm-Sein: Das Verhältnis zwischen Jesus und den Zwölf nach Markus,* Analecta Biblica 70 (Rome: Biblical Institute Press, 1975); Günther Schmahl, "Die Berufung der Zwölf im Markusevangelium," *Trierer theologische Zeitschrift* 81 (1972); 203–313; Rudolf Pesch, *Das Markusevangelium,* vol. 1, Herders theologischer Kommentar zum Neuen Testament 2/1 (Freiburg: Herder, 1976), 202–9, 325–32 (literature).

19. See Karl Kertelge, "Die Funktion der 'Zwölf' im Markusevangelium," *Trierer theologische Zeitschrift* 78 (1969): 193–206.

20. See Ched Myers, *Binding the Strong Man: A Political Reading of Mark's Story of Jesus* (Maryknoll, N.Y.: Orbis Books, 1988), 164, who stresses the political dimension of this symbolic act: Jesus forms a "kind of vanguard 'revolutionary committee.'"

it could be inferred that Mark intends to limit the preaching of the twelve to Galilee. Finally, Mark 3:13–19 and 6:6b–13 do not stress that the twelve have *to be* like Jesus but demand that as the disciples of Jesus the twelve have *to do* what Jesus did. In Mark's view Jesus is the teacher par excellence who has great authority over demons and the power to heal. Jesus' power is demonstrated by exorcisms and healing miracles. If Mark understands the twelve and all the other disciples to be the functional successors of Jesus, then it is not their maleness but their preaching, exorcising, and healing power that continue Jesus' mission.

Important too is the fact that Mark does not differentiate between but rather identifies the twelve and the disciples.[21] A comparison of Mark 11:11 with 11:14, and Mark 14:12, 14 with 14:17 speaks for the overlapping of both groups. Mark 4:10 does not provide a sufficient textual basis for a clear-cut distinction between the twelve and the disciples, since such a separation cannot be maintained for the subsequent passages (Mark 6:35–44; 7:17; 9:28; 10:10). Insofar as Mark does not stress the apostolic character of the twelve, even though he is aware of it (cf. 3:14 and 6:30), he clearly is not concerned with the theological foundation of apostolic ministry. He primarily understands the twelve as disciples and attributes to them no distinctive function and mission other than discipleship. The mission of the twelve to do what Jesus did is therefore according to Mark not restricted to the twelve but is a mission given to all the disciples.

The second part of the gospel therefore stresses again and again that the disciples have to suffer the same consequences that Jesus had to suffer for his preaching and mission. Just as the way of Jesus led to suffering and death, so does the way of the true disciple. Connected with each passion prediction are statements stressing that no possibility of discipleship exists apart from taking upon oneself its consequence of suffering. Yet again and again the twelve with their leading spokesman Peter show that they do not understand and even reject Jesus' insistence on suffering discipleship.

The twelve disciples who were called "to be with him" (Mark

---

21. Against Stock, *Boten aus dem Mit-Ihm-Sein,* who ascribes to the twelve a special function, namely to represent Jesus and to continue his work. See, however, Reploh, *Markus,* 47–48, who maintains that the twelve are included among the disciples. They have no special function distinctive from the disciples, but they are the origin and beginning of the whole church. See also Luz, *Das Evangelium nach Matthäus,* who warns not to restrict the commissioning of the twelve disciples to a limited historical circle and thereby to excuse the *ekklēsia* from practicing the ethos of discipleship.

3:14) desert Jesus in the hour of his suffering (14:50), and Peter denies him three times (14:66–72). They are not found under the cross of Jesus, nor at his burial, and it remains unclear whether they receive the message of the resurrection (Mark 16:7–8). In marked contrast to the twelve disciples, the women disciples who have followed Jesus from Galilee to Jerusalem (see 15:40f) have remained faithful until the end.

Not the twelve but the women disciples prove to be the true disciples of Jesus in Mark. The women not only accompany Jesus on his way to suffering and death but they also *do* what he had come to do, namely, to serve (*diakonein,* cf. 10:42–45 and 15:41). While the twelve disciples are unable to understand and to accept Jesus' teaching that he must suffer, it is a woman who shows such perception and acts accordingly (14:3–9). In Mark her action is the immediate cause for the betrayal of Jesus by one of the twelve (14:10f). This contrast between the twelve and the women disciples would suggest that in Mark's church the apostolic women were considered to have been the exemplary disciples of Jesus who had their place among the leaders of the Jesus-movement in Palestine.[22] In Mark's theological perspective the women disciples are the functional successors of Jesus, and they continue Jesus' mission and ministry in the "New Family" of God. Far from being the exemplars of apostolic discipleship, the twelve are the negative blueprint to right discipleship.

LUKE'S THEOLOGICAL ACCENTUATION

Since Luke-Acts has formed our theological understanding and historical imagination of early Christian beginnings, its identification of the twelve with the apostles has greatly influenced Christian theological and historical self-understanding. Nevertheless, the Lukan redaction still views the circle of the twelve as belonging to the time of Jesus and to the very beginnings of the Christian movement. The twelve's legitimation is rooted in their companionship with Jesus and in their witness to the resurrection. They have special eschatological (Q) and historical (Mark) functions vis-à-vis Israel.

---

22. See Paul J. Achtemeier, *Mark,* Proclamation Commentary (Philadelphia: Fortress Press, 1975), 92–100.

It is debatable whether Acts 1:21f makes maleness explicitly a precondition for replacing a member of the twelve.[23] According to Luke the position of Judas can be taken by "one of the men [*anēr*] who have accompanied us during all the time that the Lord Jesus went in and out among us beginning from the baptism of John until the day when he was taken up." Thus according to Luke-Acts only one of the original disciples of Jesus who were together with the eleven witnesses to the resurrection could replace Judas who was one of the twelve. However, it is not clear whether *anēr* is used in 1:21 in a grammatically generic or in a gender-specific masculine sense, since Acts often uses the address "men, brothers" (1:16; 2:29; 2:37; 7:2; 13:15; 13:26, 38; 15:7, 13; 22:1, 6; 28:17) in a grammatically generic-inclusive sense for addressing the whole community, even when women are present (see 1:14 and 1:16).

It could, however, also be argued to the contrary, that because of his theological understanding of the twelve Luke maintains that only one of the *male* followers of Jesus is eligible to become one of the twelve, since Luke 8:1–3 clearly distinguishes between the women disciples of Jesus and the twelve. Differing from its Markan source, the Gospel of Luke has the women disciples serve Jesus *and* the twelve. It qualifies their *diakonein* insofar as it specifies that the women disciples served them, i.e., Jesus and the twelve, with their possessions. Just as wealthy women provided patronage for Jewish missionary endeavors, so according to Luke wealthy Christian women support the ministry of Jesus and of the twelve apostles. Luke then seems to limit the leadership role of women in the Christian missionary movement to that of benefactors.[24]

However, Luke-Acts precludes the notion that the twelve could have appointed a line of successors, since Luke's theological perspective assigns only a very limited function to the twelve apostles. The twelve are mentioned for the last time in Acts 6:2ff. and they disappear altogether after chapter 15. It is, moreover, curious that

---

23. For Acts 1:15–26 see Ernst Haenchen, *The Acts of the Apostles* (Philadelphia: Westminster, 1971), 157–65 (literature).

24. For a different interpretation see Hans Conzelmann, *The Theology of Saint Luke* (London: Faber & Faber, 1961), 47 n. 1: "Features from the primitive community have naturally been projected back. Just as the male followers are turned into apostles, so the female followers are turned into deaconesses (v.3)." Frederick W. Danker, *Jesus and the New Age,* rev. ed. (Philadelphia: Fortress Press, 1988), 172–73, on the other hand stresses that the women are to "be included within the class of benefactors that was so esteemed in Mediterranean society," but he does not reflect on the Lukan redactional tendencies that determine this inclusion. For a feminist analysis of such Lukan tendencies see my book *But She Said* (Boston: Beacon Press, 1992).

most passages in Acts speak only of the work of one of them, Peter.
Luke-Acts does not characterize the twelve as missionaries, and
there is little evidence in Acts that they were at all active outside
Jerusalem. In Acts the apostle par excellence is Paul, who clearly
was not one of the twelve.

Luke knows likewise that the twelve were not the official local
ministers of the Jerusalem church or any other church. According
to Paul and Acts the leadership of the Jerusalem church was clearly
in the hands of James, the brother of the Lord, who was not one
of the twelve. Moreover, the twelve as a group were not replaced
when they died (see Acts 12:2). The twelve apostles had no successors. Thus it is evident that Luke knows only of a very limited
function for the twelve in the origins of the Christian movements.
Their significance appears to be limited to the very beginning of
the church and to its relationship to the chosen people of Israel.

Following Mark, Luke seems to historize the eschatological-
symbolic function vis-à-vis Israel that the twelve had in his tradition. He limits their activity to the mission within Israel. After
the Gentile mission is under way, the twelve disappear from the
historical scene. The elders and bishops in Acts are not understood
as successors of the twelve. They are either appointed by Paul and
Barnabas (14:23) or directly called by the Holy Spirit (Acts 20:28).

In conclusion: It needs to be stressed that according to Luke-
Acts the historical and symbolic function of the twelve was not
continued in the ministries of the church. Neither their symbolic-
eschatological and historical-missionary function vis-à-vis Israel
nor their function as eyewitnesses of the ministry and resurrection of Jesus is constitutive for the ministry of the church. If Luke
required that the replacement of Judas must be a male follower of
the historical Jesus, then this does not say anything about maleness as an essential requirement for the ordained priesthood or
episcopacy in the church, since Luke envisions neither an "apostolic succession" of the twelve nor an ordained priesthood. The
theological problem at hand then is whether the construct of "apostolic succession" can be maintained today in view of the historical
recognition that the twelve apostles had no successors, nor any
priestly ordination.

The historical-theological issue at stake is therefore not whether
women can be ordained as priests or appointed as successors of
the apostles if Jesus did not call any woman disciple to be a member of the twelve-circle. Rather the theological issue at hand is

whether the discipleship of equals will be realized by the *ekklēsia*, the democratic assembly of *all* citizens in the church. As long as such a vision of the *ekklēsia of women* has not become a reality, apostolic calling engages women and men in the struggle for the transformation of the patriarchal church into the discipleship community of equals.

TOWARD A LIBERATING AND LIBERATED THEOLOGY: WOMEN THEOLOGIANS AND FEMINIST THEOLOGY IN THE UNITED STATES

CONTEXTUALIZATION

This essay is a shortened form of an article that I wrote in 1978 for *Concilium,* a Roman Catholic international journal, which appears in six languages. In writing this contribution I had two goals: First, I intended to bring the situation and struggles of North American women within theological academic institutions to the attention of an international audience in the hope that women in other countries could learn from our experience. In addition, I hoped that this report would assist younger women in developing a structural, political analysis.

Second, I had observed that while feminists had provided many critical analyses of ecclesiastical hierarchy, only very few had been made of academic structures and institutions. My work with the Women's Caucus–Religious Studies, however, had made me increasingly aware of feminist tendencies to reproduce the academic separation of theory and practice, the chasm between theoretical discussion and political action for change. While the Women's Studies section has flourished because its radical theorizing fits into

the theoretical-structural framework of the academy, the Women's
Caucus, which fought for structural change, has not enjoyed such
success because the caucus does not "fit" into the established
practices and boundaries of the academic professions. Generally
speaking, women scholars in religion seem to have focused on
androcentric symbol systems, language, and traditions rather than
on political consciousness raising and change. Such a focus is not
surprising since as scholars we are members of an academic pluralistic elite who are allowed to produce theoretical scholarship
about women or gender theory as long as it remains within established academic and professional canons. As women belonging
to a marginalized group without much institutional power we can
bring about change only when we share a common vision and
political movement.

WHEN IN 1847 ANTOINETTE BROWN wanted to study theology and to take a theological degree from Oberlin, she met with
considerable resistance from her parents, friends, and advisers.
Nevertheless she persisted in her goal. After considerable debate,
the faculty at Oberlin decided that they could not deny her the
privilege of applying herself to religious studies. However, after
Antoinette Brown completed her program of theological studies in
1850, she and another female student were not allowed to graduate.
Only in 1878 did Oberlin grant her an honorary M.A. degree and
in 1908 an honorary doctor of divinity degree. In 1853 she was the
first woman ordained in the United States, but consistent with her
growing religious liberalism, she resigned from her pastorate a year
later. Nevertheless she inspired other women to pursue theological
studies and to enter the ministry.[1]

WOMEN SEMINARIANS AND THEOLOGIANS

Today the number of women students in theological schools and
seminaries steadily increases. In prestigious Protestant seminaries women already constitute up to 50 percent of the student

1. B. M. Solomon, "Blackwell, Antoinette Louisa Brown" in *Notable American
Women 1607–1950: A Biographical Dictionary,* ed. Edward T. James (Cambridge,
Mass.: Belknap Press of Harvard University Press, 1968), 3:158–61.

body. Women's caucuses within theological schools have pressured faculty and administration to take women's problems and questions more seriously. Most major theological schools therefore offer women's studies courses and support women's centers. Yet most institutions still count only a very few women among their regular tenured faculty members. Moreover, theological faculties are often neither aware of their covert or overt sexism, nor do they have academic training or qualifications in women's studies in religion or in feminist theology. Therefore, feminists in theology and religious studies have sought to create the institutional space necessary for women to shape their own theological questions, to define new research areas, to transform educational curricula and requirements, and to explore alternative ways of practicing ministry and theology. One most successful attempt, the Seminary Quarter at Grailville was initiated by Church Women United and by the Grail movement in order to model a different process of theological education.[2] That it has attracted students from theological schools all over the country during the summer months also indicates that women cannot ask their own theological questions and pursue feminist studies during the regular school year.

In short, despite well-meaning attempts to integrate women into theological seminaries and to develop their perspective in theological education, the situation of women graduating from seminary is not so different from that of Antoinette Brown. True, like their male colleagues, women graduates receive theological degrees; but only about one-third of the clergywomen are able to move into ministerial positions immediately upon the completion of their seminary training.[3] Most of them find themselves in subordinate positions, especially in educational work with women and children; only very rarely is a woman hired for an indepen-

---

2. See the report issued each summer from Grailville, Ohio. The Seminary Quarter is a six-week program. It attempts to explore not only new forms of theology but new ways of learning. Facilitators seek to foster a living-learning community: resource faculty assist students in exploring their individual theological projects and helps in the preparation of group projects. Topics explored are liberation theology and a feminist critique; language, myth, and symbol; sexuality and spirituality; curriculum for Christian feminism; self as source for theologizing; assumptions about institutional and social change; biography as theology; exploring ministry; and wholeness and worship. (Unfortunately, this experiment has not survived.)

3. E. Wilbur Bock, "The Female Clergy: A Case of Professional Marginality" in *The Professional Woman,* ed. A. Theodore (Cambridge, Mass.: Schenkman Publishing Co., 1971), 599–611; A. R. Jones, "Differential Recruitment of Female Professionals: A Case Study of Clergy Women," in *Professional Woman,* 355–65.

dent pastorate or pulpit. The increase in the number of students in seminaries and theological schools does therefore not indicate a greater influence of women in the professional ministry. Since liberal theological schools often do not attract enough qualified male applicants and struggle for their financial survival, the greater number of highly qualified women admitted to the student body does not imply an actual increase of women's presence in professional theology and ministry.

Whereas the biographical dictionary of *Notable American Women 1607–1950* lists many names of ministers, evangelists, missionaries, religious educators, founders, and leaders, it does not have an entry with the category of "theologian," even though it acknowledges women historians, psychologists, classical and literary scholars, and archaeologists. The history of women in the academic profession of theology and women's contributions to religious studies still needs to be written. Today [1978] about two to four hundred (among them only a very few women of color) women qualify as professional theologians in the United States insofar as they have a doctorate in theology or religious studies or are near its completion.[4] Women teach religious studies and theology in colleges, universities, and theological schools.

The majority of women faculty are, however, either in less prestigious colleges and schools with heavy teaching loads and little emphasis on research, or they are found in the junior nontenured entry-level positions as instructors or assistant professors. A growing number of women with doctoral degrees are not able to obtain a teaching position at all. Because of explicit or implicit "nepotism" rules, married women are often still barred from full-time faculty. They are relegated to underpaid adjunct positions or are forced to take jobs in inferior institutions. Wife-husband teams are especially vulnerable, since patriarchal administrators still assume that women will quit their jobs when they get pregnant or that the wife will move and give up her career if the husband is denied tenure or a renewal of contract.

In spite of the ecclesiastical rhetoric in defense of the Christian family, theological institutions do not hesitate to destroy marriages and families in order to preserve the patriarchal and clerical academic system that has no room for married women who are

---

4. It is difficult to obtain exact statistics. The Registry of the Women's Caucus–Religious Studies lists about 230 names. Yet this list is far from being complete.

scholars in their own right.[5] The dedication in books to wives or female collaborators, if their labor is mentioned at all, indicates the extent to which male academic careers are built on the support services of women who not only perform auxiliary tasks such as housekeeping or typing but also research and often compose the whole book. The widely published relationship between Karl Barth and Charlotte von Kirschbaum is a well-known example of this practice.

Very few women scholars hold senior-level, permanent tenured faculty positions and are free to develop their own theological interests and style. Likewise women seldom achieve the higher administrative ranks of theological institutions, and at present only one is the head of a theological school. Because of the political pressures of the academic women's movement and governmental affirmative action plans in general, and because of the work of the Women's Caucus–Religious Studies in particular,[6] a few women have been appointed in the past five years to the governing boards of major theological professional societies and to the editorial boards of leading theological journals, and only two women have served as presidents of theological societies.

The impact of these women on policy issues and on the power structures within the professional societies of theological studies, however, remains for the most part negligible. Since women scholars are often chosen who seem to be compliant "team players," the "old boys' club/network" remains intact. Women board members therefore tend to serve the purpose of token liberalism more than they are able to influence and change the power structures and ideologies of the theological professions. Because of the dismal prospects of the job market the impact of women on the theological profession will probably decline even more and not improve in the foreseeable future. The little progress that has been made in past years is in danger of being obliterated again.

Not much has changed in the century and a half since An-

---

5. See Arlie Russel Hochschild, "Inside the Clockwork of Male Careers" in *Women and the Power to Change*," ed. Florence Howe (New York: McGraw-Hill, 1975), 47–80.

6. The Women's Caucus–Religious Studies was initiated at the national annual American Academy of Religion/Society of Biblical Literature convention in Atlanta in 1971. It publishes a registry of women theologians to facilitate the placement of women graduate students and faculty and a quarterly newsletter to provide a public forum for women in the profession. It also sponsors working sessions on women in religion at the annual conventions to facilitate public discussion on feminist theological issues. The best papers of these sessions are published.

toinette Brown entered the theological field. Only grudgingly admitted to a clerical, male profession, women students as well as faculty remain marginal to the theological enterprise. They are at best tolerated by male colleagues and academic administrators and at worst are permanently turned away from theological studies and research altogether. In any case, they do not have any substantial impact on the way in which theology is done. The professional theologian remains in the public consciousness "he" and a "gentleman." This marginality of women in the theological profession is, however, not typical merely of the North American situation, but of other countries as well.

On my last visit to Germany, I asked one of my university professors whether a woman held a regular professorship at a traditional Protestant or Catholic theological faculty. He assured me that lay-men can now be "habilitated" and become professors of Roman Catholic faculties. When I stressed that I was not interested in lay-men but in knowing whether a woman theologian was a member of an established Roman Catholic faculty, he turned to his housekeeper and asked sarcastically: "Do you want to become my successor?" Apparently, for him, a housekeeper with no theological education was in the same position vis-à-vis academic theology as I who had just shared with him my theological accomplishments and involvement. Qualifications and publications seem not to matter. The only fact that counts seems to be that we are women. No wonder German theological faculties do not even sense the need for educating women as professional theologians. Since young women lack any professional role models of women who have been successful in establishing themselves as scholars, they are not motivated to work for advanced theological degrees.

FEMINIST ANALYSIS
OF ACADEMIC THEOLOGICAL INSTITUTIONS

This incident, however, made it clear to me that the situation of women theologians in North America *is* different from that of their European sisters. An American colleague might have had the same sentiments but he would never have voiced them with such candor. Because of the women's movement in the United States "androcentrism," or sexism and discrimination against women, is exposed more and more as structural evil and personal fault. Liberal professors of theology would no more risk the accusation of sexism than that of racism. They are aware that American women are no longer grateful to be tolerated on the fringes of the professions but seek full participation in them.

Feminist analyses of culture and religion have, however, shown that full participation of women in academic life and research will be possible only when the patriarchal and sexist structures of academic institutions are changed. Therefore, women do not just demand to be tolerated by the academy and to be integrated into the clockwork of male careers. By organizing professional women and by initiating legislation and affirmative action plans, feminists seek to change the patriarchal systems of the academy as well as the patriarchal-sexist attitudes of male academicians and students so that women can participate fully in intellectual work and academic research. Yet at the same time feminists realize that it does not suffice simply to incorporate more women into the academic system. What is necessary is to overcome the sexual stereotyping of the academic professions in general and of academic theology in particular.

Although numerous critical analyses of church and clerical structures exist, critical evaluations of theological professions and academic structures as such are still scarce. Liberation theologians have pointed out that theology in European and North American contexts is white and middle-class and as such shares in the cultural imperialism of Europe and the United States.[7] Theology as the domain of white clergy reflects the interests of the white middle-class community. Since theologians, theological schools, and publishing houses depend on grants and money from the rich, they have to cater to the interests of the white establishment.

Feminist theologians claim that this analysis of the life-setting of the theological discipline does not probe far enough. Christian academic theology is not just white, middle-class, and establishment but white, middle-class, and *male,* and shares in the sexual stereotyping of academic institutions and the professions. The androcentric character of the discipline is as pervasive and personally threatening as race and class issues are. Theology can become *humanized* and liberated from oppressive sexual stereotyping only when male scholars take seriously the challenges of the femi-

7. See, e.g., Frederick Herzog, "Liberation Theology Begins at Home," *Christianity and Crisis* (May 13, 1974), and his "Liberation Hermeneutics as Ideology Critique," *Interpretation* 28 (1974): 387–403.

nist critique and begin to analyze their own privileges and practice as men in a male-typed clerical profession.

The institutions of the theological discipline share the androcentric character of other academic institutions.[8] The public image of the theological profession is sex-typed, and recruitment to the profession generally has functioned to exclude or to discourage women from seeking admission to the academic or ministerial ranks of the discipline. Moreover, interactions – especially in the top echelons of the profession – are exclusive and informal, based on unstated norms and implying a social, male solidarity within an exclusive, club-like, and often clerical environment. Not so much qualifications but the prestige of the school and sponsor-protégé relationships determine access to financial resources and to the inner circles and power centers of the discipline. The *Doktorvater* system treats male students as potential professors and successors with preference insofar as it makes scholarships available to them, provides important connections with established colleagues in the field, and fills influential senior positions by informal recommendations.

Aware of the male orientation of the theological profession, professors are not inclined to sponsor and to support the career of female students with the same enthusiasm. They implicitly recognize that women will not be able to establish themselves as scholarly "authorities" in the field and therefore will not expand their own power, increase the academic standing of their *Doktorvater,* or continue his scholarship as his successors after his retirement. Male students on the other hand do not gain the same means of advancement by working with a woman professor since she is not a fully accepted member of the informal, professorial "male club." Women theologians and scholars in religion are thus not able to infiltrate successfully professional networks and to succeed in a male-typed theological profession.

Furthermore, the judgment of whether a theologian is of "top" rank usually depends on his or her affiliation with prestigious institutions and association with the leading men in the field, and on the publicity received in reviews or discussions of publications and research. On all three counts women theologians are likely

---

8. Cynthia Fuchs Epstein, "Encountering the Male Establishment: Sex-Status Limits on Women Careers in the Professions," in *Professional Woman,* 39–51; P. A. Graham, "Women in Academe," in *Professional Woman,* 720–40; Adrienne Rich, "Toward a Woman-Centered University," in *Women and the Power to Change,* 15–46.

Spiritualities of the Heart ed Annice Callahan
NY Paulist 1990

Brian Wren What Language Shall I Borrow? God-talk - Worship:
A Male Response to Fem Theol
NY Crossrood 1989

Marjorie Farley Personal Commitment: Beginning-Keeping; Changing-Hope 1986
* "New Patterns of Relationship: Beg B. a Moral Revolt't" T.S. 1975
627-46

John E . & Mary ed Contemporary Xology: Rahner + Schillebeeckx
Eglises et Théologie 1984

Ruether, Ford + H. Rhodes J Sexuality
Bible

Ruether, York Sexism ~ God-talk

McFague (worlds of God) Metaphorical Theo; Models of g. Redmp

Schneider Women + the Word: The Gender of God in NT+
Sply of Wm

Christ + Plaskow
Womanspirit Rising; A Feminist Reader ~ Rel

Elsa Tamez ed. Through Her Eyes: Women's Theo from Lat Ame
maryknoll Orbis 1989

Mary Daly Beyond God the Father: Toward a Phil of Wm?
Liberat Bost Beacon 1973

to be disadvantaged. They usually do not have senior positions in prestigious theological schools, they are not promoted by senior men to the same degree as their male colleagues, and their research and publications receive relatively little attention from men or women, since men are the supposed authorities in the field. Moreover, women students are often channelled through doctoral dissertations into fringe areas of theology. In my opinion it is no accident that in New Testament studies, for instance, women are overrepresented in Gnostic studies or in research on Revelation, a New Testament book widely neglected by serious exegetes.

Because women do not "fit" into a male-typed theological discipline, their presence in professional networks and departmental committees, moreover, causes considerable role-confusion. Men, students as well as faculty, often do not know how to relate to women as academicians but fall back on the traditional social norms governing male-female relationships. Women are treated like perpetual daughters dependent on the fatherly authority of their teachers, as secretaries or research assistants, as caring mother-figures, as aggressive "bitches," or as erotic objects for flirtation. Men rarely know how to relate to women as interesting colleagues and as theological authorities in their own right. A letter of a young woman theologian highlights this point. She reports that expressing interest in the work of established senior colleagues often leads to dinner invitations and to sexual advances. "Like her male counterparts, she needs colleagues to confirm the validity and importance of her ideas. But she finds herself in a position where she never can know whether a colleague was interested in her ideas or in her body."[9]

In addition, women themselves have deeply internalized their inferior status and blame their lack of success on their own personal failure. Many women students sincerely believe that they have equal access to education, jobs, and careers if they are "good enough" in their fields. They are worried about "reverse discrimination" since affirmative action supposedly has done away with discrimination against women and minority men. Just recently a doctoral student assured me that she had never experienced any discrimination and that she had gotten her faculty appointment because she was qualified and not because she was a woman. Since I knew for a fact that she was hired over other women, I pointed

---

9. *Women's Caucus–Religious Studies Newsletter* 2 (1974): 5.

out to her that she was successful against other applicants because she clearly stated that she was not interested in feminist questions but only in academic questions. Since women deeply want to believe that they are treated fairly and equally as scholars, she could not entertain the thought that she won out because the seminary was threatened by an affirmative action suit and badly needed to appoint a compliant token woman.

Finally, if white women have great difficulties in entering theological institutions and achieving faculty positions, the difficulties for women of color to do so are almost insurmountable. Yet as long as women of color are absent from the ranks of students and faculties in theological schools, their voice and perspective cannot be heard in feminist theology. The indictment of feminist theology as a white, middle-class women's affair should therefore more appropriately be directed against established academic institutions and theological education that are predominantly white, middle-class, and European-American.

FEMINIST THEOLOGY AND
THE LIBERATION OF THEOLOGY

Feminist theologians argue for the full inclusion of women in the theological profession not just because of their desire to advance their theological careers in a male-typed institution but also because they are convinced that theological and ecclesial structures have to be liberated from all forms of racism, classism, and sexism if they are to serve people and not contribute to their oppression. Sexism in theology is not just a personal fault but a structural evil that distorts Christian theology and corrupts the academic integrity of religious studies.

Feminist theology shares such an understanding of racism, sexism, and class exploitation as structural evil with liberation theology. However, insofar as women belong to all races, classes, and cultures and throughout the centuries have been silenced and excluded from positions of leadership in church and academy, the scope of a feminist liberation theology is more global and radical than that of the critical and liberation theologies that have been articulated by men.

Since the origins and subsequent history of Christian theology were immersed in cultural and ecclesial patriarchy, women, whether white or black, rich or poor, married or not, could never take a significant rather than marginal part in the formulation and definition of Christian faith and theology. The writers of the Hebrew Bible lived in Palestine, Augustine in North Africa, and Thomas in Europe. Yet their theology is no less formulated from a male perspective than that of Barth, Niebuhr, or Teilhard de Chardin. Because theology has been and is rooted in male experience, traditional theology has not only ignored but also suppressed the experience and contributions of women.[10]

Therefore, a hermeneutical revision of Christian theology does not suffice, since it is apparent that the Christian past and present and not just its theological interpretations and records have marginalized and victimized women and minority men.[11] It is not enough merely to understand the Christian tradition and adequately perceive its symbolic frameworks. Any understanding of Christian theology as "the actualizing continuation of the Christian history of interpretation"[12] overlooks how the tradition of theology and church is a source not only of truth and liberation but also of repression and domination. Therefore, theology must critically evaluate and reject those traditions that have contributed to the exclusion and oppression of women. Just as Christian theology has rejected the traditions of anti-Judaism, even when found in the Bible, so it has now to reject all sexist traditions even if they are deeply rooted in Christian Scriptures and traditions.

The recent Vatican statement against the ordination of women documents the negative consequences of androcentric God-language for the role of women in the church. The document's insistence on the maleness of Christ and on the masculine rather than human character of salvation serves, however, not so much as an argument against the ordination of women. It rather demonstrates that the central mysteries of Christian faith are male and exclusive of women. As long as the central Christian symbols of

---

10. For an analysis of the theological understanding of sin rooted in male experience see Valerie Saiving Goldstein, "The Human Situation: A Feminine View," in *Journal of Religion* 40 (1960): 100–112; Judith Plaskow, *Sex, Sin and Grace: Women's Experience and the Theologies of Reinhold Niebuhr and Paul Tillich* (Washington: University Press of America, 1980).

11. See the contention of Mary Daly that Christian faith and symbols are inherently sexist, Daly, *Beyond God the Father: Toward a Philosophy of Women's Liberation* (Boston: Beacon Press, 1973).

12. See Edward Schillebeeckx, *The Understanding of Faith* (London: Sheed and Ward, 1974).

faith are expressed in male language and imagery, feminist theologians have to insist that the language and symbolism of God are one-sided and need to be balanced by female imagery and symbolism rooted in women's experience. We must learn to speak of God as Father and Mother, as Son and Daughter, as she and he. Unless female God-language is commonly accepted in Christian theology and worship, women will not be able to recognize themselves in the image and likeness of God.[13]

In conclusion: Feminist theologians are well aware that their vision of a nonsexist church and nonoppressive God cannot be embodied in "old wineskins" but has to be expressed in new theological structures and language. If change is to occur, a spiral movement is necessary.[14] On the one hand, efforts concentrated on bringing women's experience to bear on theology will not succeed unless theological institutions are changed to accept the presence and expertise of women as well as to allow for feminist theologizing. On the other hand, efforts to change established theological institutions cannot be far-reaching enough if theological language, myth, and symbols are not changed but continue to maintain women's marginal status and secondary role in theology and church. Structural change in theology and the evolution of a feminist theological consciousness and theory have to go hand in hand.

---

13. Feminist theologians therefore seek to revise liturgical language and to create new symbols and liturgies. See Nelle Morton, "The Dilemma of Celebration," in *Women in a Strange Land*, ed. Clare Benedicks Fischer, Betsy Brenneman, Anne McGrew Bennett (Philadelphia: Fortress Press, 1975); Arlene Swidler, *Sistercelebrations: Nine Worship Experiences* (Philadelphia, 1974) has an excellent collection of feminist liturgies.

14. This is also emphasized by Sherry B. Ortner, in "Is Female to Male as Nature is to Culture?" in Michelle Zimbalist Rosaldo and Louise Lamphere, *Woman, Culture, and Society* (Stanford: Stanford University Press, 1974), 67–87.

10 ———————————————

TO COMFORT OR TO CHALLENGE? THE SECOND WOMEN'S ORDINATION CONFERENCE

CONTEXTUALIZATION

As its title, "New Woman, New Church, New Priestly Ministry," indicated, the Second Women's Ordination Conference, held in Baltimore in November 1979, took a stronger feminist direction than the first. In the time span between 1975 and 1979, the Vatican statement against the ordination of women had caused much discussion on both a theological and on a popular level. The Catholic Theological Society of America (CTSA) had issued a research report titled "Women in Church and Society," for which I served as a consultant. Moreover, as a board member of the Catholic Biblical Association, I had worked for the appointment of a task force to address the question of biblical warrants against or for women's ordination. This task force submitted a report in 1979 concluding "that the New Testament evidence, while not decisive by itself, points toward the admission of women to priestly ministry."[1]

In preparation for the conference, WOC had decided to use a feminist collective process that called for group involvement on the local level. The organizers had sent out a set of questions in order to facilitate this process of theological reflection. Since I in

---

1. "Women and Priestly Ministry: The New Testament Evidence," *Catholic Biblical Quarterly* 41 (1979): 608–13.

129

turn was asked to reflect on this preconference process theologically, I presented my conclusions beforehand to the organizers
at a meeting in Chicago. After this meeting I was informed that
the program was too crowded and that the plenary session on the
preconference process was likely to be canceled. It was obvious
to me that some members of the organizing committee believed
my proposals calling for "partial identification" and a "spiritual
hunger strike" were too radical. Nevertheless, to the credit of
WOC, freedom of speech was safeguarded and the plenary session
was allowed to take place.

In retrospect, it seems clear that my introductory remarks were
colored by this experience. Before my speech I worried that I
would lose the attention of the audience because I was too "far out"
for the majority of women attending the conference. On the after-
noon before my talk, I noticed an informal invitation to a women's
liturgy that was scheduled to take place at the same time as the
official liturgy celebrated by a priest. In the evening I went with
trepidation to the hotel suite where the bilingual liturgy was to
take place, since I feared to find only a handful of people present
who shared my theological perspective. To my great surprise, the
room was packed, and I experienced one of the most moving liturgies of my life. Before my eyes and ears my theological convictions
"became flesh."

Women as baptized members of the church reclaimed their gifts
to celebrate and proclaim G–d's power for the liberation and salvation not only of women but also of men. I no longer felt I was on the
"radical fringe" but realized that on the next morning I could claim
as my audience the center of the women's ordination movement.
Nevertheless, this address ended up being a "costly" speech. It
not only foreclosed several job opportunities in Catholic theological schools, but also generated letters of protest to the president of
Notre Dame University, threatening to cut off donations and public
support if I were not censured or fired from the university.

WHEN I PREPARED THIS LECTURE several people cautioned,
"Elisabeth, don't forget that you speak not only to the women
present at the conference but also to the male hierarchy who will
not be present. Churchmen do not understand the language of feminist critique nor the attitude of setting one's own agenda. Don't

challenge them too much!" This counsel of caution reminded me of the experience I had when I decided to study theology.

Because I was the first woman in Würzburg to do so and had a government scholarship requiring documentation that I was pursuing professional education, I needed the permission of the local bishop. Since the bishop knew me personally and over the years had followed my work in the youth ministry of the diocese, I was confident that I would receive his permission without any difficulties. To my surprise my bishop did not enthusiastically support my intention. Instead, he argued against it.

Finally, after all the technical arguments were exhausted, my bishop confessed his real misgivings: "Your problem," he argued, "is that you clearly recognize the wounds of the church. But instead of spreading the cover of love over them, you point your finger at them." I was very hurt by this criticism but managed a reply: "Your Excellency, if I believed that the patient was dead I would spread the blanket of love over the corpse. However, because I believe in the vitality and recuperation of the church, I persist in challenging ecclesiastical failures for the sake of the people of God who still identify with the church."

THEOLOGICAL ANALYSIS
OF THE PRECONFERENCE PROCESS

This incident happened twenty years ago. Nevertheless, the same hurt and outrage over the failures of the hierarchical church still echo through the narratives of the preconference process. If today we challenge the establishment church by the mere fact that we are having this conference, then we are doing this in the conviction that healing and comfort are possible only after the wounds have been cleansed and the festering evil of patriarchal sexism has been excised.[2] Because we love the church and are committed to the gospel, we will have to challenge the male leadership of the Roman Catholic Church. Such a critique and challenge reverberates in the accounts of the preconference process.

The expressed purpose of the preconference process was to

---

2. I understand "patriarchalism" in the sense of a social system maintaining male dominance and privilege based on female submission and marginality. The word "sexism" was coined by analogy to racism. It denotes all those attitudes and actions that relegate women to a secondary and inferior status.

initiate reflection groups that were to come together to "look at
their lived experience, to reflect upon priesthood as they presently know it, to analyze the ministries women are carrying out
today and to see how such ministries would profit from ordination." The second part of the process, which will be addressed by
the panel on "Chains That Bond," will ask what a renewed church
and ministry would look like. Thus the preconference process concentrated on the issues of ordination, ministry, women's ministry,
and church.

Since the answers we receive are dictated by the questions we
ask, a discussion of the process must analyze not only the responses
but also the questions that were asked. It is therefore important
to reflect on the theological presuppositions and questions of the
preconference process before interpreting the responses to it theologically. This needs to be done not in order to criticize those who
formulated the preconference questions, but in order to delineate
the strength and the limitations of this process.

The preconference process was not only directed to women or
to women in ministry, but was addressed to all "justice people."[3]
Almost five hundred people in fifty-three groups responded to the
invitation: 18 percent of them were men, 29 percent were women
in ecclesiastical communities, and the majority, 53 percent, were
women from other communal settings. The demographic data do
not provide information on how many groups were called together by nuns nor do we know how many of the participating
women were actively involved in ministry. The majority of the respondents were highly educated, middle-class, white, urban, and
regular participants in church life and liturgy. The respondents
appear, therefore, to be church-identified persons, although their
answers show that their identification with the Roman Catholic
Church is a partial and critical one. There is, however, not enough
information on the reaction of both those women who are nominal
Catholics and those women who have relinquished their church
identification because of the sexist character of the church. However, since the preconference process did not call together groups

---

3. The preconference data are twice removed from actual experience. The group
discussions and responses were recorded and thus already interpreted by the group
facilitator or another group leader. They were then summarized by members of the ordination conference task force. I also want to apologize to all those women whose stories
I quote without giving credit to them. However, these stories were not yet available to
me in an edited form and some of them did not have names on them.

of women to reflect on their experiences *as women* within the Roman Catholic Church and its ministry, it did not provide us with much direct information on how *women as women* experience the church and priesthood today.

The small local group in which I participated was made up of women in ministry and in theological education. We felt that the preconference perspective was somewhat "churchy" and insinuated reverse "clericalism." We missed questions on the interconnectedness between church and society, on the experiences of tokenism and co-optation, on the discrimination and trivialization experienced by those women who are already ordained in other Christian churches. Moreover, no specific structural issues within the Roman Catholic Church were raised: Why do Catholics generally experience nuns as a quasi-clerical class? Why do clerics and bishops insist that the leadership of the women's movement in the church has to be in the hands of women religious? Which present ecclesiastical structures are especially inimical to women? Where do we find new structures of ministry? How do we identify them? Why are women not "coming out of the closet" to make public their present leadership in liturgical and sacramental celebrations? How do we get from here to there, from our present experience of church and ministry to the future of a new priesthood and a new church?

The preconference process also did not include explicit questions on sexism and misogynism within the Roman Catholic Church. We therefore do not find much information on the God-question, on the understanding of Christ or Mary, on the experience of androcentricism in church liturgy, symbolism, and language. The narrow focus on church and ministry gives the impression that the preconference process did not sufficiently grapple with the issues of women's liberation as a precondition for the transformation of ministry and church. In short, insofar as the preconference process focused on personal experience and not also on structural issues, and insofar as it did not explicitly ask for women's experiences *as women* in a patriarchal church and ministry, it does not provide us with sufficient information on the "lived" experiences of women's oppression. The responses are therefore informative with respect to ecclesiology and ministry but less critical with respect to women's contribution to the ministry of the church today and in the future.

In addition to initiating reflection groups the organizers of the

preconference process asked those women who believed themselves to be called to the priesthood to submit accounts of their
personal experience and theological understanding of their call
to ministry. I personally did not participate in the second task of
the preconference process. When a friend challenged me on this
point I somewhat facetiously replied: "I do not feel myself called
to become a priest and to live my life in obedience to a bishop in
a job that no male wants to take on." The experiences of ordained
women in other Christian churches confirm that women's role in
the Roman Catholic Church will be the same as that in society,
namely, second-class citizenship. Moreover, when I was a child I
never said Mass but I did hear confessions! In an essay that I wrote
when I was seven, I confidently expressed that one day I would be
pope! I clearly had no intention of taking second place.

　　This somewhat flippant response was triggered by deep theological misgivings. Is the women's ordination movement, despite
all its assurances to the contrary, only interested after all in getting a few women into the present clerical structures? Will it
be a step backward theologically, since it seems to presuppose
a cultic understanding of priesthood that has been theologically
undermined since Vatican II? Will this movement mean a strength-
ening of the present clerical structures and a clericalization of
women? Does the movement miss the boat by shunning the theological questions of power and is it therefore in danger of co-opting
women's creativity and gifts for the present clerical system? After
having read the accounts of the women who responded, I must say
that my misgivings were either dispelled or at least muted. Yet it
became evident that the hurt and the courage expressed in these
stories told by women need to be grounded in a critical-theological
analysis and a constructive theological conceptualization. These
experiences of women must become deprivatized if they are to
have a pastoral-theological impact on the church.

FEMINIST THEOLOGICAL REFLECTION

Contrary to popular belief, there is no single expression of Roman
Catholic theology but a plurality of theological systems and approaches and a multiplicity of ways to do theology and to spell out
Christian hope, faith, and love. Biblical studies have shown that a
pluriformity of theological reflections and expressions has found

its way into the New Testament. Early Christian theology is not concerned with the formulation of timeless principles and doctrinal infallibilities but with theological responses to various pastoral situations. The Second Vatican Council has reasserted this pastoral approach of theology and of the magisterium thereby opening up a variety of new ways to reflect and to express Christian truth and faith. Since neo-scholastic theology is no longer the sole form of Roman Catholic theology, there is no longer one Catholic theology or one type of Catholic theologian.

Every theologian and theology has therefore to account for their presuppositions, conceptuality, and commitment. As a biblical scholar I have learned to think theologically not in terms of abstract principles and ecclesiastical doctrines but in terms of the Christian community and its theological and practical needs. Revelation is given for "the sake of our (i.e., women's) salvation." As a feminist theologian my self-identification and my allegiance are with women. However, in my feminist-theological understanding salvation and liberation cannot be derived from women's nature, from her specific feminine qualities or her biological powers, but only from a critical reflection on women's experience of oppression and women's struggle for liberation. Feminist theology is therefore in my understanding a "critical theology of liberation."

Since feminist theology is concerned with women's experience of oppression and has as its goal the liberation of both sexes, it has developed the tools and methods to make explicit the theological significance of women's experience and struggle for equality. Three feminist approaches present themselves. They are not mutually exclusive, but are dialectically related to each other. All three approaches understand women's present position in church and ministry as that of inequality and injustice. The exclusion of women from sacramental ministry is a violation of the equal rights that women have by virtue of their baptism as full members of the church. The hierarchy has therefore to change its present policy of the exclusion of women from ordination.

The first approach emphasizes "the unique gifts that feminine persons can offer to leadership and ministry in the church."[4] This theological approach presupposes the complementarity of the sexes and seems to be shared by many of the preconference

---

4. See Fran Ferder, *Called to Break Bread* (Mt. Rainier, Md.: Quixote Center, 1978), 48, whose psychological evaluation of the women called to priesthood seems to presuppose this approach.

respondents. When describing women's ministry today and characterizing the "new priesthood" of the future, respondents often use so-called feminine qualifications such as "more personal in style, homey, earthy, gentle, compassionate, touching, nurturing, supportive, sensitive, warm, giving, connecting people, more understanding, flexible, probably a little softer and rounder, less selfish, more encompassing, showing greater natural flair in their ministry." Although there is some awareness that women's ministries are privatized and lack implementing powers in their subordinate silent partnership, the respondents do not explore why they hold women's ministry to be more humane and more Christian than male ministry. Since they do not reflect on how women have internalized the "false consciousness" of femininity, they are in danger of projecting sexist and merely negative features onto male ministry.

Theological defenders of the Vatican declaration against women's ordination to the priesthood, as for instance David Burrell and Michael Novak, have moreover argued that the sexual differentiation between men and women justifies a sex-typed ministry and a "dual-sex" Eucharist.[5] They have advocated women's participation in all ministries of the church except the sacramental priesthood. Such an exclusion of women from the sacramental symbol system is according to Burrell required so that:

> the Church could reflect in her manifold ministries the maleness and femaleness of God's original plan, and the ordained priest would be able to see himself as the Declaration sees him: a performer of actions . . . in which Christ Himself, the author of the Covenant, the Bridegroom and the Head of the Church is represented exercising His ministry of salvation.[6]

Such theological support for the declaration's androcentrism makes one wonder whether the argument that women should be ordained in order to complement the masculine ministry of the church could in the end be fatal for women's equality in the church and jeopardize a nonsexist future of the church. Those arguing for the ordination of women on the basis of women's special nature

---

5. Michael Novak, "Dual-Sex Eucharist," *Commonweal* 103 (December 17, 1976): 813–16: "The priest is ordained to be an *alter Christus.* A woman might be consecrated as an altera Ecclesia. A dual-sex liturgy would symbolically unite, in a way hardly possible in previous centuries, Christ with his church, the masculine with the feminine."

6. David Burrell, "The Vatican Declaration: Another View," *America* (April 2, 1977): 291–92.

and particular feminine gifts are in danger of providing a theological justification for the exclusion of women from the sacramental priesthood and relegating women to "feminine" subsidiary ministries.[7] Although so-called feminine qualities must be intrinsic to the priesthood of women *and* men because they are *Christian* values, their privatization and distortion by sexism must first be confronted.[8] If the qualities of love, compassion, gentleness, sensitivity, and nurturance continue to remain restricted to women and to the ministry of women, they continue to be distorted by sexism and serve psychologically to adjust and conform women's ministries to the present structures of inequality in church and society.

The second type of feminist theology claims that Christianity is a patriarchal religion and therefore inherently sexist. Insofar as Christian theology justifies women's subordinate and inferior position theologically, any attempt to incorporate women into the present structures of the patriarchal church will contribute even more to the sexist exploitation of women. To be a feminist and a member of the Roman Catholic Church and hierarchy compares to being black and a member of the Ku Klux Klan. It is impossible to shed the "false consciousness of sexism" when one continues to internalize its values by praying to a male God and a masculine Savior and by obeying the Fathers of the Church. The post-Christian Catholic theologian Mary Daly spells out this contention in a succinct way: "Since God is male, the male is God. God, the Father, legitimizes all earthly God-Fathers. The idea of a unique divine incarnation in a male . . . is inherently sexist and oppressive. Christolatry is idolatry."[9]

In insisting on the maleness of Christ the Vatican declaration against the ordination of women to the priesthood seems merely to confirm Mary Daly's assertion:

> When Christ's role in the Eucharist is to be expressed sacramentally, there would not be this "natural resemblance" which must exist be-

7. See the commission report of the Congregation for the Evangelization of Peoples on "The Role of Women in Evangelization," *Origins* 5 (1977): 702ff, and Nadine Foley, "Women in Vatican Documents: 1960 to the Present," in *Sexism and Church Law,* ed. James A. Coriden (New York: Paulist Press, 1977), 82–108.

8. See esp. Rosemary Radford Ruether, *New Woman, New Earth: Sexist Ideologies and Human Liberation* (New York: Seabury Press, 1975).

9. Mary Daly, "The Qualitative Leap beyond Patriarchal Religion," *Quest* 1 (1974): 21. See also her book *Beyond God the Father: Toward a Philosophy of Women's Liberation* (Boston: Beacon Press, 1973).

tween Christ and his minister if the role of Christ were not taken by a man: in such a case it would be difficult to see in the minister the image of Christ. For Christ himself was and remains a man. Christ is, of course, the first-born of all humanity, of women as well as man.... Nevertheless the incarnation of the Word took place according to the male sex; this is indeed a question of fact, and this fact, while not implying an alleged natural superiority of man over woman cannot be disassociated from the economy of salvation.[10]

This statement marks a theological watershed. For the first time a church document justifies the exclusion of women from the priesthood not on anthropological but on theological and christological grounds.[11] Christology has become androlatry and therefore idolatry. When the official church risks heresy in order to exclude women from the sacramental ministry, then the hierarchal church must feel that the ordination of women is a theological and structural issue of the first order.

The androlatry of the Vatican declaration has redefined the question of the ordination of women. While previously the question was whether the hierarchy will admit women into its ranks, now the theological issue is whether women can belong to an intrinsically sexist church destructive as it is of women's identity *as women* and *as Christians,* as Christ-like persons. Or as a friend expressed it:

I no longer can participate in a male-centered mass if I do not want to relinquish my faith in God and in the Christian gospel. To witness the concelebration of ten or more men is to witness the demonstration of exclusive male power. The Eucharist has been perverted and become destructive of my Christian faith.

As long as we do not personally undergo the deep anguish and alienation experienced by women at the celebration of every male Eucharist, we will not be able to recognize the depth of our alienation and anger. Sr. Betty Carroll, R.S.M., aptly expresses the deep pain and alienation of Roman Catholic feminists:

Prayer today is a battleground. Public prayer, especially the Eucharist, becomes a locus of almost unbearable pain. The oppressive quality of a male priesthood... overwhelms me. The insensitivity to language

10. "Vatican Declaration: Women in the Ministerial Priesthood," *Origins* 6 (1977): 518–24.422.

11. See the "Commentary on the Declaration of the Sacred Congregation for the Doctrine of the Faith on the Question of the Admission of Women to the Ministerial Priesthood," which insists that the traditional exclusion of women is not based on the Fathers' "prejudices against women."

which excludes women from the saving act of redemption makes it almost impossible for me to be at peace enough to receive the Eucharist. To trust a God who is all-male is impossible. In every prayer there is a struggle: . . . Why does the Church not recognize women as God-worthy, capable of leading people in prayer and worship, capable of receiving all sacramental power.[12]

The third approach of feminist theology therefore seeks to reflect theologically on the alienation, pain, and oppression of those Catholic women who against all hope have cast their lot with the people of God and consider themselves to be Christian feminists. It seeks to mediate between the "complementarity of the sexes" position and the post-Christian stance. I have called this third approach "a critical theology of liberation" because it acknowledges and critically analyzes the oppressive sexist structures of Christian church and tradition while at the same time rediscovering the liberating traditions and elements of Christian faith and community.[13] This approach urges us to take seriously the post-Christian feminist critique of Christian religion and church while pursuing the full equality of women in the church. It does not ask for the integration of women into sexist structures nor does it advocate utopian separation, but looks for the transformation of women as well as of the church. However, in distinction to the first two approaches it does not base its theology and strategies on the *special* feminine nature, powers, and experience of women but on *women's experiences of and their struggles against oppression* in church and society. While the first approach wants to complement male hierarchical structures with the qualities women can bring to ministry and the second approach wants to withdraw women's powers and abilities from church ministries in order not to be co-opted, the third approach insists on the conversion of the church as well as of women.

However, critical theology should not be understood as negative and judgmental. A participant in the preconference process warns in a "letter to the editor": "According to your press release these stories will be studied by theologians. Please advise the theologians that I am studying them. 'Blessed is the man [sic] who finds

---

12. Elizabeth Carroll, R.S.M., "Prayer as Life's Alchemy," in *The Wind Is Rising: Prayer Ways for Active People*, ed. William R. Callahan and Francine Cardaman (Mt. Rainier, Md.: Quixote Center, 1978), 5.

13. See my article "Feminist Theology as a Critical Theology of Liberation," *Theological Studies* 36 (December 1975): 605–26 (included as chapter 5 in the present volume).

no stumbling block in me.' " Not only does this woman assume that
theologians are men but she also expects that their approach will
be judgmental. Critical theology must not be so understood. We
must rather see it in the Johannine sense of *crisis.* Feminist theology as a critical theology explores the crisis-situation of women
within the church and that of the church itself. It seeks to surface
the questions and to illumine our self-understanding as individuals
and as church in such a way that it frees us from oppressive theological justifications and leads to the transformation of personal
consciousness and of ecclesial structures. This approach therefore
seeks to formulate the theological quest for women's ordination
not in terms of feminine values and in terms of equal but different
ministries, but rather in terms of patriarchal-sexist oppression and
liberation in Jesus Christ. The theological categories that present
themselves for such a reformulation of the problem are those of
"patriarchal sexism as structural sin" and "repentance and partial
identification with the church."

PATRIARCHAL SEXISM AS STRUCTURAL SIN

While we generally understand sin as a personal transgression
or an individual act of infidelity against God, liberation theologians urge us to perceive sin not just in personal, individual terms
but also in terms of structures and institutions.[14] Sexism as structural sin encompasses the dehumanizing trends, injustices, and
discriminations of institutions, the theology and symbol system
that legitimate these institutions, and the collective and personal
"false consciousness" created by sexist institutions and ideologies and internalized in socialization and education. This "false
consciousness" permits oppressed people and groups to accept
their oppression and to internalize the values of the oppressor.[15]
This understanding of patriarchal sexism as structural sin and evil
power institutionalized in societal and ecclesial oppressive structures is akin to St. Paul's understanding of sin as a transpersonal,
destructive power whose ultimate expression is the life-destroying
power of death.

14. See Gregory Baum, *Religion and Alienation: A Theological Reading of Sociology*
(New York: Paulist Press, 1975), 197–226.
15. See Paulo Freire, *Pedagogy of the Oppressed,* 8th ed. (New York: Seabury Press,
1973), 48ff.

The preconference responses abundantly diagnose the destructive impact of sexism on present ecclesial structures. Characterizations abound that speak of the present priesthood as "distant, judgmental, opinionated, ritualistic, hierarchical instead of pastoral, lacking ability to show love, stiff, irrelevant, remote, exclusive, sterile, stifled, regressive, paternalistic, male-dominated, full of (expletive deleted), patriarchal, impersonal, frustrating." These characterizations can be summarized in the following statements: "The institutional church no longer mediates between the people and God." "The official church consolidates the existing structures in society thus oppressing women and other groups."

One preconference participant names the structural sin of patriarchal sexism as brokenness when she writes in her epistle to Archbishop Roberto Sanchez:

> One encounter with the living God is denied me, not by God but by law. This denial is based on my sex and is rooted in a sexism within our Roman Catholic tradition which has grown over the centuries and has brought us, you and me, to this moment of brokenness.... This brokenness means that an important way of releasing the power of God within me is being denied me and the community which desires my ordination and services.

The understanding of patriarchal sexism as evil transpersonal power and as structural sin helps us to trace the impact it has on the sacramental symbol system of the church. It helps us to understand the deep-seated, almost irrational refusal of the male institutional church to admit women to the sacramental priesthood. It helps us to understand why the structural sin of sexism cannot but engender the symbolic sin of patriarchal sexism. Elizabeth Janeway points out that the mythology of sexism is the product of profound cultural interests and emotional wishfulness.[16] In her opinion it is useless to show that a myth or mythology has no basis in fact, that it does not correspond to our experience, and that it defies all logic. Nor can one qualify myth and mythology as false and nonsensical because they correspond to the interests of the institutions and express the emotions of the dominant group.

Since Christian mythologies and theologies are created mostly by men they reflect the emotions and interests of men. These emotions and interests shaped by sexism are perpetuated by religious

---

16. Elizabeth Janeway, *Man's World, Woman's Place: A Study in Social Mythology* (New York: Dell, 1971).

and theological patriarchal structures. We have therefore to recognize that the theological argument for women's ordination will not be won on logical and intellectual grounds. Logical and intellectual arguments will produce only further legitimations for existing sexist structures.

First, by arguing that the sacramental priesthood should be restricted to men only, the Vatican declaration and its theological defenders risk christological heresy in order to maintain the present patriarchal church structures and ideologies. By including women in all functions of ministry and excluding them only from celebrating the Eucharist and pronouncing absolution, church leadership degrades these sacramental actions to the level of juridical magic. That such a magical understanding of sacrament does not do justice to Christian sacraments is pointed out frequently in the responses to the preconference process. Yet such a degradation of the sacraments becomes more comprehensible in the light of cultural anthropology.

In cultures and periods when the mother was the only known parent and her pregnancy was easily attributed to the wind or ancestral spirits, the power of women to create life was understood as a magical force. In the very earliest forms of art, the swollen breasts, the bellies, and the huge buttocks of the female signify female power to give life. Moreover, in recent times anthropologists have found numerous peoples who are still unaware that the male seed is as necessary to procreation as the female ovum and womb.

Scholars of religion and feminist scholars suggest that the myth of the magic power of the female to give life led to the worship and religion of woman, which later was usurped by patriarchal religion.[17] In patriarchal religion the ritual act becomes as significant to the process of human maturation as pregnancy and birth. Patriarchal initiation ceremonies at which one of the elders of the tribe confers adult status on the boys are efforts by men to act out the rite of birth. Though women give birth to children in the ordinary course of events, by enacting the sacred rites of passage men "rebirth" the initiates and turn them into full members of the clan.

The Christian sacraments are all rites that mediate life. Baptism is understood as rebirth, the Eucharist is the "bread of life," religious instruction is compared to "mother's milk." The sacrament of

17. See esp. Merlin Stone, *When God Was a Woman* (New York: Dial Press, 1978); Carol P. Christ, "Why Women Need the Goddess," *Heresies* (1978): 8–13, a volume entitled "The Great Goddess."

reconciliation restores life to its fullness, the sacrament of marriage protects and sanctifies the source of life, whereas the sacrament of the sick heals and strengthens life threatened by death. We begin to see why churches with a sacramental priesthood are most insistent on the exclusion of women from the celebration of these life-giving rituals. In maintaining a male sacramental system they seek to preserve the magic-religious character of the sacraments, since the sacraments as male rituals of birthing and nurturing imitate the female powers of giving birth and of nurturing life.

Second, the juridic-magic framework of the liturgy seems to be one of the major reasons why male clerics perceive the quest for the ordination of women to the priesthood as the struggle of women to seize control of religious power. Although women studiously avoid raising the issue of power but speak of the priesthood mainly in terms of service to the community, male clergy perceive the access of women to the Christian priesthood as a loss of male power and prestige. The magic roots and the mysterious character of the sacral priesthood serve in modern times as a reassurance of clerical masculinity in a profession that in our culture is perceived as "feminine."[18]

Since women are culturally and theologically considered to be the "weaker sex," women's access to ordination implies for male clerics that they themselves will be reduced to the low status of women and that the church will be "feminized" and thus become second rate and powerless. This fear is expressed again and again by priests when discussing women's ordination. After all the theological arguments are exhausted, sooner or later someone will raise the problem that the ordination of women will mean the complete feminization of the church. Since today most active members of the church are women and since the few remaining men will not respect a female clergy, it is feared that women will completely take over the church, thus making it obsolete for men and society.

While women seek ordination in order to serve the people of God, the male clergy cannot hear what women are saying because they fear female participation in the priesthood will demasculinize their own professional status. This psychological threat of women priests to a male clergy is compounded by the fact that our culture considers the Christian values of love, compassion, nurturance, ser-

---

18. See Ann Douglas, *The Feminization of American Culture* (New York: Avon Books, 1978).

vice, and so forth to be "feminine" qualities, which are appropriate in the private sphere but do not determine public and political life. As long as these qualities remain stereotyped as "feminine" values and are not developed as institutional and public power, men will need to project these human and Christian values onto women because they feel they cannot practice them in a masculinized culture. While the church preaches "feminine" values, its own praxis remains thereby determined by the masculine values of our culture.

As long as the sacramental priesthood remains masculinized it will not be nurturing, enabling, and serving but will continue to represent male clerical power over the spiritual life of the laity who are perceived in a "feminine" role. Equally, as long as women are not accepted into the sacramental priesthood the sacraments will not lose their magic-male character and Christian ministry will not become an institution of service to the people. The structural sin of patriarchal sexism corrupts the heart of the Christian priesthood.

Third, if the structural sin of sexism is at the root of the male hierarchy's refusal to ordain women to the sacramental priesthood, then rational theological arguments will not alleviate the problem. The only possible Christian response can be repentance and conversion. The overriding task conversely is to expose patriarchal sexism wherever we encounter it. This requires first of all that we ourselves repent of our internalized "false consciousness" of sexism. Such a repentance will have to take different forms for women and for men since women's and men's Christian self-understanding and ecclesial functions are differently affected by patriarchal sexism.

If the structural sin of patriarchal sexism is the main obstacle to the ordination of women to all ministries of the church, then we must insist that the institutional church publicly repent of its theological, symbolic, and institutional sexism. As the institutional church has officially rejected all forms of national and racist exploitation and publicly renounced all anti-Semitic theology, so it is now called to abandon all forms of patriarchal sexism. Until the hierarchy heeds this call, feminist theology will have to remain predominantly a "critical theology" that rejects a total identification of women with a male hierarchical church but persists in a "partial identification" with the church.[19]

---

19. For this theological concept see Heinz Schlette, "On So-Called 'Partial Identifica-

As long as the institutional church does not hear the call to repentance, the ordination of women cannot become a liberating reality. If patriarchalism is sinful and evil, then women or men can accept ordination into such sexist-sinful structures only in order to change them. As long as the official church does not hear the call to repentance, our conversion should express itself both in "institutional disobedience" and in "anticipatory obedience" to the vision of a nonsexist community. As long as the official church does not publicly repent, our conversion has to express itself in consistent resistance to patriarchal ecclesial structures, refusing to tolerate androcentric theologies and to participate in sexist rituals.

As long as the official church restricts the representation of Christ in the sacraments to the male and thereby affirms and continues its institutional sexism, we have to expose this sexism for what it is and to demand at the beginning of every sacramental celebration a public confession of the sin of sexism. As long as women cannot represent Christ in the eucharistic celebration, our participation at the table of the Lord remains a perversion of the eucharistic community intended by Jesus. Perhaps we should consider the appropriateness of a public spiritual hunger strike to expose the distortions of the Eucharist by the sin of sexism.

If there are any among us who would instinctively shy away from Christian confrontation, I would urge them to read again Galatians 2, where Paul speaks of his confronting the false consciousness and praxis of Peter. As Paul withstood Peter because the latter destroyed the unity of the Eucharist and of the community, so we today have to insist publicly that the exclusion of women from the sacramental priesthood corrupts the Eucharist and the Christian church. The ordination of women to the fullness of the sacramental priesthood, the episcopate, is not just a "women's" issue but a theological and spiritual issue affecting the credibility and life of the whole church.

Such repentance of the whole church for the structural sin of sexism is however possible only when both women and men identify with the struggle of women for societal and ecclesial equality and liberation. Such repentance requires that both women and men respect women in theology and ministry and so affirm the work of the Spirit among women today. It is therefore neces-

tion' with the Church," in *Perspectives of a Political Ecclesiology, Concilium* 66, ed. Johann B. Metz (New York: Herder and Herder, 1971), 35–49.

sary that women stop pleading for ordination and justifying it in
the face of sexist church traditions. Instead, we should positively
affirm women's ministries and spiritual powers wherever we encounter them. We are called to affirm publicly and institutionally
women's ministries as theologians and pastors, as preachers and
dispensers of the sacraments, as church officials and leaders, as
spiritual directors and community builders, as healers, reconcilers,
and prophets.

This conversion from ecclesial sexism demands from us the
courage to "come out of the closet" and to make public that we
as Christian women have power to image Jesus sacramentally, to
break bread in community, to reconcile people with God and each
other, to proclaim the truth and power of the Christian gospel. If
our conversion from ecclesial sexism is genuine, then we will experience that the power of God's Spirit is mightier than that of a
hierarchical male establishment dedicated to the preservation of
ecclesial patriarchalism. Repentance for the structural sin of sexism will free us to risk our careers and our lives to exercise partial
disobedience to the institutional church for the sake of a renewed
church liberated from institutional patriarchalism.

TOWARD A RENEWED CHURCH

The preconference process documents that many women have
already committed themselves to the struggle for a renewed priesthood in a church liberated from all sexism. This commitment
leads them to the prophetic refusal of identifying with a patriarchal hierarchy and institutional church that does not repent of
its institutional sexism. At the same time many participants in the
preconference process affirm that in their sacramental and pastoral ministry they make already present the sacramental grace of
a liberated and liberating church.

Despite their critical understanding of priesthood and ecclesial
structures, the majority of the preconference responses do not
identify the church with oppressive hierarchical male structures
but redefine it in terms of the people of God as a pilgrim people.
Instead of allowing themselves to be pushed out of a church so
unjust and oppressive to women, many of the respondents opt for
a *partial identification* with the church. Hierarchical male structures and the pronouncements of the male hierarchy are no longer

uncritically identified with the will of God or with the Christian community. One woman expresses her acute sense of alienation and partial identification when she introduces herself in this way: "I am called Catherine. I am a priest according to the order of Jesus Christ, not according to the order of Rome."

Many of the preconference respondents therefore do not understand their call to the priesthood in terms of the institutional church, personal piety, or cultic sacrifice. Rather they perceive their call and authority as empowerment by the Spirit to accept the call of the people of God. One voice may stand for many:

> I recall being called to pray with a group of prostitutes in Brazil because one of their friends had died and the "priest" in the area refused them use of the official church building for the services of the dead woman. We had our own service in their village and together we carried the dead woman to her place of burial and together we prayed and we blessed the body of this 15-year-old girl. . . . Time and time again I was called forth by the people to share sacramental moments of life and death with them.

Such an understanding of her call and authority as derived from the people of God allows this woman to continue in her ministry despite all obstacles brought to bear by the official male church.

> These days I don't worry about my own personal ordination. I just exercise my ministry. If someday the church catches up with me and officially ordains me, that may make some difference to the church authorities, but it won't make much difference to me. For the last thirty years I have been fully committed to the church.[20]

Although many women continue to live their call and ministry within the established structures of the church, their position in it has become "increasingly on the margin, the growing edge." Dolly Pommerleau expresses so well what it means for Roman Catholic women to live on the "cutting edge" in "partial identification" with the church:

> I have made the links between patriarchal oppression and my own alienation from structural church. I recognize the overt and subtle discrimination, the attempts to divide women, the promise made and not kept. . . . I was raised a "religious object." . . . I am in the process of becoming a "religious subject" — someone who names and creates her own spirituality, someone who joins hands with other oppressed women and caring men to create a renewed church.[21]

---

20. Peg Fitzgerald, "Female Clerics — A Faraway View," *WOC Newsletter* (October 1977): 7.
21. "Spirituality Has Its Trials," in *The Wind Is Rising,* 17.

This commitment to a renewed church, in which women can be religious subjects, compels many women today to ritualize and actualize God's grace and the community of faith in the celebration of the sacraments. Since the sacraments, and especially the Eucharist, are the symbolic center of the Christian community, they are not the private possession or privilege of the hierarchy but rightfully belong to the whole church. Church hierarchy and ecclesial office are not an end in themselves but exist to serve the people of God. The community has the right to receive the sacraments, and the male hierarchy sins gravely when it deprives the people of God of the Eucharist rather than ordain women. The exclusion of women from the sacramental priesthood goes against the church's very own teaching on the centrality of the liturgy for the symbolic actualization and theological understanding of church.

The hierarchy's refusal to ordain women also endangers the universal character of the sacraments insofar as it limits sacramental grace to institutionalized male rituals. Karl Rahner has argued in his essay "Personal and Sacramental Piety" that we should shift from a merely juridical to a more ontological understanding of sacraments in which sacramental grace is present wherever sacramental symbols are enacted. Such an ontological understanding of sacrament stresses that

> reception of the sacrament continues the life of faith and lets this identical faith grow up into the fullness of its being. . . . Explicit expression is given now to the relationship all grace has to the *Church,* by the fact that the Church takes a visible part by its [her] tangible action. In short, what had already been happening previously, now becomes a qualified tangible event and appears *publicly* in the form of a means of grace which had already sustained the previous events and which is the Church.[22]

Ritual celebration of the sacraments therefore means an intensification of the sacramental grace already present in the private act of the individual.

If we extend this analysis to the sacramental ministry women exercise today, then we can say that sacramental grace is present in every act of women ministers that reconciles people with God and mediates God's grace to people. Insofar as women act as ministers of the church they publicly make visible the "relationship all grace has to the Church." This happens for instance when

22. Karl Rahner, *Theological Investigations II: Man in the Church* (London: Darton, 1963), 128–29. I owe this reference and its possible interpretation to Francis Schüssler Fiorenza.

persons confess their sins to women or when women ministers break bread in community. One could argue that these sacramental acts of women ministers lack the *public* dimension of church insofar as they lack juridical legitimation through ordination. This argument overlooks, however, that the denial of juridical ordination of women to the priesthood is engendered by the structural sin of patriarchal sexism. Since the symbolic sin of sexism destroys the universal character of the sacrament, one can argue to the contrary that women's sacramental ministry symbolizes (i.e., sacramentalizes) fully the sacramental grace of the church insofar as "Christ's deed and the vitality of the church" is not distorted by sexist symbolism. By refusing to publicly and officially acknowledge women's sacramental ministry through ordination, the male hierarchy distorts Christ's act of salvation and the character of the church as the universal sacrament of salvation.

In conclusion: The preconference process has shown that on the one hand most women do not seek ordination into the present male hierarchal structures. On the other hand women already act on their call to the sacramental priesthood, which they understand themselves to have received from the Spirit and from the people of God. My critical theological reflection on the preconference responses sought to understand this new consciousness of women and the theological refusal of the male hierarchy to acknowledge publicly women's sacramental ministry through the ordination to the priesthood.

Two ways of action suggest themselves for all those who struggle not for ordination into the present male structures of the church but for a renewed ministry and a renewed church. This struggle for a renewed priesthood in a renewed church demands first of all a prophetic refusal to identify with a male hierarchy and institutional church that does not repent of the structural sin of patriarchal sexism. Second, such a refusal to accept the structural sin of ecclesial sexism has to entail the affirmation of women *as women*, and especially the affirmation of those women who in their sacramental ministry already make present the sacramental grace of a renewed church.

It is therefore time to call publicly to repentance anyone, be it man or woman, clergy or lay, who espouses sexism as a Christian value. We have to do this not because women want to be ordained into patriarchal church structures, not because women want a share in the "ecclesiastical pie," but because the credibil-

ity of the Christian gospel and church is at stake. In doing so we
have to follow Jesus, who paid for his resistance to the religious
and cultural establishment of his day with his life. We have to follow Jesus, who broke religious law because he cared for the weak,
the sick, the outcasts, and women. Luke 13:10-17 thus becomes a
paradigm for Jesus' and our own praxis of liberation:

> One Sabbath Jesus was teaching in a synagogue and there was a woman
> there possessed by a spirit that had crippled her for eighteen years. She
> was bent double and quite unable to stand up straight. When Jesus saw
> her he called her and said: "You are rid of your infirmity." Then he laid
> his hands on her, and at once she straightened and began to praise God.
>
> But the president of the synagogue, indignant with Jesus for heal-
> ing on a Sabbath, intervened and said to the congregation. "There are
> six working days: come and be cured on one of them, and not on the
> Sabbath."
>
> The Lord gave him this answer. "What hypocrites you are," he said.
> ... "Here is this woman, a daughter of Abraham, who has been kept
> prisoner by Satan for eighteen long years. Was it wrong for her to be
> freed from her bonds on the Sabbath?"
>
> At these words all his opponents were covered with confusion while
> the mass of the people were delighted at all the wonderful things Jesus
> was doing.

The problem is not, as the preconference participants asserted
again and again, ordination of women into sexist structures. At
stake is whether the gospel and its ecclesial proclamation can still
set free the liberating power of God that enables women to walk
upright.

11 _____

"YOU ARE NOT TO BE CALLED FATHER": EARLY CHRISTIAN HISTORY IN A FEMINIST PERSPECTIVE

CONTEXTUALIZATION

Unfortunately the "history" of this article has confirmed my analysis of patriarchal scholarship and its institutions. I was invited to prepare this paper for a scientific symposium, which was to take place in January of 1979, celebrating the sixty-fifth birthday of Professor Rudolf Schnackenburg. The theme of this symposium, which was sponsored by a circle of his former and present doctoral students, was "Problems in the History of Early Christianity." After I suggested and presented the following paper, I was assured orally and in writing that it would be published in the Schnackenburg *Festschrift* since it fit well into the overall topic. Subsequently, however, the editorial committee decided not to publish it – a decision it made without giving any professional evaluation of the scholarly merits of the paper. Instead, the editors explained their unexpected decision by saying that mine was the only contribution whose content was so timely and burning that it went clearly beyond the boundaries set by the topic "From the History of Christian Origins: Aspects and Canons of Its Development."

In a letter to the members of the Schnackenburg student association (December 28, 1979), which announced the appearance of the *Festschrift* in the series Quaestiones Disputatae (no. 87), the editors repeated the same argument: "It was especially the explosive surplus of timeliness, which distinguished the lecture of our fellow student from the other contributions, that compelled the editors not to publish it." However, they pointed out that in their opinion the topic deserved further discussion, especially since "the reports about recent papal statements in America" confirmed their judgment. At the same time they invited contributions for the next symposium, which was to discuss "Woman in Early Christianity,"[1] even though (or because) they knew quite well that the research of my paper was to be published in book form.[2] Obviously, established scholarship is compelled to neutralize, control, and co-opt research of and about women, especially if such research challenges established patriarchal canons and frameworks.

———— ❖ ————

FOR MANY CHRISTIANS the reconstruction of early Christian history is not a problem. The impression remains widespread that Acts accurately reports what actually happened in the beginning of early Christianity. Exegetes and historians of early Christianity, however, know all too well that this is not the case. However, while most exegetes would agree that Jesus did not have a blueprint for the organization of the church, their image of the actual development of early church history varies considerably. Questions regarding the historical importance of the twelve, the relationship between charism and office, the juxtaposition of Paulinism and early Catholicism, the issue of apostolic succession and heresy, and the practical-ecclesial implications of early Christian history are answered in different ways.[3] Moreover, exegetes today more

---

1. Gerhard Dautzenberg, ed., *Die Frau im Urchristentum*, Quaestiones Disputatae 95 (Freiburg: Herder, 1983).
2. *In Memory of Her: A Feminist Theological Reconstruction of Christian Origins* (New York: Crossroad, 1983) appeared in the same year as their volume. However, the theoretical approach of my work is quite distinct from theirs insofar as it is not just about women in early Christianity but seeks to reconstruct early Christian history by placing women in the center of its attention. Moreover, my book modifies the "egalitarian" reconstructive model of this article by stressing the *tension and struggle* between egalitarian and patriarchal early Christian self-understandings and structures. Finally, it seeks to indicate that the history of this struggle can be traced throughout Christian history and is still ongoing.
3. Arnold Meyer, *Die moderne Forschung über die Geschichte des Urchristen-*

readily acknowledge that a value-free interpretation of early Christian texts and an objectivist reconstruction of early Christian history are a scholarly fiction that fails to account for its own presuppositions and scientific models.

The question whether women had a leading position in the development of the early church intensifies all these interpretative problems and at the same time formulates the debated issues in a new perspective.[4] Nevertheless, most scholars have been hesitant to perceive this question as an exegetical-historical problem, but continue to understand it as a "woman's issue."[5] Seen as a "woman's issue," the question belongs to conferences and papers about and for women and has no place on the program of an exegetical-scientific symposium or in a scholarly *Festschrift.* In this way most scholars continue to perceive it only as a topical or thematic issue, not as an issue of heuristic value for the interpretation of early Christian texts and history.

One usually justifies this attitude by pointing out that a feminist topic is ideologically suspect and does not derive from historical scientific interest since it is inspired by the women's movement, and thus determined by ecclesial-societal modern concerns. Such an argument, however, overlooks the fact that all scholarship on early Christian history is inspired by contemporary questions and interests. Moreover, insofar as the Bible is not just a document of ancient history but Sacred Scripture, it claims authority and validity in the contemporary church. Therefore, *biblical* inquiries are always engendered by ecclesial and societal interests and questions.

---

tums (Leipzig and Tübingen: J. B. C. Mohr, 1898); Dieter Lührmann, "Erwägungen zur Geschichte des Urchristentums," *Evangelische Theologie* 32 (1972): 452–67; Rudolf Schnackenburg, "Das Urchristentum," in *Literatur und Religion des Frühjudentums,* ed. Johann Maier and Josef Schreiner (Würzburg: Echter, 1973), 284–309; Josef Blank, "Probleme einer Geschichte des Urchristentums," *Una Sancta* 30 (1975): 261–86; Siegfried Schulz, *Die Mitte der Schrift: Der Frühkatholizismus im Neuen Testament* (Stuttgart: Kohlhammer, 1976); Ferdinand Hahn, "Das Problem des Frühkatholizismus," *Evangelische Theologie* 38 (1978): 340–57; H. Paulsen, "Zur Wissenschaft vom Urchristentum und der alten Kirche – ein methodischer Versuch," *Zeitschrift für die neutestamentliche Wissenschaft* 68 (1978): 200–230.

4. Since this article presupposes the methodological studies about the history of early Christianity as well as the research on women in antiquity and in early Christianity, it is impossible to quote all the literature pertaining to this topic. Adequate discussion of divergent hypotheses and opinions must be reserved for a more extensive book-length treatment, which has appeared in *In Memory of Her.*

5. This is evident in the fact that the studies on women in early Christianity have not influenced the scholarly reconstruction of Christian beginnings.

This rootedness of historical-critical research in contemporary Christianity and society has been pointed out by Josef Blank: "The interest in legitimization but also in the critique and reform of contemporary Christianity in all its forms and expressions is probably an essential, and even the most fundamental motive for the study of the history of early Christianity."[6] The objection that the search for the role of women in the early Christian movements is greatly determined by societal and ecclesial political interests, and is therefore unscientific, applies to any reconstruction of early Christian history that is inspired by the quest for the identity and continuity of contemporary Christianity with the early church. An androcentric reconstruction of early Christian history, therefore, is not value-free and objective but, whether consciously or not, legitimates the present hierarchical-male structures of the contemporary church.

Historical reconstructions are based on selective, contemporary analyses of the past in the present; they are not only limited to the extant sources but are conditioned by the societal perspectives of the present. The understanding of the past is never just antiquarian but always related to the contemporary situation of the historiographer. The hermeneutic discussion has shown that historians, like other scholars, can never totally free themselves from their existential presuppositions, experiences, ideologies, and commitments.[7] The personal presuppositions and societal position of the historian and interpreter determine the selection and definition of what was important in the past, and what needs to be studied today. The hermeneutical discussion and the sociology of knowledge have driven home this recognition that historiography is determined by the experiences and interests of those who write history. However, this hermeneutic consensus seems to be forgotten whenever scientific historiography and theology are shown to be "male" conditioned. The problem is not only that most scholars are men but that our very understanding of reality is androcentric.

It is not enough, however, to expose the existential presuppositions of male exegetes and scholars; one must also analyze the interpretative models according to which they reconstruct the

6. Josef Blank, "Probleme einer Geschichte des Urchristentums," 262.

7. This is illustrated by the work of Gerhard Heinz, *Das Problem der Kirchenentstehung in der deutschen protestantischen Theologie des 20. Jahrhunderts,* TTS 4 (Mainz: Mathias-Grünewald, 1974). Heinz highlights the theological presuppositions underlying different reconstructions of early Christian beginnings. For the sociology of the biblical exegete see also Richard L. Rohrbaugh, *The Biblical Interpreter* (Philadelphia: Fortress Press, 1978).

history of early Christianity. While descriptive historical studies analyze the available information and texts of early Christianity and tacitly assume a certain understanding of early Christian history, a constructive historiography makes this assumption explicit by developing heuristic and interpretative models that enable us to reconstruct a comprehensive view of early Christian development.[8] Such interpretative models place diverse information into a coherent interpretative whole that enables readers to see the intellectual contexts and practical patterns of action in a certain perspective. An interpretative model should, therefore, not only be judged by whether it adequately lists various traditions and information, but must also be scrutinized as to whether it provides a comprehensive vision of early Christian history, making its emancipatory life-praxis and theology available to contemporary church and society.

ANDROCENTRIC INTERPRETATION AND REDACTION

The topical approach to "women in the Bible" overlooks the fact that its references to women are already filtered through androcentric interpretation and redaction. The systemic androcentrism of Western culture is evident in that nobody questions the fact that men have been historical subjects and agents in the church. The historical role of women and not that of men is problematic because maleness is the norm, while femaleness constitutes a deviation from this norm. Whenever we speak of "man" as the scientific and historical subject we mean the male.[9] For the Western understanding and linguistic expression of reality, male existence is the standard of human existence. "Humanity is male and man defines woman not in herself but relative to him. She is not regarded as autonomous being. He is the subject, the absolute; she

---

8. For the notion of "model" see Thomas S. Kuhn, *The Structure of Scientific Revolutions* (Chicago: University of Chicago Press, 1970); Ian G. Barbour, *Myth, Models, and Paradigms* (New York: Harper & Row, 1974). Josef Blank, "Zum Problem 'ethischer Normen' im Neuen Testament," *Konzilium* 7 (1967): 356–62, uses "model" in a somewhat different way.

9. See Vera Slupik, "Frau und Wissenschaft," in *Frauen in der Universität*, 6 (Munich: Frauenoffensive, 1977), 8–20; Ilse Kassner and Susanne Lorenz, eds., *Trauer muss Aspasia tragen* (Munich: Frauenoffensive, 1976); Marielouise Janssen-Jurreit, *Sexismus: Über die Abtreibung der Frauenfrage* (Munich: Carl Hanser, 1976), 11–93; Hilda Smith, "Feminism and the Methodology of Women's History," in *Liberating Women's History*, ed. Berenice A. Carroll (Urbana: University of Illinois Press, 1976), 368–84.

is the other."[10] Therefore, our societal and scientific structures define women as derivative from and secondary to men. This androcentric definition of being human not only has determined the scholarly perception of men but also that of women. In such an androcentric worldview woman must remain a historically marginal being. This androcentric scholarly paradigm thematizes the role of women as a societal, historical, philosophical, and theological problem but cannot question its own androcentric scholarly horizon.[11]

Since scientific reconstructions of early Christianity share in the androcentric paradigm of Western culture, they cannot integrate texts that speak positively about early Christian women into their overall interpretational framework. Because they generally presuppose that only men, and not women, developed missionary initiatives and central leadership in early Christianity,[12] texts that do not fit such an androcentric model are quickly reinterpreted in terms of its androcentric perspective. This happens in various ways. For example, most modern interpreters assume that Romans 16:7 speaks about two leading men who had become Christians before Paul and had great authority among the apostles. However, there is no reason to understand "Junian" as a shortened form of the male name Junianus since Junia was a well-known female name. Even patristic exegesis understood it predominantly as the name of a woman.[13] Andronicus and Junia were an influential missionary team who were acknowledged as apostles.

10. Simone de Beauvoir, *The Second Sex* (New York: A. Knopf, 1953), 10; Elizabeth Janeway, *Man's World, Woman's Place* (New York: Dell, 1971), characterizes this as "social mythology."

11. See my articles "Für eine befreite und befreiende Theologie," *Konzilium* 14 (1978): 287–94 (included as chapter 9 in the present volume); "Feminist Theology as a Critical Theology of Liberation," *Theological Studies* 36 (1975): 605–26 (included as chapter 5 in the present volume); Valerie Saiving, "Androcentrism in Religious Studies," *Journal of Religion* 56 (1976): 177–97; Beverly W. Harrison, "The New Consciousness of Women: A Socio-Political Resource," *Cross Currents* 24 (1975): 445–62.

12. See my article "Die Rolle der Frau in der urchristlichen Bewegung," *Konzilium* 12 (1976): 3–9. For the relative emancipation of women in Hellenism see Gerhard Delling, *Paulus' Stellung zu Frau und Ehe* (Stuttgart: Kohlhammer, 1931), 2–56; Carl Schneider, *Kulturgeschichte des Hellenismus* (Munich: C. H. Beck, 1967), 1:78–117; Leonard Swidler, "Greco-Roman Feminism and the Reception of the Gospel," in *Traditio-Krisis-Renovatio aus theologischer Sicht,* ed. Bernd Jaspert and Rudolf Mohr (Marburg: Elwert, 1976), 39–52; Wayne A. Meeks, "The Image of the Androgyne," *History of Religion* 13 (1974): 167–80.

13. This is the reason why Marie-Joseph Lagrange, *Saint Paul, Epître aux Romains* (Paris: Librairie Lecoffre, 1916), 366, decided in favor of a woman's name although this textual reading had been abandoned by Protestant exegetes.

Another example of androcentric interpretation is found with reference to Romans 16:1-3. In this passage Phoebe is called the *diakonos* and *prostatis* of the church at Cenchreae, the seaport of Corinth. Exegetes attempt to downplay the importance of both titles here because they are used with reference to a woman. Whenever Paul calls himself, Apollos, Timothy, or Tychicos *diakonos*, scholars translate the term as "deacon." Yet when the expression refers as here to a woman, exegetes render it as "servant," "helper," or "deaconess." While Kürzinger, for instance, translates *diakonos* in Philippians 1:1 as "deacon," in the case of Phoebe he explains that "she works in the service of the community," and in a footnote he characterizes Phoebe as "one of the first pastoral assistants."[14] Hans Lietzmann also understands the office of Phoebe in analogy to the later institution of the deaconesses, which, in comparison to that of the deacon, had only a very limited function in the church. He characterizes Phoebe as an "apparently well-to-do and charitable lady, who because of her feminine virtues worked in the service of the poor and the sick and assisted in the baptism of women."[15] Origen had already labelled Phoebe as an assistant and servant of Paul. He concluded that women who do good works can be appointed as deaconesses.[16]

However, the text does not permit such a feminine stereotyping of Phoebe. As we can see from 1 Corinthians 3:5-9, Paul uses *diakonos* parallel to *synergos* and characterizes with these titles Apollos and himself as missionaries with equal standing who have contributed to the upbuilding of the community in different ways.[17] Since Phoebe is named *diakonos* of the church at Cenchreae, she receives this title because her service and office were influential in the community. That Phoebe could claim great authority within the early Christian missionary endeavor is underlined by the second title, *prostatis/patrona*. In a similar way 1 Thessalonians 5:12 and Romans 12:8 characterize leading persons as *prohistamenoi*. Therefore, when Paul calls Phoebe a *prostatis*, he characterizes her in analogy to those persons who

14. *Das Neue Testament* (Augsburg: Pattloch, 1956), 214.
15. Hans Lietzmann, *Geschichte der alten Kirche* (Berlin: Walter de Gruyter, 1961), 1:149.
16. *Commentaria in Epistolam ad Romanos 10, 26* (PG 14, 1281B) *10, 39* (PG 14, 1289A).
17. See E. Earl Ellis, "Paul and His Co-Workers," *New Testament Studies* 17 (1970-71): 4939; Mary Ann Getty, "God's Fellow Workers and Apostleship," in *Women Priests,* ed. Arlene and Leonard Swidler (New York: Paulist Press, 1977), 176-82.

had influential positions as representative protectors and leaders in Hellenistic religious associations.[18] G. Heinrici points out that in antiquity religious and private associations received legal protection and derived social-political influence from the patronage of eminent and rich members.[19] Nevertheless, E. A. Judge insists on interpreting the patronage of women in the early church in an androcentric fashion:

> The status of women who patronized St. Paul would particularly repay attention. They are clearly persons of some independence and eminence in their own circles, used for entertaining and running their salons, if that is what Paul's meetings were, as they saw best.[20]

This misinterpretation reduces the influential role of women in the early Christian movement to that of "lady of the house" permitted to serve coffee after Paul's lectures!

Since scholars take it for granted that the leadership of early Christian communities was in the hands of men, they assume that those women mentioned in the Pauline letters were the help-mates and assistants of the apostles, especially of Paul. Such an androcentric interpretive model leaves no room for the alternative possibility that women were missionaries, apostles, or heads of communities independent of Paul and equal to him.[21] Since Paul's position was often precarious and in no way accepted by all the members of the communities, it is even possible that the influence of some women was equal to or even greater than that of Paul. Texts such as Romans 16:1–3 or 16:7 suggest that leading women in the early Christian missionary movement did not owe their position to Paul. It is more likely that Paul had no other choice but to cooperate with these women and to acknowledge their authority within the communities.

We must ask, therefore, whether it is appropriate to limit all leadership titles in the New Testament that are grammatically masculine to males alone. Predictably enough, androcentric exegesis

---

18. This is stressed by Ramsay MacMullen, *Roman Social Relations* (New Haven: Yale University Press, 1974), 74–76, 124.

19. "Die Christengemeinde Korinths und die religiösen Genossenschaften der Griechen," *Zeitschrift für wissenschaftliche Theologie* 19 (1976): 465–526.

20. "St. Paul and Classical Society," *Jahrbuch für Antike und Christentum* 15 (1972): 28.

21. See my article "Word, Spirit and Power: Women in Early Christian Communities," in *Women of Spirit: Female Leadership in the Jewish and Christian Traditions,* ed. Rosemary Radford Ruether and Eleanor McLaughlin (New York: Simon & Schuster, 1979), 29–70.

interprets grammatically masculine terms in a twofold way, namely as generic and as gender specific.[22] Grammatically masculine terms such as "saints," "the elect," "brothers," and "sons" that serve to characterize members of Christian communities are usually understood to refer to both men and women. Exegetes do not go so far as to understand Christian community in analogy to the Mithras-cult and to limit church membership or the application of New Testament admonitions and injunctions to men.[23] However, every time the New Testament uses grammatically masculine titles such as "prophet," "teacher," "deacon," "missionary," "co-worker," "apostle," or "bishop," titles that refer to leadership functions within the Christian community, exegetes assume that these refer exclusively to men. Scholars lack interpretive heuristic models that could do justice to the position and influence of women like Phoebe, Prisca,[24] or Junia or could adequately integrate them into their conception of early Christian leadership. Such androcentric interpretations are easily misused to legitimate the patriarchal practice of the contemporary church.[25]

One could reject such a critique and maintain that the androcentric interpretation of early Christianity is conditioned and justified by our sources because they speak about women and their role in the early church only rarely and mostly in a polemic argument. The historical marginality of women, one could argue, is not simply created by contemporary exegesis, but by the fact that women were marginal in the discipleship of Jesus and in the early Chris-

---

22. For this distinction see Casey Miller and Kate Swift, eds., *Words and Women: New Language in New Times* (New York: Anchor, 1977), esp. 64–74.

23. Small sectarian groups separate themselves from the world and distinguish between their members as insiders and the outsiders who are conceived as "the others." Not women but the non-Christians are the "others" in early Christianity. There is no evidence that church membership was restricted to males only, although the address for Christians is usually grammatically masculine. See my article "The Study of Women in Early Christianity: Some Methodological Considerations" in *Critical History and Biblical Faith: New Testament Perspectives*, ed. J. T. Ryan (Villanova: College Theology Society, 1979), 30–58, and the contribution of Wayne A. Meeks, "Since Then You Would Need to Go Out of the World: Group Boundaries in Pauline Christianity," in the same volume, 4–29.

24. Hans Conzelmann, *Geschichte des Urchristentums* (Göttingen: Vandenhoeck & Ruprecht, 1971), Appendix 1, mentions only Prisca among the leading figures in the Pauline churches.

25. This was already recognized and deplored by Elizabeth Cady Stanton, *The Woman's Bible* (1895–1898; reprint, New York: Arno Press, 1972), in the last century. It is regrettable that the recent Vatican declaration against the ordination of women confirms this experience. For a discussion of this document in an international context see Leonard Swidler, "Roma Locuta, Causa Finita?" in *Women Priests,* 3–18.

tian church from its very beginnings. Jesus was a man, the apostles were men, the early Christian prophets, teachers, and missionaries were men. All New Testament writings are assumed to be written by male authors and the theology of the first centuries is called the "theology of the Fathers." Women do not seem to be of any significance in the early churches nor are they permitted to exercise any leadership or teaching functions. The Christian marginality of women, it is argued, has its roots in the patriarchal beginnings of the church and in the androcentrism of Christian revelation.

Such a theological conclusion presupposes, however, that early Christian writings are objective factual reports of early Christian history and development. It presupposes that the scarcity of women's mention in early Christian sources adequately reflects the actual history of their activity in the early church. Such an assumption, however, neglects the methodic insights of form, source, and redaction criticism which have pointed out that early Christian writings are not at all objectivistic factual transcripts but pastorally engaged writings. The early Christian authors have selected, redacted, and reformulated traditional sources and materials with reference to their own theological intentions and practical objectives. None of the early Christian writings and traditions is free from any of these tendencies. All early Christian writings, even the gospels and Acts, intend to speak to actual problems and situations of the early church in order to illuminate them theologically. One therefore can assume that this methodological insight applies equally to the traditions and sources about women in early Christianity. Since early Christian communities and authors lived in a predominantly patriarchal world and participated in its mentality, it is likely that the scarcity of much of the information about women was conditioned by the androcentric traditioning and redaction of the early Christian authors. This applies especially to the gospels and Acts since these were written toward the end of the first century. Many of the traditions and information about the activity of women in early Christianity are probably irretrievable because the androcentric selection or redaction process saw these as either unimportant or as threatening.[26]

The contradictions in early Christian sources indicate such an androcentric process of redaction, which qualifies information

---

26. Many studies on women in the Bible do not perceive this process because they are often motivated by an apologetic defense of the biblical writers.

that could not be omitted. The gospels indicate that women were disciples of Jesus and witnesses of the resurrection, but do not count any of them among the twelve. Jesus healed women and spoke with them but no gospel tells us a story about the call of a woman to discipleship. The images of the parables draw on the world and experience of women but the God-language of Jesus is predominantly masculine. The gospels tell us that women discovered the empty tomb but the true resurrection witnesses seem to have been men.

Acts tells us about women, especially rich women who supported the early Christian missionary endeavor with their hospitality and wealth. However, the historical elaboration of Luke gives the impression that the leadership of the early Christian mission was in the hands of men. We find short references to widows and prophetesses, but Luke does not tell us any stories about their activity or function. Thus Luke's conception of history is harmonizing and does not acknowledge a "women's problem" in the early church.

Such a problem emerges, however, when one reads the Pauline letters. The meaning of the Pauline texts that speak directly about women is still unclear, although numerous attempts at interpretation have been made.[27] Exegetes are divided on the question of whether the influence of Paul was negative or positive with respect to the role of women in early Christianity. Paul presupposes in 1 Corinthians 11:2-16 that women speak as prophets in the community's worship but demands that in doing so they adapt to the prevailing custom. It is not clear, however, what the actual bone of contention is between Paul and the Corinthians or how the individual arguments of Paul are to be evaluated and understood. The negative result of the injunction in 1 Corinthians 14:33-36 is clear-cut, but exegetes are divided as to whether the famous *"mulier taceat in ecclesia"* is a later interpolation, since it seems to contradict 1 Corinthians 11.

In Galatians 3:28 Paul proclaims that all distinctions between Jews and Greeks, free and slave, male and female are obliterated, but he does not repeat in 1 Corinthians 12:13 that maleness and femaleness no longer have any significance in the body of Christ. Therefore, no exegetical consensus is achieved on whether

---

27. See my article "Women in the Pre-Pauline and Pauline Churches," *Union Seminary Quarterly Review* 33 (1978): 153-66.

Galatians 3:28, like 1 Corinthians 12:13, applies to the Christian community, or to the eschatological future, or refers to the spiritual equality of all souls. The Pauline lists of greetings mention women as leading missionaries and respected heads of churches, they are not univocal on how much they owe their leadership positions to Pauline approval and support. It is true that Paul values women as co-workers and expresses his gratitude to them. Yet he probably had no other choice than to do so because women like Junia or Prisca already occupied leadership functions before him and were on his level in the early Christian missionary movement.

That early Christian sourcε ·εxts are unclear and divided about women's role in early Christiۃnity also becomes evident when one compares their informatio. The Pauline letters indicate that women have been apostles, missionaries, patrons, co-workers, prophets, and leaders of communities. Luke, on the other hand, mentions women prophets and the conversion of rich women but does not mention any instance of a woman missionary or leader of a church. He seems to know of such functions of women, as his references to Prisca or Lydia indicate, but this knowledge does not influence his portrayal of early Christian history. Whereas all the gospels know that Mary Magdalene was the first resurrection witness, the pre-Pauline tradition of 1 Corinthians 15:3-5 does not mention a single woman among the resurrection witnesses. The Fourth Gospel and its tradition ascribe to a woman a leading role in the mission to Samaria, while Acts knows only of Philip as the first missionary of this area. While Mark knows of the discipleship of women (*akolouthein*), Luke stresses that the women who followed Jesus supported him and his male disciples with their possessions.

Reference to the Lukan works, the major source of our knowledge of early Christian history, demonstrates how much the androcentric interests of the New Testament authors determined their reception and depiction of early Christian life, history, and tradition.[28] Since Luke is usually regarded as the New Testament writer most sympathetic to women,[29] such a hypothesis may sound strange. However, such an androcentric tendency becomes evident

28. See my plenary address "Women's Discipleship and Leadership in the Lukan Writings," at the 1978 Catholic Biblical Association annual meeting in San Francisco.

29. See, e.g., Constance F. Parvey, "The Theology and Leadership of Women in the New Testament," in *Religion and Sexism*, ed. Rosemary Radford Ruether (New York: Simon & Schuster, 1974), 137-46.

when one analyzes the Lukan Easter narratives. The discussions of Paul with his opponents indicate that the leadership function of the apostle was of eminent importance for the developing Christian church. However, according to Paul, the apostolate is not limited to the twelve but includes all those who had received an appearance of the Resurrected One and whom the Resurrected One had commissioned to work as Christian missionaries (1 Cor. 9:4). Luke not only limits the apostolate to the twelve but also modifies the criteria mentioned by Paul;[30] only those males who had accompanied Jesus in his ministry from Galilee to Jerusalem and had become witnesses of his death and resurrection (Acts 1:21f) were eligible to replace Judas as apostle. In terms of these criteria, Paul cannot be called apostle because he did not know the earthly Jesus, but some women would qualify. According to Mark, women were witnesses of the public ministry of Jesus in Galilee and Jerusalem.[31] They were the only ones who were eyewitnesses of his execution since the male disciples had fled, and women were the first to receive the resurrection news (Mark 15:40f, 47; 16:1-8). Whereas Mark does not tell us of an appearance of the Resurrected One to anyone, Matthew and John report that Mary Magdalene, and not the male disciples, was the first to see the Risen One.

Luke does not know of any appearance of the risen Jesus to women. His androcentric redaction attempts in a subtle way to disqualify the women as resurrection witnesses. He emphasizes that the twelve who heard about the empty tomb from the women did not believe them but judged their words as gossip (24:11). When the men checked out the message of the women, it proved to be true (24:24), but this did not provoke a faith response from the male disciples. Not until the appearance of the Risen One to Simon (24:34) did the men believe in the resurrection of Jesus. However, this appearance to Peter is not narrated but proclaimed in a confessional formula. This formula corresponds to the tradition quoted by Paul in 1 Corinthians 15:3-5, which mentions Cephas and the eleven, but not Mary Magdalene and the women, as witnesses of the resurrection. That Luke is interested in excluding women from

---

30. See my articles "The Twelve" and "The Apostleship of Women in Early Christianity," in *Women Priests*, 114-22 and 135-40 for literature.

31. Paul J. Achtemeier, *Mark* (Philadelphia: Fortress Press, 1975), considers the possibility that the gospel was authored by a woman, since the Gospel of Mark portrays women positively. Although the tradition ascribes all New Testament writings to male authors, historical-critical scholarship has shown that we do not know the authors of most New Testament writings.

apostleship is also supported by his condition that only one of the male disciples is eligible to succeed Judas (Acts 1:21).

This Lukan stress on Peter as the primary Easter witness must be situated within the early Christian discussion of whether Peter or Mary of Magdala qualifies as the first resurrection witness. This discussion understands Peter to be in competition with Mary Magdalene insofar as he complains constantly that Christ has given so many revelations to a woman. The Gospel of Thomas reflects this competition between Peter and Mary Magdalene.[32] The gnostic writing *Pistis Sophia* and the apocryphal Gospel of Mary further develop this motif. In the Gospel of Mary it is asked how Peter can be against Mary Magdalene because she is a woman if Christ has made her worthy of his revelations.[33] The Apostolic Church Order evidences that this discussion presupposes an actual ecclesial situation. While the Gospel of Mary argues for the authority of Mary Magdalene on the grounds that Christ loved her more than all the other disciples, the Apostolic Church Order argues for the exclusion of women from the priesthood by letting Mary Magdalene herself reason that the weak, namely, women, must be saved by the strong, namely, men.[34] This dispute about the resurrection witness of Mary Magdalene shows, however, that Mary, like Peter, had apostolic authority in some Christian communities even into the third and fourth centuries. It also makes clear that the androcentric interpretation of egalitarian primitive Christian traditions functions to serve a patriarchal ecclesial praxis.

PATRISTIC INTERPRETATION AND CODIFICATION

Such an androcentric interpretation of early Christian traditions provokes the question whether the early Christian traditions and sources canonized by the Fathers manufactured the historical marginality of women in the church. In other words, was early Christian life and community totally and from its very beginnings patriarchally defined or was the patriarchal marginality of women

---

32. Logion 114, pl. 99, 18-26. See Edgar Hennecke and Wilhelm Schneemelcher, eds., *New Testament Apocrypha* (Philadelphia: Westminster Press, 1963), 1:522.
33. Ibid., 343.
34. See John Peter Arendzen, "An Entire Syriac Text of the Apostolic Church Order," *Journal of Theological Studies* 3 (1902): 71.

in early Christian sources a by-product of the "patristic" selection and canonization process? Is it possible to unearth an emancipatory tradition in the beginnings of Christianity or is the question of the liberating impulses of Christian faith historically illegitimate and theologically inappropriate? This question becomes all the more pressing since scholars of antiquity point out that the "woman's question" was much debated in antiquity and the legal position of women was quite good in the Greco-Roman world. In order to address this question one must first challenge the patristic interpretative model that understands early Christian history and community as an antagonistic struggle between orthodoxy and heresy.[35]

The classic understanding of heresy presupposes the temporal priority of orthodoxy. According to Origen all heretics were at first orthodox but then erred from the true faith.[36] According to this model of interpretation heresy is not only a freely chosen defection but also an intended mutilation of the true faith. The orthodox understanding of history is said to know that Jesus founded the church and gave his revelation to the apostles, who proclaimed his teaching to the whole world. By its witness the orthodox church preserves the continuity of revelation in Jesus Christ and safeguards it through the construct of apostolic succession, which maintains the continuity of church offices with Jesus and his first apostles.

Since this understanding of Christian beginnings is shared by all groups of the early church, they all attempt to demonstrate that their own group and teaching is in apostolic continuity with Jesus and the first disciples. Montanism, gnostic groups of various persuasions, and the patristic church claim apostolic tradition and revelation in order to substantiate (and to legitimate) their own authenticity. Both parties, the opponents as well as the advocates of the ecclesial leadership of women, claim apostolic tradition and

---

35. See Adolf Hilgenfeld, *Die Ketzergeschichte des Urchristentums,* new ed. (Darmstadt: Wissenschaftliche Buchgesellschaft, 1963); Walter Bauer, *Orthodoxy and Heresy in Earliest Christianity* (Philadelphia: Fortress Press, 1971); Hans Dieter Betz, "Orthodoxy and Heresy in Primitive Christianity," *Interpretation* 19 (1965): 299–311; Jaroslav Pelikan, *The Emergence of the Catholic Tradition* (Chicago: University of Chicago Press, 1971).

36. Origen, *Commentary to the Song of Songs* 3.2.2; similarly also 1 Clem 42; Tertullian, *De Praescriptione* 20; Eusebius, *Eccl. History* 4.22.2–3: see also John G. Gager, *Kingdom and Community: The Social World of Early Christianity* (Englewood Cliffs, N.J.: Prentice-Hall, 1975), 76–92.

succession for such a leadership.[37] The advocates point to Mary of Magdala, Salome, or Martha as apostolic disciples. They stress the apostolic succession of women prophets in the Hebrew Bible and the New Testament and call attention to the women of apostolic times mentioned in Romans 16. They legitimate their egalitarian structures of community with reference to Galatians 3:28. Others preserve the Acts of Thecla as a canonical book.

The patriarchal opposition, on the other hand, appeals to the example of Jesus, who did not commission women to preach or admit them to the last supper.[38] They quote texts like Genesis 2–3, 1 Corinthians 14, the deutero-Pauline household codes, and especially 1 Timothy 2:9–15. Whereas egalitarian groups trace their apostolic authority to Mary Magdalene and emphasize that women as well as men have received the revelations of the resurrected Christ, so-called patristic authors pit the authority of Peter against that of Mary Magdalene. While groups that acknowledge the leadership of women search the Jewish Scriptures and the Christian writings for passages that mention women, patristic authors attempt to explain away or play down the role of women whenever they are mentioned. Origen, for instance, concedes that women have been prophets, but stresses that they did not speak publicly and especially not in the worship assembly of the church.[39] Chrysostom confirms that in apostolic times women traveled as missionaries who were preaching the gospel. But then he goes on to explain that women could do this only because in the beginnings of the church the "angelic condition" permitted it.[40] Whereas the Montanists legitimate the prophetic activity of women with reference to the Scriptures, the extant Church Orders justify the institution of deaconesses,[41] which granted women only very limited and sub-

---

37. For extensive references see my article "Word, Spirit, and Power," in *Women of Spirit.*

38. See *Didascalia* 15 and *The Apostolic Church Order,* III, 6.9; J. Kevin Coyle, "The Fathers on Women's Ordination," *Eglise et Théologie* 9 (1978): 51–101; Carolyn Osiek, "The Ministry and Ordination of Women According to the Early Church Fathers," in *Women and Priesthood,* ed. C. Stuhlmüller (Collegeville, Minn.: Liturgical Press, 1978), 59–68.

39. Origen, *Commentarii, in Iam Epistulam ad Corinthios* 14.34–35. See C. Jenkins, "Origen on I Corinthians," *Journal of Theological Studies* 10 (1908–9): 41ff.

40. Elisabeth A. Clark, "Sexual Politics in the Writings of John Chrysostom," *Anglican Theological Review* 59 (1977): 3–20; Donald F. Winslow, "Priesthood and Sexuality in the Post-Nicene Fathers," *Saint Luke's Journal of Theology* 18 (1975): 214–27.

41. See especially A. Kahlsbach *Die altkirchliche Einrichtung der Diakonissen bis zu ihrem Erlöschen* (Freiburg: Herder, 1926), and R. Gryson, *The Ministry of Women in the Early Church* (Collegeville, Minn.: Liturgical Press, 1976).

ordinate ecclesial functions by appealing to the prophetesses in Israel and the earliest church.[42] While women who preached and baptized claimed the example of the apostle Thecla, Tertullian attempts to denounce the Acts of Thecla as a fraud.[43] This example indicates that the process of the canonization of the early Christian documents was affected by the polemics and struggle concerning the leadership of women in the church. Our canon of Scriptures reflects a patriarchal selection process and has functioned to bar women from ecclesial leadership.

The caustic polemics of the Fathers against the leadership of women indicate that the question of women's ecclesial office was still debated in the second and third centuries. It also demonstrates that the progressive patriarchalization of church leadership did not happen without opposition but had to overcome an early Christian theology and praxis that acknowledged the leadership claim of women.[44] We owe to these polemics the few surviving bits of historical, though prejudiced, information about women's leadership in various groups of the early church. Unfortunately, early Christian historiography does not understand them as the outcome of bitter polemics but as historically adequate descriptive information that has theological authority.

The polemics of patriarchal authors against women's ecclesial leadership and office ultimately resulted in the linkage of women's leadership with heresy. The progressive equation of women and heresy had as a theological consequence the misogynist defamation of Christian women. For example, the author of the Book of Revelation prophesies against an early Christian woman prophet whom he abuses with the name Jezebel.[45] This prophet apparently was the head of an early Christian prophetic school and had great influence and authority in the community of Thyatira. Since

42. *The Apostolic Church Order* III, 6.1–29.
43. Tertullian, *De Baptismo*, 17; for the Acts of Thecla see C. Schlau, *Die Akten des Paulus und der Thekla* (Leipzig: Hinrichs, 1877); W. M. Ramsay, *The Church and the Roman Empire*, 375–428, and the very interesting dissertation of Ross Kraemer, *Ecstatics and Ascetics. Studies in the Function of Religious Activities of Women* (Ann Arbor: University Microfilms, 1976), 142–49.
44. See also F. Heiler, *Die Frau in den Religionen der Menschheit* (Berlin: DeGruyter, 1977), 114. He surmises, however, that in heretical communities women in office were not disciplined enough.
45. The accusation of sexual licentiousness is a stereotypical accusation leveled by pagans against Christians and by Christians against each other. See Klaus Thraede, "Frau," in *Religion in Antike und Christentum* 8 (Stuttgart, 1973): 254–66; L. Zscharnack, *Der Dienst der Frau in den ersten Jahrhunderten der christlichen Kirche* (Göttingen: Vandenhoeck & Ruprecht, 1902), 78ff.

the author of Revelation stresses that despite his warnings and denunciations this prophet continued to be active in the community, her authority seems to have at least equaled that of John, whom she, in turn, might have perceived as a false prophet. Her influence seems to have been lasting since Thyatira in the middle of the second century became a center of the Montanist movement, where women prophets had significant leadership and influence.

The attacks of Tertullian give evidence as to how prominent women's leadership remained even toward the end of the second century. Tertullian is outraged about the insolence of those women who dare to "teach, to participate in theological disputes, to exorcise, to promise healings, and to baptize." He argues that it is not permitted for women "to speak in the church, to teach, to baptize, to sacrifice, to fulfill any other male function, or to claim any form of priestly functions."[46] He legitimates such an exclusion of women from all ecclesial leadership roles with a theology that evidences a deep misogynist contempt and fear of women. Tertullian accuses woman not only of causing the temptation of man but also that of the angels. According to him woman is the "devil's gateway" and the root of all sin. In like manner Jerome not only attributes to women the origin of sin but of all heresy.

> With the help of the prostitute Helena, Simon *Magus* founded his sect. Crowds of women accompanied Nicholas of Antiochia, the seducer, to all impurity. Marcion sent a woman before him in order to prepare the minds of men so that they might run into his nets. Apelles had his Philumena, an associate in the false teachings. Montanus, the mouthpiece of an impure spirit, used two wealthy women of noble origin, Prisca and Maximilla, in order to first bribe many communities and then to corrupt them....Arious' intent to lead the world astray started by misguiding the sister of the emperor. The resources of Lucilla supported Donatus to corrupt so many wretched in Africa with his staining rebaptism. In Spain the blind woman Agape led a man like Elipidius to his grave. He was succeeded by Priscillian who was an enthusiastic defender of Zarathustra and a Magus before he became a bishop, and a woman by the name of Gall supported him in his endeavors and left behind a stepsister in order to continue a second heresy of lesser form.[47]

---

46. *De Praescriptione* 41.5 and *De Baptismo* 17.4. See also J. K. Coyle, "The Fathers on Women's Ordination," 67ff.
47. Jerome, *Adversus Iovinianum,* 1.48.

PATRIARCHALIZATION AND INSTITUTIONALIZATION

The process of ecclesial patriarchalization, which climaxed in the identification of women's leadership with heresy, was also operative in the selection and formulation of the canonical New Testament writings. This becomes explicit in the later writings of the New Testament, which in turn serve to reinforce and to legitimate the patriarchalizing tendencies in the patristic church.

Since the genuine Pauline letters know of leadership roles of women in the beginnings of the church and since exegetes debate the meaning and authenticity of 1 Corinthians 11:2-16[48] and 1 Corinthians 14:33-36,[49] scholars discuss whether or not this process of patriarchalization was initiated, or at least supported, by Paul. However, there is no question that the early Christian tendencies of patriarchalization claimed Paul for their cause and determined the history, theology, and praxis of the church in his name. Such an interpretation of Pauline theology is continued by modern historical-critical exegesis. Scholars presuppose the interpretative model of orthodoxy and heresy when they label the opponents of Paul as "gnostic" or "gnosticizing." Christian women in the community of Corinth, who apparently occupied an equal position in the leadership and worship of the community, are thereby qualified as "heretical," whereas the theological admonitions and arguments of Paul are understood as "orthodox."[50]

The theological-historic claim of Galatians 3:28 is disqualified in a similar way when it is classified as a "gnostic" baptismal formula and denounced as enthusiastic spiritualization and illusion.[51] Although the validity of this model for a historiography of early Christianity has been questioned, its patriarchal implica-

---

48. See Winsome Munro, "Patriarchy and Charismatic Community in Paul," in *Women and Religion*, ed. Plaskow and Romero (Missoula, Mont.: Scholars Press, 1974), 189-98; W. O. Walker, "I Cor 11:2-16 and Paul's View Regarding Women," *Journal of Biblical Literature* 94 (1975): 94-110; J. Murphy-O'Connor, "The Non-Pauline Character of I Cor 11:2-16," *Journal of Biblical Literature* 95 (1976): 615-21.

49. For literature and discussion of this text see G. Fitzer, *Das Weib schweige in der Gemeinde* (Munich: Kaiser, 1963), and my article "Women in the Pre-Pauline and Pauline Churches."

50. Paul's reaction is often understood as inspired by his Jewish past. For the danger of anti-Judaism in such an exegetical feminist explanation see Judith Plaskow, "Christian Feminism and Anti-Judaism," *Cross Currents* 28 (1978): 306-9.

51. See W. Schmitthals, *Die Gnosis in Korinth* (Göttingen: Vandenhoeck & Ruprecht, 1956), 227 n. 1; W. A. Meeks, "The Image of the Androgyne," 180ff; R. Scroggs, "Paul and the Eschatological Woman Revisited," *Journal of the American Academy of Religion* 42 (1974): 536.

tions are not yet exposed. Even though exegetes disagree on Paul's own stance toward women, they acknowledge explicit tendencies of patriarchalization in the deutero-Pauline and post-Pauline literature. The so-called household-codes of the deutero-Pauline literature accept and legitimate the patriarchal family order.[52] Ephesians especially gives a theological justification for the patriarchal relationship between husband and wife or slave and master, insofar as the author legitimates the relationship of subordination with reference to the hierarchically defined relationship between Christ and the church.[53] 1 Peter, which belongs to the area of Pauline influence, identifies the missionary vocation of women with their subordination to their husbands, whom they can win over to Christianity without many words. The author admonishes women to imitate the example of obedience given by the women of the Hebrew Bible. Sarah becomes a prime example for the Christian woman because she acknowledged Abraham as her "lord." The husbands, in turn, are admonished to treat their wives with understanding since they are the "weaker sex." The expression "weaker vessel" implies the corporal, spiritual, intellectual, and social inferiority of woman. Peter concedes that women are also "heirs of the life," but theologically legitimates their secondary position. Indeed, the text not only justifies the submission of woman, but also demands the submission of all Christians to the patriarchal political-societal order (2:13). With reference to the sufferings of Christ, slaves are most especially enjoined to submit to patriarchal domination. The authors of 1 Peter and of Ephesians do not shy away from developing a Christian theology that supports the patriarchal-hierarchical claims of the Greco-Roman state and society.[54]

1 Timothy 2:10–15 does not speak about the subordination of women to the patriarchal family order; but like 1 Corinthians 14:33–36, it explicitly demands the silence and subordination of women in the Christian community. The goal here, a patriarchaliza-

---

52. See James E. Crouch, *The Origin and Intention of the Colossian Haustafel* (Göttingen: Vandenhoeck & Ruprecht, 1972); W. Leslie, *The Concept of Women in the Pauline Corpus* (Ann Arbor: University Microfilms, 1976), 188–237.

53. See J. Paul Sampley, *And the Two Shall Become One Flesh* (Cambridge: University Press, 1971), and my article "Marriage and Discipleship," *The Bible Today* (April 1979), 2027–34.

54. See the excellent analysis of David Balch, *"Let Wives Be Submissive...." The Origin and Apologetic Function of the Household Duty Code (Haustafel) in 1 Peter* (Ann Arbor: University Microfilms, 1974).

tion of ecclesial leadership functions, is evident in the injunction of the author that women should learn in total submission and his categorical prohibition of women from teaching and having authority over men. This patriarchal injunction is theologically substantiated by the argument that man was created first and that woman sinned first.[55] This negative theological understanding of woman's functions is used to legitimate the exclusion of women from leadership and office in the church. Woman's vocation is not the call to discipleship or to mission; it is her patriarchally defined role as wife and mother that accomplishes her salvation.

This demand of the Pastorals for the subordination of women is formulated in the context of the progressive patriarchalization of large parts of the church and its leadership functions. The Pastorals require that the structures and leadership of the Christian community should be patterned after the patriarchal family structure. This comes to the fore in the criteria for the election of male leaders: they should be married to one woman and have demonstrated their patriarchal leadership qualities in their own household; they should know how to rule their children and to administer and order their household authoritatively.[56] Such a patriarchal church order, by definition, has no room for women's leadership.

It is clear, however, that such a patriarchal leadership structure was advocated in conflict with a more egalitarian church practice, which it sought to replace. It goes hand in hand with an ideological legitimation of the exclusion of women from church leadership. Thus it becomes obvious that the misogynist expressions of patristic theology are not only rooted in a faulty anthropology of woman but are also provoked by ecclesiastical-patriarchal interests to theologically legitimate the exclusion of women from ecclesiastical offices. Such an exegetical-historical reconstruction of the patriarchalization of church offices does not prove, however, that such a development was historically necessary and unavoidable; it does not call for theological justification but for critical-theological analysis.[57]

Today exegetes and theologians usually understand the process

---

55. See S. Roth Liebermann, *The Eve Motif in Ancient Near Eastern and Classical Greek Sources* (Ann Arbor: University Microfilms, 1975).

56. See A. Sand, "Anfänge einer Koordinierung verschiedener Gemeindeordnungen nach den Pastoralbriefen," in *Kirche im Werden,* ed. J. Hainz (Paderborn: Schöning, 1976) 215–37, 220.

57. For a positive interpretation of this development see, for example, W. Schrage, "Zur Ethik der neutestamentlichen Haustafeln," *NTS* 21 (1974): 1–22.

of ecclesial patriarchalization as the necessary development from charism to office, from Paulinism to early Catholicism, from a millennialist radical ethos to a privileged "malestream" establishment, from the radical Jesus movement within Judaism to an integrative love-patriarchalism[58] within the Hellenistic urban communities, from the egalitarian charismatic structures of the beginning to the hierarchical order of the Constantinian church. Unlike the orthodoxy-heresy model, this interpretative framework does not justify the patriarchalization process of the early church on theological grounds, but argues with it in terms of sociological and political factors.

It implicitly maintains that, from a sociological-political point of view, the gradual patriarchalization of the early Christian movement was unavoidable. If the Christian communities were to grow, develop, and survive historically, they had to adapt and take over the patriarchal institutional structures of their society. The institutionalization of the charismatic-egalitarian early Christian movement could not but lead to the patriarchalization of ecclesial leadership functions – that is, to the exclusion of women from church office or to the reduction of their ecclesial functions to subordinate, feminine, marginal positions. The more the early Christian movement adapted to the dominant societal institutions, thus becoming a genuine part of its patriarchal Greco-Roman society, the more women had to be excluded from church leadership and office. They were reduced to powerless fringe-groups or had to conform to the feminine stereotypes of the hegemonic Greco-Roman culture. For example, the patristic offices of widow and deaconess had to limit themselves to the service of women, and finally disappeared from history. Moreover, these leadership functions could no longer be exercised by all women but only by those who had overcome their femaleness by remaining virgins.

This interpretative model of early Christian development seems accurately to describe the consequences and casualties of the gradual patriarchalization of the Christian church. However, it does not reflect on its own theological androcentric presuppositions, insofar as it overlooks that the history of early Christianity is writ-

---

58. For this expression see Ernst Tröltsch, *Die Soziallehren der christlichen Kirchen und Gruppen* (Tübingen: Mohr, 1923) 1:67f. and especially Gerd Theissen, *Sociology of Early Palestinian Christianity* (Philadelphia: Fortress, 1978) and his various articles. However, in my opinion Theissen too quickly ascribes love-patriarchalism to the early Christian missionary movements in the Greco-Roman urban centers.

ten from the perspective of the historical winners.[59] Christian history and theology reflect those segments of the church that have undergone such a patriarchalization process and have theologically perpetrated it in the formulation of the canon. Insofar as this reconstructive sociological-political model presents the elimination of women from ecclesial office and their marginalization in a patriarchal church as a historical necessity, it justifies the patriarchal institutionalization process as the only possible and historically viable form of institutional church structure. It overlooks, however, that the institutional structures of the patriarchal household and state were not the sole institutional options available to and realized by early Christians; some collegial private associations, philosophical schools, guilds, and mystery cults accepted women and slaves as equal members and initiates. Like the early Christians, these groups, however, were always politically suspect because their egalitarian ethos challenged the patriarchal structures of Roman society. Since women such as Phoebe or Nympha were founders and leaders of house churches, the missionary house churches seem to have been patterned after such egalitarian private organizations and not after the patriarchal household.

The theological implications of a patriarchal sociological model for the reconstruction of early Christian history are obvious: Women can occupy only subordinate positions in the contemporary church since they could only do so in the early church. The patriarchal character of church office is given with the institutionalization of the church. Women who claim to be called to church office and leadership violate the essence of ecclesial tradition and institution. An androcentric sociological model for the reconstruction of early Christian history unwittingly supports theological claims that patriarchal church structures are divinely revealed, and thus cannot be changed.

Both the androcentric theological model and the sociological-cultural model for the reconstruction of early Christian life and community presuppose and argue that the process of the patriarchalization of the church is a historical given. They claim that the early Christian theology and praxis that acknowledged women

59. See Gustavo Gutiérrez, "Where Hunger Is, God Is Not," *The Witness* (April 1977): 6: "Human history has been written by a white hand, a male hand, from the dominating social class. The perspective of the defeated in history is different. Attempts have been made to wipe from their minds the memory of their struggles. This is to deprive them of a source of energy, of an historical will to rebellion."

as equal Christians and disciples was either "heretical" or "charismatic," and hence theologically or historically not viable. Neither
model can conceive of a Christian church in which women were
thought to be equal. Therefore, it does not suffice merely to interpret biblical texts that speak about women in early Christianity.
What is necessary is to challenge the traditional interpretative models for the reconstruction of early Christianity and to search for
new models that can integrate both egalitarian and "heretical" traditions. Insofar as such interpretative models presuppose and are
based on the equality of all Christians, they could be called feminist. If such models should comprehend the basic social equality
of all Christians within the early Christian church, they have to
employ sociological analysis.

AN EGALITARIAN INTERPRETATIVE MODEL

The interpretative model presented here is based on the insight
that Christianity has not been patriarchally determined from its
very inception and has not been an integrated segment of its
dominant patriarchal Jewish or Greco-Roman societies. If one
asks which as yet unrealized emancipatory impulses in early
Christianity are still historically accessible today in spite of the patriarchalizing tendencies of tradition and church, then one must
adopt a reconstructive model that can bring to the surface the egalitarian impulses not only of the early Christian movements but also
of their surrounding Jewish and Greco-Roman societies.

Despite obvious patriarchal tendencies in the transmission and
redaction of the Jesus traditions, the New Testament sources do
not attribute to Jesus misogynist statements about women. This is
remarkable if one considers that the gospels were written at a time
when the patriarchalization process of the Christian community
was well underway. Even New Testament texts that insist on the
patriarchal submission of Christian women do not buttress their
injunctions with reference to a word or action of Jesus but with
reference to cultural custom or biblical texts such as Genesis 2-3.

The Jesus traditions are not defined in a misogynist fashion.[60]
The opposite seems the case. They reflect both that Jesus was crit-

---

60. See also Evelyn and Frank Stagg, *Woman in the World of Jesus* (Philadelphia:
Westminster, 1978), 102.

icized because he took women seriously, and that women were disciples and primary witnesses in the early church. Since membership in the community of disciples dissolved and replaced traditional family bonds (Mark 3:35), the women disciples are defined by the patriarchal order of marriage and family. Not biological motherhood but faithful discipleship is decisive. The commitment and fidelity of the women disciples is especially underlined in the Markan Gospel. Women persevered with Jesus in his sufferings and execution. The women disciples were the primary witnesses to the empty tomb and the resurrection. Thus Mark's three passages about the women disciples indicate that women were the primary witnesses for the three basic data of early Christian faith and kerygma: the death, burial, and resurrection of Jesus. These three women texts seem to parallel the confessional formula "Christ died, ... was buried, ... was raised" of 1 Corinthians 15:3-5.[61]

The gospel tradition about the women disciples, especially that of Mary of Magdala, as primary witnesses and guarantors of the Christian gospel stands up to the critical criteria that historical scholarship has defined for determining authentic Jesus traditions.[62] This tradition is found in two different forms in the synoptic and the Johannine traditions. It cannot be derived from contemporary Judaism where, as far as we know, women were not considered as competent witnesses. It also does not owe its formulation to early Christian community interests, since, as we have seen, later documents attempt to play down the importance of the women disciples. In addition, patristic and later church traditions speak of Mary of Magdala as the "apostle to the apostles," even though they are interested in diminishing rather than enhancing her importance. In the long run Mary of Magdala becomes in Western liturgy and memory the "prostitute" and "sinner." Even modern interpreters attempt to explain away the significance of this woman as the primary witness and guarantor of Christian resurrection faith when they stress that, in distinction to Peter, the witness of Mary Magdalene was "unofficial."[63]

These gospel traditions about the role of women in the disci-

---

61. See Martin Hengel, "Maria Magdalena und die Frauen als Zeugen," in *Abraham unser Vater,* ed. Otto Betz and Martin Hengel (Leiden: Brill, 1962), 246.

62. For a short discussion of these criteria see Norman Perrin, *What Is Redaction Criticism?* (Philadelphia: Fortress, 1971).

63. See, e.g., Raymond E. Brown, "Roles of Women in the Fourth Gospel," *Theological Studies,* 692, n. 12.

pleship of Jesus fit into the understanding of the Jesus movement that has been worked out by the sociological interpretation of early Christianity.[64] As an inner-Jewish renewal movement the Jesus movement stands in conflict with its dominant patriarchal society and is "heretical" with respect to its dominant religious community. The earliest Jesus traditions expect a reversal of all social conditions through the eschatological intervention of God; this is initially realized in the ministry of Jesus. Therefore, the Jesus movement can accept all those who, according to contemporary societal standards, are marginal people and who are, according to a strict interpretation of the Torah, "unclean" — the poor, the exploited, public sinners, publicans, the maimed and sick, and of course women in all these groups. In distinction to other Jewish renewal movements, such as the Qumran community, the Jesus movement was not exclusive but inclusive; it made possible the solidarity of those who would not be accepted by some other Jewish renewal groups because of religious laws and ideologies.[65]

In the Jesus movements women of all walks of life could become disciples, although they were socially marginal, religiously inferior, and for much of the time cultically unclean. The sevenfold transmission[66] of a Jesus-saying in the synoptic tradition, which states that the first and the leaders should be last and slaves, indicates that Jesus was remembered as having radically questioned social and religious hierarchical and patriarchal relationships. The fatherhood of God radically prohibits any ecclesial patriarchal self-understanding. The lordship of Christ categorically rules out any relationship of dominance within the Christian community (Matt. 23:7–12). According to gospel traditions Jesus radically rejected all relationships of dependence and domination.[67] This demand for inclusiveness and domination-free structures in the Jesus move-

---

64. In addition to the work of Gerd Theissen, John Gager, Ross Kraemer, and Wayne A. Meeks see also the article by Robin Scroggs, "The Earliest Christian Communities as Sectarian Movement," in *Christianity, Judaism and Other Greco-Roman Cults*, ed. Jacob Neusner II (Leiden: Brill, 1975), 1–23; J. A. Wilde, "The Social World of Mark's Gospel," in *SBL Seminar Papers 1978*, II (Missoula, Mont.: Scholars Press, 1978): 47–70.

65. See M. Völkl, "Freund der Zöllner und Sünder," *Zeitschrift für die neutestamentliche Wissenschaft* 69 (1978): 1–10; Luise Schottroff, "Das Magnifikat und die ältesten Traditionen über Jesus von Nazareth," *Evangelische Theologie* 38 (1978): 298–312, and especially her excellent book, Luise Schottroff and Werner Stegemann, *Jesus von Nazareth: Hoffnung der Armen* (Stuttgart: Kohlhammer, 1978).

66. See Mark 9:35; 10:41–45; Matt. 18:4; 20:25–28; 23:11; Luke 9:48; 22:24–27.

67. See Paul Hoffmann and Volker Eid, *Jesus von Nazareth und seine christliche Moral* (Freiburg: Herder, 1975), 199ff.

ments provides the theological basis for the acknowledgment of women as full disciples.

This ethos of the Jesus movements also finds expression in the early Christian missionary movements. In them social status privileges based on race, religion, class, and sex are not valid.[68] All Christians are equal members of the community. Galatians 3:28 is a pre-Pauline baptismal formula that Paul quotes in order to prove that in the Christian community all religious-social distinctions between Jews and Gentiles have lost their validity. This pre-Pauline baptismal confession clearly proclaims values that are in total opposition to those of the Greco-Roman culture of the time. Like the Jesus movement, Christian missionary communities did not tolerate the religious-social structures of inequality that characterized the dominant Greco-Roman society. This new Christian self-understanding sought to do away with all religious, class, social, and patriarchal relationships of dominance. It made it possible not only for Gentiles and slaves but also for women to assume leadership functions within the urban missionary movements. In these movements women were not marginal figures but exercised leadership as missionaries, founders of Christian communities, apostles, prophets, and leaders of churches.

Contemporary exegetes, therefore, do not do justice to the text when they label this pre-Pauline baptismal formula as "gnostic," because it negates traditional differences.[69] Just as Christian Jews remained racially Jews, so women remained biologically female although their patriarchally defined gender roles and subordinate status were no longer of any socioreligious significance in the Christian community. Moreover, Galatians 3:28 does not claim, as later gnostic and patristic texts do, that "maleness" is the full expression of being human and Christian, and that women, therefore, have to become "male" in Christ. In addition, Galatians 3:28 may not be misunderstood as purely spiritual or eschatological, since the text does not maintain the Christian equality of Jews and Gentiles regarding their souls or with respect to the eschatological future.

---

68. See, e.g., Hans Dieter Betz, "Spirit, Freedom, and Law: Paul's Message to the Galatian Churches," *Svensk Exegetic Arsbok* 39 (1974): 145–60.

69. It is often claimed that the text is "gnostic" because it does away with the creational differences between women and men. However, such a judgment in my opinion does not sufficiently distinguish between biological sex and social gender roles. For such a distinction and its cross-cultural documentation see Ann Oakley, *Sex, Gender, and Society* (New York: Harper Col., 1972).

Finally, Galatians 3:28 should not be misinterpreted as purely charismatic but must be seen as applying to the structures and organization of the Christian community. Egalitarian structures were not unthinkable at the time. Such communal, organizational forms, which eliminated the societal differences between slaves and free as well as between male and female, are found in religious and secular associations of the time, even though these were always suspected of promoting sedition and of undermining the dominant social, patriarchal order.[70] Like other cultic associations, especially Judaism and the cult of Isis, Christian communities had to face the accusation that they upset the traditional patriarchal order of the household and, therefore, the order of the Roman state and society, by admitting women and slaves to equal membership. Hence the thesis of Gerd Theissen that the radicalism of the counter-cultural Jesus movement was assimilated by the earliest urban Hellenistic missionary communities into a "family style love patriarchalism," in which the societal distinctions survived although in a softer mitigated form, must be questioned.

The household-code texts of the Pauline tradition do not prove that such love patriarchalism existed in the initial stages of the early Christian missionary movements in the Hellenistic urban centers.[71] They are better understood as advocating a cultural development of patriarchal adaptation that they deemed necessary because the early Christian missionary movements were seen as counter-cultural movements that caused conflict because they undermined the patriarchal structures of the Greco-Roman political order. In short, an egalitarian model for the reconstruction of early Christian history can do justice both to the egalitarian traditions of woman's leadership in the church and to the gradual process of adaptation and theological justification of the churches to their dominant patriarchal Greco-Roman culture and society.

To sum up: I have attempted to sketch a critical analysis of both the theological and sociological androcentric models that inform historical and theological reconstructions of early Christian history and theology. I have also argued that such models must be replaced with an egalitarian reconstructive model, which can not

---

70. See the documentation and elaboration of this point by David Balch, *"Let Wives Be Submissive....,"* 115-33,

71. The interrelation between the organizational forms of private or religious associations and the house-churches needs to be clarified. See A. J. Malherbe, *Social Aspects of Early Christianity* (Baton Rouge: Louisiana State University Press, 1977), 92.

only do justice to conflicting early Christian traditions but also does not need to eliminate or downplay the traditions of women's discipleship and leadership in the Jesus movement and in the early Christian missionary movements. Like other historical interpretations, an egalitarian reconstruction and interpretation of early Christian history is not only descriptive but also constructive. It is not only motivated by interest in the past. It also attempts to set free emancipatory impulses and to recover forgotten traditions in the interest of the present and the future.[72] Such a reconstruction of early Christian beginnings seeks to engender an emancipatory praxis of church and theology that could historically and socially recapture the emancipatory impulses of the Jesus movement in Palestine and of the early Christian missionary movements not only for transforming Christian religion but also for changing patriarchal society and culture.

---

72. See H. M. Baumgartner, *Kontinuität und Geschichte: Zur Kritik und Metakritik der historischen Vernunft* (Frankfurt: Suhrkamp, 1972), 218.

12 ——————————————

WE ARE STILL INVISIBLE:
A THEOLOGICAL ANALYSIS
OF THE LCWR STUDY
ON WOMEN AND MINISTRY

CONTEXTUALIZATION

Between 1978 and 1980, the Ecclesial Role of Women Commission and its steering committee in the Leadership Conference of Women Religious (LCWR) sponsored a study on women's ministerial roles in the Roman Catholic Church. To publicize and analyze the results of this study, LCWR adopted a threefold procedure: First, LCWR commissioned a national survey of *women in ministry,* which was conducted by the Center for Applied Research in the Apostolate (CARA); second, LCWR ordered a national survey of women and men as *recipients of ministry,* which was undertaken by the Princeton Religion Research Center. Both surveys were published by CARA in 1980.[1] (Page references are to this study.) Third, in the spring of 1981 LCWR invited fifty church leaders and representatives of Roman Catholic organizations to reflect on these studies. The article that follows was presented at this symposium. The symposium was published under the title *Women and Ministry,* although several speakers and participants objected that this

---

1. *Women and Ministry: A Survey of the Experience of Roman Catholic Women in the United States* (Washington, D.C.: CARA, 1980).

title was misleading. In my opinion, both the study as well as the symposium would have been better entitled: *Women's Work in Support of the Patriarchal Church.*

The twelve recommendations that participants of the symposium made to various church bodies dealt with issues ranging from theological education and appointment and placement services, to women's preaching and the circulation of the study. I would like to single out here those recommendations pertaining specifically to women's ministry in the Roman Catholic Church. Given the present repressive ecclesiastical climate, one cannot expect that these recommendations will be executed by "official" church bodies such as LCWR. Rather, goals and tasks spelled out in these recommendations need to be taken up by feminist organizations such as the Women's Ordination Conference (WOC) or Women's Alliance for Theology, Ethics and Ritual (WATER) with the financial support of LCWR and other ecclesial organizations concerned with women in ministry. Projects emerging from an exploration of the recommendations could include, for instance, a national resource center, a journal for women in ministry, support for feminist research and publications on women in ministry, national archives dedicated to preserving the history of all women, continuing theological education, advocacy and mediation, an international organization for women in ministry, and, finally, supportive networks for enabling nun-women and lay-women, women of different ethnic groups, races, and sexual persuasions, part-time and full-time ministers, Catholic, Jewish, Muslim, and Protestant pastoral leaders to share their experiences in ministry and to support each other.

———— ❖ ————

WHEN I WAS ASKED to explore theologically the LCWR study on "Women and Ministry," I could not possibly decline because "Women in Ministry" is not only one of the key topics of my theological work, but it has also decisively formed and inspired my own life and self-understanding. In one way or another I have been involved in ministry since I was thirteen when I became a leader of a parish girl scout group. Since then I have primarily been involved in ministering to other women within a church context, although I have come only very slowly to recognize women as my own people to whom I am accountable in a special way. Consid-

ering my involvement in ministry and my personal engagement
with the topic, my theological analysis will be neither neutral nor
abstract. But that is true of all theological discussion.

In order theologically to get a hold on the study whose sociological method and conclusions I will not discuss here, I should
like to start with my own experience. About twenty years ago,
when I decided to study for an M.Div. degree, I was not only the
first woman to do so at my university but the undertaking was
also theologically "illegitimate." The new theology of my professors like Albert Auer, Karl Rahner, or Yves Congar, which found
its way into the documents of Vatican II, defined the vocation of
the clergy and of "religious" as ministry to the church, while the
mission of the laity was said to be directed toward the world. As
a woman I was by definition a lay-person and therefore had no
business whatever studying theology in order to work within the
context of the church. Yet I was fascinated by theology and had
always had the vocation to ministry.

Since at the time it did not dawn on me to question the so-called
lay-clergy dualism that prevailed even in the "new" theology, I attempted to show in my first book that this prevailing theology did
not correspond to the German pastoral situation where women
had been working full-time and professionally within the institutional structures of the church since the early twentieth century.
I therefore gathered all the available materials on full-time women
ministers within the German Catholic church, as well as within an
international and ecumenical context. At the same time I sought
to develop a theological understanding of ministry that would be
inclusive of clergy and laity. Since women were "laity," according
to Canon Law, and did not have the option of becoming clergy, I
took "women ministers" as examples to prove my point. However,
I did not articulate the problem as a problem of women, although
I myself was a woman. I was not interested in women's situation
and their role in the church, but in promoting and documenting
a theology and ministerial practice of church that was not clerical
but based on the "priesthood of all believers."

In the process of writing the thesis, however, I learned that
I could not just deal with "laity" as a problem because I had
overlooked (or repressed) that "women" had a special role and
position according to theology, church law, and pastoral praxis.
Therefore, I came to focus more and more on "women," so that
when the book was published in 1964, it read like an argument for

women's ordination, although at the outset I was not interested in the clericalization of women but in the declericalization of the church.

I have spoken here of my own work so much, not in order to prove to you my credentials for analyzing the topic, but in order to indicate where I come from and what direction my theological evaluation and critical analysis will take. To put it in a nutshell: Like my own work on ministries of women in the church, the present study, *Women and Ministry,* seems to be riddled with theological inconsistencies and must therefore be carefully examined for what it proves and what it does not. I would submit that it is fundamentally flawed because this study did not start with women's experiences and ministries but with the prevailing ecclesiological framework. Its major concern is not women's ministry but the advancement of church and ministry.

While my book sought to establish a participatory model of church as the people of God by pointing to the de facto clerical status of women in the German church, LCWR initiated this study in order to document the ecclesial leadership and creative ministries of women in the post–Vatican II North American church. Yet in my opinion this study could not do so and could not get hold of women's experiences in ministry because it used as its heuristic theological-sociological model of church that of the patriarchal hierarchy, which by definition and by law is exclusive of the independent leadership of women and can tolerate women's ministry only in subsidiary positions and auxiliary roles.

Interestingly enough the crucial indicator in both studies is the theological understanding of laity. While I used it as my heuristic starting point because it expressed most adequately my own theological self-understanding formed by the biblical liturgical and Catholic Action movements, the initiators of the LCWR study expected to document the leadership of "women religious" and ended up by documenting the contributions of "lay-women" to parish life.[2]

---

2. Here another language problem needs to be addressed: The study consistently uses "lay-women" but describes nuns not in canonical but religious terms. Therefore, I use here "lay-women" and "nun-women" in order to characterize both groups with ecclesiastical categories. I do so not in order to deepen our alienation from each other but to alert my sisters to the alienating language permeating the study. I can understand that they cringe to be called "nun-women" just as I do when I am labelled "lay-woman."

THEOLOGICAL MODELS OF CHURCH

If we ask what kind of theology and reality of church underpins the CARA study, then the term "lay" points to two quite different experiences and theological models of church today. The term implies a clerical classification as well as an active participation within the ministry of the church. These divergent, if not sometimes contradictory meanings of "laity" are engendered by two different theological models of church that in this century and especially since Vatican II have coexisted alongside or within each other and have done so with more or less tension. Both models of church are not related to each other as the real church to the ideal church nor are they totally exclusive of each other in their concrete actualizations. Rather, both models are alternative self-understandings and self-actualizations of church that are not "neutral" with respect to women's leadership and ministry in the church.

In the first model the term "laity" is derived from the Greek term *laikos,* whose structural counterpart is *kleros.* Laity in this sense are the nonordained, the nonprofessionals, the "ordinary" believers as objects of pastoral power or pastoral care. They are distinct from those who by ordination, training, or celibate lifestyle are set apart as "clergy." Women who like myself are professionally trained or who live a celibate lifestyle and perform a ministry in the church do not "fit." The church according to this model consists of the laity and the clerical-sacerdotal hierarchy in such a way that the laity is always of a lower order and subsidiary class. Whenever laity enters into the ministerial domain of the clergy, they are relegated to the role of a supporting cast and subordinate agency. Insofar as the clerical-sacerdotal structures of hierarchy are by law exclusive of women as women, these structures are sexist, i.e., they discriminate against women on the basis of sex, and patriarchal, i.e., they constitute a social system of male ranks and hierarchies.

This first type of church is found in its most canonical-traditional form in the local church of the parish and diocese, or in the Vatican and its hierarchical dependencies. It is patriarchal in its structures because one ordained male — usually older — stands on top of the pyramid and has "jurisdiction" over younger clergy bound to him in obedience as well as over the laity, men and women. Even the new code of Canon Law defines jurisdiction as "the power of ruling" that is validated by sacred orders (Canon 126).[3] This model of church sustains communal life by control from the top to the bottom. Obedience and loyalty to the pope, the bishop, the pastor, the superior, and the husband are the required response from those who are "subordinates."

This patriarchal model of church can admit women into its ordained ranks only when they are willing to accept their "wife-role" as it is defined by the patriarchal family. This is not only apparent in the practice and policy of those Christian churches that ordain women, but is also documented by the CARA study that we discuss here. While post-Vatican II liberal Catholic theology has critically analyzed the hierarchical and clerical character of church office, it has not paid sufficient attention to the patriarchal aspect of this model of church and its theological function. In the discussions on "women in the church" this patriarchal element comes more and more to the fore as *the* foundational and integral moment of church. Hence feminist theology as a critical theology of liberation compels feminists to raise the issue of sexism as a structural evil and sin so that the incorporation of women into the ministry of the church does not lead to women's further alienation and oppression.

The second model of church does not define laity as the opposite of clergy, but derives its meaning from the Greek work *laos*. It therefore understands church as the people of God. The constitutive sacrament in this theological model of church is not ordination but baptism. The church as the pilgrim people of God stands in continuity with Israel and in solidarity with all the peoples of the world. In Christ Jesus the radical separation between the old and the new covenant people as well as that between the sacred and the profane, the church and the world, is overcome. All the baptized constitute church and are empowered and responsible for building up church. Ministry is a function of the whole people of God vis-à-vis the whole world. Those ministries directed toward the nurturing and "building up" of the faith-community are the prerogative and vocation of all those baptized. Ministry in this model of church has a twofold function: it is outer-directed toward the "world" in proclaiming the gospel and in ministering to those who are weak and powerless. At the same time ministry is inner-directed toward the "church" in nourishing, empowering,

---

3. See *National Catholic Reporter,* February 6, 1981, 10.

enabling, and building up the faith-community. Neither function of ministry can be divided and parceled out to laity and clergy. Ministry in its twofold form is the responsibility of all; it is not a prerogative or privilege of a clerical class or of one sex, but it is rooted in the baptism of all believers. In the past twenty years or so this model of church has engendered very different forms of faith-community and ministry. It has enabled all members of the church, especially women, to become actively involved in ecclesial as well as sociopolitical ministries. I would therefore like to call this model the participatory-inclusive (Catholic) model of church.

Canonical communities of women have most forcefully addressed the issue of structural-economic change and sought to embody the second participatory-inclusive model of church in their own institutions and structures of decision making. The LCWR study *Patterns in Authority and Obedience* (published May 15, 1978) has established that canonical women's communities have undergone a thoroughgoing structural change from the patriarchal or matrilineal (the "uncle" still has the power) hierarchy model to that of participatory decision making and community. This structural change toward the participatory-inclusive model of church often runs on collision course with the patriarchal-hierarchy model as the study states:

> Enabling and participative modes of leadership/decision-making prevalent in many congregations seem in direct conflict with traditional authoritarian modes still current in the institutional church. Some bishops evidence little grasp and deep suspicion of emerging collaborative structures. (13)

The study points out that this shift in authority/obedience patterns is based on a theological awareness of church "as a community of persons distinctively gifted by the Spirit" (9) and has engendered "a strong affirmation of the basic rights of women to define themselves and to have access to the decision-making that shapes their lives" (11).

However, the LCWR study explicitly restricts these structural and theological changes to women's canonical communities and does not explore them as the structural-theological emergence of a new type of church. Therefore, it does not seek to extrapolate them for all areas of the church. Because the study does not question nun-women's privileged status engendered by the clerical-patriarchal hierarchy model it does not sufficiently understand the structural contradictions in which women's canonical communities find themselves today. Enabling and participative modes of leadership and ministry within the church have first of all to abolish the canonical dualism between lay-women and nun-women engendered by the patriarchal hierarchy model, as the study under discussion here so forcefully documents. As I have stressed elsewhere, I would like to emphasize again that women committed to the second model of church must have as their primary goal the overcoming of this lay-nun dualism that separates us as ecclesial sisters from each other.

Both models of church have found their way into the documents of Vatican II and both models of church are Catholic and orthodox. In the past two decades they have co-existed with more or less tension and conflict. It seems, however, that the corrective coexistence of both models of church and ministry is now at a critical juncture. Whether we move toward the participatory Catholicity of the second model or reconfirm the clerical-patriarchal structures of the first model of church will depend on how we resolve the "women's issue." Since the study *Women and Ministry* can be used in both directions it is important to evaluate it critically. Seen within the historic development of the contemporary Catholic Church, the CARA study clearly is situated within the patriarchal hierarchy model of church, although its impulse and goal were derived from the participatory Catholic model.

THE STUDY ON "WOMEN AND MINISTRY"

The indebtedness of the study to the patriarchal hierarchy model of church and ministry comes to the fore in the way in which the study was conducted and especially in its definition of ministry (30). The pastor was first contacted and it was he who named women ministers who were then contacted and interviewed. Thus it is not surprising that women like my friend Ann, who runs a shelter for homeless women, my friend Kathleen, who works with prostitutes, or my friend Margarita, who works with migrant workers, are not mentioned. Women like myself and others who do not work within hierarchical-ecclesiastical context "invisible" in this study.

Yet I would submit that most women who are exploring new forms of ministry cannot be found in the patriarchal diocesan-parish context. Hence it seems that not just the statistical method of the study, as the author suggests, but even so its location within the patriarchal hierarchy model of church explains why women's creative initiatives in ministry and in ecclesial leadership do not come to the fore. Because of this theological-ecclesial location, the study excludes women who are not willing to work as auxiliaries to male clergy in conformity and subordination to hierarchical leadership. And thereby excludes much of women's leadership in the North American church. Ministry as conceived in this study is exclusive of women's leadership. In her presentation Dr. Rosenberg has conceded as such. No wonder that all of us who are actively involved and committed to new forms of ministerial leadership are deeply disappointed when reading the study. We are still invisible and our story is not yet told. However, the study proves that this story cannot be told within the framework and presuppositions of the patriarchal hierarchy model of church.

One is even more surprised to find this theological location of the CARA study within the patriarchal hierarchy model of church when one considers LCWR's initiative in bringing about the project. Hence it is not surprising that the researchers first approached pastors and not member communities of LCWR, individual members, or other women publicly recognized for their commitment to ministry in the church. These women would have been able to provide lists of names for a so-called snowball approach to the study. A method that would have first identified women in ministry could have avoided the patriarchal hierarchy structures as primary resources as well as the nun-lay dualism. It would have been based on *women's* recognition of women in ministry. In my view only such an approach would have been theologically appropriate and sociologically feasible. While some might have questioned its sociological adequacy, it would have been methodologically less deficient than the present study.

The second theological flaw that permeates the study is the presumption of lay-nun dualism, which in the long run could prove even more fatal. Since the patriarchal hierarchy model defines *all* women (including nuns) as laity, the researchers had to introduce another heuristic theological category in order to delineate the role of nun-women ministry as distinct from that of lay-women. This heuristic theological category introduced into the study is the dualism between church – defined as Roman Catholic – and world, or between sacred and secular. This pattern allows nuns – although they are *as women* laity – to become an integral element of the sacred sphere of the church, which is structurally coextensive with the patriarchal hierarchy and excludes women from the clergy. Operating within this theological mindset, the study therefore interprets the expansion of women's auxiliary ministries primarily in terms of lay-women moving "full-time" into areas that were held previously by nun-women (e.g., schools or hospitals). Conversely the nun-women are said to have moved into quasi-clerical, professional, full-time parish ministry that previously was occupied by the male clergy only. The study therefore does not even discuss or mention lay-women like myself who exercise a full-time professional ministry in the church. However, it does discuss such nun-women, although they do not show up statistically. It points out that they do not receive the same financial remuneration and ecclesial status as the male members of the hierarchy.

Hence one is not surprised that the study's definition of ministry draws the boundaries between church and world, ministry and Christian life, in terms of the family. A woman who teaches the Bible to her own children, according to the study, is not performing a ministry, while a woman who teaches the Bible to her neighbor's kids as part of a parish Bible school program is performing a ministry. Such a boundary between ministry and Christian duty, between church and world, which comes to the fore in the study's definition of ministry, corresponds to the clerical boundary of the patriarchal hierarchy model that also demands as prerequisite for ordained ministry that one "lives" without family and practices celibacy. But whereas in the study the family boundary is functional, in the ecclesial definition of clergy it assumes the character of lifestyle. Because their lifestyle conforms to the clerical lifestyle nun-women can be admitted as quasi-clergy and can hold subordinate paid positions within the parish-diocesan hierarchy. Within the mindset of the patriarchal hierarchy model of church, therefore, this reverence for "women in ministry" actually means "nuns in ministry."

What then is the positive result of the CARA study *Women and Ministry?* For me its value consists in the extensive and comprehensive documentation of women's work for the patriarchal-hierarchical church and especially of lay-women's unacknowledged contributions to the parish. When I declare this result as "positive" I am not being facetious. Any cure of the patient depends on a good diagnosis of her "disease". Insofar as the study documents this illness of the patriarchal hierarchical church living off the unpaid work of women, it might contribute more to ecclesial renewal than a study on women's leadership in ministry could have done. However, this disease needs to be diagnosed correctly. It would be fatal if the study would claim to be the *definitive* study on Women in Ministry, rather than an important documentation of ecclesial sexism engendered by the patriarchal hierarchy model of church, which excludes the jurisdictional and sacramental leadership of women. In short, the study documents sexism as a structural ecclesial sin on all three levels of church: the economic-social, the theological, and the personal levels.

The Economic-Structural Level

The study provides overwhelming evidence that the church is built not only on women apostles and prophets but also on the unpaid and unrecognized labor of women. In my opinion the study's conclusion is the most devastating theological indictment of the patriarchal church:

> Women who are heads of households and women in low income brackets very likely cannot afford ministry, however they might like to engage in it. They must work to support themselves and others and most ministries do not pay enough for the woman who has no other income. (33)

Ministry as unpaid or minimally paid labor is a commodity that only the upper middle-class woman can afford. If women move as full-time professional workers into the lowest ranks and auxiliary positions of the patriarchal hierarchy, they are paid minimally. Thus the patriarchal hierarchy structure of church exploits women's labor and religious engagement to its own ends. Yet this exploitation of women as unpaid and low-status laborers by the patriarchal church affects nun-women and lay-women differently: Nun-women, who are according to the study more critical of the patriarchal system and more self-identified as women, are effectively prohibited from using their economic resources for ecclesial change because they receive only subsistence salaries. Although they are inspired by the participatory inclusive model of church, they lose their economic and institutional power to bring it about.

Lay-women who are married are even more exploited because they are not remunerated for their work at all, or are only minimally paid; their economic status is completely determined by that of their husbands. Hence women "without husbands" cannot afford ministry. The study limits a married woman's ministry theologically: Because women are supposed to be financially supported by their husbands, the study does not recognize women's economic exploitation. Ministerial involvement thus appears to have a definitely conservative, retarding function for women. It channels the anger and frustrations of many well-educated but economically dependent married women into religious, auxiliary activities that are dependent on male decision making and power. Thus ministry that requires much time and energy of women but does not adequately remunerate them deepens the economic and personal dependency of married women and this at a time when many educated middle-aged women are moving into the marketplace in order to attain economic independence and personal autonomy. Hence it is not surprising that the women in the study are more conservative and less open to change than the men, and that they do not identify with the feminist movement. If ministry is to become a liberating force in the lives of women, it has to enable them to become economically and personally more independent rather than to reinforce the societal discrimination and economic exploitation of all women.

The Theological-Structural Level

Economic-social exploitation and theological co-optation of women's gifts and energies are targeted by the study's definition of ministry as "service." The categories of "service" or "selfless," "sacrificing" love have always allowed society and the church to exploit women and to "keep them in their place" and in low-status, low-pay, servant-type occupations. That the study shares this societal understanding of women's work comes to the fore in its qualifications of ministry and in its predictions for the future. A theological definition of ministry defines ministry as "contributory service." Ministry may not be "an end in itself" or a "means to greater status, remuneration, or extrinsic reward" (30). Whenever it is doubtful whether or not a person is a minister, these additional criteria allow one to decide who is a minister and who is not. For instance, since my lecture here will be remunerated and because of my paid professorial status, I, as a woman, do not perform a ministry, whereas my colleagues who share the podium with me and are ordained may charge and still perform their ministry according to the study's definition.

In line with this theological understanding of ministry the authors predict that there will be an increasing formalization of women's ministerial roles in the future but no remuneration for it. Formal training and certification programs will lead to a growing group of professional volunteers who perhaps will gain greater "official" status; however, this development will not lead to ministry as a "paid occupation." Although I am not as confident as the authors of the study are that more and more women will volunteer for unpaid auxiliary ministries, I would like to point out that such a development, should it occur, will lead to greater exploitation of women because *ordained* male ministry is and will remain a "paid occupation." Moreover, any plans to legitimate the economic exploitation of women ministers and their auxiliary status through "official" ecclesial ritualization would lead to the deepening of ecclesial sexism as a structural sin.

In contrast to the study's definition of women's ministry as auxiliary service, many women in ministry understand their ministerial function in terms of power. They understand their ministry as empowering, nourishing, and enabling rather than as service. This comes clearly to the fore in the experiential statements collected before the Second Women's Ordination Conference in Baltimore or in those of "Women Ministering: Testimonies of New York Women in Non-Ordained Ministries," statements collected by the Women's Ordination Conference of New York. These women have articulated their experience of their call to ministry as being both "empowered" by the community or by the women among whom their ministry takes place, and as "power for," enabling the faith community. Ministry has to empower rather than to exploit women and the whole church. Only such an understanding of ministry as both "power for" and as "accountability to" others will lead to a redefinition of the patriarchal-hierarchical ministry that is understood as "ruling power over others." Jesus asked "service" from those who were first and in power, but he empowered those who were weak and exploited by their society and by institutionalized religion. Ministry "as power for" actualizes God's power for salvation.

The Personal Level

Considering the theological location of the study and its definition of ministry, one is not surprised to learn that the women interviewed have internalized their second-class status in the church. Since the study samples only those women who had been named by their pastor, one is not astonished to find that "the pastor's attitudes are very similar to those of women in ministry" (90). Moreover, it is also to be expected that those women who are economically most dependent because of age or lesser education are most opposed to change within the church because any change, especially ecclesial-religious change, would threaten their precarious hold on the world. On the other hand, their activity in charismatic groups indicates that even these women long for active religious participation, although they enact it in a sphere where it is most acceptable and least threatening to the status quo of their lives.

Given the study's definition of ministry as auxiliary service, ecclesiastically controlled formalized education for such ministry would contribute even more to their self-alienation as women and their internalization of patriarchal values and dependencies. Hence education of women for ministry first of all must be conceived as conscientization or consciousness-raising. Since the study has shown that nun-women are more self-identified as women and have more resources and support, I would suggest that LCWR organize such consciousness-raising groups. If the common experience of women in ministry is their economic exploitation and their auxiliary, subordinate status within the patriarchal model of church, then this experience must become the basis on which the bonding between lay-women and nun-women can take place. Consciousness-raising groups of women ministers exploring their common experience of work and sexuality in the patriarchal church should be initiated across the country. The National Assembly of Women Religious has made a good beginning, but these efforts need to be extended to *all* women in ministry, some of whom are identified by the CARA study.

Most importantly, for the first time in history women can claim theology and spirituality "as our own affair." We must therefore do everything in our power to end the spiritual, theological, and liturgical colonialization of women and to develop our own institutions for theological education and spiritual formation, as centers of empowerment. We have to do this not in order to segregate women from men but in order to develop structurally the participatory-inclusive model of church. Women's professional education for ministry as it presently takes place in male-directed theological schools will in the long run only lead to increasing alienation either from ourselves or from the church.

CONCLUSION

I have critically analyzed the theological presuppositions and methods of the study *Women and Ministry,* not in order to detract from the enormous work that was accomplished but in order to name the product "theologically." In documenting the extent of the co-optation of women's energies and talents in the patriarchal model of church, the authors of the study have provided an invaluable service to the North American church. Some of us might be inclined to disown the study because we do not find our own experience of ministry and church reflected in its results and conclusions. I would, however, caution that we should look more carefully into the mirror held up to us. Then we might come to recognize ourselves. Yet I also insist that the study needs to be named anew if it is not to do a serious disservice to women in ministry and to jeopardize the participatory-inclusive model of church that has inspired all of us and that women religious have brought into being in their own communities during the past two decades.

Since this study documents only how women are co-opted and exploited as subsidiary auxiliaries but not how they act as decision-making participants within the patriarchal model of church, it must be complemented by a study that can equally show the ministry of women who walk and work in the power of the Spirit. The story of women in ministerial leadership still needs to be told in stories, songs, and celebrations. We need a "Dinner Party" of our own to which not only our foresisters are invited but all those women who today act in the power of the Spirit. Such a celebration of women's leadership in the church needs to be rooted in the participatory-inclusive model of church. It cannot be told through statistics because statistics will only demonstrate the status quo as the so-called reality to be accepted. Statistics, however, would have captured neither the ministry of Jesus nor that of Prisca. In a poem about Käthe Kollwitz, Muriel Rukeyser asks, "What would happen if one woman told the truth about her life?" and she answers: "The world would split open." Maybe the same will happen to the church if and when the truth of Women in Ministry — the whole truth — is told.

13 ───────────

GATHER IN MY NAME*:
TOWARD A CHRISTIAN
FEMINIST SPIRITUALITY

───────────────────────────────────

CONTEXTUALIZATION

In the spring of 1981, the Center of Concern held a conference entitled "Women Moving Church." The purpose of this conference was to assess the impact of the women's movement on the Roman Catholic Church in the United States. In preparation for this conference around five hundred leading Catholics across the country were asked for their appraisal of the situation. The responses were divided. Some emphasized that the women's movement had great influence on the church; others thought that its effects were minimal or nonexistent. However, all the respondents agreed that the women's movement had a profound impact on Roman Catholic women.

Since the conveners of the conference, Diann Neu and Maria Riley, wanted to model a feminist process, they did not plan keynote speeches but several panel discussions instead. In order to prepare the actual event on the basis of the responses received, the organizers called together the invited speakers for a workshop. However, the group had a difficult time focusing the question into program objectives, since the responses were so contradictory.

───────────────────────

*I owe this title to the black poet Maya Angelou.

During these discussions it became clear to me that we were framing the question in the wrong way. The question and title of the conference presupposed that the church was identical with the hierarchy and that women were not a part of it. The church is here and women are there. (A similar androcentric framing is at work in the call of the World Council of Churches to celebrate the decade of women, in which the churches are asked to be in solidarity with women.) The title "Women Moving Church," I realized, evokes the image of women pushing and pushing a church such as the National Shrine in Washington or St. Peter's in Rome in order to move it. Even if a miracle happened and the church moved several inches, nothing would have been changed. Hence it was necessary to correct the androcentric framework of the question and to frame it in such a way that women could move into the center of our attention. If we were to replace the title "Women Moving Church" with "Women as Church on the Move," I argued, the conference could focus on the "moving" energies and changes that *women as church* are in the process of bringing about. Therefore, I sought to capture the notion of *women as church* with the German expression *Frauenkirche,* which Diann Neu rendered into English as *women-church.* Although this expression was used in theological discourses of the 1960s in a pejorative way to characterize the "feminization" of the church, I thought to reclaim *Frauenkirche/* women-church as a positive term and did so by substituting for *Kirche*/church, which derives from the Greek word *kyriakē* (belonging to the Lord), the term *ekklēsia* (assembly of the people), the Greek word used for "church" in Christian Scriptures. Since *ekklēsia* as the democratic assembly of "the saints" has never been fully realized historically, I qualified it with the phrase "of women," in order to indicate that *ekklēsia* will become historical reality only when women are fully included.

——— ❖ ———

ONE OF THE RESPONDENTS to our question regarding the impact of the women's movement on the Roman Catholic Church summed up her answer in the following way:

> What is clear is that the Women's Movement has played an important role in raising women's consciousness of their basic dignity as equal human persons. It has been a source of courage and support in questioning lack of that equality both in the market-place and in the church.

Within the church it has been a catalyst in calling women to recognize and respond to their baptismal call: a call to be and to do that is no respecter of sex.[1]

Since another panelist will address the impact of feminist spirituality on our personal-individual self-understanding, self-affirmation, and calling as women, I would like to explore here theologically what it means for women's spirituality to be "church on the move." I will seek to articulate a feminist spirituality that can engender the bonding of women for the empowerment of women, the gathering of women for the "birthing" of a new vision of community and church. Such an "ecclesial spirituality" of the women's movement is articulated in the response of a medical student:

The Women's Movement threatens the institution, ... challenges the community to go beyond, to transcend the earlier senses of duty, ... is an avenue by which the church *could* metamorphize if it has the courage and vision needed to follow the spirit, ... has given the community more of a sense of community and experiential spirituality than church did, ... has moved many from the religious to the spiritual, ... has given support that used to be gotten through church, ... has given us permission for other ways of naming and looking at the mystery transcendent in our lives.[2]

However, in finding her own spirituality this Catholic woman like so many others sees herself moving to the fringe and identifying herself as a "sporadic" in the church. In the past couple of years or so the experience of feminist spirituality in community has moved more and more feminist Catholics to a "partial identification" with the institutional church in order to form basic spiritual communities of sharing and empowerment for each other. How then can we forge our feminist experience of bonding in sisterhood and our rediscovery of our baptismal call to the discipleship of equals into a new Catholic-Christian vision that would allow us to build a feminist movement not on the fringes of the church but as the central embodiment and incarnation of a "renewed church" in solidarity with the oppressed and the "least" of this world, the majority of whom are women and children dependent on women?

It is usually assumed that spirituality has something to do with the life of the "soul," with prayer-life and worship, with meditation and mystical union, with "waiting" for God's will to come to

---

1. Response of Nadine Koza, O.S.F., Campus Minister.
2. Response by Kathi Antolak as communicated by Loie Lenarz.

pass and religious experience of the divine. In this understanding spirituality concentrates above all on prayer and meditation, on "spiritual" direction and Christ's indwelling of the soul, on ascetic and religious exercises as the precondition for progress on the spiritual journey of the soul from one level to another. In a similar fashion feminist spirituality can be occupied with meditation and incantations, spells and incense, womb chant and candle gazing, feminine symbols for the Divine and trance induction. Such an understanding of spirituality in terms of religious rituals and practices is found in all religions and not limited to Christianity. Therefore, it does not capture the specific vision of Jesus and the movement initiated by him.

The gospel is not a matter of the individual soul; it is the communal proclamation of the life-giving power of Spirit-Wisdom. It is God's vision of an alternative community and world. The experience of the Spirit's creative power releases us from the life-destroying powers of structural sin and sets us free to choose an alternative life for ourselves and for each other. The focal point of early Christian self-understanding was not a holy book or a cultic rite, not mystic experience and magic invocation, but a set of relationships: the experience of God's presence among one another and through one another. To embrace the gospel means to enter into a community; the one cannot be obtained without the other. The gospel calls into being the *ekklēsia* as a discipleship of equals that is continually being recreated in the power of the Spirit. Jesus' ministry, his healings and exorcisms, his promise to the poor and challenge to the rich, his breaking of religious law and his table community with outcasts and sinners, made experientially available God's new world, not, as we used to think, *within* us but *among* us. God's presence is found in the "midst of us" (Luke 17:21). The name of Jesus is Emmanuel, "God with us." The God of Jesus is divine Wisdom-Spirit whose power is gentle and whose yoke is light.

Like Jesus' own ministry so the community called forth by Jesus, the messenger of Divine Wisdom, is not an end in itself. In the power of the Spirit the disciples are sent to do what he did: to feed the hungry, heal the sick, liberate the oppressed, and announce the inbreaking of God's intended world and humanity here and now. In every generation Divine Wisdom commissions prophets — women and men — and makes them friends and children of God. To embrace the gospel means to enter a movement, to become a member of God's people who are on the road that stretches from Christ's death to Her return in glory. *Ekklēsia* – the Greek term for church – expresses this dynamic reality of Christian community. It is not a local, static term; it is not even a religious expression; it means the *actual* gathering of people, the assembly of free citizens in a town called together in order to decide matters affecting their own welfare.

In the First Testament *ekklēsia* means the "assembly of the people of Israel before God." In the Second Testament *ekklēsia* comes through the agency of the Spirit to visible, tangible expression. It is realized in and through the gathering of God's people around the table, eating together a meal, breaking the bread and sharing the cup in memory of Christ's passion and resurrection. *Christian* spirituality means eating and drinking together, sharing together, talking with each other, receiving each other, experiencing God's presence through each other, and in doing so proclaiming the gospel as God's alternative vision for everyone, especially for those who are poor, outcast, and battered, the majority of whom are women and children dependent on women. As long as Christian women are excluded from breaking the bread and deciding their own spiritual welfare and commitment, *ekklēsia* as the discipleship of equals is not realized and the power of the gospel is greatly diminished. The true spiritual person according to St. Paul is the one who *walks* in the Spirit. It is she who brings about the alternative world and family of God over and against all oppressive powers of this world's enslaving patriarchal structures.

A feminist Christian spirituality therefore calls us to gather together the *ekklēsia of women* who in the angry power of the Spirit are sent forth to feed, heal, and liberate their people who are women. It unmasks and sets us free from the structural sins and alienation of sexism, racism, and exploitation, and propels us to become children and spokeswomen of God. It rejects the idolatrous worship of maleness and articulates the Divine Image in female human existence and language. It sets us free from the internalized demands of altruism and self-sacrifice, from a mindset that is concerned with the welfare and work of men first to the detriment of our own and other women's welfare and calling. It enables us to live "for one another" and to experience the presence of God in the *ekklēsia* as the gathering of wo/men. Those of us who have heard this calling respond by committing ourselves to the liberation struggle of women and all peoples, by being accountable to women and their future, and by urging solidarity within the *ekklēsia* of women. Commitment, accountability, and solidarity in community are the hallmarks of our calling and struggle.

Two major objections are usually raised at this point: The first is that the *ekklēsia* of women does not share in the fullness of church. This is correct, but neither do male-dominated hierarchical assemblies as the actual gathering of the people of God. Such women's religious communities have always existed within the Catholic tradition. They were generated as soon as local church structures became patriarchal and hierarchical and relegated women to subordinate roles or eliminated them from church offices altogether. The male hierarchical church in turn has always sought to control these communities by colonizing them through male theology, liturgy, law, and spirituality, but was never quite able to do so. By abolishing these religious communities of women the Protestant Reformation strengthened patriarchal church structures and intensified male clerical control of women's communities in modern times. In the last centuries, however, there have arisen again and again women leaders of their people who have sought to gather communities of women free from clerical and monastic control. A Catholic feminist spirituality claims these communities of women and their history as our own heritage and seeks to transform them into the *ekklēsia* of women by claiming our own spiritual powers and gifts, by deciding our own welfare, by standing accountable for our decisions, in short, by rejecting the patriarchal structures of lay-women and nun-women, which deeply divide us along sexual lines.

The second objection made to the expression "*ekklēsia* of women" is the charge of reverse sexism and the appeal to "mutuality with men" whenever women gather together as the *ekklēsia* of women in Her name. However, such an objection does not sufficiently realize the gravity of the issues of patriarchal oppression and power. It looks too quickly for easy grace after having paid lip-service to the structural sin of sexism. Do we call it "reverse imperialism" if the poor of South and Central America gather together as a people? Or do we call it "reverse colonialism" whenever Africans or Asians gather together as a people? We do not do so because we know too well that the coming together of those who are exploited does not spell the oppression of the rich or that the oppressed are gaining power over white Western men and nations; rather it means the political bonding of oppressed people in their struggle for economic and cultural survival. Why do men then feel threatened by the bonding of women in the struggle for liberation? Why then can churchmen not understand and accept that Christian women gather together for the sake of our spiritual survival as Christians and as women? It is not over and against men that we gather together but in order to become *ekklēsia* before God, deciding matters affecting our own spiritual welfare and struggle.

Because the spiritual colonialization of women by men has entailed our internalization of the Divine as male, men have to relinquish their spiritual and religious control over women as well as over the church as the people of God, if mutuality is to become a real possibility. Women in turn must reclaim their spiritual powers and exorcise their possession by male idolatry before such mutuality can become reality. True, "the dream of a common language" belongs to God's alternative world of co-humanity engendered by the power of the Spirit. Yet it can become reality among the people of God only when male idolatry and its demonic structures are rejected in the confession of the structural and personal sin of sexism, and the fullness of *ekklēsia* becomes a possibility in a genuine conversion of individual persons and ecclesiastical structures. Not women, but churchmen exclude women from "breaking the bread and sharing the cup" in eucharistic table community. Churchmen, not women, prevent us from proclaiming the presence of God in our midst.

Images have a great power in our lives. For almost two hundred years two biblical images have dominated the American women's movement in and outside of organized religion. Today the image of *Eden-Home* determines the arguments and appeals of the so-called Moral Majority, while that of *Exodus* has inspired radical feminism calling us to abandon the oppressive confines of home and church. The "cult of true womanhood" proclaims that the vocation of women is "homemaker." The fulfillment of her true nature and happiness consists in creating the home as a peaceful island in the sea of alienated society, an Eden-Paradise to which men can retreat from the exploitations and temptations of the work-world. Women must provide a climate of peace and happiness, of self-sacrificing love and self-effacing gentility, in the home, in order to "save the family." Therefore, the spiritual calling of women is superior to that of men. This glorification of femininity conveniently overlooks that poor and unmarried women cannot afford to stay "at home," it overlooks the violence done to women and children

in the home, and it totally mistakes patriarchal dependency for
Christian family.

The *Exodus* image on the other hand compels women to leave
everything they treasure: loving community with men, shelter and
happiness, children, nurturance, and religion because all these
have contributed to their oppression and exploitation in the patriarchal family and church. Women have to move away from "the
fleshpots" of patriarchal slavery and institutions and live "in a new
space and time." The image of the Exodus calls women to move out
from the sanctity of the home, to leave the servitude of the patriarchal family, and to abandon the certitudes of patriarchal religion.
The spirituality of Exodus overlooks not only that the patriarchal
oppression of "Egypt" is everywhere, but also that God is present
not just on the boundaries but also in the center. God is "in the
midst of us" wherever and whenever we struggle for liberation.

These two biblical images – that of Eden and that of Exodus –
place us before the alternatives: Either to become Martha serving
Jesus in the home or to become Miriam, the sister of Moses, leading
her people into the desert. They, however, do not lead us into
the center of patriarchal society and church, "giving birth to" and
bringing about God's vision of co-community in our struggle and
solidarity with each other.

The Roman Catholic variant of these alternative biblical images
is the image of Martha as lay-woman serving Jesus and the family
in the home and that of Mary as nun-woman leaving the world of
family and sexuality and serving Jesus in "religious life" and patriarchally defined ecclesiastical orders. The dichotomy evoked by
the images of Exodus and Eden becomes structurally expressed
in a dichotomy of lifestyles: virgin-mother, religious-lay, spiritual-
biological. Women's sexual or spiritual relationship with men, or
lack of it, becomes constitutive for their Christian vocation. The calendar of saints therefore marks women, but not men, as "virgins"
when extolling their sanctity.[3]

Rather than define women's relationship to God by their sexual
relationship to men and through the patriarchal structures of family and church, a feminist Christian spirituality defines women's
relationship to God in and through the experience of being called
to the discipleship of equals, the assembly of free citizens who

---

3. This was pointed out by Sister Joyce Brogan in her paper "Christian Feminist
Theology: Liturgical Implications."

decide their own spiritual welfare. The image of the *ekklēsia* of women, the gathering of women as a free and decision-making assembly of God's people, replaces the other biblical images mentioned — that of Eden-home, Exodus-world, and Virgin-Mother — by integrating them with each other. It can do so however only if the structural-patriarchal dualisms are overcome in which these alternative images have their spiritual roots. The *ekklēsia* of women as the egalitarian model of church can only be sustained if we overcome the structural-patriarchal dualisms of lay-women and nun-women, homemakers and career women, active and contemplative, married women and single women, physical mothers and spiritual mothers, church and world, the sacral and the secular, heterosexual women and lesbian women — if we overcome them through and in solidarity with all women. The patriarchal divisions and competitions among women must be transformed into a movement of women as the people of God. Feminist Christian spirituality must be incarnated in a historical movement of women struggling for liberation. It must be lived in prophetic commitment, compassionate solidarity, consistent resistance, affirmative celebration, and grassroots organizations of the *ekklēsia* of women.

Such a movement of women as the people of God is truly ecumenical not only insofar as it has in common the experience of patriarchal ecclesiastical sexism, but also because it shares a central integrative image: the biblical image of God's people that is common to Jewish as well as to Christian religion. Moreover, it is distinctive but not separated from the so-called secular women's movements. Any battle against the structural sin of sexism won for Episcopalian, Jewish, or Mormon women benefits the liberation struggle of all women and vice versa. Solidarity in the struggle with poor women, women of color, Third World women, lesbian women, welfare mothers, or older and disabled women is our primary spiritual commitment and accountability.

Although most women's lives are defined by the birthing and upbringing of children the feminist movement on the whole has not paid sufficient attention to the needs of children and of women with children. The movement of women as the people of God therefore must recover the meaning of baptism as initiation into the *ekklēsia* of women, which can provide "god-mothers" who become intimately involved with the upbringing and socialization of children and young people. As a feminist ecclesial community of adults it can model the discipleship of equals from which children can receive their bodily and spiritual sustenance. Children are not just the responsibility of mothers, not even just the responsibility of both parents. Their well being and rights are given into the care of all of us, not because we are women but because they are our future.

Women as the *ekklēsia* of God have a continuous history that can claim Jesus and the early Christian movement as its roots and beginnings. This history of women as the people of God must be exposed as a history of oppression and reconstructed as a history of conversion and liberation. When I speak of the *ekklēsia* of women, I have in mind women of the past and of the present, women who acted and act in the power of the life-giving Spirit-Wisdom. Such an understanding of Catholic sisterhood that spans all ages, nations, and continents does not need to deny our hurt and anger or to cover up the injustice and violence done to women in the name of God and Christ. It also does not need to claim salvific powers for women or to narrow its understanding of sisterhood to those women who are the elect and the holy. It need not expect salvation from women because it knows that women have also internalized the structural sin of sexism and therefore can act against our own spiritual interests and leaders. It calls us to solidarity with all women of the present and the past. Such a solidarity in sisterhood allows us to treasure and recover our heritage as Christian women and as Catholic Christians. As Judy Chicago has pointed out: All the institutions of our culture seek to persuade us that we are insignificant by depriving us of our history and heritage. "But our heritage is our power."

Finally, a feminist Christian spirituality is rooted in the *ekklēsia* of women as the "body of Christ." Bodily existence is not detrimental or peripheral to our spiritually becoming *ekklēsia* but constitutive and central to it. Not the soul or the mind or the innermost self but the body is the image and model for our being church. How can we point to the eucharistic bread and say "this is my body" as long as women's bodies are battered, raped, sterilized, mutilated, prostituted, and used for male ends? How can we proclaim "mutuality with men" in the Body of Christ as long as men curtail and deny reproductive freedom and moral agency to us? As in the past so still today men fight their ideological-religious wars on the battlefields of our bodies, making us the targets of their physical or spiritual violence. Therefore, the *ekklēsia* of women must reclaim women's bodies as the "image and body of Christ." It has to denounce all violence against women as sacrilege and to maintain women's moral power and accountability for deciding our own spiritual welfare that encompasses body and soul, heart and womb.

The *ekklēsia* of women gathers together to reject the idolatry of maleness in ourselves and to call the Christian brotherhood to repentance. Yet our primary task is to nurture and support one another. In breaking the bread and sharing the cup we celebrate not only the passion and resurrection of Christ but also that of women.

14

INVOCATIONS

CONTEXTUALIZATION

In Germany prayerbooks for women are very popular. When I received the invitation to contribute to a feminist prayerbook that Susanne Kahl-Passoth edited and published in 1984,[1] I selected the following meditations and invocations for submission. I include a translation of them here not only because they speak in a different genre, but also because prayers say something not just about G–d but also about our own spiritual engagement and vision.

CREATIVE DARKNESS

Creative Darkness
You have sent to us the Sun of Justice
who reveals your truth to all your people.

Liberating Strength
You have made known
through your messengers and prophets
throughout the ages
that you are
the God of Life and not of death
the God of freedom and not of bondage

---

1. Susanne Kahl-Passoth, ed., *Was meinst du dazu, Gott? Gebete von Frauen,* GTB Siebenstern 485 (Gütersloh: Gerd Mohn, 1984).

the God of love and not of domination
the God of creativity and not of division

Strengthen your people
Holy Sustainer
that we might struggle
against exploitation and for happiness
against injustice and for liberation
against every deprivation of body and soul.

And always may we know
Your Strength
And your Love.
Nurture us,
Gentle Wisdom,
Now and in the times
Of our despair. Amen.

GLORY TO GOD-WITH-US

and peace to her people

We glorify you
we praise you
we give thanks to you
because of your overflowing grace.

Holy One

Source of all Life
Power of the Powerless
Sun of Justice
Sustaining Vision in Struggle

Hear our prayers
and let your face shine upon us.

Amen.

HOLY ONE, MOTHER OF ALL LIFE

We have sinned against you
through lack of self-respect
through lack of self-affirmation
through lack of self-love
through lack of solidarity with other women.

How can we worship you
whose image and likeness we are
if we do not respect ourselves?

How can we praise your glory
    whose image and likeness we are
    if we do not affirm ourselves?

How can we love our sister neighbor,
    if we do not love ourselves?

Forgive us our trespasses
    as we forgive those who have trespassed against us:
    those who trivialize us
    those who do not respect us
    those who weaken us
    and rob us of our power
    those who engender self-loathing
    in our hearts and minds.

And lead us not into temptation
but deliver us from the evil of patriarchal domination.

Amen.

EVEN IF A MOTHER
WOULD FORSAKE HER CHILDREN

Even if a mother would forsake her children
I will not forsake you.

The poor of this world
The hungry of this world
The rape victims of this world
The battered of this world
The violated of this world

Are women.

Women
exploited and harassed
locked away in insane asylums
prostituted and abused
maimed by beauty standards
killed in illegal abortions

and yet they do not forsake their children

children
plagued by hunger and cold
bitten by rats
imprisoned without hope
stolen for bourgeois adoption

without playgrounds and sun
held hostage by welfare bureaucracies
playthings of our society

Women cry out
    for their rights and the welfare of their children
    the right to their bodies and souls
    the right of their children to be "legitimate"
    the right to work, to equal pay, and to housing
    the right to be human in freedom and responsibility

God Our God
Holy One with a Woman's Face
    raped and prostituted
    impoverished and exploited
    hungry and without a future
    pregnant in the slums of our world

You ask all of us
    Where are your sisters?

What you have done to the least of my sisters
that you have done to me.

DIVINE WISDOM

Holy One
Invoked with a Myriad of Names

God our mother
God our sister
God our Goddess
    Holy One have mercy on us

Christ our friend
Christ our nurture
Christ our justice
    Holy Wisdom have mercy on us

Spirit of Life
Spirit of Courage
Spirit of Truth
    Holy One have mercy on us

God we have turned you into a moloch
God we have turned you into an old man
God we have turned the male into God
    Forgive our sin

You are neither Father nor Mother
You are neither Male nor Female
You are neither God nor Goddess

Our language is insufficient
Our intellect does not grasp you
Our imagination cannot get hold of you
Although we do not know what to call you
we are called by you

Your Wisdom cherishes us
Your Faithfulness remains with us
Your Justice sustains us
Your world of well-being is promised to us
Your struggle will not fail us

Everywoman is precious in your eyes
Everywoman is close to your heart
Everywoman shares in your power
Everywoman deserves dignity and justice
Everywoman will become free

Holy, most Compassionate One
Take us home in the hour of our death.
Amen

15 _____

PATRIARCHAL STRUCTURES AND THE DISCIPLESHIP OF EQUALS

A BLESSING SONG

Bless you my sister,
Bless you on your way. . . .
So go gently my sister,
Let courage be your song
You have words to say, in your own way
And stars to light your night
   And if you ever grow weary
   And your heart's song has no refrain
   Just remember we'll be waiting
   To raise you up again
And we'll bless you our sister . . .

                  —Marsie Silvestro

CONTEXTUALIZATION

In 1981 the core commissioners of the Women's Ordination Conference (WOC) decided to hold its next international conference at the "grassroots" level, bringing together women in local and regional conferences so that not just women who had the financial resources to travel and to pay for hotel costs could participate. This

---

This paper was prepared for and presented at the first Dialogue for Bishops and Women, November 12–13, 1983 in Washington, D.C., sponsored by the bishops' Committee on Women in Society and in the Church.

strategy engendered the growth of small, grassroots gatherings and "base" communities in which hundreds of women were involved. These women gathered not just for the purpose of advancing women's ordination, but also for consciousness raising, mutual support, liturgy, theological study, and spiritual reflection, as well as for political organizing and action for justice. Although these groups attracted mostly white, middle-class Catholic lay-women and nun-women, some of them were ethnically and racially mixed. Such grassroots-level meetings, which were not restricted to WOC members, paved the way for the First International Woman-Church Conference, which gathered in November of 1983 in Chicago. The conference title, "From Generation to Generation Woman Church Speaks," took up the notion of women-church that had been articulated at the Women Moving Church conference in Washington, but it changed the plural form *women* to the singular form *woman,* thereby giving the definition of women-church an essentialist slant. Although the second conference changed back to the plural form *women-church,* the tension between an essentialist "feminine" and a sociopolitical-ecclesial notion of woman remains inscribed in the self-understanding of the women-church movement.

For me, one of the most memorable events of the conference was the liturgy of blessing that was celebrated to express the intrinsic link between the women-church gathering and the bishops' dialogue with representatives of Catholic women's organizations. As one of the women invited to participate and speak at this dialogue who was also present at the Second Women-Church Conference, I was commissioned and blessed by the assembly to speak in the name of women-church, a ritual that carried all the overtones of ordination. One of the women in the audience spontaneously acknowledged this interpretation by privately giving me a stole woven in Guatemala. Its multicolored symbolism, in addition to Marsie Silvestro's blessing song — "So, go gently, my sister, let courage be your song ... " — have accompanied and encouraged me well beyond these two events of great ecclesial significance.

During the same weekend in November, the ad hoc committee on Women in Society and in the Church of the National Conference of Catholic Bishops (NCCB) had brought together thirteen women's organizations — among them WOC — that represented a wide spectrum of women. Although the idea for this dialogue was engendered by the experience some of the bishops had during their dialogue with representatives of WOC, ordination was not to be a central topic in Washington. After the national dialogue meeting had already been scheduled, Pope John Paul II admonished the American bishops during their *ad limina* visit in Rome not to support groups or individuals who promote the ordination of women to the priesthood. Since, despite such pressures, the representatives of WOC and myself, the only speaker who was "officially" associated with WOC (as a speaker at both WOC conferences and as a core commission member), were not disinvited, I decided to introduce this thorny problem "tongue in cheek" by telling a story about myself.

FEMINIST THEOLOGY begins with the systematic exploration of women's experience. Hence I would like to share with you a personal story in order to address so difficult a topic as patriarchy — the topic on which I was invited to speak.

In 1963 when I completed my M.Div. and licentiate examinations, the Second Vatican Council received a petition to consider women's ordination to the priesthood. Since I was the first woman to receive a theological degree in Würzburg, the faculty assured me that they would recommend me for ordination if the council approved of it. I replied that I did not think I had the vocation to become a pastor in an isolated village lost in the woods. However, I asserted, I do have the vocation to become a bishop. "That will never happen," the dean assured me. When I asked, "Why not?" he explained: "Because then we would depend on you and owe obedience to you."

I

I have chosen to share this personal experience not because I intend to focus my remarks on ordination but because it crystallizes what constitutes the heart of patriarchy: dependence on and control by men in power. Obedience is the essence of patriarchy. Rather than explore the historical situation preceding classical patriarchy or define patriarchy simply as the rule of all men over all women, I work with a classical definition of patriarchy: Patriarchy is a complex political-economic-legal system that found its classical expression in Athenian democracy and its systemic articulation in Aristotelian philosophy.[1]

Aristotelian political philosophy was concerned with the relationship between rulers and ruled in household and state.[2] Against the Sophists Aristotle stressed that the patriarchal relationships of the household and state are based not on economic function and social convention but on "nature." He insisted that the discussion of political ethics must begin with household management and marriage, which he defined as the union between "natural" ruler and subject. Against those who argue that slavery is contrary to human nature, Aristotle maintains "that all human beings that differ as widely as the soul from the body . . . are by nature slaves" who must be ruled by patriarchal authority "just as it is natural and expedient for the body to be governed by the soul" (*Politics* 12:60a). Not only the order of the household but that of the state is jeopardized if patriarchal rule is not exercised faithfully. It is therefore the freeborn, propertied male head of the household who is both a full citizen and a truly human being.

That the categories of property, social function, and dependence are the crucial elements in classical patriarchy is already obvious in Plato's utopian thought. In the *Republic* Plato describes the ideal city-state, which is ruled by the guardians. He understands the city-state as a united patriarchal household in which private property is communalized. Freeborn women and children as well as slaves are no longer the property of individual male heads of households but the property of all elite men. Since the private household is abolished women of the aristocratic class are freed from their "natural" social-economic functions in the household and therefore can participate in the administration of the city-

---

1. "Patriarchy" is often used interchangeably with "sexism" or "androcentrism." I distinguish both and understand androcentrism and sexist dualism as ideological mindsets or legitimations generated by patriarchy, and racism, sexism, and classism as structural components of patriarchal society and ideology. An understanding of patriarchy solely in terms of male supremacy and misogyny cannot articulate the interaction of racism, classism, and sexism in contemporary society. For discussion of the different meanings of patriarchy see Veronica Beechey, "On Patriarchy," *Feminist Review* 1 (1979): 66–82.

2. Ernest Barker, ed., *The Politics of Aristotle* (New York: Oxford University Press, 1962); Lynda Lange, "Woman Is Not a Rational Animal: On Aristotle's Biology of Reproduction"; Elizabeth V. Spelman, "Aristotle and the Politization of the Soul"; and Judith Hicks Steihm, "The Unit of Political Analysis: Our Aristotelian Hangover," all three in *Discovering Reality: Feminist Perspectives on Epistemology, Metaphysics, Methodology, and Philosophy of Science*, ed. Sandra Harding and Merill B. Hintikka (Boston: D. Reidel, 1983), 1–15, 17–30, 31–43.

state household. They are no longer the sexual property of their husbands but that of all freeborn men. Hence the relative political liberation of aristocratic women does not lead to their sexual liberation nor to the economic-civil liberation of all women, since for the functioning of the ideal city-state slaves and metics (resident aliens) — women and men — remain of crucial importance. The relative emancipation of some upper-class women does not lead to the liberation of all women from patriarchal domination.

Marilyn Arthur, the classics scholar, has argued that the articulation of the polarity between the sexes and the difference in male and female nature is not yet explicit in the writings of the aristocratic period but only emerges with the introduction of Athenian democracy.[3] While previously the inferior status of women was not explicit, now the political and legal structures of the state prescribe women's subservience and exclude freeborn women from citizenship. Not polytheistic or monotheistic patriarchal religion but politics and economics are the sustaining rationale for patriarchal domination. Explicit articulation of the specific "natures" of the subordinate members of the household is occasioned by the contradiction between the social-political structures of Athenian democracy restricting full citizenship to free propertied male heads of households and the democratic ideal of human dignity and freedom first articulated in the middle-class democracy of the city-state.

In short, ideological polarity and misogynist dualism as well as philosophical justifications of social-patriarchal roles as based on distinctive human "natures" of slaves and freeborn women seem to be generated by a social-political situation where the equality and dignity of all humans are articulated but their actual participation in political and social self-determination is prohibited because they remain the economic or sexual property of freeborn male heads of households.

The same contradiction between democratic ideals and social-patriarchal political and legal structures also characterizes modern Western society. Feminist political philosophers have shown that Aristotelian patriarchal philosophy also undergirds Western

---

3. Marilyn B. Arthur, "Women in the Ancient World," in *Conceptual Frameworks of Studying Women's History,* Sarah Lawrence College Women's Studies Publication (New York, 1975), 1–15; and her "Liberated Women: The Classical Era," in *Becoming Visible: Women in European History,* ed. Renate Bridenthal and Claudia Koonz (Boston: Houghton Mifflin, 1977), 60–89.

democratic society and legal-political philosophy.[4] Although the patriarchal family has been modified in the course of history, the split between the private and public spheres has been intensified through industrialization. Capitalism has not replaced patriarchy but modified and reinforced it.[5] Contemporary political philosophy and law still work with the Aristotelian premise that the free, educated, propertied male is the full citizen, whereas all the other members of the population – women, colonialized peoples, and the "working classes"[6] – support the few free, propertied, usually older, white males who determine our economic and political life.

Even though liberalism understands society to be constituted of independent and free individuals, the family and not the adult human person is the basic political unit for liberal as well as nonliberal philosophy. Since the wife is responsible for the economic and emotional climate of the private sphere, she can take on outside responsibilities only after she has successfully taken care of her domestic responsibilities. Even minority and working-class women, who could never afford just to stay at home and take care of their own households, are responsible for household maintenance and child-rearing. Whatever professional or public function a woman fulfills, housework and childcare are her primary responsibilities.

The patriarchal separation between the public male sphere and the private female domain generates a separate system of economics for women.[7] The women's system of economics is based on the assumption that every family consists of the ideal father earning the living for the family. It is justified by the assumption that all women are either temporary workers or work for pin-money

---

4. See esp. Susan Moller Okin, *Women in Western Political Thought* (Princeton: Princeton University Press, 1979), and Hannelore Schröder, "Feministische Gesellschaftstheorie," in *Feminismus: Inspektion der Herrenkultur,* ed. Luise F. Pusch, Suhrkamp NT 192 (Frankfurt: Suhrkamp, 1983), 449–76; and Schröder, "Das Recht der Väter," in *Feminismus,* 477–506.

5. See esp. Zilla L. Eisenstein, *The Radical Future of Liberal Feminism* (New York: Longman, 1981), and Heidi Hartmann, "Capitalism, Patriarchy, and Job Segregation by Sex," in *The Signs Reader: Women, Gender & Scholarship,* ed. Elizabeth Abel and Emily K. Abel (Chicago: University of Chicago Press, 1983), 193–225.

6. According to Zilla Eisenstein the tension between the interests of capitalism and that of patriarchy come especially to the fore in the case of the working (i.e., wage-earning) wife and mother. See also Ann Oakley, *The Sociology of Housework* (Bath: Pitman, 1974).

7. See *Fact Sheets on Institutional Sexism* (New York: Council on Interracial Books for Children, 1982); Lisa Leghorn and Katherine Parker, *Women's Worth: Sexual Economics and the World of Women* (Boston: Routledge & Kegan, 1981).

because they will get married and become pregnant. Lower wages and lower-level positions for women are justified because women's wages are presumed to be supplementary. Since it is believed that housework and childcare are women's "natural" vocation, they need not be remunerated or counted in the gross national product. The result of this separate system of economics for women is the increasing feminization of poverty and the destitution of female-headed households.[8]

In 1980 a United Nations survey of eighty-six nations (including the United States) found that while women and girls are half of the world's population, they do two-thirds of the world's work hours, receive a tenth of the world's income, and own less than a hundredth of the world's property. Two out of three of the world's illiterates are women. The import of Western technology and "development" does not improve the economic status of women. To the contrary, it undermines their traditional economic resources and public influence. The patriarchal economic system of women is moreover stamped by racism. All statistics consistently show that women of color earn less than their white sisters.They suffer from multiple patriarchal oppressions because racism and poverty are economically overshadowed by sexism insofar as all American men earn more than all American women.[9]

Finally, this separate economic system for women sustains female "sexual slavery," which cuts across all lines of race, class, and culture.[10] Whereas patriarchal racism defines certain people as subhuman in order to exploit their labor, patriarchal sexism seeks to control women's procreative powers. Since children in patriarchy are considered to be the property of the father and master, female virginity before marriage and female chastity in marriage are strictly enforced in order to insure that the child is "legitimate." In classical antiquity the father had the right over the life of wife and children, the husband had the right of unlimited intercourse, and the master the right over slave women and men. Rape was viewed as an offense against the property rights of the freeborn husband, father, or master. At the heart of patriarchy is

---

8. See esp. "Who Is Poor in America? The Feminization of Poverty," *Probe* 11, no. 4 (May/June 1982).

9. For the double jeopardy of black and minority women see Diane K. Lewis, "A Response to Inequality: Black Women, Racism, and Sexism," in *The Signs Reader,* 169–91.

10. Kathleen Barry, *Female Sexual Slavery* (New York: Avon Books, 1979).

the control of women's reproductive powers and their economic dependency.

Patriarchal exploitation and control of women's reproductive powers engender domination and violence against women and children also today: One out of every three women in this country is raped in her lifetime. Fifty percent of the rape victims are under eighteen years of age; 25 percent are under twelve. One out of every two wives has been beaten by her husband. Eighty-five percent of the wives killed by their husbands made at least one call to the police, 50 percent made five or more calls to the police during prior episodes of violence, but received no help. One out of every four female children is sexually abused during childhood, usually by close family members or friends. Seventy percent of young prostitutes, while still living at home, were forced by a father or other relative to have sexual relations. Eighty percent of the women who work outside the home report being sexually harassed on the job.[11]

Violence against women and children is increasing precisely when women claim the full human rights and dignity accorded to male citizens. The fight of the political Right against the Equal Rights Amendment, their battle for the recriminalization of women and doctors in the case of abortion, and their rhetoric about the "protection of the American family" seek to reinforce women's economic dependency, to strengthen the patriarchal controls of women's reproductive powers, and to maintain the patriarchal family as the mainstay of the patriarchal state.[12]

---

11. The documentation and analysis of sexual violence against women and children is too extensive to be listed here. See E. Morgan, *The Erotization of Male Dominance/Female Submission* (New York: Putnam, 1981); Debra Lewis and Lorenne M. G. Clark, *Rape: The Price of Coercive Sexuality* (Toronto: Women's Press, 1977); Catherine A. MacKinnon, *Sexual Harassment of Working Women* (New Haven: Yale University Press, 1979); Andrea Dworkin, *Pornography: Men Possessing Women* (New York: Putnam, 1981); Judith Herman, *Father-Daughter Incest* (Cambridge: Harvard University Press, 1981); Florence Rush, *The Best Kept Secret: Sexual Abuse of Children* (New York: McGraw-Hill, 1980); Diana Russell, *Rape in Marriage* (New York: Macmillan, 1982); R. Emerson Dobash and Russell Dobash, *Violence against Wives* (New York: Free Press, 1979); and the review article by W. Brines and L. Gordon, "The New Scholarship on Family Violence," *Signs* 8 (1983): 490–531.

12. See Deirdre English, "The War Against Choice: Inside the Antiabortion Movement," *Mother Jones* (February/March, 1981): 16–32. For a comparison of the rhetoric of the political Right in America with the propaganda machine of Nazi Germany see Flo Conway and Jim Siegelman, *Holy Terror: The Fundamentalist War on America's Freedoms in Religion, Politics, and Our Private Lives* (Garden City, N.Y.: Doubleday, 1982). For a feminist proposal for a just Christian social order see esp. Beverly Wildung Harrison, *Our Right to Choose: Toward a New Ethic of Abortion* (Boston: Beacon Press, 1983).

II

The same basic contradiction between the claim to full equality of all citizens and the subordinate position of some persons in the patriarchal structures that characterize Athenian and modern Western democracy also characterizes contemporary Christianity. Such a contradiction between the call to the discipleship of equals and patriarchal ecclesial structures was introduced toward the end of the first century in the process of ecclesial adaptation to Greco-Roman society and culture. We have considerable evidence that Aristotle's patriarchal philosophy was revitalized in neo-Pythagorean and Stoic philosophy in reaction to the increased emancipation and independence of first-century women. Probably for the same reasons it was also adopted by Hellenistic Jewish writers such as Philo and Josephus.

This adoption and modification of the Aristotelian patriarchal ethos took place in the face of certain more egalitarian aspirations of Hellenistic and Roman society, since the general economic development allowed for the greater advancement of slave women and men and the greater independence of freeborn women from patriarchal control. While professing to strengthen the traditional patriarchal household, Augustan legislation actually undermined it insofar as the emperor increasingly arrogated to himself the powers of the *paterfamilias.* The same Aristotelian pattern of patriarchal submission also found its way into the New Testament.[13] The so-called household-code texts, which demand subordination and obedience from wives, children, and slaves, participate in this stabilizing reception of patriarchal political philosophy in the first centuries of our era.

Studies of the social world of early Christianity have indicated that from their very beginning early Christian community and life did not conform to the patriarchal ethos and structures of their own society and religion. Studies of the Jesus-movements in Palestine have highlighted that they were reform movements within Judaism that stressed the gracious goodness of the Sophia-Creator God who wants the wholeness of everyone in Israel without

---

13. See Klaus Thraede, "Zum historischen Hintergrund der 'Haustafeln' des NT," *Jahrbuch für Antike und Christentum,* Ergänzungsband 8 (1981): 359–68; David Balch, "Household Ethical Codes in Peripatetic, Neopythagorean and Early Christian Moralists," in *SBL Seminar Papers II,* ed. Paul J. Achtemeier (Missoula, Mont.: Scholars Press, 1977), 397–404.

exception.[14] Wholeness and inclusiveness are the distinguishing marks of the Jesus-movements. Jesus promised God's common-weal (*basileia*) not to the rich, the pious, or the learned but to the poor, the destitute, and the prostitutes. This inclusive charac-ter of the Jesus-movements allowed women as well as men, poor as well as rich, cultically unclean as well as strict observers of the Torah to become followers of Jesus. Women such as Mary of Magdala were among the most prominent and faithful dis-ciples of Jesus. The Church "Fathers" acknowledge her as the key witness and disciple when they call her the "apostle of the apostles."

Discipleship in the Jesus-movements required the breaking of natural kinship ties and household relationships. Those who followed Jesus received instead a new familial community. For example, Mark 3:31–35 contrasts Jesus' natural family, which is "outside," with his new family sitting around him "inside" the house. In Mark 10:28–30 Jesus assures Peter, the spokesperson of the disciples, that all who have left their households and severed their kinship ties will receive a much greater family – however, only under persecutions. According to Mark 13:12 such persecu-tions, sufferings, and executions will be instigated by their own families and households.

This new "kinship" of equal discipleship, however, has no room for "fathers." Whereas "fathers" are mentioned among those left behind, they are not included in the new kinship of the Jesus-movements, which the disciples acquire "already now in this time." Insofar as this new "family" has no room for "fathers," it implic-itly rejects their patriarchal power and status, and thereby claims that in its midst all patriarchal structures of domination and sub-ordination are abolished. Rather than reproducing the patriarchal relationships of the "household" in antiquity, the Jesus-movements demand a radical break with them.

The child/slave who occupies the lowest place within patri-archal structures becomes the primary paradigm for the true discipleship-community. Such true discipleship is not measured on the father/master position but on that of the child/slave. This can be seen in the paradoxical Jesus-saying: "Whoever does not receive the *basileia* of God like a child/slave shall not enter it"

---

14. For a review and discussion of the literature see my book *In Memory of Her: A Feminist Theological Reconstruction of Christian Origins* (New York: Crossroad, 1983), 69–84, 105–59.

(Mark 10:15). This saying is not an invitation to childlike inno-
cence and naiveté but a challenge to relinquish all claims of power
and domination over others.

The importance of this saying for the Jesus-movements is indicated both by its inclusion in the synoptic tradition in a sevenfold
combination and by its transmission in very different situations
and forms. The ecclesial process of interpretation applied a saying
originally addressed to the socially well-to-do in Israel to its own
relationships within the discipleship of equals. Structures of domination should not be tolerated in the discipleship-community of
Jesus, but those who would be great or first among the disciples
must be servants/slaves of all. Therefore, all patriarchal roles and
titles are rejected in Matt. 23:8–11: The discipleship of equals rejects teachers because it is constituted and taught by one, and only
one, teacher. Similarly, the kinship relationship in the discipleship
of equals does not admit of any "father" because it is sustained by
the gracious goodness of God whom alone the disciples of Jesus
call "father" (Luke 11:2–4; 12:30; cf. Mark 11:25). The "father" God
is invoked here not to justify patriarchal structures and relationships in the community of disciples but precisely to reject all such
claims, powers, and structures.

Although Paul only once calls Christians "members of the
household of faith" (Gal. 6:10), the family metaphor is also a key
image in the Pauline communities. Christians are called brothers
and sisters; as adopted children they are co-heirs with Christ (Rom.
8:14–17). God is addressed with the intimate familial name "abba."
The leaders of the missionary movements are called household
stewards (1 Cor. 4:1–2; 9:17), household servants, or slaves. At
the same time Paul can understand himself in nurturing paternal
or maternal terms. As members of the new "family," as siblings,
Christians eat common meals together and greet each other with
a "holy kiss." Conversion makes slaves, e.g., into "beloved family
members" not only in an ecclesial context but also in everyday
social interaction within the house-church (see Paul's letter to
Philemon).

True, we find analogous familial language also in the Hebrew
Bible and in Jewish theology. Israel is very early called the household of God; its members are brothers and sisters, sons and
daughters. Such familial language does not imply however the
abolition of patriarchal social relationships. A basic difference in
Jewish and early Christian self-understanding does not quite come

to the fore in "word-studies" but is succinctly pointed out by the Jewish scholar Raphael Loewe:

> The sociological basis on which Christianity rests is not the tie of kinship, as in the case of Judaism, but that of fellowship — fellowship in Christ. Such fellowship may acknowledge kinship as a potentiality ... or it may repudiate it ... Whatever position it takes the ties of kinship are for Christianity in the last resort expendable.[15]

While one is born into Judaism, the Christian movement is based solely on conversion, which does not continue the national, racial, or social status prerogatives derived from the patriarchal household. In baptism converts enter into a new kinship relationship with people coming from very different religious, cultural, and social backgrounds and patriarchal relationships. These former status differences are not to determine the social and religious structures of the new community.

It is widely recognized today that Galatians 3:28 is not a theological peak-formulation of Paul's but a pre-Pauline baptismal formula that Paul quotes in order to assert the equality of Jewish and Gentile Christians. Krister Stendahl has pointed out that the third pair of the formula refers to Genesis 1:27, which qualifies humanity created in the image of God as male and female in order to introduce the theme of family and procreation.[16] Jewish exegesis understood this qualification primarily in terms of marriage and not in terms of androgyny, just as Markan theology cites the expression in order to evoke the image of the first couple (10:6). Therefore, Galatians 3:28c probably asserts that marriage and family status are no longer constitutive for the new community in Christ. Irrespective of their marriage or household status persons are full members of the Christian movement in and through baptism.

In declaring all religious-patriarchal status differences between Jews and Gentiles, slave and free, married and unmarried as irrelevant for status in the community of Christ, Galatians 3:28 also rejects the religious prerogatives and patriarchal privileges of freeborn (Jewish) male heads of households, since Galatians 3:28 runs counter to the general acceptance of male religious privileges among Greeks, Romans, Persians, or Jews. Since social-patriarchal privileges in antiquity also implied religious privileges, conversion

---

15. Raphael Loewe, *The Position of Women in Judaism* (London: SPCK, 1966), 52ff.
16. Krister Stendahl, *The Bible and the Role of Women* (Philadelphia: Fortress Press, 1966). For a review of the literature see Hans Dieter Betz, *Galatians* (Philadelphia: Fortress Press, 1979).

of freeborn elite men to the Christian movement meant relinquishing their religious prerogatives based on their social status in the patriarchal household of antiquity. Because they accepted persons as full members irrespective of their patriarchal status and because they rejected patriarchal prerogatives and power, the early Christian missionary movements stood in tension with the dominant Greco-Roman society.

Not the "waning of eschatological expectation" or the "enthusiastic excesses" of slaves or women but the realization of an alternative egalitarian vision and egalitarian communal structures occasioned the introduction of the Aristotelian pattern of patriarchal submission into the prescriptive statements of the post-Pauline writings. Whereas the prescriptive injunctions for patriarchal submission in Colossians and 1 Peter address Christian slaves and wives living in pagan households, Ephesians and the Pastoral Epistles address slaves and wives living in Christian households. Moreover, the Pastorals begin to understand the Christian community as a whole in terms of the patriarchal household insofar as they formulate as a requirement for Christian leadership that one must have proven himself to be an excellent *paterfamilias* in terms of the dominant Greco-Roman patriarchal ethos. However, the fact that such patriarchal injunctions became necessary indicates that the communal praxis and life of the churches in Asia Minor at the end of the first century were not yet patriarchally structured.[17]

By reinforcing the patriarchal submission of those who according to Aristotle must be ruled, the household-code injunctions rob the early Christian ethos of co-equal discipleship of its capacity to structurally transform the patriarchal order of family and state. In seeking to adapt the Christian community to its patriarchal society these late New Testament texts open it up to political co-optation by the Roman empire. That such a co-optation process required centuries speaks for the vitality of the early Christian ethos of co-equal discipleship. In the process, however, the vision of *agapē* and service, mutuality and solidarity among Christians no longer connotes a "new reality" but becomes

---

17. See my "Discipleship and Patriarchy: Early Christian Ethos and Christian Ethics in a Feminist Theological Perspective," *Papers of the American Society of Christian Ethics* (Waterloo, Ont., 1982), 131–72; reprinted in *Bread Not Stone: The Challenge of Feminist Biblical Interpretation* (Boston: Beacon Press, 1984).

reduced to mere moral appeal. Submission and obedience, but not equality and justice, are institutionalized by this patriarchal ethos.

Insofar as this ethos of submission was not restricted to the household but also adopted by the church in subsequent centuries, the Christian vision and praxis of "equality from below" no longer could provide a structural-political alternative to its patriarchal Greco-Roman culture. Its preaching of the gospel and its patriarchal structures became a contradiction that robbed the gospel of its historical-structural transformative power. The gradual adaptation of the Christian movement to Roman imperialist-patriarchal structures seems to have made the church in the long run more Roman than Christian.

III

Insofar as both early Christian traditions, that of the discipleship of equals and that of the Aristotelian pattern of patriarchal submission, were incorporated into the canonical Scriptures of Christians, they have influenced Christian self-understanding and community throughout the centuries. Insofar as the gradual patriarchalization and hierarchalization of the church in subsequent centuries opened the doors for the adaptation of the church to the imperial structures of the Roman state, the patriarchal model of church has become historically dominant. However, a historical analysis can show that this model of patriarchal church is more determined by Roman imperial structures than by the Christian vision of the discipleship of equals. The Constantinian church criticized by political and liberation theology derives its structures of control from Greco-Roman patriarchy.

Just as societal patriarchy so also religious Christian patriarchy has defined not only women but also subjugated peoples and races as "the other," as "nature" to be exploited and dominated by powerful men. It has defined women not just as "the other" of men but also as subordinated and subjected to men. Since patriarchy has defined not only societal structures and ideologies but also ecclesial structures and theologies, Christian church and theology have often not only legitimated but also perpetrated societal patriarchy, which specifies women's oppression not simply in terms of race and class but also in terms of sexuality and patriarchal marriage. Today the political Right's "holy war"[18] against the women's movement in society is again fought with the weapons of patriarchal biblical religion. Over and against the religious claims of patriarchy in society and church a feminist theology of liberation insists that the victimization and dehumanization of the poorest and most despised women on earth exhibits the full death-dealing powers of patriarchal evil while their struggle for survival and self-determination expresses the fullest experience of God's grace in our midst.

Within the patriarchal model of church we find two distinct hierarchical subsystems, that of women and that of men (see the chart on p. 226). While the patriarchal male system rests on clerical obedience and sub-ordination as well as sexual control through the requirement of celibacy, that of women is built on patriarchal marriage or male control of canonical women's communities. In this patriarchal model of church the reality of the church is coextensive with that of the male hierarchy. It is best described as patriarchal hierarchy, a term used here not to label this model of church but to accurately define it. It is patriarchal in its structures because one ordained male — usually older — stands on top of the pyramid and has "jurisdiction" over younger male clergy bound to him in obedience as well as over the laity, women and men. This model of church sustains communal life by control from the top to the bottom. Obedience and loyalty to the pope, the bishop, the pastor, the superior, or the husband are the responses required of those who are the "subordinates." Religious obedience and economic dependence are the sustaining force of ecclesial patriarchy.

The church understood as clerical-patriarchal hierarchy not only is exclusive of women in leadership, but also establishes its boundaries through sexual control and celibacy. It does not center church around the strength and needs of its members or of humanity as a whole but around institutional patriarchal interests. It needs the laity either as objects of pastoral "care," as consumers of sacramental-liturgical goods, or as a subsidiary work force, but not as fully responsible ecclesial participants and decision-makers. It admits women into its patriarchal ranks only if we accept male

---

18. For this expression see Charlene Spretnak, "The Christian Right's 'Holy War' against Feminism," in *The Politics of Women's Spirituality* (New York: Anchor Books, 1982), 470–96, and Shirley Rogers Radl, *The Invisible Woman: Target of the Religious New Right* (New York: Dell Publishing Co., 1983).

"CONSTANTINIAN" ROMAN PATRIARCHAL MODEL OF CHURCH

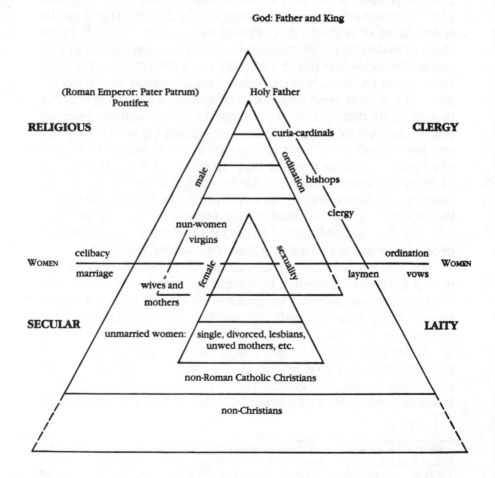

control and are prepared to fulfill the "wife-role" as it is defined by patriarchal family and society.

Those of us who according to Canon Law are "religious" and live in canonically controlled institutions are subject to patriarchal control and clerical obedience without having male clerical sacramental powers. As "brides of Christ," who in traditional spirituality have repressed their carnal femaleness as much as possible, we have clerical "wife" status within the male patriarchal pyramid. Just as the wife in patriarchal marriage cannot control her own property, cannot retain her own name, is not free to choose her own residence and lifestyle, is not paid for her labors, and is controlled in her dress and behavior, so also women in canonical, male-controlled communities are vowed to obedience to men, are economically dependent on men through their vow of poverty, are sexually controlled through the promise of virginity, have to follow men-made laws, and cannot determine their own and their sisters' spiritual-religious well-being.

Those of us who are wives and mothers are second in the rank of sexual hierarchy among women in the patriarchal model of church. We also are not permitted by the male hierarchy to control our own procreative powers, to leave oppressive marriage relationships, and to define our present and future well-being as well as that of our children. While nun-women are paid only minimally for their labors within the patriarchal church, lay-women are expected to volunteer their talents and labors so that we do not become economically independent in patriarchal marriage relationships.[19]

Those of us who are neither in canonical communities nor in patriarchal marriage relationships have no status whatever in the Constantinian patriarchal pyramid of the Roman church. No religious ceremony or sacramental rite makes us visible within the female pyramid of the patriarchal church. Single women, unwed mothers, lesbians, or divorced women are at best invisible and at worst declared to be public sinners.

Rather than seek incorporation into the male patriarchal pyramid through ordination, we must seek to become free from the spiritual and economic bondage of the patriarchal model of

---

19. For the LCWR/CARA study on "Women and Ministry" see Doris Gottemoeller and Rita Hofbauer, *Women and Ministry: Personal Experience and Future Hopes* (Washington, D.C.: LCWR, 1981), and my contribution: "We Are Still Invisible: Theological Analysis of 'Women and Ministry,' " 29–43 (included as chapter 12 in the present volume.

church. We can do so only if we cease to define ourselves in terms of ecclesial or marital status and patriarchal dependency and stop identifying ourselves in and through male structures and definitions rather than through the call to Christian discipleship.

A historical exploration of the patriarchalization of the discipleship-community of equals elucidates that the exclusion of women from church leadership and our ghettoization in male-controlled celibate communities go hand in hand with the reaffirmation of the bondage of slave women and slave men as well as with the spiritualization of poverty. Therefore, if theology and church are to cease to perpetrate the societal-patriarchal oppression of poor and marginalized women, the patriarchal model of church must be transformed into the church of self-identified women and men who identify with women's struggles. The struggles against religious-ecclesial patriarchy are at the heart of societal liberation struggles against racism, colonialism, militarism, or poverty, and vice versa.

The ecclesial reform movements of this century culminating in Vatican II have rediscovered the communal-participatory model of church actualized in the early Christian movements as well as in other reform-movements throughout Christian history. This model of church does not define church as patriarchal hierarchy but as the people of God. The constitutive sacrament for this model of church is not ordination but baptism. The church as the pilgrim people of God stands in continuity with Israel and in solidarity with all the peoples of the world. Ministry is a function of the whole church vis-à-vis the whole world. Those ministries directed toward the nurturing and "up-building" of the community are the prerogative and in the power of all those baptized. Ministry in this model of church has a twofold function: it is outer-directed toward the whole "world" in proclaiming the gospel and in ministering to those who are in need and are powerless. At the same time ministry is inner-directed toward the "church": nurturing, empowering, enabling, and challenging the faith-community.[20]

---

20. For a similar emphasis see also Edward J. Kilmartin, "Lay Participation in the Apostolate of the Hierarchy," in *Official Ministry in a New Age*, ed. James H. Provost (Washington, D.C.: Canon Law Society, Catholic University of America, 1981), 89–116. He distinguishes as competing models of church in the documents of Vatican II "juridical ecclesiology" and "christomonistic communion ecclesiology" but proposes a third ecclesiological model, which he terms "trinitarian ecclesiology." He argues that the council has made the attempt to integrate "the role of the Holy Spirit into the christological dimension of Church" but "has never made the attempt to show how

Ministry in its twofold form is the responsibility of all: it is not a prerogative or privilege of a clerical class or the male sex, but is rooted in the baptism of all believers. This model of church has engendered in the past twenty years or so very different forms of community and service within Roman Catholicism. It has enabled all members of the church, especially women, to become actively involved in ecclesial as well as sociopolitical ministries. I would therefore like to name this model the participatory-inclusive Catholic (not Greco-Roman) model of church.

This second model of church is not biblicist or archaic because it is decisively influenced by contemporary democratic-social understandings, as well as by the ecclesial-sociological change from a church into which one is born to a church which one chooses. However, this model of church is also the most "conservative" model insofar as it resembles some of the New Testament structures of church and therefore can claim Jesuanic and apostolic succession.

Insofar as Vatican II elaborated the collegial and familial "brotherhood" dimension of church, it sought to transform the patriarchal model of church. In accordance with the New Testament the council stressed the priesthood of all believers, defined the character of ecclesial office as service, emphasized that the church's mission is to the world, and asserted that other Christian churches with different institutional structures are "ecclesial" communities. The council also sought to redefine the hierarchical-clerical model of ministry by using the expression "ecclesiastical ministry" (*ministerium ecclesiasticum*) rather than hierarchy, and by stressing that such ecclesiastical ministry is divinely instituted. Whereas Trent taught that ecclesial ministry consists of the hierarchy of bishop, priest, and deacon, Vatican II teaches that ecclesial ministry is exercised in these different orders.[21]

---

the ministries of the laity and the ordained derive from the mystery of the Spirit-filled Church and are ordered to one another without the one simply being under the control of the other" (107).

21. *Lumen Gentium* 28: "Thus the divinely established ecclesiastical ministry is exercised on different levels by those who from antiquity have been called bishops, priests and deacons." *Lumen Gentium* 32 also stresses with reference to Galatians 3:28: "There is in Christ and in the church no inequality on the basis of race or nationality, social condition or sex" as well as explains the authority of ecclesiastical ministry in terms of service and nurturance of the community. It seems thus that the council at least indirectly rejects here Greco-Roman patriarchal structures, although the ecclesiological implications are not drawn out. For the translation see Walter M. Abbott, ed., *The Documents of Vatican II* (New York: Herder and Herder, Association Press, 1966), 53,

The NCCB/LCWR study of 1978 documents that this second, participatory model of church has been most actualized in canonical women's communities. In these communities a shift has taken place from pyramidal-hierarchical to circular models of government. Government is related to contemporary needs. Accountability, participation, and communication are stressed. Authority is exercised from *within* the community and not from above. Leadership functions as integrating, enabling, focusing, facilitating, inspiring, empowering, and challenging ministry to the community.[22] However, insofar as neither the theology of Vatican II nor the sisters renewal movement in the United States has directly addressed the male and female subsystems of the patriarchal church nor questioned the economic and spiritual dependency and obedience required by these subsystems, the second model of church could not yet develop its full transformative powers.

In conclusion: I have outlined the structures and destructive powers of patriarchy in Greco-Roman and contemporary society in order to point to the ramifications of ecclesiastical patriarchy. Placing the "women's issue" in the wider context of societal and hierarchical patriarchy indicates that an incorporation of women into clerical-patriarchal structures will not engender the transformation of the patriarchal model of church. The imperative to struggle against patriarchal structures in society and church comes from the realization of the dehumanizing effects of patriarchal structures fostering racism, sexism, and colonialist imperialism. Such an impetus to overcome the death-dealing powers of patriarchy is derived both from this struggle of women and from a systemic analysis of dehumanizing patriarchal structures. The early Christian ethos of the discipleship of equals provides a sustaining vision in this struggle against patriarchal domination and dehumanization wherever we encounter it.

We are at a decisive historical juncture in the Roman Catholic Church and in society. Not only the future of the church but

58ff. See also Edward Schillebeeckx, *Ministry: Leadership in the Community of Jesus Christ* (New York: Crossroad, 1981), who, however, does not address the *patriarchal* aspect of hierarchical structures.

22. NCCB/LCWR Liaison Committee, *Patterns in Authority and Obedience*, researched and authored by Sr. Lora Ann Quinonez. This study shows that the communal-participatory model of church is not purely utopian but is already realized in ecclesial communities today. It also can be found in base communities especially in Latin America and Africa, but also in North America, Europe, and Asia.

also the fate of our planet will depend on whether we are able to overcome patriarchal institutional structures and ideological mind-sets engendering the domination and exploitation of the weaker members of the human community. Crucial in this process of preventing global annihilation is the rejection of the languages of oppression – sexism, racism, class exploitation, colonialism, and militarism – that denigrate all those who are not in power. If the church continues to perpetrate the Greco-Roman patriarchal structures and language of domination, it will not be able to contribute to peace, justice, and the salvation of the world. Militaristic colonialism and the dehumanization of the dominated "other" are the hallmarks of patriarchy.

At the same time as we gather here 1,250 Catholic women meeting in Chicago have realized that it depends not the least on us whether the church becomes the church from "below," women-church, the liberating and salvific sacrament of God's alternative world. I hope that the participants in this dialogue will join women-church in the rejection of the structural sin of patriarchy in society and church and in doing so will support all those dehumanized by its language and structures of oppression in their struggle for survival and liberation. Only when the church acts in solidarity with the most dehumanized, exploited, and poorest women on earth (Redstockings), only when it relinquishes its patriarchal structures and prerogatives, will it be able to become the effective sacrament of salvation for all of humanity. Conversion and solidarity but not patriarchal control, obedience, or submission must characterize our discipleship and commitment today.

POSTSCRIPT

The discussion following the presentation of the paper centered around the question of a proposed pastoral letter by the National Conference of Catholic Bishops on "Women in Society and in the Church," which subsequently was approved by the annual meeting. Although well-intentioned as a means for a broad-based discussion of "women's issues," such a procedure could aggravate our patriarchal predicament. Not only will it produce another authoritative statement about women by men in power, since women do not share in the episcopal office, but it also will not be forced to discuss crucial issues such as the ordination of women, reproductive rights, and homosexuality because of ecclesiastical discipline. Such pitfalls, I suggest, can be averted only if the bishops' discussion moves from "women as the problem" to a systemic-theological analysis of patriarchy as an ecclesial problem and sinful structure.

16

CELEBRATION IN STRUGGLE

CONTEXTUALIZATION

Each year the Women's Ordination Conference (WOC) recognizes persons who have contributed to the movement for *New Woman, New Church, and New Priestly Ministry.* I was honored to be among the first to receive this award. The invitation to the first WOC award dinner, December 12, 1984, stated the purpose of the award as follows:

> The WOC Awards are being presented to honor those women who are for us Prophetic Figures: those who, in their respective fields of endeavor, have shown us new ways of being. We celebrate the gifts of these three women in modelling new shapes to the lives we choose to lead: as activist, as member of an inclusive egalitarian community, as intellectual who gives fully of her gifts. In a year of repression, when our sisters and brothers are being persecuted because of their commitment to ministry, it is fitting to concentrate on those women who have been signs of hope.

The following remarks are also offered as a sign of gratitude to Long Island WOC for giving me in 1989 the Teresa of Avila Award.

SISTERS, FRIENDS, AND CO-WORKERS
It remains for me to join Theresa Kane and Shelly Farabaugh in expressing my deep appreciation for this recognition. I want especially to thank Ruth Fitzpatrick and the other women who

have prepared this celebration. You have managed to prove the
Scriptures wrong: Sometimes prophets are recognized in their own
town and by their own people. I appreciate this recognition especially since I have always been a part of the "critical left" in WOC,
which has consistently insisted that we should resist the clericalization of the church and its patriarchal exploitation of women,
working instead for the feminist conversion and transformation of
the church into the discipleship community of equals.

I am happy to share this celebration with Theresa, who like me
has always insisted that she has the vocation to become a bishop
rather than that to be ordained a deacon and priest. I wished I
had known her personally in 1979, when the pope visited this
city. At the time Chris was in first grade. We were at the breakfast
table when Francis told me that the pope had reiterated his objection to women's ordination. I started a tirade on why the pontiff
would pronounce on such a sensitive issue in a country where
other churches have long ordained women and anti-Catholic sentiments are still widespread in academic circles. Chris interrupted
my explosion and asked: "What are you talking about?" I cooled
down somewhat to explain that the pope, the head of the Roman
Catholic Church, was visiting this country and had said on TV that
women could not become priests, bishops, or popes. She listened
carefully, put her spoon down, and with the superiority of a six-
year-old declared: "He ought to know better! If he does not know
that girls can be anything they want to be, he ought to listen carefully to my record 'Free to be you and me'!" Just imagine if Theresa
had given him this record with the penance to listen three times
a day to it until he gets it!

We live not only in difficult times but also in a historic moment
of women-church. We live in dangerous times when the patriarchal hierarchy resorts again to violence in order to sustain their
centuries-old power. At the same time we live in times where they
no longer have the legal power to torture and burn us at the stake.
They might try to vilify us as heretics or to make us invisible and/or
marginal. Yet they cannot succeed as long as we can claim both
the authority of the gospel and the authority of our common but
different experiences for sustaining the struggle for women's consciousness, heart, and intellect. We women are church, we always
have been church, and we always will be church. Whether we
are ordained or not we are called and empowered to minister in
women-church.

I wear this stole tonight as a sign of my "ordination." It was given to me in Chicago at the Woman Church Speaks conference, and I wore it as a sign of my feminist mission and accountability at the bishops' dialogue last November. I want to thank Mary Hunt for her words of friendship reminding me of this accountability. I could not do my work without you, without the community of women here, across the country, and throughout the world. This community of women – Catholic and Protestant, white, black, and brown, nun-women and clergywomen, academic and activist, Jewish, pagan, and agnostic feminists – has empowered me to become a minister in women-church and to find my own theological voice, albeit with a foreign accent.

Here in Washington I have experienced being "at home" working with many of you belonging to WOC, WATER, Network, Catholics for a Free Choice, the Center of Concern, the Quixote Center, and LCWR, as well as celebrating the biweekly liturgies of Sisters Against Sexism. During times that were professionally very difficult for me, I could always count not only on a sympathetic ear but also on a good argument about strategic-ecclesial and theological matters.

Tonight I feel privileged to be able to thank all of you, those who are here in this room and those who cannot be here, for listening to me and for challenging me "into speech" – to use a favored expression of Nelle Morton. I want to thank you for keeping me honest and making me laugh despite my "pessimist nature." I have been able to do my work only because of so many women who have responded to it, because of the reality of women-church, because of you, my sisters in the struggle.

Tonight we have come together to celebrate: to celebrate the courage and struggle of so many women who are less fortunate than we; to celebrate women's religious engagement and imagination; to celebrate the women's liberation movement in society and religion because it makes present God's power for liberation and salvation; to celebrate the discipleship of equals whose vision calls, inspires, and sustains us. Several months ago, I was invited to celebrate the tenth anniversary of the ordination of women in the Episcopal Church. Tonight we affirm as Catholic women the ordination of feminist women priests, ministers, rabbis, and bishops in all churches and synagogues. Women-church claims them as our own ordained ministers, bishops, and leaders.

And yet. . . . Barbara Harris, the editor of the Episcopalian journal *The Witness,* entitled her report on the tenth-anniversary
celebration in Philadelphia: "Celebrating a Dream Yet to Come
True." What is this dream that still needs to be realized? Is it the
dream that women in the Roman Catholic Church finally will be
able to call ourselves Reverend, to wear a clerical collar, to buy
ourselves vestments and receive clerical tax or travel privileges? Is
it the dream of receiving the "indelible mark" of essential difference, the promotion to "upper-class" status not only in the church
but also in heaven? Is it the dream of getting a piece of the clerical
pie even if we choke on it? Do we want to be called "Father" in
exchange for promising obedience and loyalty to a patriarchal institution and for celebrating androcentric liturgies? Or is it the dream
of creating a different ministry and priesthood, of transforming the
patriarchal hierarchy into the discipleship of equals?

It has been the genius of the Women's Ordination Conference
in this country to have always insisted on women's ordination to
a "New Priesthood in a Renewed Church." This was as true for
the first ordination conference as for the second. We celebrate tonight a dream yet to come true. The exclusion of women from the
sacramental ministry of the Catholic Church remains a powerful
sign of the structural sin of patriarchal sexism. The early Christian movement and vision of the discipleship of equals, of the
ekklēsia of women, provides a sustaining vision in our struggle
against patriarchal domination in society and church.

I ended my response at the first ordination conference in Detroit with "Sisterhood is Powerful." It may sound quaint for some
today, but it is still true: Sisterhood *is* powerful when it is impelled
by the dream of the *ekklēsia* of women that inspires our struggle
for ministry in the discipleship of equals. We are not the first ones
to follow this dream and to stand up and insist on our Christian
birthright, and we are not alone in our struggle. A "great cloud of
witnesses" surrounds us and has preceded us throughout the centuries in the discipleship of equals. We derive strength and courage
from the memory of our foremothers' and foresisters' struggles for
dignity and survival.

My thanks and appreciation go to all of you who have accompanied me on this journey in the past ten years. The power of
Spirit-Sophia be with all of us.

17

CLAIMING OUR AUTHORITY AND POWER: THE *EKKLĒSIA* OF WOMEN AND ECCLESIASTICAL PATRIARCHY

CONTEXTUALIZATION

In 1984 I was one of the members of the Catholic Committee on Pluralism and Abortion, which at the height of the presidential election campaign (October 7) placed a paid advertisement in the *New York Times* asserting that "in fact, a diversity of opinions regarding abortion exists among committed Catholics."[1] The "Catholic Statement on Pluralism and Abortion," which included among its ninety-seven signers twenty-six nun-women from fourteen different canonical communities, sought to voice publicly a Catholic opinion that differed from that of the bishops who had viciously attacked democratic vice-presidential candidate Geraldine Ferraro because of her prochoice stance.

Subsequent events provide a case study in religious patriarchal violence and the repression of dissent. Although the Vatican's censure of famous theologians was well known, its swift repressive

---

1. For documentation see Mary E. Hunt and Frances Kissling, "The New York Times Ad: A Case Study in Religious Feminism," *Journal of Feminist Studies in Religion* 3 (1987): 115–27.

reaction took some of the signers by surprise. On November 30, 1984, Cardinal Jerome Hamer of the Vatican Congregation of Religious and Secular Institutes (SCRIS) sent a letter to the religious "superiors" of the nun-signers, threatening dismissal from their canonical communities if the signers would not obey and publicly retract their action.

In response to these reprisals, especially against the nun-signers, the same committee published a full-page "Declaration of Solidarity" in the *New York Times* on March 2, 1986, insisting that Catholics who express responsible dissent and "in good conscience take positions on the difficult questions of legal abortion and other controversial issues that differ from official hierarchical positions are within their rights and responsibilities as Catholics and as citizens." In the ensuing years, the question of the right to "responsible dissent" has become even more controversial. Nevertheless, precisely this right is indispensable for the intellectual integrity of theology as well as for democratic forms of society and church.

The struggle of the nun-women signers, especially that of sisters Barbara Ferraro and Patricia Hussey, who refused to publicly retract or tacitly arrange a compromise, has been widely publicized. What is less widely discussed are the devastating effects of the Vatican's repressive action both on the spirit of reform in canonical women's communities in general, and on the individual signers in particular who, regardless of their settlement, felt battered and violated in their trust and commitment to the vision of religious community as the discipleship of equals. Also not sufficiently explored and discussed has been the impact of this incident on the women's movement in the Roman Catholic Church. The violent divide-and-conquer policy of the Vatican has left deep scars. The following theological analysis, which likened the situation to that experienced by women in abusive family situations, was written during the early days of this struggle. It appeared in an issue of *Concilium* on the "Teaching Authority of the Believers."

IN HIS ENCYCLICAL *Pacem in Terris* Pope John XXIII remarked twenty years ago that "the signs of our times" are: the economic and social advancement of the working classes, the equality of colonial peoples and races, and the participation of women in public life. The more women become conscious of our human dignity, the more we must claim the rights and duties that accord with this dignity as human persons. Just as women and men suffering from the evil of racism must claim their rights as signs of their dignity, so all women must insist that others have the duty to recognize and value our rights. Although the pope spoke only of the entrance of women into public life, women have understood this to mean also the public life of the church and have begun to claim our human *and* ecclesial dignity and rights.

In *Gaudium et Spes* Vatican II stated in a similar fashion: "Nevertheless with respect to the fundamental rights of the person, every type of discrimination, whether social or cultural, whether based on sex, race, color, social condition, language, or religion, is to be overcome and eradicated as contrary to God's intent."(29) After having asserted that "by divine institution Holy Church is structured and governed with a wonderful diversity," the Dogmatic Constitution on the Church went on to say: "Hence there is in Christ and in the Church no inequality on the basis of race or nationality, social condition or sex" and it quotes Galatians 3:28 in support of this statement (32).

In the past twenty years women in the church have taken these words of "the Fathers of this most sacred Council" seriously and have consistently argued that we be acknowledged as human and ecclesial subjects rather than as objects of patriarchal power. Yet our call to conversion from ecclesial patriarchy has met with increasing rejection by the Vatican. While Catholic women have denounced the structural and personal sin of patriarchal sexism and have claimed our ecclesial dignity, rights, and responsibilities, the Vatican has appealed to the authority of Christ, of the Apostles, and of Tradition in order to legitimate patriarchal church structures that exclude women from sacramental, doctrinal, and governing power on the basis of sex.

The struggle for women's ecclesial dignity and rights is more than a struggle to incorporate a few women into the patriarchal hierarchy in and through ordination. That patriarchal authority and "power over" is at the heart of the women's liberation struggles in society and church is also more and more recognized by ordained women in other Christian churches. As Rev. Letty Russell, professor of theology at Yale, points out: "One of the real problems that women and men have with female clergy is just this – that women

are not good representatives of authority, of 'father right.' "[2] Therefore, the women's ordination movement in the United States has
always had as its goal the renewal of church and ministry. We have
theologically articulated why the struggle for women's ordination
is not a struggle for the incorporation of some women into the
patriarchal pyramid of domination, of "authoritative ministry" exercised by "fathers" from the top.[3] Instead, we have called for the
conversion of the whole church to the discipleship community of
equals that Jesus initiated, the apostolic churches continued, and
Vatican II has reaffirmed. The expression "the *ekklēsia* of women"
or "women-church" seeks to bring to consciousness that women
are church and always have been church. It reclaims the human
and ecclesial authority and power of women, the majority of whom
are poor and triply oppressed by racism, poverty, and sexism.

PATRIARCHAL AUTHORITY:
VIOLENCE AND SUBMISSION

At the time of this writing we have entered a new phase in this
struggle. The "superiors" of thirteen different religious communities have been ordered by SCRIS to demand that twenty-four
nun-women who are among the ninety-seven signers of a statement
on "pluralism and abortion" publicly retract their endorsement or
be expelled from their communities. The "pluralism" statement
appeared in the *New York Times* (October 7, 1984) as a paid
advertisement during the Mondale/Ferraro presidential campaign.
Geraldine Ferraro, the first woman to be nominated by a major U.S.
party as a vice-presidential candidate, was viciously attacked by the
archbishops of New York and Boston for her defense of the legal-
ity of abortion in a pluralistic society. Although other male Roman
Catholic candidates for public office, Democratic and Republican,
had advocated a similar position, none of them was as harshly
rebuked by the male hierarchy. Moreover, none of the prelates insisted on outlawing artificial birth control, although it is equally
prohibited by the Vatican, and although in 1921 the archbishop

---

2. Letty M. Russell, "Women and Ministry: Problem or Possibility?" in *Christian
Feminism: Visions of a New Humanity,* ed. Judith Weidman (San Francisco: Harper &
Row, 1984), 80.

3. See the proceedings of the First and Second Ordination Conferences in, respec-
tively, Detroit, 1975, and Baltimore, 1978.

of New York had attacked Margaret Sanger in a similar fashion. Finally, the Reagan government was not chastised even though its offenses against all the other "garment of life" issues are well documented. The *Boston Globe* columnist Ellen Goodman suggests why Ferraro was a special target of the hierarchy: "Bishops like Law and O'Connor and Krol watched Ferraro go to church on Sunday and talk pro-choice on Monday. She became a challenge to authority, proof that they had lost control over Catholic women."[4]

Acknowledging the official teaching of the hierarchy, the *New York Times* advertisement stated as fact that there *is* a diversity of opinion on the issue among committed Roman Catholics (only 11 percent of Catholics surveyed disapprove of abortion in all circumstances). The signers therefore call for a public discussion without recriminations and sanctions, especially against priests, religious, theologians, and legislators. We call for candid and respectful discussion on the issues of responsible sexuality and human reproduction and state that "Catholics should not seek legislation that curtails the legitimate exercise of the freedom of religion and conscience or discriminates against poor women." The signers insist "that responsible moral decisions can only be made in an atmosphere of freedom from fear of coercion." That the majority of the signers are leading Roman Catholic women and not, as in 1968, established male theologians and clergy (only two priests and one brother were among the signers published) indicates the increasing awareness among Roman Catholic women that reproductive freedom is a basic women's rights issue. It also shows that Vatican investigations of and sanctions against male theologians and clergy have already silenced responsible theological discussion of this difficult moral problem. While a variety of opinions among Catholics are tolerated on questions such as war and nuclear armament, capital punishment and economic systems, no similar freedom of moral discussion is allowed in the case of reproductive rights.

The SCRIS letter of November 30, 1984, expects that presidents of religious congregations function as mere institutional instruments rather than decision-making partners, since no consultation whatever preceded this letter. SCRIS requests that the "superiors" collaborate in patriarchal coercion, insofar as they are expected to threaten their own sisters with the psychological-economic violence of expulsion. This most recent action of SCRIS continues the

---

4. *Boston Globe*, December 27, 1984, 13.

policy of coercion that the Vatican has pursued, e.g., against the Sisters of Mercy under the leadership of Theresa Kane or against the School Sisters of St. Francis of Milwaukee. In the latter case, no canonical cause was given or previous discussion with the order's highest authority took place before SCRIS removed the authority of the generalate with respect to one of its provinces. Just as battered wives or right-wing women collaborate with patriarchal oppression and violence for the sake of survival, so also women superiors often believe that they must remain silent and cooperative for the sake of institutional survival and in order to protect their members from "possible hurt."

The most recent action of the Vatican lays open the predicament of women who are without power in a patriarchal system except the power to maintain "father right" and ecclesiastical laws that they were not permitted to formulate. An article by a former "superior" of a congregation written before the SCRIS action and published anonymously in the *National Catholic Reporter* likens their situation to that of "battered women":

> An important fact unknown to many within the church is that superiors of religious orders in the United States are, in many cases, battered women in the church. The form of violence is not as blatant as it is in some marriages, but the physical and mental anguish is strikingly similar. The parallels to domestic violence are unmistakable; the reasons for the silence are identical. But the silence must be broken so all in the church can participate in the ministry of justice, reconciliation, and conversion.[5]

The same insight was already summed up in a press statement of a group called "Women in Dialogue" released on February 7, 1979, during the Third Conference of the Latin American Bishops in Puebla, Mexico:

> But the most oppressed woman in the Church has been the religious woman who has made a tremendous contribution to the institutional Church by her donated service, her work among the sick, the elderly, children, etc. and yet has no control over her own life and activity. One of the most important steps for the religious woman to be able to behave in a responsible and involved way is for her to obtain economic independence.[6]

---

5. "Nuns: The Battered Women of the Church?" *National Catholic Reporter*, December 21, 1984, 25.

6. Ruth Fitzpatrick, ed., *Women in Dialogue* (Mujeres para el Diálogo) (Notre Dame: Catholic Committee on Urban Ministry, 1979), 127ff.

It is not accidental that U.S. canonical communities of women have become a primary target of patriarchal institutional violence, since they have sought to implement the participatory model of church proclaimed in the documents of Vatican II. Women's communities have taken seriously the words of the council fathers that the people of God are the church, that ministry is both service to the world and to the church, that dialogue is desirable, and participatory responsibility to be commended. Nun-women have moved from being asexual religious symbols and "well-protected daughters" to a positive self-identification and self-affirmation as adult women in responsible community. It therefore seems no accident that institutional patriarchal violence breaks into the open exactly at points where nun-women have publicly identified with the struggle of all women against patriarchal control and oppression. In a similar fashion the Vatican forced the resignation of Sister Agnes Mansour, head of Michigan's welfare department, from her order last year because the welfare department funds abortions for poor women.

In each case, the Vatican threatens as "punishment" for "misbehavior" relegation of nun-women to "lay status." The "contradiction" is obvious: Nun-women are canonically speaking "laywomen," since they are excluded from sacramental and policy-making ecclesiastical powers because of their sex. Nevertheless, they are treated "as clergy" in terms of patriarchal discipline. *Canonical status* is *patriarchal status.* Just as a wife is supposed to uphold patriarchal authority, policy, and punishment in the family, so nun-women are supposed to uphold without dissent "church teaching and authority," i.e., the teaching, authority, and powers of the "church fathers" among women. The SCRIS letter sums it all up: "The signers of the ad are, therefore, seriously lacking in 'religious submission of the will and mind' to the Magisterium."[7] Consequently, the punishment threatened by the "fathers" in the Vatican is expulsion from the "patriarchal ecclesiastical family," i.e., canonical community.

In a statement issued on December 19, 1984, the nun-women also appeal to the "bonds of family." Many of the nun-women

---

7. Francis A. Sullivan, S.J., *Magisterium: Teaching Authority in the Catholic Church* (New York: Paulist Press, 1983), does not discuss the fact that because of their sex women are excluded from the magisterium as well as from official theological teaching. What are the theological implications of discriminatory (sinful) church structures for the authority of the magisterium and the "consensus fidelium"?

"emphasized that religious communities have close and sacred relationships much like those of families. Members of religious communities," they note, "frequently feel called in conscience to make statements on public issues, and they have come to trust that the relationships of community will not be broken because of such conscience positions." They state that they have "received expressions of strong personal support from their communities, though they were hesitant to draw conclusions about the final outcome of the process." The nun-signers appeal to personal support and community because they know too well that their "superiors" do not have the power to avert the patriarchal violence invoked against them and that such institutional powerlessness might turn into horizontal violence and in "blaming the victims."

THEOLOGICAL EXPLORATION: AUTHORITY, CONSENSUS, POWER

I have elaborated the most recent conflict between women-church and the Vatican so extensively because feminist theology begins with the experience of women struggling against patriarchal oppression. As a critical theology of liberation feminist theology is a second order reflection on the faith-experience and liberation struggle of women-church. It is obvious that in choosing and presenting this conflict for elaborating the topic "authority, consensus, and power" in the church I have already taken a critical stance and "advocacy position." I have linked the authoritarian action of the Vatican to the experience of "battered women" in order to show that "freedom of speech and conscience" is not possible in an institutionalized situation of patriarchal violence. It is therefore necessary to critically "name" the theological definitions and institutional issues at the heart of this conflict between patriarchal church and women-church. Only if we break through the theological mystifications and religious legitimations of patriarchal authority and power will women be able to reclaim our dignity, authority, and power as ecclesial subjects.

The concept of teaching authority espoused by the letter of SCRIS is absolutist, allowing for no dissension, discussion, or argument. It is monolithic, presenting a unified front that admits neither ambivalence nor exceptions. It demands that like the Communist party the representatives of the church—bishops, priests, nuns – maintain the official line and keep a united front even when it is a façade. It is patriarchal, giving women no real voice or power in the formulation of teaching or in the decision-making process. It rules from the top down, requests "submission of mind and will," and is prepared to use force and violence to obtain such submission. No appeal is possible, no due process instituted. *Consensus fidelium* means the unqualified, if necessary forced, compliance and obedience of the faithful. True, the Vatican no longer has the power to burn us at the stake or to incarcerate us in cloisters. Nevertheless, its decrees and actions still use threat and force rather than persuasion and consultation. The notion of authority and power that undergirds the Vatican's order "to recant or to leave" is the same as that of Augustine's appeal to the delegate of the Roman emperor: *Coge intrare* (force the Donatists to enter).[8]

While in republican Rome *auctoritas* and (*patria*) *potestas* were distinct not only conceptually but also institutionally, beginning with Augustus they were united in the person of the emperor, who claimed for himself the *patria potestas,* the power of the father over life and death of the members of the household. He was the *pater patrum,* the supreme Father with absolute power. *Auctoritas,* authority, was no longer understood as the power of persuasion and counsel rooted in personal and social integrity, capability, and prominence, but now served to legitimate absolute imperial rule and force. This political and legal concept inherited from imperial Rome has decisively influenced Roman Catholic theological tradition and its understanding of authority and power as "father power over."

The Roman imperial notion of authority and submission could be theologically appropriated because of the gradual patriarchalization of church structures during the second and third centuries. The so-called Pastoral Epistles advocate for the first time an understanding of church and ministry in terms of Greco-Roman household structures. The gradual patriarchalization of the Christian community seeks to restrict women's leadership and teaching authority to women only, and argues that they should not teach and have authority over men (Tit. 2:3–5 and 1 Tim. 2:11). The author seems to expect opposition to this prohibition since he sees the need to legitimate such an injunction scripturally with the un-

---

8. Theodor Eschenburg, *Über Autorität* (Frankfurt: Suhrkamp, 1976), 47, and for the following paragraph, 11–39.

proven assertion that "Adam was not deceived but the woman who
became a transgressor."

Misogynist theology and the exclusion of women from ecclesial
leadership go hand in hand as the subsequent centuries confirm.
Patriarchal teaching authority in the church is established at the
price of women's silence and oppression. Women are not only the
"silenced majority" of the faithful but also have been excluded from
the teaching authority of the magisterium and until very recently
from that of theologians. Resorting to the Aristotelian argument for
the patriarchal order of household and state, Thomistic theology
argues that "the female sex cannot signify any superiority of rank,
for woman is in a state of subjection" (*Summa Theologiae Suppl.*
39, 1 ad 1).

Since ecclesial authority and power are understood in terms
of "power over," women, it is said, cannot receive the spiritual
power of the sacrament of ordination because of their position of
subordination. True, more recent Vatican statements have rejected
arguments for the exclusion of women from church leadership
and power based on the inferiority of women. Instead, they advocate a "special nature and vocation" of women and refer to the
positive will of Christ and the apostles. While feminist theology
has proven the latter argument wrong on historical grounds,[9] feminist theory has shown that Aristotle developed the concept of
"women's special nature" in order to argue why they are excluded
from full citizenship although they are rational human beings.[10]
Vatican statements that replace this Aristotelian notion with the
modern construct of "femininity" are no less oppressive because
they extol rather than denigrate women's physical and spiritual
motherhood.

One must therefore ask whether the Vatican's "take it or leave
it" alternative – give your unqualified submission of will and mind
to patriarchal teaching authority or leave the church – is the only
viable alternative possible for self-affirming women. Many post-
Catholic feminists would agree with the Vatican. After having
realized the full extent of the patriarchalization of Christian faith
and church, they have chosen the "exodus from the church" as

---

9. See my book *In Memory of Her: A Feminist Theological Reconstruction of
Christian Origins* (New York: Crossroad, 1983).

10. See, e.g., Susan Moller Okin, *Women in Western Political Thought* (Princeton: Princeton University Press, 1979), 15–96, and Marilyn B. Arthur, "Review Essay:
Classics," *Signs* 2 (1976): 382–403.

the only possible feminist option. The signers of the statement and many others have chosen a different route, although in many instances we have experienced ecclesiastical injustice and violence even more deeply. Rather than abandon Christian faith and community as inherently oppressive to women we seek to reclaim the power of Christian faith and community for the liberation and wholeness of all, women and men. Realizing the oppressive as well as liberating impact of Catholic faith and church on the self-understanding and liberation struggle of all women, we affirm our ecclesial authority and insist that the patriarchal church must change into a church in which men *and* women have the authority and power of the gospel. To quote the black theologian James Cone:

> Bishops, pastors and other church leaders have a special accountability to the people whom they serve and to the God in whose name they claim the right to serve.... The church will never become an instrument of liberation as long as its leaders enslave the ones they are supposed to serve. Black church persons must rise up and claim the right to fashion church structures that are humane and liberating.[11]

Authority within the church as the discipleship community of equals must not be realized as "power over," as domination and submission, but as the enabling, energizing, creative authority of orthopraxis that not only preaches the gospel of salvation but also has the power to liberate the oppressed and to make people whole and happy. Jesus commissioned his disciples not only to preach but also to heal and to set free those dominated and dehumanized by evil powers. Leadership in the community of disciples must not be exercised as domination and power over but as service and liberation. No one in the community can claim the authority, i.e., the ruling power, of father, master, or lord. Rather than submit to the patriarchal authority presently displayed by the Vatican, we question its Christian legitimacy. No doubt its patriarchal praxis corresponds to the understanding and exercise of Roman imperial power, but does it represent the "authority of Jesus Christ"? A historical-theological study could easily show why this is not the case.[12]

---

11. James H. Cone, *For My People: Black Theology and the Black Church* (Maryknoll, N.Y.: Orbis Books, 1984), 198.
12. See, e.g., Leonardo Boff, *Church: Charism and Power* (New York: Crossroad, 1984).

However, feminist theological redefinitions of ecclesial authority and power, all our talk about women-church, could have a similar function for women in the church as soap operas and romantic novels have for abused women, if there were no real possibility for change and conversion. The most recent repressive action of the Vatican is to be seen as one further attempt of the patriarchal church to silence the call to conversion. The censure or attempted censure of First and Third World theologians, and of African, European, or North American bishops, priests, and religious in public office, the attempts to bring religious communities of women under control, and the theological rationalizations of the exclusion of women from sacramental and policy-making power in the church are indications of how embattled the Roman bureaucracy feels. By aligning itself with the oppressive powers of society the patriarchal church might be able to maintain its powers of control and domination over some of its members for a while longer. However, it does so at the risk of loosing its catholicity as well as its religious and moral authority.

We would behave like "battered women" fearfully remaining in a violent home situation if we were to repress or deny the violence of the patriarchal church because we do not believe in the possibility of change and the power of God's grace. The faith of women-church in the possibility of change needs to be sustained in solidarity and coalition with all those who work for the participatory model of church as the effective sacrament of salvation and liberation for all.[13] In a recent lecture in Washington a bishop asked rhetorically: "Can we do away with a patriarchal church tradition and institution of almost eighteen hundred years?" and to his great surprise the audience responded with a loud, "Yes, we must!"[14]

---

13. See also Maureen Fiedler, S.L., "Catholic Feminists and Church Repression," *New Women, New Church* (July 1984), 6–11.
14. In support of their response they could have quoted the Second Vatican Council (see *Gaudium et Spes,* 44).

18 _____

THE SILENCED MAJORITY
MOVES INTO SPEECH

> ... Our freedom is your only way out.
> On the underground railroad
> you can ride with us or you become the jailer.
> Harriet Tubman never lost one entrusted to her.
> Neither will we.[1]

CONTEXTUALIZATION

Over the years I have been involved in feminist explorations and meetings that sought to develop new institutional ways of doing theology. Since publications and scholarly communication are very important for academic theologians, the Jewish feminist theologian Judith Plaskow and I pooled our financial resources and our professional contacts to found a feminist journal. Such a journal intended to give women scholars the possibility of publishing their feminist research. It was to provide a forum for developing and discussing feminist studies in religion as an intellectual discipline that remains rooted in the women's liberation movement in society and religion. We felt the need for such an ecumenical, interreligious, and interdisciplinary journal because at that

---

1. From a poem entitled "Women behind Walls for the Women in Cook County Jail and Dwight Prison" by Renny Golden, in Renny Golden and Sheila Collins, *Struggle Is a Name for Hope,* Worker Writer Series 3 (Minneapolis: West End Press, 1982).

time established theological journals were not keen on publishing feminist research. Moreover, leading feminist journals were, by and large, not interested in research on religion. The first issue of the *Journal of Feminist Studies in Religion* was published in 1985, the same year in which the first issue of feminist theology in *Concilium* appeared. *Concilium,* an international Roman Catholic journal, was founded to keep alive and develop the theological visions of the Second Vatican Council. It is published six times annually in seven languages. After intense debate and argument the international foundation and editorial board of *Concilium* decided to restructure its twelve sections, which represented traditional theological disciplines, and to establish two "extraordinary" new sections, one on Third World theologies and one on feminist theology. Sister Mary Collins, O.S.B., professor of liturgy at the Catholic University of America, and myself were appointed co-editors of the introductory issue, with the theme "Women: Invisible in Church and Theology," in which part of this article appeared.

Whereas the *Journal of Feminist Studies in Religion* has adopted an interreligious, academic *feminist* studies approach, *Concilium,* which is explicitly contextualized in the discourses of Roman Catholic theology, offers the challenge of articulating a feminist liberation-theology perspective for an international audience within a "progressive" Catholic theological framework. This framework and approach of feminist liberation theology requires both a *different* structure for the feminist issues of *Concilium* and a *different* methodological approach from that of traditional theology. In this first and subsequent issues we implemented the feminist concept and method of doing theology that this article suggests. In contrast to a method that starts with ecclesial-doctrinal questions or with a history of dogma, such an approach begins with women's experience and is followed by both a feminist systemic analysis and critical theological exploration. Although the liberal theological board of *Concilium,* comprised of mostly white European and North American male theologians, has some control over the topics for the feminist theological issues,[2] we have been fortunate to single out issues of interest to a wide readership. These

---

2. Subsequently the following topical issues have appeared, edited by Professor Anne Carr, B.V.M., of the University of Chicago and myself: "Women, Work and Poverty"; "Motherhood: Experience, Institution, Theology"; "A Special Nature of Women?" and in preparation "Violence against Women," edited with Mary Shawn Copeland, O.P., of Yale Divinity School.

feminist theological issues of *Concilium* are of particular importance in Southern Europe, where they have often been the only feminist resource for women in the church.

THIS ISSUE OF *CONCILIUM* inaugurates a new section on feminist theology, which both places feminist theology on the same level with established theological disciplines and assures the articulation, analysis, and restatement of a given theological problem from a feminist perspective. Such a movement into theological discourse seeks to empower women, the silenced majority of the church, to speak for themselves. The scope and approach of this section is therefore both interdisciplinary and ecumenical, although it remains accountable especially to Catholic women around the world.

Women are not only the "silent majority," but we are also the "silenced majority" in the church. Throughout the centuries and still today the authority of the apostle Paul has been invoked against women's preaching and teaching in the church: "The women should keep silence in the churches. For they are not permitted to speak but should be subordinate . . . " (1 Cor. 14:34), and "Let a woman learn in silence with all submissiveness. I permit no woman to teach or to have authority over men; she is to keep silent. For Adam was formed first and then Eve; and Adam was not deceived but the woman was deceived and became a transgressor." (1 Tim. 2:11–14 RSV).

To quote these well-worn biblical phrases again might seem to some like pouring water into the Tiber or the Charles River. Yet women's theological silence in the church is still reinforced today. For instance, during the last visit of Pope John Paul II to the Netherlands Professor Catharina Halkes, the Roman Catholic "dean" of feminist theology in Europe, was forbidden to address the pontiff. Although women can study theology, we almost never become professors at influential theological schools and faculties. Women are excluded from preaching and articulating church policy or doctrine because we are not admitted to the episcopacy or the college of cardinals. No feminist theologian speaks with official "teaching authority," no one of us belongs to an international or papal theological commission, no one serves as *perita* of a bishop or an episcopal synod, and only a very few, if any, of us are acknowledged as "theological authorities" in our own right. Theological textbooks and research, ecclesial commissions and studies, and even "progressive" liberation and political theologies still ignore our theological work.[3]

Such a deliberate or unintended silencing of women in the church engenders our ecclesial and theological invisibility. Although women are the majority of people who still attend church and of those who join religious orders, only males can represent the church officially. Although the church is called "our mother" and referred to with the pronoun "she," it is personified and governed by fathers and brothers only. Therefore, whenever we speak of *the* church we see before our eyes the pope in Rome, bishops or pastors, cardinals and monsignors, deacons and altar boys, all of whom are men. Eucharistic concelebrations, televised bishops' conferences, or the collective laying on of hands in the ordination rite are manifestations of the church as an "old boys club." No wonder that many Christians believe that God is a male patriarch and that the male sex of Jesus Christ is salvific.

Women *as church* are invisible neither by accident nor by our own default but because of patriarchal law that excludes us from church office on the basis of sex. (Such discrimination on the basis of sex is generally acknowledged today as sexism.) The present policy and official theology of the Roman hierarchy still enforces the Pauline injunction "women should be silent in all the churches" and seeks to legitimate such a policy theologically. Hence the 1977 Vatican statement against the ordination of women argues that women do not have a "natural resemblance" to the maleness of Christ.[4] This argument, however, implies either that women cannot be baptized because in baptism Christians become members of the (male) body of Christ or that we do not remain women because those baptized have been conformed to the "perfect male." In any case, such a theology denies the universality of incarnation and salvation in order to maintain and legitimate the patriarchal structures of the church.

---

3. See the reflections of Christine Schaumberger, "Die 'Frauenseite': Heiligkeit statt Hausarbeit," in *Theologisch politische Protokolle,* ed. Tiemo Rainer Peters (Munich: Kaiser-Grünewald, 1981), 244ff.; on theological education see the Mud Flower Collective, *God's Fierce Whimsy: Christian Feminism and Theological Education* (New York: Pilgrim Press, 1985).

4. "Vatican Declaration: Women in the Ministerial Priesthood," *Origins* 6 (1977): 522.

FEMINIST THEORY AND THEOLOGY

Feminist theology seeks to unmask the oppressive function of such a patriarchal theology. It explores women's experience of oppression and discrimination in society and religion as well as our experiences of hope, love, and faith in the struggle for liberation and well-being. Feminist theology has a dual parentage: the women's liberation movement in society and church as well as the academy and theological institutions.

Feminist studies and theology are proud to be the daughters of the women's movement and at the same time ambivalent about their origin and setting in the academy. Whereas in the last century the women's movement sought access for women to the academy and the ministry by pointing to women's special "feminine" contributions, in this century it did so by claiming women's full personhood and "equal rights." However, women began to realize that it does not suffice to argue for a special sphere or domain for women or to integrate women into male-dominated society and church. What is necessary is the transformation of the patriarchal state and church into institutions that allow for the full participation of women as well as men in society and church.

In the last century women gained access to academic work and theological studies at first through special courses or seminaries for women. Then women were admitted to full academic and theological studies if they could prove that they were as good as, if not better than, their male colleagues. Although women scholars have fulfilled all the standards of academic excellence, only a very few have achieved faculty status or scholarly influence. Today feminist theologians no longer seek merely to become incorporated into the androcentric academy and theological institutions. Rather, women scholars have come to realize more and more that all intellectual institutions and academic disciplines need to be redefined and transformed if they are to allow women to participate fully as subjects of academic research and theological scholarship. Feminist studies, therefore, seek to engender, in the words of Thomas Kuhn, a paradigm shift from the male-centered scholarship that is produced by the patriarchal academy and church to a feminist comprehension of the world, human life, and Christian faith.

Just as feminist studies in general have affected all areas of academic inquiry, so also feminist theology has worked for the transformation of theology. It seeks to integrate the emancipatory struggles for ending societal and ecclesial patriarchy with religious vision, Christian faith, and theological reflection. If theology is "faith seeking understanding," then feminist theology is best understood as the reflection on Christian faith-experiences in the struggle against patriarchal oppression. If theology, as Karl Rahner puts it, has the vocation to engage the whole church in self-criticism, then feminist theology has the task to engender ecclesial self-criticism, not just of the church's androcentrism but also of its historical patriarchal structures.

Feminist theology thus begins with the experience of women struggling against patriarchal exclusion and for liberation and human dignity. Just as other liberation theologies so a critical feminist theology of liberation understands itself as a systemic exploration and "second order" reflection on this experience. Its methods are therefore critical analysis, constructive exploration, and conceptual transformation. As a critical theology feminist theology identifies not only the androcentric dynamics and misogynist elements of Christian Scriptures, traditions, and theologies but also those structures of the church that perpetrate patriarchal sexism as well as racism, classism, and colonialism in and outside the church. As a constructive theology feminist theological studies seek both to recover and reconstruct all those theological symbols and expressions that reflect the liberative faith experiences of the church as the discipleship community of equals, the experiences of the people of God who are women.

However, it must be noted that feminist studies articulate emancipatory struggles and liberatory perspectives in different ways and with the help of varying philosophical or sociological-political analyses.[5] While liberal feminisms, for example, emphasize the autonomy and equal rights of the individual, socialist or Marxist feminisms see the relationship between social class and gender within Western capitalism as determinative of women's societal oppression. Third World feminisms in turn insist that the interactions of racism, colonialism, and sexism are defining women's oppression and struggle for liberation.[6] Such a variety of analy-

---

5. See D. Griffin Crowder, "Amazons and Mothers? Monique Wittig, Hélène Cixous and Theories of Women's Writing," *Contemporary Literature* 24, no. 2 (1983): 117–44, who underlines these differences in her discussion of French and American feminism.

6. See, e.g., S. A. Gonzales, "La Chicana: Guadalupe or Malinche?" in *Comparative Perspective of Third World Women: The Impact of Race, Sex, and Class,* ed. Beverly Lindsay (New York: Praeger, 1980), 229–50.

ses and theoretical perspectives results in different conceptions of feminism, of women's liberation, and of being human in the world.

A diversity in approach and polyphony in feminist intellectual articulations are also found in feminist theology and in feminist studies in religion.[7] It is therefore misleading to speak of feminist theology in the singular or of *the* feminist theology without recognizing many different articulations and analyses of feminist theologies.[8] These articulations not only share in the diverse presuppositions and theoretical analyses of women's experience but also work within diverse theological frameworks, e.g., neo-orthodoxy, liberal theology, process theology, evangelical theology, or liberation theology. As theological articulations they are rooted in diverse ecclesial visions and pluriform political-religious contexts. I have defined my own approach as a critical feminist theology of liberation that is indebted to historical-critical, critical-political, and liberation-theological analyses and is rooted in my experience and engagement as a Catholic Christian woman.[9]

Insofar as feminist theology does not begin with doctrines about God and revelation but with the experience of women struggling for liberation from patriarchal oppression, its pluriform vision is articulated by the voices of women from different races, classes, cultures, and nations.[10] These theological voices challenge androcentric forms of liberation theology to articulate the preferential "option" for the poor and oppressed as the option for poor and oppressed *women,* because the majority of the poor and exploited today are women and children dependent on women for survival. As the African theologian Mercy Amba Oduyoye has pointed out:

7. See Anne Barstow Driver, "Review Essay: Religion," *Signs* 2 (1976): 434–42; Carol P. Christ, "The New Feminist Theology: A Review of the Literature," *Religious Studies Review* 3 (1977): 203–12; Carol P. Christ and Judith Plaskow, eds., *Womanspirit Rising: A Feminist Reader in Religion* (San Francisco: Harper & Row, 1979), 1–17.

8. See Catharina Halkes, *Gott hat nicht nur starke Söhne: Grundzüge einer feministischen Theologie* (Gütersloh, 1980); Elisabeth Gössmann, *Die streitbaren Schwestern: Was Will die feministische Theologie?* (Freiburg: Herder Verlag, 1981).

9. In addition to the chapters of the present book see also my "Claiming the Center," in *Womanspirit Bonding,* ed. Mary Buckley and Janet Kalven (New York: Pilgrim Press, 1984), 293–309.

10. See especially Marianne Katoppo, *Compassionate and Free: An Asian Woman's Theology* (Geneva: World Council of Churches, 1979); Elsa Tamez, *The Bible of the Oppressed* (Maryknoll, N.Y.: Orbis Books, 1982).

[Feminist theology] is not simply a challenge to the dominant theology of the capitalist West. It is a challenge to the maleness of Christian theology worldwide, together with the patriarchal presuppositions that govern all our relationships as well as the tradition; a situation in which men (male human beings) reflected upon the whole of life on behalf of the whole community of women and men, young and old.[11]

If the primary theological question for liberation theology is not "How can we believe in God?" but "How can the poor achieve dignity?" then a critical feminist theology of liberation must articulate the quest for women's dignity and liberation ultimately as the quest for God. The hermeneutical privilege of the poor must be articulated as the hermeneutical privilege of poor women. Liberation theologies of all colors must address the patriarchal domination and sexual exploitation of women.[12]

In short, feminist theologians do not limit themselves either to studies about women or to the academy. They do not seek to articulate a theology of woman nor restrict their questions to women. Rather, they understand themselves as charting a different method and an alternative perspective for doing theology. Therefore, a critical feminist theology of liberation constructs theology neither in terms of the traditional taxonomies and dogmatic *topoi* of theology such as God, Christ, creation, church, sacraments, or eschatology[13] nor in terms of an academic religious studies approach. Both approaches are valuable and necessary, but they attempt to chart new visions and roads with the help of the old maps of doctrinal or academic theology.

Instead, a critical feminist liberation theology seeks to adopt an interdisciplinary approach and framework that does not reinscribe professional divisions among the various theological disciplines but uses their methods as tools for investigating women's theological questions. It does not envision theology as a doctrinal system

11. "Reflections from a Third World Woman's Perspective: Women's Experience and Liberation Theologies," in *Irruption of the Third World*, ed. Virginia Fabella and Sergio Torres (Maryknoll, N.Y.: Orbis Books, 1983), 250.

12. See especially also J. Grant, "Die schwarze Theologie und die schwarze Frau," in *Frauen in der Männerkirche*," ed. Bernadette Brooten and Norbert Greinacher (Munich: Kaiser, 1982), 212–34; Eng.: "Black Theology and Black Woman" in *Black Theology: A Documentary History*, ed. Gayraud S. Wilmore and James H. Cone (Maryknoll, N.Y.: Orbis Books, 1979).

13. For such an approach see Catharina J. M. Halkes, "Feministische Theologie: Eine Zwischenbilanz," in *Frauen in der Männerkirche*, 158–74, and the excellent work of Rosemary Radford Ruether, *Sexism and God-Talk: Toward a Feminist Theology* (Boston: Beacon Press, 1983).

but as an active theological reflection on liberation struggles, as an emancipatory way of "doing" theology. Hence feminist theological studies seek dialogic, participatory, nonhierarchical processes of doing research and teaching that cultivate the gifts and talents of everyone. In short, feminist studies demand not just the admittance of women to the academy and the recognition of women's intellectual contributions in the past and the present. They also require a reconceptualization and revision of accepted theoretical assumptions and frameworks that until very recently have been based entirely on the experiences and studies of "educated" men.

FEMINIST SYSTEMIC ANALYSIS

A critical feminist theology of liberation calls for a paradigm shift in theological and ecclesial self-understanding. It insists that the androcentric-clerical theology produced in Western universities and seminaries no longer can claim to be a Catholic Christian theology if it does not seek to become a theology inclusive of the experiences of all members of the church, women and men, lay and clergy. Dominant theology cannot even claim to be a Christian theology proclaiming the "good news" of salvation if it does not take seriously its call to be a theology subversive of every form of sexist-racist-capitalist patriarchy.

As a critical theology of liberation feminist theology conceives of feminism not just as a theoretical worldview and analysis but as a women's liberation movement for societal and ecclesial change.[14] Patriarchy in this view is not just a "dualistic ideology" or androcentric world-construction in language, not just the domination of all men over all women, but a sociocultural political system of graded subjugations and dominations. Sexism, racism, and militaristic colonialism are the roots and pillars of patriarchy. Since the silence and invisibility of Catholic women are generated by patriarchal laws and structures of the church and maintained by androcentric, i.e., male-defined, theology, a critical feminist liberation theology seeks to investigate in what ways androcentric language, theoretical frameworks, and theological scholarship sustain and perpetrate patriarchal structures in society and church.

---

14. For a review of the present discussion see Carter I. Heyward, "An Unfinished Symphony of Liberation: The Radicalization of Christian Feminism among White U.S. Women," *Journal of Feminist Studies in Religion* 1 (1985): 99–118.

The term "patriarchy" is often used interchangeably with "sexism" and "androcentrism." However, these feminist analytical categories must be distinguished. Androcentrism or androcentric dualism is to be understood as a world-construction in language. It indicates a framework, mindset, or ideology that legitimates patriarchy. Patriarchy in turn is a societal system of domination and exploitation that is structured by heterosexism, racism, nationalism, and classism.

Patriarchal sexism is enforced by female "sexual slavery"[15] that cuts across all lines of race, class, and culture. Whereas patriarchal racism defines certain people as subhuman in order to exploit their labor, patriarchal sexism seeks to control women's procreative powers and labor. Violence against women and children is increasing at a time when women claim the full human rights and dignity accorded to male citizens. The political Right's attack on feminism, its battle for the recriminalization of women and their doctors, and its rhetoric for the "protection of the Christian family" seek to reinforce women's economic dependency, to strengthen the patriarchal controls of women's procreative powers, and to maintain the patriarchal family as the mainstay of the patriarchal state.[16] Sexual violence against women and children in and outside the home sustains the patriarchal order of male dominance:

> Anonymous verbal and bodily assault: rape — rape in general, racial rape, marital rape, wartime rape, gang rape, child rape — wife and women battering; abortion and birth control laws; involuntary sterilizations; unnecessary hysterectomies; clitoridectomies and genital mutilations; prostitution and female slavery; sexual harassment in employment; aggressive pornography.[17]

All these and more are forms of sanctioned violence against women. Whereas sociobiologists view rape as a natural, biological tendency in males, as a *biological* imperative, feminist studies

---

15. For this expression see Kathleen Barry, *Female Sexual Slavery* (Englewood Cliffs, N.J.: Prentice-Hall, 1977). The literature on sexual violence against women is too extensive to be listed here. For a review see W. Brines and L. Gordon, "The New Scholarship on Family Violence," *Signs* 8 (1983): 490–531.

16. See, e.g., S. Rogers Radl, *The Invisible Woman: Target of the Religious New Right* (New York: Delta Books, 1983). For a comparison of the rhetoric of the political Right in America with the propaganda of Nazi Germany see Flo Conway and Jim Siegelman, *Holy Terror: The Fundamentalist War on America's Freedoms in Religion, Politics, and Our Private Lives* (Garden City, N.Y.: Doubleday, 1982).

17. Ruth Bleier, *Science and Gender: A Critique of Biology and the Theories on Women* (New York: Pergamon Press, 1984), 184.

have documented that rape and other forms of institutionalized violence against women are a *social* imperative necessary to uphold patriarchy by force.

The struggle against the violence and dehumanization of societal and religious patriarchy in Western societies is at the heart of all liberation struggles against racism, colonialism, militarism, and poverty. Feminist theology does not just reflect on these struggles; it is also shaped by them and in turn inspires them. Androcentric legitimations of patriarchal domination and victimization become more pronounced and forceful whenever claims to equality and self-determination gain public recognition and broad acceptance. Feminist thought is labeled extremist, subversive, irrational, or abnormal because it seeks to put forward an alternative to patriarchy as the basis of Euro-American society or church. It demystifies and rejects cultural or religious values of male domination and subordination, which are the very standard of reasonableness, veracity, and knowledge.

Therefore, liberal theologians and churchmen who are "for" the ordination of women are often opposed to "feminist theology" that places women's liberation at the center of its thought. They label "feminist theology" as a "so-called theology" that is at best trivial and incompetent and at worst man-hating propaganda and unfeminine revolt. Instead, they advocate a "theology of woman" or of "femininity." Therefore, they are quick to play out the token woman theologian – the "good woman" who respects male scholarship and expertise – against the feminist theologian – the "bad woman" who radically questions them. If women are admitted to the clergy they are ordained as long as they promise to shore up the patriarchal structures of the church and to perpetuate its androcentric theology and symbol system. Liberal churches and theologians are willing to allow women to become visible in the church and to let us preach and teach as long as we are prepared to represent the patriarchal church and its androcentric theology and liturgy.

Because Catholic feminists have learned from the experience of ordained women in other Christian churches and from our own experience in theology and ministry, the Roman Catholic women's ordination movement in the United States has always insisted that the incorporation of some token women into the patriarchal hierarchy does not suffice. Roman Catholic women experience anger and pain daily because our church is corrupted by the structural and personal sin of patriarchal sexism. Hence the ordination of some women to the lower ranks of the patriarchal hierarchy would not eliminate the evil of patriarchal sexism; it would merely conceal its destructive powers. Catholic feminists have come to understand that the "woman question" facing the church is not simply a question of ordination but that it requires an intellectual paradigm shift from an androcentric worldview and theology to a feminist conceptualization of the world, human life, and Christian religion.

If societal and ecclesiastical patriarchy generate misogynistic legitimation and androcentric knowledge of reality, then political struggle for women's rights and not feminist theory seems to be called for. Therefore, segments of the women's movement have often eschewed theory and scholarship as a male "head trip" that co-opts women for its own patriarchal ends. Many women have found academic scholarship, argumentative reasoning, and abstract thought very much removed from their daily experience. Women students have often experienced that academic education has not only alienated them from their own intellectual questions and intuitions, but also co-opted and undermined their intellectual power and self-confidence.

This has been true also for women in religion and in theology. Since most of us still cannot study with feminist professors, rarely find feminist works on the required reading lists for courses, and often have our questions declared "nonquestions," women in theological schools have been rightly suspicious of academic education and theological systems. Yet such a healthy suspicion of androcentric scholarship easily can turn into feminist anti-intellectualism that unwittingly serves patriarchal interests in excluding women from defining the issues. I remember at one of the earliest conferences of women ministers and scholars in religion in 1972 it was seen as elitism when I called myself a theologian since we were all said to be doing theology. However, no one had any problem with the title "minister" or "Reverend" that introduced clerical distinctions among us. While access to the ordained ministry was considered a feminist achievement, access to theology was regarded as male elitism.

In the meanwhile many of us have recognized that knowledge *is* power and that androcentric language and patriarchal ideology produce meaning for the sake of domination. Therefore, the alternative between societal-ecclesial struggle against patriarchy or critical analysis and change of androcentric language and scholarship is a false one, in my view. Women's invisibility in the intellectual interpretations of the world and our forced silence in academy and church are in the interest of patriarchy. That we are excluded from defining the world and the meaning of human life and society is an integral part of our oppression. To break the silence and to reclaim the "power of naming that was stolen from us" (Mary Daly) must therefore become an integral element in our struggles for liberation from patriarchal structures.

Feminist scholarship unveils the patriarchal functions of the intellectual and scientific frameworks generated and perpetrated by male-centered scholarship that makes women invisible or peripheral in what we know about the world, human life, and cultural or religious history. Placing women's experience and subjectivity at the center of intellectual inquiry has challenged the theoretical frameworks of all academic disciplines. In all areas of scholarship feminist studies are in the process of inaugurating a scientific revolution or paradigm shift from an androcentric – male-centered – worldview and intellectual framework of discourse to a feminist comprehension of the world, human culture, and history.[18]

FEMINIST ANALYSIS OF LANGUAGE

Whereas androcentric scholarship defines woman as the "other" of man or of a male God and reduces us to "objects" of male scholarship, feminist studies insist on the reconceptualization of our language as well as of our intellectual frameworks in such a way that women as well as men can become the subjects of human culture and scholarly discourse. A feminist critical analysis of the ideological functions of androcentric language and scientific knowledge not only challenges the claims of male scholarship to universality but also highlights its patriarchal bias. Far from being objective or descriptive, androcentric texts and knowledge maintain the silence and invisibility of women engendered by a patriarchal society and church. Women's invisibility in androcentric culture and our concealed oppression in Western language,

18. The literature is too extensive to be listed here. For a comprehensive discussion see Alison M. Jaggar, *Feminist Politics and Human Nature* (Sussex: Harvester Press, 1983). However, the black feminist scholar bell hooks argues forcefully that much feminist theory lacks a broad and inclusive analysis because it has emerged from privileged women's experience. See her book *Feminist Theory: From Margin to Center* (Boston: South End Press, 1984).

religious symbol systems, historical records, and scientific theories
have therefore been the core problem and focal point of feminist
studies.

The most basic liberating insight of feminism has been that
the personal *is* political, that our personal questions are not just
our private problems. Simone de Beauvoir's adage that "women
are made, not born" has stimulated much feminist research on the
social construction of sex and gender as well as on the socialization
of children into cultural masculine and feminine roles. When Chris
was in the so-called questioning phase, she would ask constantly:
Why can only men be presidents? Why are all the priests men? Why
do women earn less than men? Why does God have only sons and
not daughters? Why are women against equal rights for women?
Why can't boys wear dresses? Why were all the great figures in
history men? Why does the teacher always say "boys and girls" and
not "girls and boys"? Why is God He? Why don't women keep their
own names, when they get married? Why does Jessica's mother do
all the housework? Why don't all children have enough to eat? Why
do women wear makeup? Why, why, why?

These questions express women's early experiences of inferiority and "otherness" in a patriarchal society and religion. It is the
experience that the "world" does not make sense. It is the experience that we are "out of place," that we don't matter, and that we
have no power to define and change the world in such a way that
it corresponds to our experience of self-worth and to our image
of how the world should be. Such critical experiences of women
in patriarchal society and church, however, are silenced through
socialization and education into patriarchal language and value systems. Therefore, girls internalize this experience of alienation and
believe that anger is just their own personal problem, that something must be wrong with *them* and that they have to accept and
adapt to things *as they are.*

Crucial for the internalization of "secondary status" is what
Casey Miller and Kate Swift have called "semantic roadblocks"[19]
and Pierre Bourdieu has termed "symbolic violence."[20] Since
language not only reflects the world but also shapes our self-

19. Casey Miller and Kate Swift, *Words and Women* (Garden City, N.Y.: Anchor
Books, 1977). See also Dale Spender, *Man Made Language* (Boston: Routledge & Kegan,
1980); Senta Trömel-Plötz, ed., *Gewalt durch Sprache* (Frankfurt: Fischer TB, 1984);
Luise F. Pusch, *Das Deutsch als Männersprache* (Frankfurt am Main: Suhrkamp, 1984).
20. See the critical discussion of Pierre Bourdieu's work by John B. Thompson,

understanding and our understanding of the world, the very process of learning to speak socializes us into a world in which male and masculine is the standard of being human. "Those of us who have grown up with a language that tells them they are at the same time men and not men are faced with ambivalence – not about their sex but about their status as human beings."[21] Feminist studies have documented over and over again how much androcentric world-constructions in and through language inculcate both the self-affirmation of men and the self-alienation of women.

Insofar as boys and girls learn to express themselves and to define the world in grammatically masculine "generic" language that subsumes women under "men" and "he," they learn to understand themselves in terms of patriarchal superordination and subordination, of being in the center or being on the margins. That is why women's oppression is so "commonsense" in Western society and culture. Therefore, it is so difficult for both women and men to recognize the oppressive character of grammatically masculine language that renders women invisible and marginal. Moreover, such androcentric language makes poor women, women of color, or colonialized women doubly invisible. Insofar as we speak of those who suffer from patriarchal oppression and are disadvantaged in our society as the poor, blacks, Native Americans, Africans, Asians, *and as women*, androcentric language makes poor, black, Native American, African, or Asian women doubly invisible.

Sacred language legitimates and intensifies women's alienation in an androcentric language structure.[22] For centuries women have had to "listen in" on the theological talks and sermons addressed to men. We have had to think twice in order to know whether we were meant or not with the address "brothers," "faith of our fathers," "brotherhood of men," or "sons of God." Take for instance the following statement:

> God, who has fatherly concern for everyone, has willed that all men should constitute one family and treat one another in a spirit of brotherhood. For having been created in the image of God, who "from one man

---

Studies in the Theory of Ideology (Berkeley: University of California Press, 1984), 42–72.

21. Miller and Swift, *Words and Women*, 34ff.

22. See esp. the collected essays of Nelle Morton, *The Journey Is Home* (Boston: Beacon Press, 1985).

has created the whole human race...," all men are called to one and
the same goal, namely, God Himself.[23]

Do women belong to the "family of men" and do we share in the
"spirit of brotherhood"? Not only are men or humans "he," but so
also is God "Himself" in whose image we are made. Women do not
figure in the language about divine reality and in the theological
articulation of the "world."

WOMEN'S INTELLECTUAL-RELIGIOUS HERITAGE

Not only in and through language-socialization but also through
education and acquisition of knowledge women and men learn to
respect men but not women, to internalize the patriarchal values
of domination and submission, to adopt the patriarchal interpretation of the world and human life. However, one must never forget
that educated *men* have produced such androcentric interpretation and knowledge; they have defined the world and human
life.

> We had believed, I guess, that women and men participate equally in
> a noble republic of the spirit and that both sexes are equal inheritors
> of a "thousand years of Western culture." Rereading literature by both
> women *and men,* however, we learned that, though the pressures and
> oppressions of gender may be as invisible as air, they are also as in-
> escapable as air, and, like the weight of air, they imperceptibly shape
> the forms and motions of our lives.... The treasures of Western culture,
> it began to seem, were the patrimony of male writers, or put in another
> way, Western culture itself was a grand ancestral property that edu-
> cated men had inherited from their intellectual forefathers, while their
> female relatives, like characters in a Jane Austen novel, were relegated
> to modest dower houses on the edge of the estate.[24]

It is still true what Virginia Woolf observed almost sixty years
ago: Almost all the books on the shelves of our libraries are written by men, even those on women. In the service of patriarchy
educated men — consciously or not — have allocated to women all
the qualities they do not value in themselves. We all know the
stereotypes: Men are intellectual, assertive, logical, active, strong,

23. *Gaudium et Spes* II, 24. For the English translation see William M. Abbott, *The Documents of Vatican II* (New York: Herder and Herder, Association Press, 1966).
24. S. M. Gilbert, "What Do Feminist Critics Want?" in *The New Feminist Criticism,* ed. Elaine Schowalter (New York: Pantheon Books, 1985), 33.

born leaders, competent, have authority, etc., while women are emotional, intuitive, receptive, passive, beautiful, compassionate, religious, gossipy, submissive, self-sacrificing, silly, frivolous, etc. While some men have feared woman as whore, sinner, temptress, snare, or devouring mother, others have praised the "eternal feminine" as the only salvation of men.

Women's subordination and powerlessness, we are told, is either the result of our inferior nature or interpreted as a special feminine sphere of womanly qualities that enable us to fulfill our special role in life. Traditional catechesis and theology would answer that sin came into the world through a woman, that patriarchy is willed by God, our Father, and that His Son ordained only men to become his successors and leaders of the church. In any case women learn early that we are the "secondary sex," and we internalize our own inferiority and invisibility. Self-worth and power can be derived only from men and/or a male God. The masculinity of theological and liturgical God-language is therefore not a cultural or linguistic accident but an act of domination in and through proclamation and prayer. While androcentric language and intellectual frameworks make patriarchal domination "commonsense," masculine God-language in liturgy and theology proclaims it as "ordained by God."

Although women have questioned these explanations and internalizations of femininity throughout the centuries, we have remained ignorant of our own intellectual traditions and foremothers.[25] All "great" philosophers, scientists, theologians, poets, politicians, artists, and religious leaders seem to have been men. For centuries they have been writing and talking to each other in order to define God, the world, human community, and existence as "they saw it." Needless to say, this does not mean that women have not been "great" thinkers and leaders. Their thoughts and works have not been transmitted and become classics of our culture and religion because patriarchy requires that in any conceptualization of the world men and their power have to be central. This is why women's thought, culture, history, and religion have so effectively disappeared or have been marginalized and trivialized. Women's words are censured, misrepresented, ridiculed, and eliminated in a male-dominated society, and then women are blamed

---

25. See especially Dale Spender, *Women of Ideas (And What Men Have Done to Them)* (Boston: Ark Paperbacks, 1983).

because no "great" thinkers, scientists, artists, or theologians have emerged among us.

If one has understood the ideological function of androcentric texts, theological scholarship, and ecclesiastical authority in the maintenance of societal and religious patriarchy, one must develop a "hermeneutics of suspicion" in order to perceive what is said and what is not said about women's reality under patriarchy and our historical struggles against patriarchal oppression. Although women are neglected in the writing of history and theology, the effects of women's lives, thoughts, and struggles are a part of the historical reality and theological meaning that is concealed from us.

Just as other feminist scholars so also feminist theologians seek to break the silences, inconsistencies, incoherences, and ideological mechanisms of androcentric records and scholarship in order to reappropriate the patriarchal past of women.[26] Women have not only suffered the pain and dehumanization of patriarchal oppression but have also participated in its social transformation and prophetic critique as well as provided a vision of the church as an alternative community to patriarchy. Making visible our foresisters' struggles and religious experiences of liberation empowers us to affirm the validity of our own religious consciousness, spiritual experience, and historical struggles.[27]

In every generation women have to challenge anew the patriarchal definition of reality; we have "to reinvent the wheel," so to speak, over and over again because patriarchy cannot tolerate the conscientization of the oppressed. Feminist theology has shown that our societal oppression and ecclesial exclusion are not women's "fault"; they are not the result of Eve's sin nor are they the will of God or the intention of Jesus Christ. Rather they are engendered by societal and ecclesiastical patriarchy and legitimated by androcentric world-construction in language and symbol systems. Insofar as religious language and symbol systems function to legitimate the societal oppression and cultural marginality of women, the struggle against ecclesiastical silencing and ecclesial invisibility is at the heart of women's struggles for justice, liberation, and wholeness.

---

26. See the series and first volume edited by Elisabeth Gössmann, *Das wohlgelahrte Frauenzimmer,* Archiv für philosophie- und theologiegeschichtliche Frauenforschung, Bd.1 (Munich: Judicium Verlag, 1984).

27. See my book *In Memory of Her: A Feminist Theological Reconstruction of Christian Origins* (New York: Crossroad, 1983).

Feminist theology not only reflects on these struggles but also seeks to explore whether religion and church can provide resources and visions in these struggles and are able to account for the hope that lives in and among us.[28] It seeks to make explicit that divine presence and revelation are found among the people of God who are women. Women are church, and always have been church, called and elected by God. Throughout the centuries and still today patriarchal church and androcentric theology have silenced and marginalized women, made us invisible, and kept us without theological or ecclesiastical powers because we are women. Nevertheless, women have always heard God's call, have mediated God's grace and presence, and have lived church as the discipleship community of equals.

In short, a critical feminist theology of liberation seeks to interrupt the patriarchal silencing of women in order to make women visible and audible as God's agents of grace and liberation. It shows that the need to silence women and to make us invisible in male linguistic systems and theological frameworks will no longer exist when the church transforms its patriarchal structures of superordination and subordination that are exclusive of women or can admit us only in marginal and subordinate positions. The full participation of women requires not only the conversion and transformation of the patriarchal church and its ministry into a discipleship community of equals but also the articulation of a new theology.

Such a feminist liberation theology is committed to the struggle of all women against patriarchal oppression in church and society; it seeks to transform an androcentric, i.e., male-defined, clerical theology that legitimates patriarchal oppressions into a theology that promotes and enhances the liberation of the people of God, the majority of whom are women. Matilda Joslyn Gage aptly articulated this task of feminist theology precisely one hundred years ago: "The most important struggle in the history of the church is that of women for liberty and thought and the right to give that thought to the world."[29]

---

28. See Elisabeth Moltmann-Wendel, *A Land Flowing with Milk and Honey: Perspectives on Feminist Theology* (New York: Crossroad, 1986), and E. (Helga) Sorge, *Religion und Frau: Weibliche Spiritualität im Christentum* (Stuttgart: Kohlhammer TB, 1985).

29. Matilda Joslyn Gage, *Woman, Church & State* (first publ. 1893; Watertown, Mass.: Persephone Press, 1980), 237.

Almost fifty years ago Virginia Woolf insisted that women have to set the conditions under which we are willing to join the "procession of educated men" and to ask where this procession will lead us if we join its ranks. She concluded that it will lead us to war, exploitation, elitism, the greed for power, and the degeneration of the human race and our natural environment. Christian theology and church must ask today the same questions. If the Christian God is a God of liberation and salvation for *all* rather than a God of dehumanization and destruction, then Christian theology cannot but become more and more a feminist theology of liberation. As long as this is not the case, however, we need a special section of Concilium committed to the articulation and development of such a Catholic Christian feminist theology.

19 ——————————————

KOINŌNIA:
CONSENSUAL PARTNERSHIP

During the winter holidays [of 1985] when in preparation for this essay I started to study the official documents of the extraordinary synod of bishops in 1985, I became increasingly "blocked." The topic, "the main task of theology in the postsynodal period," provoked the terse response "so what?" According to the synodal pronouncements the main task for Catholic theology seems to be the study and exegesis of the documents of Vatican II and the explication of the forthcoming universal catechism. How boring! — to use a favored expression of Chris.

But she also had some words of advice: "When I have a difficult assignment I always write and rewrite the topic sentence. If you get the topic sentence right the rest will flow from it." It was obvious; I needed a new topic sentence. First, I tried Peter Steinfels's headline "So far, so good, so what?" but I quickly realized that I had to change it to: "So far, so bad..." The reasons for this change are obvious. The synod had been a visual demonstration of the patriarchal church or, in the words of the "Holy Father," an "act of ecclesi[astic]al fraternity." Moreover, the phallic pronouncements of cardinals arguing that women cannot be ordained because Christ was a man had become theologically embarrassing.

Since Catholics in North America saw the "women question" as one of the major issues to be addressed by the synod, bishops sought to scale down such expectations in the presynodal period. Cardinal Carter of Toronto, e.g., spoke in a pastoral letter under the

heading "The Church Ad Extra" about "the vexatious subject of the
role of women in the church" and made clear that he did "not subscribe to the sometimes shrill clamor that women are second-class
citizens in the church." According to the cardinal women need to
feel that they are wanted and that their gifts are "put to good use."
In his view, "some attention along these lines by the extraordinary
synod would do much to calm the present unrest. The majority of
Catholic women are very happy in their allegiance."[1]

When speaking of problems that have affected Catholic life
negatively in the past twenty years in the United States, Bishop
James Malone, the head of the bishops' conference, stated: "I think
of such things as ... confusion about sexual morality, widespread
breakdown of marriage and family, and the emergence of aggressive, secularized feminism."[2] Representatives of Women-Church
Convergence protested at the annual meeting of the National Conference of Catholic Bishops against this attempt to lay the blame
for the problems of the church on women: "Women are becoming for the bishops the scapegoat that secular humanism is for the
religious right. Women are, as they have ever been since Eve, described as the problem."[3] Those of us who had believed that some
of the bishops had heard our call to conversion from the sin of patriarchal sexism realized that we were again betrayed in the name
of "fraternal unity." Nothing has changed!

Without question the synod was a splendid manifestation of patriarchal church. Not only — as was to be expected — were there no
Catholic women members of the extraordinary synod but we were
also absent from the ten ecumenical observers. Not just the Roman Catholic but the whole Christian church was represented by
men only. Why couldn't the other Christian churches send women
priests, bishops, ministers, preachers of all colors to make up what
the Roman Church is lacking in catholicity and universality?

Not surprisingly, the sin of patriarchal sexism was never mentioned. The "message to the people of God" has a formidable list of
the "ills of the world": lack of respect for human life, suppression
of civil and religious liberties, contempt of the rights of families,
racial discrimination, economic imbalance, insurmountable debts,
problems of international security, and the race for more power-

1. *Origins* 15 (1985): 350.
2. Ibid., 36.
3. *Probe* 8 (1985): 8.

ful and terrible arms,[4] but it does not mention patriarchal sexism, which dehumanizes and exploits half of the world's population.

Although the final report of the synod does not link secularism with feminism, it treats the "vexatious subject" of women in the church under the heading "participation and co-responsibility in the church on all levels." It states: "May the church [i.e., the patriarchal hierarchy?] do its utmost so that they [women] might be able to express, in the service of the church, their own gifts and to play a greater part in the various fields of the church's apostolate."[5] Curiously, women are declared here to be a separate group constituting a distinct level of the church, insofar as we are mentioned after bishops and priests, deacons and religious, clergy and laity. Surely the synod did not want to say that women are fifth-class rather than second-class citizens! "So far, so bad . . ."

The year changed from 1985 to 1986 and I still had not found a topic sentence. Chris advised me to look for the key words or key paragraphs in my reading materials. Even a cursory reading of the synodal statements indicates that such a key word is "mystery." Since Chris and I are both fans of "Murder She Wrote," I was tempted to write a topic sentence like "postsynodal Roman Catholic theologians must become mystery writers" producing headlines such as "synod releases mystery story but there is no corpse!"

This last topic sentence, however, was not feasible because I knew of too many "casualties." Theologians such as Leonardo Boff and Charles Curran are still silenced or threatened with loss of their teaching jobs; feminist nuns are asked to acquiesce or to be expelled from their communities; divorced and remarried Catholics are barred from the sacraments; teenagers become pregnant and are expelled from schools, although Catholic institutions do not teach responsible and effective birth control; bishops like Thomas Gumbleton or Francis Murphy are not rewarded for their ecclesial leadership, while others have become cardinals despite their support for the Reagan government, which is responsible for increasing poverty and militarism. If Catholic theology in the postsynodal period is to serve the whole church and not just those "in secular or spiritual power," its main task, I suggest, will be to defend its intellectual freedom and ecclesial integrity.

---

4. *Origins* 15 (1985): 443.
5. Ibid., 449.

The final report of the synod witnesses "an increase in hunger, oppression, injustice and war, sufferings, terrorism and other forms of violence of every sort." But rather than reflect on the causes of such injustice and violence and the church's participation in them, the synod advocates a theology of suffering and the cross. "It seems to us that in the present-day difficulties God wishes to teach us more deeply the value, the importance and the centrality of the cross of Jesus Christ."[6] I had an old teacher of dogma who used to warn us: "Never use the word 'mystery'! Whenever a theologian uses the word 'mystery' he [and theologians at the time were all *he!*] has something to hide. 'Mystery' theology is bad theology!" I couldn't agree more.

However, it seems to me that the second theme proposed by the synod, "the church as *koinōnia*/communion,"[7] is pregnant with possibilities for Roman Catholic theology and ecclesiology in the postsynodal period. However, this Greek term needs to be better translated and understood. In his study *Pauline Partnership in Christ*, J. Paul Sampley has shown that *koinōnia* is a Greco-Roman legal term and was used as such by St. Paul.[8] It is best translated as shared partnership and commitment. Such consensual partnership is operative as long as the partners are of the "same mind" about the purpose and commitment upon which the partnership was founded in the first place. The common purpose and commitment of all Christians is, according to the synod, the witness to "the mystery of God through Jesus Christ in the Holy Spirit." This is spelled out, e.g., as "the child [son] of God became human [man] in order to make people [men] children of God. Through this familiarity with God, persons [man] are raised to a most high dignity. Therefore, when the church preaches Christ it [she] announces salvation to everyone [mankind]."[9] Catholic theology and episcopal teaching have to come clear on the question of whether my inclusive translation of this text is justified or not. Does the "salvific love of God for the world" include women? Have Christian women entered into the consensual partnership with God, Christ, and the Holy Spirit in the church for the salvation/well-being of everyone? *Not aggressive secular feminism* but *ecclesial femi-*

---

6. Ibid.

7. Ibid., 448.

8. J. Paul Sampley, *Pauline Partnership in Christ* (Philadelphia: Fortress Press, 1980).

9. *Origins* 15 (1985): 446.

nism raises the most difficult theological issues for the patriarchal hierarchy.

In a remarkable statement the synod report rejects a "purely hierarchical understanding of the church" but warns: "We cannot replace a false unilateral vision of the church as purely hierarchical with a new sociological conception which is also unilateral."[10] Instead, it advocates an ecclesiology of *koinōnia* as the "foundation for order in the church." This ecclesiology provides the sacramental foundation for collegiality and co-responsibility, ecumenical partnership and mission to the world, especially "in the service of the poor, the oppressed and the outcast,"[11] the majority of whom – I would add – are women and children dependent on women.

By way of conclusion, I would like to make two practical suggestions: First, as long as the college of bishops is restricted to men, that of cardinals should become restricted to women. Since the college of cardinals does not go back to Jesus nor stand in apostolic succession nor require ordination, no theological obstacle can be fabricated that would prohibit the implementation of such a suggestion. If it were adopted, the next synod or council of the Roman Catholic Church would then be able to live and model *koinōnia*, consensual partnership on an international and ecumenical level. In their article "We Are Catholics and We Are Feminists," M. Congo, M. Goodwin, and M. Smith have provided the theological symbolism for the self-understanding of future women cardinals electing the next pope:

> What must we do to change this institution which betrays women who have served so faithfully? Perhaps we should wear some sign, some signal that says: "I am woman – and what my sister endures, I too endure." Perhaps we should wear red. Red to acknowledge courage. Red to acknowledge that we are angry. Red to acknowledge that we are passionate. Red to acknowledge that we are sexual and like our sisters of herstory are still officially barred from the sanctuary because we menstruate. Red to acknowledge the blood that flows from us with each birth, with each abortion, with each battering and with each assault. Let us cloak ourselves in solidarity with our sisters who are in pain. Then we could wear red, speak the unspeakable, and take our place in the sanctuary. Then we could wear red... and proclaim: It is OUR church. WE are CHURCH. And we will not disappear.[12]

---

10. Ibid., 447.
11. Ibid., 450.
12. *Probe* 8 (1985): 8.

Second, the synod declares "reciprocal dialogue between bishops and theologians" as necessary "for the building up of the faith and its deeper comprehension."[13] Such a permanent reciprocal dialogue between bishops and feminist theologians ought to be instituted on a national and international level to foster a deeper comprehension of the church as a discipleship of equals in consensual partnership. The appointment of such theological commissions on diocesan, national, and international levels would acknowledge women as ecclesial and theological subjects in the postsynodal period.

---

13. *Origins* 15 (1985): 447f.

20 ──────────────────────

COMMITMENT
AND CRITICAL INQUIRY:
HARVARD DIVINITY SCHOOL
1988 CONVOCATION

───

CONTEXTUALIZATION

This address marks several professional changes, including my move from a predominantly Catholic university to an ecumenical theological environment. It marks the transition from an ecclesial theological context to a pluralistic, interreligious academic setting. I had enjoyed my sabbatical year at Union Theological Seminary in New York in 1974–75, but I felt that my social-ecclesial home was Catholicism. When after almost fifteen years of teaching I debated whether to move from the University of Notre Dame to the Episcopal Divinity School (EDS) in Cambridge, Massachusetts, a distinguished Catholic colleague encouraged me to accept the invitation. He reasoned that in the next decade(s) an intellectually responsible Catholic theology – one that would be "worth its salt" – would not be possible in Roman Catholic institutions

───────────────────────────────

For reading drafts of this address I am grateful to: Constance Buchanan, Katie Cannon, Karen Sorensen, Margaret Studier, and Ronald Thiemann. Obviously, I am responsible for the final form of this presentation.

but only in theological environments that guaranteed freedom of speech and research.[1]

The dean of EDS, a strong supporter of women's ordination to the priesthood, persuaded me that the school would provide a conducive environment for articulating a *different* Christian theology — a theology that could overcome the church's misogynism and provide a vision for a church in which the ordination of women was not a concession but the *sine qua non* of its existence. Hence EDS seemed the ideal place to engage in theoretical feminist reflection on and theological development of ministry. I envisioned working for a feminist Doctor of Ministry program that could provide an institutional framework and research time for women ministers to explore theoretically their ministerial experiences and theologies, especially if this program were integrated into an institutional center that could provide resources for research and dialogue. I felt that a center that could bring together women in ministry and women in academic theology was necessary since much of feminist theology in general, and feminist liberation theology in particular, was written by women based in theological schools and religious studies departments of universities. Compelled by this vision, I wrote a proposal for establishing such a Resource Center for Feminist Liberation Ministry and Theology at EDS, which my colleague Katie G. Cannon suggested naming the Pauli Murray Center:

> The center should be dedicated to the education of future feminist ministers and to the articulation and exploration of feminist theology and ministry. To my knowledge no such center exists to date in this country. There are community-based and movement-based feminist theological centers but none within the context of a traditional theological educational institution. Since Christian religion and church have been involved — consciously or not — in the legitimation and continuation of patriarchal oppression, it becomes necessary in a disciplined way to explore the patriarchal elements and functions of ecclesial ministry and theology. EDS therefore could make a great contribution to the wider church and its feminist praxis of theology and ministry by the establishment of such a resource center.
>
> The work of the center would consist in offering the M.A. and D.Min. degrees in the area of feminist liberation ministry and theology, in initiating research, bibliographic documentation, and a wide range

---

1. I am saddened to say that the "Instruction on the Ecclesial Vocation of the Theologian," issued by the Vatican's Congregation for the Doctrine of the Faith on May 24, 1990, proved his point.

of publications, in sponsoring conferences and continuing education events, and in serving as a resource center for feminist theology and ministry.

My proposal went on to spell out the institutional conditions and implications for the creation of such a center. However, my Episcopal women colleagues did not believe that it was feasible to argue for such a bold venture. Since the establishment of such a center would entail the creation of a "school within the school," they argued, this proposal would have no chance of being approved by the board of trustees and the male faculty. Instead, we decided to focus on an important part of the proposal, the implementation of a Doctor of Ministry program and, at a second stage, that of an M.A. program and degree in Feminist Liberation Theology and Ministry as a part of the established D.Min. and M.A. programs. In the school year 1986–87 we received the approval of the faculty and were ready to launch the M.Div. program in Feminist Liberation Theology and Ministry, for which I was responsible as the first coordinator. Since that time, the Feminist Liberation Theology and Ministry programs have attracted many students, dramatically changing educational perspectives and processes with the influx of students from different cultural and racial contexts.[2]

My decision to move from EDS to Harvard Divinity School (HDS) was equally difficult to make. Not only was I committed to the programs in Feminist Liberation Theology and Ministry at EDS, but I was also well aware of the powers of neutralization and co-optation in the academy. To put it facetiously, this move seemed like taking on a post in the Vatican in the interest of promoting feminist liberation theology and critical biblical interpretation. It implied a conscious decision to move to a "liberal," pluralistic, interreligious, academic environment, in which, in the words of one of my students, a "critical feminist liberation theology" is as much out of place as "a fish with a bicycle." My convocation address at the beginning of my tenure at HDS sought to speak to this tension and paradox. While the "minority" population of the school greeted it with enthusiastic affirmation, the address was largely passed over with "institutional silence." Like the patriarchal church so also the

---

2. See Alison M. Cheek, "A Theological Seminary's Bold Venture: Teaching Feminist Liberation Theology," in *Changing Women, Changing Church*, ed. Marie Louise Uhr (Newton, Australia: Millennium Books, 1992), 123–34.

academy has a difficult time changing its structures of exclusions and kyriocentric – master-centered – mindsets.

Readings: Sir 24:1-8, 13-21
          Mark 7:24-30

WE ARE CALLED TOGETHER here to mark the beginning of a new school year with a symbolic act – *convocatio*. As cultural anthropologists tell us, such ritual symbolic acts function simultaneously to induct participants into the common life-world of a community and to hold up to them shared values and visions. The convocation address provides an opportunity to reflect critically on the ritual act itself and on the shared visions and values it embodies. Such an exploration can uncover tensions and contradictions in how the community sees itself and the world, contradictions that provide openings and challenges for change. By reflecting on these tensions I seek to display the first step in a feminist theological practice. The inclusion of the previously excluded as theological subjects, I argue, calls for a paradigm shift from a value-detached scientism to a public rhetoric, from a hermeneutical model of conversation to a practical model of collaboration.

Kuhn's categories of scientific paradigm and heuristic models provide a theoretical framework for such an argument.[3] A paradigm, such as liberal theology, articulates a common ethos and constitutes a community of scholars who are formed by its institutions and systems of knowledge. Moreover, paradigms are not necessarily exclusive of each other but can exist alongside and in corrective interaction with each other until they are replaced by a new paradigm. By envisioning the Divinity School as a heterogenous public and our work as critical collaboration, I hope to contribute to the conversations on critical theological education and public theological discourse that Dean Thiemann initiated in his inaugural convocation address and programmatic alumnae/i day lecture of 1987.[4]

---

3. Thomas S. Kuhn, *The Structure of Scientific Revolutions* (Chicago: University of Chicago Press, 1962).

4. "Toward a Critical Theological Education," *Harvard Divinity Bulletin* 17 (1986): 6–9, and "Toward an American Public Theology," *Harvard Divinity Bulletin* 18 (1987): 4–6, 10. See also his "The Scholarly Vocation: Its Future Challenges and Threats," *ATS Theological Education* 24, no. 1 (1987): 86–101.

I

The contradictions marking this public event are obvious. For instance, we are an academic community in the context of a modern research university, but we have chosen the religious language of ritual to express our common identity and vision. I was asked to select readings from Jewish and Christian Scriptures but at the same time told that the genre of the convocation address is not that of the homily but that of the academic lecture. However, it was to be a short lecture, not longer than twenty minutes, that is, as short as a good sermon is supposed to be. This ambivalence in our choice of language and ritual seeks to do justice – I would submit – to the rich religious, confessional, and academic diversity of HDS's constituency and at the same time to retain our biblical-historical roots as a Christian divinity school in a university setting.

My own ritual location discloses these contradictions and tensions in the self-presentation of the school. Ritual positions me on high – I speak from a pulpit, cast in the role of the authoritative preacher to whom not only students but also faculty must look up in silence. At the same time I wear the insignia of the academic tradition that has replaced the sermon with the lecture. My academic position configures these institutional contradictions. As a biblical scholar I am to research only what the text meant in its first-century contexts, whereas as a faculty member of practical theology I am to teach the meaning and significance of the Bible for contemporary communities of faith.

I also speak here as a woman scholar. As a biblical scholar I am positioned at the center of the Christian paradigm. As a woman I belong to an outsider group that until this century has not been allowed to speak publicly and for centuries has been excluded from theology by religious law and academic convention. To be sure, my ritual position also signals change. Because of the bitter struggle of our foresisters, women have gained access to ministry, theological education, and scholarship in most but not in all religious communities. Under the leadership of Constance Buchanan the "Women in Religion Program" at Harvard has become a national and international center for gender studies in religion. Year after year it attracts scholars from around the world to teach and do research on women. For many of us this program is one of the major reasons why we are here today in such large numbers.

Yet I stand here not simply as a woman scholar but also as an educated white woman speaking with a German accent. While my gender position marks me as a member of the silenced majority in church and academy, my racial-cultural position designates me as heir to the privileges of white Western Christianity and to the mindset of the Euro-American academy. As a feminist liberation theologian I am challenged by the voices of my Afro-American, Native American, Asian-American, and Hispanic sisters to use these privileges in the interest of women suffering from multiple oppressions. To this end I need to collaborate with women from different cultural and religious subject-locations in articulating a "different" theological discourse.

Yet such a critical collaboration remains a "problematic potentiality" as long as women entering religious studies have to adopt the languages of those clerical and academic communities that have silenced us, have defined us as the "other of the Divine" or as the "other" of "the Man of Reason,"[5] have relegated us to social, ecclesial, and intellectual nonsubjects or — to use the expression of Gustavo Gutiérrez — to "nonpersons."[6] In order to become speaking theological subjects, women must "master" the clerical and academic discourses of the Fathers. For in Kuhn's terms, to become a member of the community of scholars students have to internalize the entire constellation of beliefs, values, techniques, shared worldviews, and systems of knowledge as maps or guidelines for thinking "scholarly."

This intensive process of academic socialization could be likened to immersing oneself in the languages and customs of a foreign culture. In the course of this socialization students experience contradictions between their own social or religious life-worlds and those of their discipline until they speak and think in its idiom. Such a process of inculturation, of becoming "a Harvard man," is less alienating for those who share a gender, racial, social, cultural, or religious background with those who have shaped the discipline.

Women who enter theological education have three choices. Either we embrace the languages, traditions, theories, or world-

---

5. See, e.g., G. Lloyd, *The Man of Reason: "Male" and "Female" in Western Philosophy* (Minneapolis: University of Minnesota Press, 1984), and my contribution, "The Politics of Otherness: Biblical Interpretation as a Critical Praxis for Liberation," to the Gustavo Gutiérrez *Festschrift*.

6. See, e.g., Gustavo Gutiérrez, *The Power of the Poor in History* (Maryknoll, N.Y.: Orbis Books, 1983).

views of theology, which has silenced, marginalized, and objectified us *as women,* and risk muting our own theological voice and creativity. Or we reject theological inquiry as white male scholarship because we recognize its destructiveness for women's self-definition and self-affirmation. However, this second choice deprives us of the intellectual skills and tools for finding our own theological voice and for changing theology in the interest of women and all other nonpersons. A third option compels us to critically articulate the experiences of contradiction between our own cultural-political-religious ethos and that of the discipline and to keep them in creative tension. For to vary Audre Lorde's dictum, the master's tools will dismantle the master's house as long as we use them for building our own house and not for executing the master's mindset and discursive blueprints.[7]

Feminist liberation theologians who consciously seek to work in the interest of women and other nonpersons realize that our existence and practice as feminist liberation theologians and as theological scholars is *contradictory.* As women marked by race, class, and culture we belong to a marginalized and exploited group, whereas as theological scholars we share in the educational privileges of the white-male academic elite. This contradictory subject-position of feminist liberation scholars in religion provides a rich source of inspiration, energy, and creativity for doing our theological work.[8] By consciously taking the standpoint of "women," defined by gender, race, class, culture, and religion, the feminist scholar in religion seeks both to deconstruct oppressive religious and theological practices and to reconstruct a religious heritage and theological voice for women. To that end she must not only reconstruct the discourse of her own discipline but also collaborate in articulating a different paradigm of religious scholarship and theological knowledge. Theology in a different key would no longer constitute itself by excluding or silencing the religious experience and theological voice of the subordinated Others. Rather, by constituting itself as a heterogeneous polyphonic public, theology would be able to develop critical collaboration and discursive practices in the interest of a democratic public no longer confined to elite male citizens in church and nation.

---

7. Audre Lorde, *Sister Outsider* (New York: The Crossing Press, 1984), 110–13.

8. See also Patricia Hill Collins, "Learning From the Outsider Within: The Sociological Significance of Black Feminist Thought," *Social Problems* 33 (1986): 14–32.

The Divinity School as a public forum for critical collaboration would encourage especially those who have been excluded from theological discourse to articulate their religious self-understandings, to create religious-moral meanings, to find their particular theological voice, to reconstruct religious history, and to reshape the theological knowledge and moral values of the past as a heritage for the future.

Critical collaboration as the metaphor for naming our common task of "doing theology" from different subject-locations and standpoints not only takes into account the pains, long hours, and exhaustion of hard labor but also evokes the anticipation, satisfaction, and exhilaration of creative work. It reminds us that our task is not simply to understand religious communities and traditions but to change them as well. It insists that as researchers, students, staff, teachers, or administrators we contribute in different ways to the "common task" of "doing" theology. Critical collaboration also has negative overtones, as in "collaboration with the enemy," which warn us that unless theological institutions allow for the equal participation of those previously excluded, collaboration easily spells co-optation or treason.

Such a paradigm of theology as critical collaboration invites the study and assessment of cultural-religious practices as rhetorical practices. Cultural-religious practices include not only discursive practices such as language, texts, ideas, or theories, but also non-discursive practices such as institutions, social systems, or gender, race, and class divisions. Cultural-religious practices are rhetorical practices. By rhetorical I do not mean mere rhetoric as linguistic manipulation, technical skill, or stylistic ornament but as communicative praxis that links knowledge with action and passion. It does not deny the Others or set them at a distance. Rather it insists that as sociopolitical practices discourses call for public discussion and moral judgment. Theology understood as rhetorical or communicative praxis unmasks the value-detached scientistic posture of religious studies as well as the doctrinal certainty of theology narrowly conceived. At the same time it reconstitutes theology as a religious-ethical practice of critical inquiry and particular commitments.[9]

---

9. For a fuller development of the notion of biblical studies as rhetorical see my *Society of Biblical Literature* presidential address.

II

Allow me to clarify this proposal for a different theological paradigm with reference to Edward Farley's discussion of the university in the Enlightenment tradition[10] in order to indicate the oppositions such a paradigm shift will have to overcome. The ideal of the Euro-American Enlightenment was critically accomplished knowledge in the interest of human freedom, equality, and justice under the guidance of pure reason. Its principle of unqualified critical inquiry and assessment does not exempt any given reality, authority, tradition, or institution. Knowledge is not a given but a culturally and historically embodied language and therefore always open to probing inquiry and relentless criticism. This critical principle of the Enlightenment was, however, institutionalized as the empiricist paradigm of knowledge that gives primacy to experienced data and empirical inquiry. Its "logic of facts" relies on abstraction for the sake of rigor, evidence, and precision.

The critical principle of the Enlightenment has also engendered three historical correctives that underline the complexity, particularity, and corruption of reality. The esthetic-romantic corrective stresses intuitive imagination over selective abstraction, the religious-cultural corrective insists on tradition as wisdom and heritage, and the political-practical corrective asserts that there is no pure reason as instrument of knowledge that can lead to a just society. In the beginning was not pure reason but power. The institutions of so-called pure reason – the sciences, scholarship, and the university – hide from themselves their own complicity in societal agendas of power. These three correctives introduce the hermeneutical principle as a second principle of critical inquiry.

However, I would suggest that a fourth corrective is in the process of being articulated, for in interaction with postmodernism and critical theory so-called minority discourses question the Enlightenment's notion of the universal transcendental subject as the disembodied voice of reason. These discourses assert that the political-social and intellectual-ideological creation of the devalued Others goes hand in hand with the creation of the "Man of Reason" as the rational subject positioned outside of time and space. He is

---

10. Edward Farley, *The Fragility of Knowledge: Theological Education in the Church and the University* (Philadelphia: Fortress Press, 1988).

the abstract knower and disembodied speaker of Enlightenment science.

But in distinction to postmodernism, minority discourses insist that the colonialized Others cannot afford to abandon the notion of the subject and the possibility of defining the world.[11] Rather, the subordinated Others must engage in a political and theoretical process of becoming the subjects of knowledge and history. We who have previously been excluded from the academy have to use what we know about the world and our lives to critique the dominant culture and to construct a heterogeneous public that fosters appreciation of difference.

To be sure, the argument of these four correctives is not with empirical research, analytical scholarship, or critical abstraction itself but with an uncritical conception of reason, knowledge, and scholarship. The atrophy and anorexia of the critical principle in the modern university have engendered a scientistic ethos of allegedly disinterested impartial research, a proliferation of techniques and specializations in ever narrower fields of professionalization – practices that are reenforced by the university's reward system. Insofar as the scientific paradigm fails to apply the critical principle of the Enlightenment to its own self-understanding and its institutions of knowledge, it cannot recognize its own scientistic character as rhetorical but has to marginalize its four correctives as "ideological." Yet by doing so, the modern research university fails to advance the Enlightenment goal of a just and democratic society. Therefore, the voices calling for value-clarification and moral education in higher education[12] can effect change only if the university relativizes its dominant paradigm by institutionalizing rather than marginalizing the four correctives of Enlightenment reason.

III

Although the research-oriented Divinity School has been fashioned in the likeness of the empiricist-scientific paradigm of the modern

11. See, e.g., Nancy Hartsock, "Rethinking Modernism: Minority vs. Majority Theories," *Cultural Critique* 7 (1987): 187–206; Linda Alcoff, "Cultural Feminism Versus Poststructuralism: The Identity Crisis in Feminist Theory," *Signs* 13 (1988): 3–17.

12. See, e.g., President Derek Bok's report for 1986–87 to the Board of Overseers, which was issued in April 1988.

university, it has nevertheless sought to embrace a more complex paradigm of knowledge insofar as it has adopted not only the critical but also the hermeneutical and practical principles of knowing. However, as long as doctoral education perpetuates the ethos of specialism and scientism theological discourse will remain part of the problem rather than contribute to the articulation of public ethics and moral vision.

Traditionally theology has been understood as the science of God or as the systematic exploration of biblical and church teachings on doctrine and morals. In contrast to such a doctrinal or confessional understanding of theology biblical, historical, and religious studies have developed their own self-understandings as critical scientific studies in terms of the modern research university. Freed from the fetters of doctrinal commitments and ecclesiastical controls, scholarship supposedly pursues critical inquiry with utmost value-neutrality, detachment, and objectivity. It is descriptive rather than evaluative.

The so-called hard sciences such as biblical and historical studies distinguish themselves from theological studies in terms of descriptive objectivity over against confessional commitment. This posture of value-detached scientism has however been thoroughly challenged by philosophical hermeneutics, the sociology of knowledge, and critical theory. Although the progressive vanguard in my own discipline, for instance, utilizes insights from philosophical hermeneutics, the sociology of knowledge, and cultural anthropology for the interpretation of early Christian practices, it often uses them as scientific rules and prescriptions. Insofar as the discipline fails to apply a critical analysis to its own rhetorical practices or to use critical theory for investigating the function of biblical texts in contemporary church and society, it falls short of its claim to be a critical discipline.

The hermeneutical models of theology as narrative and of theology as conversation focus on the internal story of the community and center on the classics of the tradition. Theology construed as conversation admits of a plurality of voices and disciplines. It not only allows for the participation of those previously excluded from theology, ministry, and the academy but also seeks to compel the various discrete theological disciplines — or intellectual villages as Clifford Geertz calls them[13] — to engage in dialogue. This is not an

---

13. Clifford Geertz, *Local Knowledge* (New York: Basic Books, 1983).

easy task since the specialism of the graduate school encourages, for instance, biblical students to master the technical skills of their area of specialization but does not invite a hermeneutical exploration of their theological frameworks or foster the cultivation of a "common theological language."

Yet theological scholarship that makes its hermeneutical commitments plain for others to examine is not less but more scientific; it is not less but more critical than an inquiry that hides its own interests and goals or denies its particular social location. Since what we see depends on where we stand, our socioreligious location or rhetorical context decides how we see the world, construct reality, or explore religious practices. When we do theology from a variety of experiences and standpoints we enhance rather than hinder theological work.

The creativity and excellence of a theological school rests not simply on technical competence but on the presence of scholars who speak from diverse experiences. Theology as conversation depends on how much we are able to form an intellectual theological "rainbow-coalition" and to hold our differences in creative tension. If the excellence of a theological school rests on diversity rather than conformity, then in evaluating students or hiring faculty members, for instance, we cannot just look for signs of excellence in their respective disciplinary specialties. We must also look for evidence that candidates are able to cross the narrow boundaries of their disciplinary village; in other words that they are not *Fachidioten,* specialized idiots, but that they have communicative competence and moral vision.

Liberation and feminist theologies, however, have criticized the model of theology as conversation for mystifying relationships of power in discourse not only by advocating a value-neutral pluralism but also by giving the impression that we all enter the conversation on equal terms. Moreover, by hypostatizing the text as a partner in the conversation this model obfuscates the real relationship between text and interpreter, between the classics of a culture or religion and structures of domination. By aiming for domination-free conversation and consensus this model idealizes the practices of theology and religious studies that are embedded in relationships of power. If this is recognized, the distinction between theology as committed confessional inquiry and religious studies as impartial objective inquiry breaks down. Both constitute political-rhetorical practices that are shaped by the Western "Man of Reason."

The "inclusion" of the previously excluded as theological subjects, I argue, entails a paradigm shift from a scientistic to a rhetorical genre, from a hermeneutical model of conversation to a practical model of collaboration. Since rhetorical practices display not only a referential moment about something and a moment of self-implication by a speaker or actor but also a persuasive moment of directedness to involve the other, they elicit responses, emotions, interests, judgments, and commitments directed toward a common vision.

In my presidential address to the Society of Biblical Literature I have extended this argument in terms of my own discipline to include not only the rhetorical practices of biblical texts but also the way we understand our function as scholars and in whose interests we do biblical scholarship. Since the sociohistorical location of rhetoric is the public of the *polis,* to be understood today in terms of global interdependence, a rhetorical paradigm shift situates biblical studies in such a way that public discourse and political responsibility become an integral part of our research and educational activities. If, as Krister Stendahl has argued,[14] the Bible has become a classic of Western culture because of its status as Holy Scripture, New Testament scholars must study not only its historical-rhetorical practices but also its functions in contemporary society.[15] Biblical scholarship in collaboration with other disciplines must therefore articulate public-ethical criteria for rejecting the religious authority claims and identity formations of destructive religious discourses inscribed in sacred texts. Today, when right-wing political movements forcefully employ the languages of hate encoded in religious scriptures and traditions, biblical scholars can no longer withdraw into our academic and clerical ivory towers but must become critical participants in the competing public discourses on the Bible.

If theological discourse is to contribute to a religious critical consciousness and cultural moral imagination, it must take seriously the particular social and religious locations of those "doing theology" in the interest of the "common good." Rather than

---

14. Krister Stendahl, "The Bible as Classic and the Bible as Holy Scripture," *Journal of Biblical Literature* 103 (1984): 10.

15. See also Helmut Koester's convocation address "The Divine Human Being," *Harvard Theological Review* 78 (1985): 243–52.

striving for consensus and integration, it must aim for a pluralistic collaboration that respects the particular social locations and religious reference communities of its practitioners and seeks connections between diverse theological-cultural discourses.[16] Since it invites a plurality of often contradictory responses to the problems at hand, it produces deeply felt tensions that will turn into sectarian divisions if they are not articulated in terms of a shared vision of well-being for all.

Let me try to illustrate my point: In his 1982 presidential address to the American Academy of Religion our colleague Gordon Kaufman reminded scholars in religion of our responsibility to face the nuclear devastation of our planet.[17] He called on theologians to deconstruct and reconstruct the central Christian symbols in such a way that Christian theology and community will not foster the mentality and culture of possible atomic annihilation but help to avert them. Sharing Kaufman's conviction the feminist Goddess theologian Carol Christ has argued that the Christian theology of finitude, body, and nature are at the heart of the nuclear mentality.[18] In her book *Models of God* the Christian theologian Sallie McFague in turn has rearticulated Kaufman's project in feminist terms but has come more and more to understand the ecological deterioration of the earth as the major problem.[19] And liberation theologians of all colors have insisted on the oppression of peoples due to racism, sexism, class exploitation, homophobia, militarism, and colonialism as the practical and ideological condition of nuclear mentality. While a theological conversation between these diverse theologians will never reach consensus because of their fundamental theological differences, they nevertheless can collaborate with each other because they share a common theological commitment, ethos, and passion.

---

16. For the importance of pluralism in theological articulation see Diana L. Eck, "Darsana: Hinduism and Incarnational Theology," *Harvard Divinity Bulletin* 17 (1987): 10–11, and in theological education see Margaret R. Miles, "Hermeneutics of Generosity and Suspicion: Pluralism and Theological Education," *ATS Theological Education* 23 Supplement (1987): 34–52.

17. Gordon Kaufman, "Nuclear Eschatology and the Study of Religion," *Journal of the American Academy of Religion* 51 (1983): 13.

18. Carol P. Christ, *The Laughter of Aphrodite: Reflections on a Journey to the Goddess* (Boston: Beacon Press, 1987), 214.

19. Sallie McFague, *Models of God: Theology for an Ecological Nuclear Age* (Philadelphia: Fortress Press, 1987).

IV

In place of a conclusion, I would like to recall the two women of the biblical readings we have heard: one human, the other divine. Both represent the religious-theological voice that has been excluded, repressed, or marginalized.

Whether we locate the rhetorical practice of the Markan text in the life of Jesus or in that of the early church, its argument discloses religious prejudice and exclusive identity. The Syrophoenician woman is characterized ethnically and culturally as a religious outsider. She enters theological argument, turns it against itself, overcomes the prejudice of Jesus, and achieves the well-being of her little daughter. As distinct from all other controversy stories, Jesus does not have the last word. Rather, the woman's argument prevails and her daughter is freed from her destructive spirit.

The other voice is that of Divine Wisdom, "who speaks with pride among her people." She offers life, rest, knowledge, and the abundance of creation to all who accept her. She is all-powerful, intelligent, unique, people-loving, an initiate of God's knowledge, a collaborator in God's work. She is the leader on the way out of the bondage of Egypt, the preacher and teacher in Israel, and the architect of God's creation. She shares the throne of God and lives in symbiosis with the Divine. Reading the biblical texts that speak of her one can sense how much the language struggles to characterize Chokma-Sophia as divine in the theological framework of monotheism.

The theology of Divine Wisdom has been suppressed and cut off not only in Jewish but also in Christian theology. Yet traces of her theology, of sophialogy, have been rediscovered by New Testament scholarship. Earliest Christian theology understood Jesus first as Divine Wisdom's messenger and prophet and then as Sophia-Incarnate. Nevertheless, most Christians have never heard of her. The Sophia-God of Jesus could not make her home among her people. Her offer of well-being, beauty, and knowledge presents rich possibilities for the future of theology in a different key.

21 _____

FEMINIST MINISTRY
IN THE DISCIPLESHIP OF EQUALS

CONTEXTUALIZATION

When I was invited by St. Bernard's Institute to give the commencement address as one of the recipients of an honorary doctorate[1] at the 1990 graduation ceremonies, I was conscious and appreciative of the courage it took for a Roman Catholic institution to extend such an invitation. However, I was not sufficiently aware of how much courage it took in the face of increasing ecclesiastical repression.

In the months following this graduation I experienced first hand the ecclesiastical politics of silencing, defamation, and manipulation. In celebration of its one hundredth anniversary, the theological faculty of the prestigious University of Fribourg/Freiburg, Switzerland, had planned a symposium on the topic "Theology in Intercultural Dialogue." The faculty had appointed a task force to prepare an event that would celebrate the catholicity of the faculty and its theology. This task force had proposed a week-long symposium on the goal of engendering a critical dialogue between European theology, which was for centuries the theology exported to the whole world, and theologies of other continents.

Unpublished Commencement Address, St. Bernard's Institute, Rochester, N.Y., May 4, 1990.

1. I also want to thank the faculty and trustees of St. Joseph's College in West Hartford, Conn., and of Denison University in Granville, Ohio, for honoring my work in this way.

For this dialogue-celebration the faculty invited Gustavo Gutiérrez from Peru to represent Latin American theology, Jean-Marc Ela from Cameroon to represent African theology, Tissa Balasuriya from Sri Lanka to represent Asian theology, and myself from the United States to represent feminist theology. Although it was hoped to confer the honorary doctorate on all four scholars, academic custom required that the honorees would officially learn of this honor only at the university's *dies academicus* in November, the official conclusion of the centennial celebration.

Though the University of Freiburg/Fribourg is a state university, its Roman Catholic theology faculty is sponsored by the Dominican order and is thus subject to Vatican oversight. Since the faculty had had difficulties in the matter of conferring honorary degrees in previous years, some members unofficially inquired in Rome whether these four theologians would be able to receive the *nihil obstat.* Two of the four, they learned, would not. (The names of these two scholars are still not known, but I was assured that my name was not among the two who were rejected!)

To avoid negative publicity, the faculty revised the list and officially recommended to the Vatican Congregation for Education five different candidates for the honorary doctorate, among them Archbishop Rembert Weakland of Milwaukee; South African anti-apartheid theologian Albert Nolan; Swiss Reformed theologian and a past president of the World Council of Churches Dr. Marga Bührig; Archbishop Arturo Rivera y Damas of San Salvador; and Dr. James A. Sanders, an American Presbyterian biblical scholar. This time the Vatican's Congregation for Education, headed by former U.S. pronuncio Pio Laghi, did not object to the two Protestant candidates, but it vetoed the honorary doctorate for both Archbishop Weakland and Dominican Father Nolan.[2]

As an official reason for the refusal of the *nihil obstat* to Archbishop Weakland, the Vatican congregation cited his statements on abortion. Weakland was the sole American bishop who had held pastoral hearings for women in his diocese on the difficult moral questions of birth control and abortion. Such hearings revealed "how far the gap is between the official teaching" of the church forbidding the use of birth control and the views of "some very conscientious women."[3] Although the Swiss univer-

2. See the newspaper reports of November 8, 10, and 16, 1990, in *Freiburger Nachrichten* and of November 15, 22, and 24, 1990, in *Vaterland.*
3. See Peter Steinfels, "Vatican Bars Swiss University from Honoring Archbishop

sity had chosen Archbishop Weakland primarily because of his central role in drafting the American bishops' pastoral letter on the economy, the Vatican explicitly referred to the archbishop's statements on abortion in explaining its refusal. Allegedly these statements had caused "a great deal of confusion among the faithful."

In protest the members of the Catholic Theological Faculty of the University of Freiburg/Fribourg voted on October 24, 1990, not to grant any of the five honorary doctorates. According to the American press, the theological faculty and the Dominican order apologized to Archbishop Weakland and presumably to the other "official" candidates for the honorary doctorate. To my knowledge, however, neither the faculty nor the order has extended such an apology to the other four "unofficial" candidates whom it had invited for an intercultural theological dialogue. In light of these subsequent events, the action of St. Bernard's Institute has become for me a special sign of courage and hope.

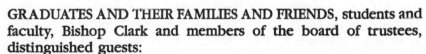

GRADUATES AND THEIR FAMILIES AND FRIENDS, students and faculty, Bishop Clark and members of the board of trustees, distinguished guests:

First of all allow me to express my deep appreciation to all the members of St. Bernard's Institute community, especially to the faculty and board of trustees, for choosing me as this year's commencement speaker and as a recipient of the honorary doctorate in divinity. I deeply appreciate your recognition of my work in these difficult times. I draw courage and hope from this tribute and accept it as a sign of your desire to honor women's work and contributions to the theological discourse of the church.

We have gathered here tonight to celebrate the accomplishments of the graduating class and the successful completion of their theological studies. We have come together here to ritualize the transition from study to ministry, from theological reflection to ministerial commitment and struggle. Tonight I invite you to explore with me what it means theologically to commit one-

of Milwaukee," *New York Times,* November 11, 1990; Pat Windsor, "Vatican Vetoes Doctorate for Weakland," *National Catholic Reporter,* November 16, 1990.

self in the last decade of this century to the ministry of the church in an ever-expanding world community. As many of you know, I speak here from the perspective and struggle of feminist theology. For centuries the voices and visions of women and so-called lay-men have been excluded from ecclesial decision making, theology, and ministry. Nevertheless, many of the baptized have envisioned and engendered church as *ekklēsia*, as the discipleship community of equals. In its focus on women feminist theology is not exclusive of men. Rather, it invites men, those who are ordained and those who are not, to identify with women's struggle for ecclesial equality, authority, and citizenship, for a patriarchal-hierarchical church construes all the baptized in cultural-ecclesiastical terms as "feminine" subordinates or as immature "children."

Our visions and hopes for the future are conditioned and limited by our experiences in the past and present. Almost thirty years ago when I started to study theology, rumor had it that Karl Rahner was going to be silenced. At that time I made a solemn promise: If Rahner were condemned I would not continue with my theological studies, since I firmly believed that intellectual integrity and religious freedom of speech were absolutely necessary for ministry in the church. As we all know, the Second Vatican Council happened instead. It opened "windows and doors" to the world and engendered new theological and ministerial possibilities. The church on the whole became oriented toward the future rather than bent on defending its monarchical repressive structures of the past. Rahner emerged as one of the great "church fathers" of the twentieth century.

Through the conciliar process the early Christian vision of the discipleship of equals has been incarnated as a lived reality among the people of God. Women have emerged as creative, articulate, and trail-blazing members in the church and its ministry. This was possible because the vision of church as the discipleship community of equals understands all members of the church to be fully responsible democratic citizens and does not restrict ecclesial leadership to male clerical elites. Such a vision of church has early Christian roots and is engendered by the teachings of Vatican II. Churches all around the world have sought to translate this vision into ecclesial practice. In many parts of the world the Roman Catholic Church has become in the past twenty-five years or so a force for social justice, radical democracy, and global peace. It has moved from a form of Roman-imperial, Eurocentric[4] Catholicism to a pluralistic actualization of World Catholicism that utilizes the gifts and talents of all its people.

And yet, twenty-five years after the council we seem to have come almost full circle. Theologians such as Hans Küng, Jacques Poiher, Edward Schillebeeckx, Charles Curran, or Leonardo Boff are silenced. Attempts are made again and again to pressure European and North American bishops' conferences and local churches into conformity, while African, Latin American, and Asian churches are measured by Eurocentric colonial standards. Reactionary powers in the Vatican and in national episcopal conferences are supported by "big money" and capitalist interest groups that work under the disguise of being "true defenders of pure doctrine." Anyone interested in a careful documentation and analysis of this struggle between those advocating a Constantinian capitalist model of church and those inspired by the vision of the discipleship of equals should read Penny Lernoux's book *The People of God*, which carefully records "the extent of the Vatican crackdown, along with the attempts to resist the Restoration by continuing reforms begun by Vatican II. At stake are two different visions of faith: the church of Caesar, powerful and rich, and the church of Christ – loving, poor, and spiritually rich."[5]

Woman especially have taken the vision of the discipleship of equals very seriously. We have consistently maintained that we must be acknowledged as human and ecclesial subjects with equal rights and dignity rather than remain objects of patriarchal theology and clerical governance. Yet our call to conversion from ecclesial patriarchy is often met with outright rejection or subtle co-optation. While we have denounced the structural and personal sin of patriarchal sexism and have claimed our ecclesial dignity, rights, and responsibilities, those who advocate theological restoration of the pre–Vatican II patriarchal model of church have appealed to the maleness of Christ. They have produced the ideology of essential gender and sacramental difference in order to legitimate church structures that exclude from sacramental, doc-

---

4. On the important subject of Eurocentrism see Samir Amin, *Eurocentrism: Critique of an Ideology* (New York: Monthly Review Press, 1989).

5. Penny Lernoux, *People of God: Struggle for World Catholicism* (New York: Penguin Books, 1990), 1. See esp. pp. 206–57 on the Roman Restoration in the United States and 283–364 on the international Catholic Right.

trinal, and governing power all women and those men who are associated with women.

The church understood as clerical-patriarchal hierarchy not only is exclusive of women in leadership, but also establishes its clerical territorial boundaries as a women-free zone through celibacy. Resorting to the Aristotelian argument for the patriarchal order of household and state, Thomistic theology has insisted that "the female sex cannot signify any superiority of rank, for woman is in a state of subjection" (*Summa Theologiae Suppl.* 39, 1 ad 1). Since it understands ecclesial authority and power in terms of "power over," it has argued that women cannot receive the spiritual power of the sacrament of ordination because of their position of subordination. Women are to remain the silenced majority of the faithful who are not allowed to preach the gospel. The sin of patriarchal sexism still seems to prevail over the vision of the discipleship of equals that Christ offers to the patriarchal church today. Nevertheless, we must be careful not to construe our struggle for the transformation of the patriarchal church into the discipleship community of equals in dualistic oppositional terms. There are many members of the patriarchal hierarchy that seek to realize the discipleship community of equals, just as women and other ecclesial nonsubjects still have to struggle with our religious internalizations of patriarchal values and visions.

The structural sin of sexism is like an evil spirit of possession that threatens to destroy the ecclesial future of our daughters and sons. When I was working on this talk a young woman student came to my office to discuss with me her program of studies. Although she had enrolled in the M.Div. program at Harvard and was committed to ministry, she did not intend to be ordained because she did not want to join an institutional church. It turned out that she had been a Roman Catholic who now considered herself a practicing Christian without church affiliation. Her negative experiences as a parish youth minister after college had brought about a profound alienation. One year of involvement with the patriarchal church on the parish level had estranged her from her community and heritage.

She reminded me of a doctoral student in theology who sat crying in my office after Father Curran was censured. "They are taking away my church," she lamented. "The only church I have known is the post–Vatican II church." She had grown up in a local church practicing the discipleship of equals and was shocked by the violence exerted by the patriarchal hierarchy against its most faithful members. Many women students in theological studies have confessed that they dread the day of graduation; for their fellow seminarians this is the step to ordination, but their own gifts for ministry are neglected or rejected by the official church. Their commitment to ministry in the discipleship of equals is greeted with silence or derision rather than with appreciation and encouragement.

Mark's Gospel tells a story about a Greek woman from Syrophoenicia whose little daughter was possessed by an evil spirit. She asks Jesus to heal her daughter, but Jesus refuses, likening the Gentiles to dogs who should not steal the food of the children. But the woman does not give up in the face of such an insult. As a cultural and religious outsider, she enters into theological argument with Jesus about the exclusion of Gentiles from the life-giving power of God's reign. The woman turns Jesus' argument against itself and overcomes his prejudice. No one should be excluded. God's power of salvation is without boundaries. And because of her argument her daughter is freed from the evil power destroying her life and her future. The Syrophoenician whose adroit argument opened up a future of freedom for her daughter has become the apostolic foremother of world Catholicism by advocating the inclusion of people of different religions, cultures, and races. She has achieved the setting of a new table to which all are invited, under which no one must grovel and beg for crumbs.

Just as the Syrophoenician so feminist ministers and theologians today argue with those representatives of Jesus who fear the transformation of the patriarchal church into the inclusive discipleship community of equals, a transformative process that has been underway in world Catholicism for most of this century. Rather than to allow women to preside at the eucharistic table, they prefer to withhold the eucharistic bread from the faithful altogether. Feminist ministers and theologians cannot accept silently such violation of the right of the baptized to the sacraments. Therefore, we do not move away from the center of the argument to the fringes of the church or leave it altogether, but we continue to struggle for change.

We do so because we have a dream that one day in the not too distant future the patriarchal church will be freed from its bondage to Caesar's imperial structures. We still have a dream that one day the patriarchal clerical pyramid will be transformed into the "round table" of equal discipleship, a dream that one day the Euro-centered, male-dominated, Roman-imperial church will become *ekklēsia* — the decision-making citizenry of all the baptized around the whole world. Those of us who have been called to Catholic ministry therefore must redefine ministry in terms of this vision of church as a discipleship of equals. We must both reject the notion of ministry as loyalty and service to patriarchal structures and at the same time reconceive ministry as a challenge to these structures.

In one of the earliest systematic feminist theological works, the Jewish feminist theologian Judith Plaskow argued that theological terms, categories, and concepts function differently with respect to women than men.[6] Building on the insights of Valerie Saiving she analyzes the understanding of sin and grace in the work of two major Protestant theologians: Reinhold Niebuhr and Paul Tillich. She concludes that neither the understanding of sin as pride and rebellion against God nor that of sin as estrangement reflects women's experience and socialization. Rather, women's sin is self-denial, self-abnegation, and self-sacrifice in the service of others, the failure to become a self.

Such a failure is not inherent in women's nature but due to women's cultural and religious socialization. Insofar as Christian theology does not take into account this difference in women's and men's self-understanding and experience but takes men's experience as a "universal" standard, it turns women's failure to become a self into virtue and grace. Its preaching of grace and salvation therefore cannot be liberating for women since it enforces feminine cultural stereotypes. A similar theological argument can be developed for the theological notion of ministry as service, since it has been differently interpreted for women and men.

The Greek term *diakonia,* which means literally "waiting at tables," is usually translated as "service" or "ministry."[7] We can distinguish two different meanings in the biblical usage of the word-cluster *diakonia/diakonos/diakonein,* which have become

---

6. Judith Plaskow, *Sex, Sin and Grace: Women's Experience and the Theologies of Reinhold Niebuhr and Paul Tillich* (Washington, D.C.: University Press of America, 1980). This is a revision of her 1975 Yale dissertation.

7. See H. W. Beyer, *"diakoneō,"* in *Theological Dictionary of the New Testament (TDNT)*, ed. Gerhard Kittel (Grand Rapids: Eerdmans, 1964), 2:81–93; K. H. Rengstorf, *"doulos,"* ibid., 261–80; K. H. Hess, "serve," *New International Dictionary of New Testament Theology,* ed. Colin Brown (Grand Rapids: Zondervan, 1975), 3:544–49; R. Tuente, "slave," ibid., 592–98.

paradigmatic for later theology: In a religious-spiritualized sense the word-cluster signifies an honorary activity, a person standing in the service of the god/s, in the service of a city or common-wealth, or in the service of great ideas or ideals. When used in this sense the word-cluster characterizes Christian preachers and mis-sionaries like Paul or Phoebe as representatives and messengers of God.

However, in its original sense the terms mean actual material service, waiting at table and other menial tasks. The "servant" had a low social position, was dependent on her or his master/mistress, and could not command respect. Despite the debasing negative social connotations of its original meaning, "service" has become the key symbol for the revival of a "servant ecclesiology" with pro-gressive intentions. Feminist theological attempts to salvage this biblical symbol in the face of the stringent feminist critique of its cultural-political functions in the oppression of women share the assumption of such a "servant ecclesiology," that selfless "service" is central to Christian identity and community.

Since the early 1960s the image of the servant-church has come to dominate progressive Roman Catholic and Protestant ecclesiolo-gies and ministerial self-understandings. This revival of a theology of *diakonia* went hand in hand with a change in the church's at-titude to the "world." For instance, the Pastoral Constitution on the Church in the Modern World of Vatican II teaches in Article 3 that just as Jesus Christ became human not to be served but to serve so also the church seeks to serve the world by fostering "the brotherhood of all men." In his book *Models of the Church* Avery Dulles points out that a similar servanthood ecclesiology motivates official statements of other churches.[8]

Such a servanthood ecclesiology insists with Bonhoeffer "that the Church is the Church only when it exists for others."[9] Yet insofar as this theology does not critically analyze the social un-derpinnings of servant-language, it is not able to recognize it as "theological double-speak." Since the theology of service has dif-ferent implications for men and women, black and white, ordained and nonordained, powerful and powerless, the understanding of

---

8. Avery Dulles, *Models of the Church* (Garden City, N.Y.: Doubleday, 1974), 87. See also John E. Booty, *The Servant Church* (Wilton, Conn.: Morehouse-Barlow, 1982).

9. Dietrich Bonhoeffer, *Letters and Papers from Prison,* rev. ed. (New York: Macmillan, 1967), 203.

ministry as service has quite different implications for socially subordinated groups.

Hand in hand with this servanthood ecclesiology goes a diversification of "ministry" in the Roman Catholic context. Theologians argue that ministries are functional, that they are a specific gift and service to the community. They exist for the building up of the community and do not consist in special status, lifestyle, or sacred office. Since the servant church as the ministerial community is said to be prior to its ministers,[10] the church can officially sanction new ministries that complement the traditional hierarchical ministries of bishop, priest, and deacon.[11] Thus this servant theology does not seriously challenge the church's structures of patriarchal hierarchy and the "class" division between ordained and nonordained ministries but exhorts those who have patriarchal clerical status and ecclesiastical powers to serve the laity and those in need.

In Roman Catholicism this ecclesiology has developed in response to the shortage of priests in many parts of the world, which has engendered an explosion of specialized ministries. These ministries seek to serve not only the needs of the church but also those of the world. This development has allowed women to exercise ministerial functions, although the official stance against the inclusion of women in the ordained ministry has increasingly hardened.

In short, the "progressive" theology of ministry as service has supported not only a variety of ministries but also the participation of women in the ministry of the church.[12] Yet at the same time this servant ecclesiology has also motivated women and other subor-

---

10. See, e.g., Edward Schillebeeckx, *Ministry: Leadership in the Community of Jesus Christ* (New York: Crossroad, 1982), 147; David Power, *Gifts That Differ: Lay Ministries Established and Unestablished* (New York: Pueblo, 1980), 106.

11. See John A. Coleman, "A Theology of Ministry," *The Way* 25 (1985): 15–17, with reference to Peter Chirico, "Pastoral Ministry in a Time of Priest Shortage," *Clergy Review* 69 (1984): 81–84.

12. The first list of proposals made by the 1987 Synod on the Laity contained the following recommendation, which reflected the mind of the synod: "Because of the fundamental equal dignity of the disciples of Christ, all offices and tasks in the church except the ministries which require the power of orders should be open to women as well as men, with due regard to local sensibilities."

However, this and the recommendations to study the admission of women to the ministry of deaconesses as well as to that of "altar-servers" disappeared without any convincing explanation from the subsequent drafts. See Peter Hebblethwaite, "Reports Reveal Curia Derailed Lay Synod," *National Catholic Reporter* 24 (February 5, 1988): 28.

dinates to acquiesce to their "second-class" ministerial status and prevented them from insisting on their rights as church workers. Several years ago I met with a group of pastoral assistants in Germany who complained that as women they were not allowed to preach whereas permanent deacons were able to do so although they had much less theological education and pastoral experience. When it was suggested that all the pastoral assistants in the city should "go on strike" in protest against such blatant discrimination, the women were horrified because, as one of them put it, they had dedicated their life to the service of the church.

According to Canon Law only those in orders can receive jurisdiction, i.e., the power of decision making, and are officially entitled to exercise sacramental powers. Women are therefore relegated by law to subservient tasks, auxiliary roles, and secondary status in ministry. While the Vatican has acknowledged that the majority of people in evangelization are women,[13] a U.S. study on women in ministry has documented that most women in ministry do unpaid volunteer work or are minimally paid if they are remunerated at all. Women engaged in such volunteer ministry are mostly middle-aged, middle-class married women whose children have left the home, who have no professional career, and whose husbands are able to support them. At the price of their continuing economic dependence they can "afford" ministry, whereas poor women and welfare mothers are not able to do so. The double-speak of "ministry" is illustrated by this study: men exercise ministry by virtue of ordination, whereas women's work is qualified as ministry only when they do not receive financial, social, or professional gains.[14]

Such subservient and secondary ministerial status of women is also still found in Christian churches that ordain women.[15] Governing boards and decision-making positions are often restricted to

---

13. "The Role of Women in Evangelization," issued by the Pastoral Commission of the Vatican Congregation for the Evangelization of Peoples. The text can be found in *Origins* 5 (April 1976): 702–7.

14. *Women and Ministry: A Survey of the Experience of Roman Catholic Women in the United States* (Washington: CARA, 1980). See my analysis of this study: "We Are Still Invisible: Theological Analysis of 'Women and Ministry,' " in *Women and Ministry: Present Experience and Future Hope*, ed. Doris Gottemoeller and Rita Hofbauer (Washington: LCWR, 1981), 29–43 (included as chapter 12 in the present volume).

15. See Jackson W. Carroll, Barbara Hargrove, and Adair Lummis, *Women of the Cloth* (San Francisco: Harper & Row, 1983); Judith L. Weidman, ed., *Women Ministers* (San Francisco: Harper & Row, 1981); A. Schilthuis-Stokvis, "Women as Workers in the Church Seen from the Ecumenical Point of View," *Concilium* 194 (1987): 85–90.

male clergy. Women clergy are not infrequently relegated to small rural parishes, are paid less than men with comparable qualifications, and remain at the level of assistant ministers. At the same time as ordained professionals clergywomen are better off than other female church workers and volunteer staff. In the churches as in society at large the majority of social-charitable volunteer workers are women.[16] The servanthood of the church thus seems to be represented by women.

In a ministerial situation of institutional inequality, the theology of ministry as service and its underlying servant ecclesiology help to internalize and legitimate the patriarchal-hierarchical status quo in theological-spiritual terms. Despite its progressive intentions such a servant ecclesiology reproduces the asymmetric dualism of power between church and world, clergy and laity, religious and secular, men and women that is generated by patriarchal-hierarchical church structures. Insofar as ecclesial relationships are structured and conceptualized in such a way that the church, clergy, religious, and men still remain the defining subjects, a servant ecclesiology deceptively claims service and servanthood precisely for those who have patriarchal-hierarchical status and exercise spiritual power and control. For instance, the "Holy Father" has supreme authority and power in the Roman Catholic Church but at the same time is called *servus servorum dei*, the servant of God's servants. As long as actual power relationships and status privileges are not changed, a theological panegyric of service must remain a mere moralistic sentiment and a dangerous rhetorical appeal that mystifies structures of domination.

A theology of servanthood becomes even more questionable when its cultural-social contexts come into view. In Western cultures women are socialized to selfless love in order to perform unpaid services in the family as well as volunteer services in the public domain. The myth of "true womanhood," romantic love, and domesticity defines women's nature as "being for others" and women's identity as derived from service to their husband and children. Women are expected to sacrifice their names, their careers, and their resources for the well-being of their families and personal "relationships" of love. Mothers especially are to sacrifice their lives in the service of their children and all those in need.

---

16. See, e.g., G. Notz, "Frauenarbeit zum Nulltarif: Zur ehrenamtlichen Tätigkeit von Frauen," in *Studium Feminale*, ed. Arbeitsgemeinschaft Frauenforschung der Universität Bonn (Bonn: Nora Frauenverlag, 1986), 134–51.

Whereas men are socialized into the masculine roles of self-assertion, independence, and control, women's true nature and destiny are said to be self-sacrificing service and loving self-surrender. The cultural socialization of women to selfless femininity and altruistic behavior is reinforced and perpetuated by the Christian preaching of self-sacrificing love and self-denying service. Since Jesus Christ humbled himself and sacrificed his life for the salvation of others – this theology argues – the notion of self-sacrificing love and humble service is at the heart of Christian ethics. Not only Christ, the perfect servant and sacrifice of God, but also Mary, the obedient handmaid of God, are the models of true Christian womanhood.

However, this Christian theology of service must be scrutinized not only for its cultural androcentric presuppositions and implications. It must also be analyzed with respect to its classist, racist, and colonialist underpinnings. Already Aristotle had argued that the propertied, educated, freeborn Greek man is the highest of mortal beings and that all other members of the human race are defined by their functions in his service. Freeborn women as well as slaves and barbarians, both women and men, are by "nature" inferior to him and therefore destined to be the instruments of his well-being.[17] Modern political and philosophical anthropology continues to assume that propertied, educated white Western Man is defined by reason, self-determination, and full citizenship whereas women and other subordinates are characterized by emotion, service, and dependence.[18] They are seen not as rational and responsible but as emotional and child-like.

In short, patriarchal society and culture are not only characterized by the sexual and economic exploitation of all women, which is sustained and legitimated by the cult of true womanhood, the myth of femininity, romantic love, and education to domesticity;[19] patriarchal society and church also need for their functioning a "servant class," a "servant race," or a "servant people," be they slaves, serfs, house servants, kulis, or mammies. The existence of such a "servant class" is maintained through law, education, so-

17. Susan Moller Okin, *Women in Western Political Thought* (Princeton: Princeton University Press, 1979), 73–96.
18. See Elisabeth List, "Homo Politicus – Femina Privata: Thesen zur Kritik der politischen Anthropologie," in *Weiblichkeit in der Moderne: Ansätze feministischer Vernunftkritik*, ed. Judith Conrad and Ursula Konnertz (Tübingen: edition diskord, 1986), 75–95.
19. See Brigitte Weisshaupt, "Selbstlosigkeit und Wissen," in ibid., 21–38.

cialization, and brute violence. It is sustained by the belief that members of a "servant class" of people are by nature or by divine decree inferior to those whom they are destined to serve.[20]

In addition, the cultural "hierarchy of service" implicates women in the exploitation of other women. The noble lady of the castle or the white lady of the plantation was to be subservient to her father or husband as the "lord and master of the house." Nevertheless, such subservience allowed her to delegate labor to a "servant group" of people, especially to that of impoverished, uneducated, and colonialized women.[21] The cultural assumption of women's sexual and domestic subservience to the "Boss-Man" therefore pits women against women in a patriarchal society insofar as elite women must control and supervise the low-paid domestic service and work of other women. However, with the erosion of the economic power of lower- and middle-class males, women of the upper economic strata also have to shoulder more and more the triple burden of unpaid housework, care of children as well as of the elderly and infirm, and low-paid work outside the home.[22] True, African-American and Hispanic lower-class women workers always had to do so. Yet because of their segregation in low-paying domestic and service jobs, today they and their children are increasingly forced to join the ranks of the poor.

Finally, the increase of virulent right-wing prejudice in the past decade — such as racism, anti-Semitism, work-fare programs for the poor, biblicist fundamentalism, militarist colonialism, and "the new cult of femininity and the family" — seeks to maintain the servanthood of exploited people by insisting that some groups of people are superior and others subservient by "nature." When ecclesiastics insist anew today that women must live their true womanhood in complementarity with men as well as that the ordained differ "in essence" from the laity, such an insistence must be seen in this cultural right-wing context. As Letty Russell so succinctly states:

---

20. See, e.g., the biographical reflection and analysis of apartheid as an ideology and institution to maintain a "servant people" by Mark Mathabene, *Kaffir Boy: The True Story of a Black Youth's Coming of Age in Apartheid South Africa* (New York: Macmillan, 1986).

21. See, e.g., Martha Mamozai, *Herrenmenschen: Frauen im deutschen Kolonialismus,* Rororo 4959 (Rheinbeck: Rowohlt Taschenbuchverlag, 1982).

22. See the contributions in *Women, Work, and Poverty, Concilium* 194, ed. Elisabeth Schüssler Fiorenza and Anne Carr (Edinburgh: T. & T. Clark, 1987).

Regardless of what we say about ministry as a function, we [the clergy] are still placed in a position of permanent superiority in the life of the church. In this sense ordination becomes an indelible mark of caste rather than the recognition of spiritual gifts for a particular ministry in the church.[23]

The theological language of ordained ministry as servant leadership does not abolish the ecclesial "class" division between clergy and laity but mystifies and perpetuates it.

It must therefore be asked whether the notion of ministry as service should be completely discarded by those who understand their ministry as dedicated to the vision of the discipleship of equals. I would suggest that the notion of *diakonia* can be reclaimed by feminist ministers only when it is understood as a critical category challenging those who have actual power and privilege in patriarchal church and society. Since oppressions are interstructured, hierarchized, and multifaceted women who do not live on the bottom of the patriarchal pyramid are not just exploited, they also benefit from the structures of domination and service.

Those of us who are marginalized and subordinated as women but at the same time are privileged by virtue of ordination, education, wealth, nationality, race, health, or age must use our privileges for bringing about change. We should seek to become ministers not in order to be incorporated into the lowest ranks of the patriarchal hierarchy as altar-servers, lectors, deaconesses, or even priests but in order to subvert clerical-hierarchal structures and to transform the church into a discipleship of equals.

Such a critical accentuation of the word-cluster *diakonia/ diakonos/diakonein/doulos* corresponds to its meaning in the gospel traditions. The core saying of Mark 10:42–44, which in some form is assumed to go back to the historical Jesus, juxtaposes "great/servant" and "first/slave." The subject under discussion is the contrast between societal structures of domination and the "discipleship of equals."[24] The saying clearly presupposes a society in which those who "rule and have authority over" are the kings and great ones, whereas those who are servants and slaves are required to take orders, render obeisance, and provide ser-

23. Letty M. Russell, "Women and Ministry: Problem or Possibility?" in *Christian Feminism: Visions of a New Humanity,* ed. Judith L. Weidman (San Francisco: Harper & Row, 1984), 89.

24. For the following see my book *In Memory of Her: A Feminist Theological Reconstruction of Christian Origins* (New York: Crossroad, 1983), 148–51.

vices. It challenges those in positions of dominance and power to become "equal" to those who are powerless. Masters should relinquish domination over their slaves and servants and step into their shoes.

The importance of this saying is indicated by its inclusion in the Synoptic tradition in a sevenfold combination (Mark 10:42-45 par. Matt. 20:25-27; 23:11; Luke 22:26; Mark 9:33-37 par. Matt. 18:1-4; Luke 9:48). Its content is also stressed in the Johannine tradition (John 12:25-26 and 13:4-5, 12-17). The ecclesial process of interpretation applied a saying originally addressed to the whole people of Israel to its own structures and relationships. Structures of domination and servanthood should not be tolerated in the community of equals. True leadership in the community must be rooted in solidarity with each other. But whereas Mark and Matthew acknowledge no "great" and "first" in the community at all, Luke does so. His only requirement is that their style of leadership orient itself on the example of Jesus.

This saying of Jesus and its ecclesial adaptation does not exhort all Christians to become servants and slaves but only those who have status and power in the societal or ecclesial patriarchal pyramid. It seeks to create "equality from below" not by incorporating those on the bottom of the patriarchal pyramid into its lower ranks. Rather it rejects the patriarchal-hierarchical pyramid as such and seeks to level it by urging those on the top of the pyramid to join the work and labor of those on the bottom, thereby making a "servant class" of people superfluous. By denying the validity of the positions of master and lord and by ironically urging those who "would be" great and leaders to live on the bottom of the patriarchal pyramid of domination, this Jesus-saying and its variations paradoxically rejects all patriarchal-hierarchical structures and positions.

Luke and later theologians have no longer understood the radical paradox of the discipleship of equals when they called those in positions of wealth and power to "charitable service," which did not question but confirm patriarchal status privileges. It must also not be overlooked that the gospels preserve and adopt this Jesus-tradition of "equality from below" at a time when the post-Pauline traditions in the interest of "good citizenship" advocate the adaptation of the Christian community as "the household of God" to its patriarchal societal structures. Since the latter trend has defined mainline Christian self-understanding and community and has institutionalized structures of "domination and authority over," a feminist praxis of ministry must reject such a patriarchal Christian self-understanding rather than perpetuate it by valorizing the notion of service and servanthood. Those of us who are called to ministry can no longer understand our work as "service" or as "waiting on someone" but as the praxis of "equality from below" in solidarity with all those who struggle for survival, self-love, and justice.

One hopes that this celebration and ritualization of our call to ministry will empower the graduates and all of us to dedicate ourselves anew to the vision and practice of equal discipleship in the power of the Spirit.

22

DAUGHTERS OF VISION
AND STRUGGLE

> Each one must pull one...
> Each one, pull one back into the sun
> We who have stood over
> so many graves
> know that no matter what they do
> all of us must live
> or none.
> —Alice Walker[1]

CONTEXTUALIZATION

Since the Second International Women-Church Conference, which took place in Cincinnati on the weekend of October 9, 1987, I have received numerous international requests to speak on the subject of the women-church movement in the United States. The following lecture was presented during 1989–92 in various "incarnations" in Switzerland, Germany, Austria, Spain, and Australia. Parts of it were also discussed at the occasion of the fiftieth anniversary celebration of the Grail in the United States in December 1990. I am grateful to the women of the international women-church movement – too numerous to be mentioned here by name – who have prepared and organized these lectures. In the face of growing

---

1. "Each One, Pull One (Thinking of Lorraine Hansberry)," in *Horses Make a Landscape Look More Beautiful: Poems* (San Diego: Harvest/HBJ Books, 1984), 52f.

repression in society and church, it has been a privilege to experience the tenacious courage and vibrant vision of the women's movement in the churches. Without so many prayers and letters of encouragement from women around the globe, I could not persist in my work.

•

Feminist liberation theologies reflect on the religious and societal oppression of women. They seek not only to overcome the theological silencing and marginalization of women but also to rearticulate theology in a feminist key. The difficulty of changing theological discourses and of placing feminist analyses in the center of theological debates became very clear to me some years ago when I attended an international ecumenical consultation in Prague. This meeting became bogged down in debate on the question of correct method in theology. Should theology start with the doctrinal system and self-understanding of the church and then, in a second step, fit experience into this system? Or must ecclesiology be articulated and changed on the basis of theologically reflected experience? In light of hermeneutics and critical epistemology, it was surprising – to say the least – that the proponents of the traditional way of doing theology claimed to be "scientific" and accused their opponents of having replaced theology with sociology. Women theologians and ministers who sought to bring their own religious experience and theological analysis to ecclesiological male-defined discourses were labeled as doing sociology rather than theology. At the same time this vocal minority both denied the ecclesial legitimacy of women's ordination and classified women's ministry as social work.

Although the majority of the participants were ordained women, it proved impossible to change the discourses of the consultation in such a way that patriarchal church and ministry – and not women – became its central problem. Women participants were not able to raise their own questions and to discuss strategies for change. Rather they were once again held responsible for causing the existing difficulties in ecumenical dialogue and for preventing ecclesial "reunification." Since prior to or during the meeting the women participants had no way of developing structures of communication among themselves nor space for articulating a common feminist ecclesial analysis, they were unable to change the meeting in such a way that its work could serve women's interests.

The strategy of the women participants at a congress in Geneva in 1983, to which the Ecumenical Association of Third World Theologians (EATWOT) had invited theologians of the so-called First World, was quite different. The Third World women scholars successfully resisted attempts of some male participants to divide and play against each other women of color and white feminists. They not only insisted that the conference schedule should be changed in such a way that they could participate both in the workshops of their own continents and in those of feminist theology, but they also managed to have all participants spend an entire morning exploring feminist analyses of women's oppression. Moreover, the women participants secured the organizational and financial support of EATWOT for women's conferences dedicated to the development of feminist liberation theologies on different continents. To these conferences we owe a rich theological analysis of different global contexts from women's perspectives.[2] In contrast to the women at the Prague consultation, the feminist theologians present at the Geneva congress were able to use their power of solidarity for theological-ecclesial change because they shared a common liberation theological perspective and systemic analysis of oppression.

This experience has taught me that the articulation of feminist theological strategies must fulfill three criteria: Firstly, feminist strategies for change must be rooted in a common systemic analysis; second, in order to foster solidarity and collaboration a critical feminist theology of liberation must avoid constructing differing feminist strategies as exclusive oppositions; and, third, feminist theology must seek to articulate a common vision that can inspire diverse movements of liberation.

SYSTEMIC ANALYSIS OF OPPRESSION

BOTH CONSERVATIVE AND PROGRESSIVE CHURCHMEN often argue that in distinction to the poor or the peoples of the Third

---

2. See Virginia Fabella and Mercy Amba Oduyoye, eds., *With Passion and Compassion: Third World Women Doing Theology* (Maryknoll, N.Y.: Orbis Books, 1988).

World, women are not oppressed. The women's movement is said to represent the interests of privileged middle-class women of the First World who have never experienced oppression. Although this objection might be fueled by some segments of the women's movements in church and society, it hides the fact that women also belong to the Third World and that the majority of the poor are women and their children. Moreover, this objection overlooks that today in every culture, society, and religion women's status is lower than men's. To be sure, not all women are oppressed equally and to the same degree. Hence one must ask whether women's secondary status around the world is sufficient to speak of the oppression and liberation of women.

Feminist political scientists such as Iris Marion Young have developed the following five criteria with which to ascertain whether and how much social groups are oppressed:[3]

1. Exploitation: International women's research has documented that women in all countries of the world are exploited economically, culturally, and politically. Internationally women receive between one- and two-thirds of the income that men of their own class and race earn. At the same time, women shoulder the greatest load of unpaid childcare and household maintenance work. Similarly, the unpaid volunteer work of women sustains for the most part cultural and religious institutions.

2. Marginalization: In all cultural, religious, and academic institutions women are underrepresented. Their participation in cultural production, history, science, and theology is only rarely — if at all — recorded. Women are either not present in political and cultural leadership positions or they function as "token" women without any effective power and influence of their own.

3. Powerlessness: Although women are able to vote in most countries of the world, they have very little representation in most governments and not much political decision-making powers in them. Women's interests are not perceived as public interests and their influence is restricted to private life. Women who are leading in national liberation movements are often pushed aside "after the revolution." According to cultural notions of femininity women are presumed to exercise manipulative, indirect influence; but they are not supposed to exercise real power.

---

3. Iris Marion Young, "Five Faces of Oppression," in *Justice and the Politics of Difference* (Princeton: Princeton University Press, 1990), 38–65.

4. *Cultural Imperialism* stereotypes marginal peoples and at the same time makes them invisible. Women are not perceived as human persons in their specific particularity, but are always portrayed as *women*. At the same time, language and scientific knowledge make invisible the contributions and struggles of women in the accounts of Western culture – accounts that understand elite white man as the paradigmatic human being, positioning all other people in relation to him. This Western understanding of world and humanity then becomes universalized and identified as human culture par excellence.

5. *Systemic Violence:* Violence against women is often understood not to be a violation of human rights, although women are physically and mentally abused, ill treated, battered, tortured, maimed, and killed just because they are women. In antiquity as today, more girls than boys have been abandoned; in many cultures women receive only the food left over by men; advertising and mass media objectify women as sexual objects and visual consumer goods, as seductive vampires inviting men to sexual abuse and mistreatment; murder and violence against women has become a "commonsense" everyday event.

To these five criteria of women's oppression I would like to add two more that especially apply to church and theology.

6. *Silencing:* Throughout the centuries women have not been allowed to speak in public either in church or society or to have access to the academy. Ever since the fateful injunctions of St. Paul and his students that "women must be silent in the assembly and are not allowed to speak or to teach men," Christian women have been the silenced majority of the people of God. Throughout the centuries and still today, women are prohibited from preaching and from the official teaching office of the church. Until very recently they have not been allowed to study and teach theology or to define moral and ecclesial policy.

7. *Vilification and Trivialization:* In Western thought and theology women have been the source of all evil and the fountain of all falsehood. Beginning with the Pastoral Epistles the sin of Eve looms large. Since Tertullian woman has been declared to be the "devil's gateway." Not only the witch hunts of the inquisition, but also the cosmetic mutilations of today's multimillion dollar beauty industry seek to "correct" the deficient and evil nature of women.

If more than one of these criteria apply, Young argues, one

can speak of women's oppression. The variation and combination of several criteria serves to explicate the specific forms of women's oppression. For instance, in comparison to the black or brown woman who cleans her office, a privileged academic white woman like myself is much less exploited economically, has more influence and possibilities in daily life, and is less socially marginalized or stereotypically dehumanized, although she is also likely to be abused and battered in her home or to be raped when she goes out at night. In comparison to her male colleagues, however, a professional woman generally receives a lower salary, has fewer chances for professional advancement, and exercises less influence in her field. Indeed, her scholarship is often trivialized, co-opted, or passed over in silence, thereby limiting her power to change cultural and religious institutions. If both the cleaning woman and the professor are Roman Catholics they will not be admitted to ordination regardless of their social standing.

OVERCOMING DUALISTIC STRATEGIES

In light of such an analysis of women's oppression, feminist theory and the feminist movement have developed different strategies for change. Yet such strategies for change and transformation cannot develop their full power if they remain caught up in the cultural patriarchal framework of androcentric dualism. Although feminist theology from its very inception has severely criticized dualistic patriarchal thinking that is modeled after asymmetric gender dichotomy, it has nevertheless been unable to avoid it entirely in its own conceptualization and strategies of either-or positions: either reformist or radical, either Christian or post-Christian, either religious or secular, either feminist or womanist, either inclusive or exclusive of men, either in the church or outside of it, either oppressed or liberated, either in the center or on the margins of patriarchal society and religion.

This dualistic either-or positioning is engendered by the origin of feminism in Enlightenment thought. In the context of Western democratic revolutions, feminism has been articulated either in liberal terms as the struggle for equal rights or in romantic terms as the myth of the "eternal woman." Whereas classical philosophy and Augustinian-Thomistic theology had argued for the exclusion of women from government and from positions of authority on grounds of deficient female reason and nature, Western bourgeois romanticism postulates a special feminine sphere, essence, and refinement of woman that is represented by the civilizing image of the "white Lady." Such a "feminine sphere" is complementary to the masculine domain of work and politics. By contrast, liberal equal rights advocates have rejected the notion of complementarity and have argued instead that women must have the *same* rights and opportunities as men.

In order to overcome these totalizing either-or strategies, one needs to position and envision feminist movements and strategies for change differently: Beyond the romantic-liberal dualistic framework, different forms of the women's movement in society and religion must be critically analyzed and assessed. They must not be isolated as disjunctive doctrinal positions or played against each other as irreconcilable oppositions. Rather one needs to envision the different articulations of the feminist movement as the disparate strands of a rope. To be sure, they have the strength to bind the evil power of patriarchy and to pull us into the future only if they become intertwined and twisted together. To use another image: These divergent strategies can be visualized as different eddies that, by flowing together into one stream, can swell into a rapid torrent that will wash away the rock of patriarchy. A careful look at the "different strands of the rope" or the "various eddies of the stream" allows one to see their interaction and tensions with each other, their appeal to biblical symbols and images, their generation of "power" for women and all other nonpersons, as well as their pitfalls and dangers.

Feminists in biblical religions have also remained caught up in the modern dualistic alternative of liberal or romantic feminisms. They too have articulated their diverse visions and strategies in a dualistic fashion with the alternative biblical images of Eden/ home or Exodus/liberated community. A critical feminist theology of liberation must seek to overcome this dualistic biblical imaging of the women's movement in the churches, replacing it with a plurality of images that can capture diverse feminist strategies and movements for transforming patriarchal relations of domination and exploitation.

THE WOMEN'S MOVEMENTS IN THE CHURCHES

Here I will attempt to sketch a pluriform typology of feminist strategies and movements of women. As with any classification, such a typology cannot but simplify and generalize. Nevertheless, it allows for a critical inspection and assessment of the strength of the rope that we have fashioned for pulling women "back into the sun." Rather than as separate and isolated groups, the various embodiments and strategies of the women's movement are best envisioned as diverse strands that when braided and twined together makes up the strong rope called the women's movement. This braided rope of strategies can be visualized with the images of (1) Family, (2) Altar and Sanctuary, (3) The Word, (4) Body, (5) The Divine Feminine, (6) "Rainbow Coalition," (7) Base Community of Justice-Seeking Friends, (8) Feminist Parish, and (9) Public Forum or Women's-Synod. By introducing the image of the *ekklēsia of women* I have proposed a possible common vision that conceives of the different "cords of the women's movements' rope" in the churches as intertwined, overlapping, and mutually reinforcing rather than as discrete exclusive positions.

1. The Family: The "conservative" women's movement that has arisen in response to liberal feminism is well organized and politically powerful. As in the last century, so also today conservative women appeal to a "true womanhood" and to Christian family values, insisting that the vocation of women and the fulfillment of their true nature is to protect the home, to create in it the tranquility and beauty of Eden, and to fashion the home and church as a refuge to which men and children can retreat from their labors in the marketplace and from the temptations of a secularized, godless world.

Because woman's feminine powers are said to fashion a spiritual island of wholeness, love, and happiness, the religious calling of women is superior to that of men. The hallmark of this calling can be summed up in the slogan *"Kinder, Küche, Kirche,"* i.e., children, kitchen, church. Such a calling, however, is not restricted to married women; for it also applies to those women in canonical orders who follow the higher calling of their spouse Christ to spiritual motherhood, nurturance, and service.

Critical feminist analyses have pointed out that the political and religious Right manipulates women's fears of male violence and patriarchal oppression by promising them and their children safety, shelter, rules, and love based on clearly defined gender roles with different spheres of accountability. If women keep their part of the bargain by being submissive, obedient, nurturing – in short, by doing "God's will" – then men in turn will assume the responsibility for women and children's economic support, for providing a secure home, and for maintaining marriage and family as well as political, spiritual, and ecclesial institutions. Of course, the experience of most women conflicts with this ideology of femininity and motherhood. Women who "keep their end of the bargain" are still exposed to rape, male violence, wife beating, sexual abuse of children, poverty, homelessness, low-paid and low-status work, psychological and spiritual crippling, and betrayal of the marriage contract day in and day out.

Since the political and religious Right recognizes that women's anger and fear constitute a potential revolutionary force when directed against patriarchal institutions, it manipulates these fears by quieting and redirecting them. The Right employs biblical religion to inculcate the subordination and special nature of women as "divinely ordained." Women can fulfill their feminine vocation by living the ideal of true complementarity. The Christian Right offers women the love of Jesus, the perfect man, the one man to whom they can submit absolutely without being sexually violated or abused. The power of Christ enables willful women to become submissive in the Lord so that they can subordinate themselves to the leadership of their husbands or pastors.

A second way that the political Christian Right manipulates women's anger and fear consists in scapegoating "equal rights feminists." By utilizing traditional sexual moral teachings right-wing groups redirect women's fear of patriarchal violence and exploitation against feminists who publicly assert their rights. In particular, the misnamed "right to life" movement has galvanized women against feminists who insist on reproductive freedom. Women who "break the patriarchal rules" – such as "unwed" mothers, pregnant teenagers, lesbians, sexually promiscuous women, radical feminists, women eschewing the traditional feminine roles of "baking cookies and serving tea" – all these women and many more provoke fear, public rejection, and irrational anger.

In short, the political and religious Right redirects the fear and anger of women by clearly delineating groups such as blacks, socialists, terrorists, Jews, gays, or feminists as dangerous outsiders. They, and not patriarchal institutions, are held responsible for the

violence, economic insecurity, poverty, trivialization, and insignificance of women's lives. Whereas the expression of anger and fear
against other minority groups who might be women's allies is con-
doned, any anger expressed toward the control of men is censured
as "unfeminine" and/or against Christian love. Christian feminists
who invite women to move "beyond anger" and to use ritual and
spirituality for doing so play into the hands of the political and
religious Right.[4]

I have elaborated this first strategy of women for survival in patriarchal society so extensively because it is usually not analyzed in
terms of its feminist potential for change. The women's movement
on the whole can learn from these strategies. We must not only
acknowledge the organizational talents, courageous commitment,
and hard work of "traditional" women, which the Right exploits for
patriarchal ends. Feminists must also recognize that some of these
traditional values are also important for emancipatory movements.
In realizing that nurturing, "at-homeness," personal "touch," loving relationships, care for children, religious meaning, and ritual
celebrations *are* important values that are missing in modern tech-
nologized and bureaucratized societies, "traditional" women seek
to maintain "children, home, and religion" as spheres of women's
relative power, spheres that in the past have sustained women's
culture and religion. Any feminist strategy for changing patriarchal
relationships and structures must recognize these values as essential "human" values while seeking to set them free from patriarchal
deformation. Partial identification and solidarity with conservative
women's struggle – rather than total negation – will strengthen
the "powers of the weak."[5]

2. *Altar and Sanctuary:* The women's rights movement within
the churches and different branches of Judaism has organized
primarily around the access of women to ordination. Its biblical
symbol is not the "household of God" but the sanctuary, altar,
and pulpit. Although this movement has argued for women's
ordination either in terms of "equal rights" or in terms of "feminine-
masculine complementarity," it has not yet sufficiently articulated
what women's ordination will contribute to the struggle against
the patriarchalization of the church as a structural ecclesial evil.

4. See esp. Shirley Rogers Radl, *The Invisible Woman: Target of the Religious New
Right* (New York: Dell Publishing Co., 1983); Sara Diamond, *Spiritual Warfare: The
Politics of the Christian Right* (Boston: South End Press, 1989).
5. Elizabeth Janeway, *Powers of the Weak* (New York: Alfred A. Knopf, 1980).

To be sure, only when this movement does so will it be able to avoid co-optation and tokenism or the misuse of women's relational powers for shoring up the patriarchal hierarchy. If the struggle for women's ordination is not to result in the incorporation of some women into the lowest ranks of the patriarchal hierarchy as deaconesses or as "honorary clergymen," the ordination movement must be articulated as a struggle for both women's ecclesial dignity and spiritual power on one hand, and as a struggle for changing church and ministry into the discipleship of equals on the other. By focusing on changing patriarchal leadership and power the women's ordination movement acknowledges that all institutions need power and leadership. At issue is not the rejection of all institutional power and leadership but the right structuring of it.

To achieve its goal, the struggle for the ordination of women must not just critically analyze the theological arguments against women's ordination. Rather, it must first withhold consent to those ecclesiastical structures, dogmatic concepts, and spiritual teachings that sustain patriarchal authority and power of subordination. Since the churches' power of coercion is no longer political but only "spiritual," the withholding of consent to spiritual ecclesiastical authority over women is one way the subordinated and silenced majority can generate power for institutional ecclesial change.

3. The Word: Whereas the women's ordination movement insists on the sacredness of women, the women's theological movement seeks to reclaim the intellectual power and voice of women. Since the beginning of this century European and North American Protestant women have sought to gain entry into academic institutions and to study and teach theology. Although in Europe Roman Catholic women have been theological students since World War I, in the United States they gained access to theological institutions only in the 1960s. Moreover, only with the advent of the second wave of the feminist liberation movement have women begun to reclaim their intellectual powers, attempting to find their own theological voice. In the past twenty years, the explosion of women's studies in general and feminist studies in religion in particular has not only enriched our knowledge about women; it has also challenged the universality of positivist androcentric frameworks and objectivist scientific paradigms.

At the same time, women entering theological schools still have to adopt the language and categories of those clerical and academic

communities that have silenced us, defining us as "the other" of
the Divine or as the "other" of the academic "man of reason."
Moreover, after the right to theological education and ordained
ministry has been won, many women entering theological schools
seek assimilation into the clerical or academic establishment hop-
ing to prove themselves as serious scholars either by distancing
themselves from feminist theology or by co-opting it into androcentric patriarchal frameworks. For in order to become speaking
"academic" subjects, women must not only "master" the academic
discourse of the "fathers," but they must also disown their own
intellectual voice.

Thus women who enter theological education have a choice
among three strategies: We can embrace and internalize the languages, traditions, and theories of theology that have silenced,
marginalized, and objectified us *as women.* Or we can totally
reject theological studies as male head-tripping because we recognize their potential destructiveness to our own self-affirmation
and intellectual voice. However, this second option would deprive
women of the intellectual tools, skills, and theories necessary for
changing the subject matter of theology in the interest of women
and other nonpersons. A third option allows women in theology to use the "master's tools" for dismantling his intellectual
house. By consciously adopting the vantage point of women – defined by gender, race, class, culture, and religion – the feminist
theologian learns to use such intellectual tools for deconstructing
oppressive religious-theological structures and for reconstructing
the religious heritage and theological voice of women.

4. Body: Although it has become commonplace that biblical
religion and theology have identified woman with sexuality and
sin, the movement for the sexual rights and self-determination of
women in all its different forms has not received as much attention
as the women's ordination movement among religious feminists.
To take an example from my own confessional context in the
United States: The reproductive rights movement Catholics for
a Free Choice or the Conference for Catholic Lesbians, founded
in 1983, have only very slowly received equal public voice and
membership in the Catholic women's movement organized in the
Women of the Church Coalition. Although their reasons were not
officially stated, some groups who had previously been affiliated
with the Women in the Church Coalition withdrew their sponsor-
ship and support before the First Woman-Church Conference in

November 1983. As Mary Jo Weaver suggests, this was probably due to the high visibility of Catholic Lesbians and the presence of Catholics for a Free Choice among the organizing groups.[6] The aim of the lesbian movement has been to struggle for "civil rights" inside and outside the church, to articulate a different understanding of sexuality, and to indict all forms of homophobia and hetero-sexism. Whereas in Protestant churches the rights of lesbians to ordination is still curtailed, in the Roman Catholic Church civil and ecclesial rights are at stake. As long as the words "this is my body" spoken at the height of the Christian eucharistic celebration do not also include women's bodies in all their diversity, the struggle for sexual self-determination and rights must remain central to the women's movement in the churches.

This struggle received unusual visibility with the intervention of the Vatican Congregation for Religious and Secular Institutes (SCRIS) in late 1984 against the nun signers of the *New York Times* advertisement on "Pluralism and Abortion," which Sister Maureen Fiedler, a nun signer, has called "one of the most important events in recent Women-Church herstory."[7] The need for an international religious sexual self-determination movement has increased with the efforts of the Reagan/Bush governments, of the Catholic hierarchy, and of religious fundamentalist groups to severely restrict access to safe and legal family planning for poor, young, and isolated women, and for all Third World women; to prohibit condoms for protection against infection by the AIDS virus; and to criminalize again women's termination of pregnancy. Such a movement is necessary in the face of a right-wing politics that curtails civil rights for lesbians and so-called illegitimate mothers in the name of "family values," the Right's code-word for blatant sexism and the patriarchal control of women's sexuality and reproductive power. In sum, whereas the women's ordination movement seeks to reclaim women's ecclesial powers, feminist studies in religion attempt to rediscover women's theological heritage and intellectual voices, and the sexual self-determination movement in the churches insists on freedom from sexual control.

5. *The Divine Feminine:* Although women's movements in the

---

6. Mary Jo Weaver, *New Catholic Woman* (San Francisco: Harper & Row, 1985), 245 n. 84.

7. See her talk at the Second Women-Church Conference entitled "Claiming Our Power as Women in the Midst of Political Struggle," which was published in an expanded form in *Conscience* 9 (1988): 1.

churches struggle for civil rights, the so-called secular women's movements in society or in the academy often totally neglect or reject religion, which they see as "part of the problem, but not part of the solution." Hence the feminist spirituality movement stresses the importance of the powers of religion for women's liberation struggles. Consequently, it has called for an Exodus from patriarchal Christianity and Judaism because they have co-opted or destroyed women's religious powers by fashioning the Divine in the image and likeness of elite men. Instead, the women's spirituality movement seeks to create a "liberated" space for women on the boundaries of patriarchy or in the "other-world." Whereas Mary Daly has conceived of sisterhood as antichurch and the women's liberation movement as cosmic covenant, Elga Sorge understands women-church as providing rituals and sacraments that could replace the services of the institutional patriarchal church. Both conceptualize feminist community as Exodus community and as a liberated space. Other spirituality feminists utilize Jungian psychology to celebrate the feminine Divine.

Carol Christ has articulated one of the most cogent arguments for the reconstruction and re-creation of Goddess religion in the interest of women.[8] The Goddess, she argues, symbolizes that the divine principle, the sustaining and saving power, is female. Therefore, women no longer need male figures as saviors or as mediators of the divine. The Goddess is thus the symbol of female power. The "power of naming" the Divine, of ritualizing Her presence, of constructing a female symbolic universe is regained by women.

Such a positive affirmation of women's spiritual-ritual powers and recovery of divine ultimate power in women's image must also be claimed by Christian faith communities if they are to become an empowering force in women's struggle for ecclesial justice and religious self-affirmation. Hence Christian feminists have insisted that androcentric language for God, the liturgical language, and the biblical language of proclamation must be changed. Patriarchal symbols and androcentric imagery for God must be replaced by female language and symbols if so-called inclusive, gender-neutral language is not to continue to function as masculine. However, if Goddess-spirituality appeals to an ontological feminine reality, its insistence on female divine images and on women's

---

8. Carol P. Christ, "Why Women Need the Goddess: Phenomenological, Psychological and Political Reflections," in *Womanspirit Rising: A Feminist Reader in Religion*, ed. Carol P. Christ and Judith Plaskow (San Francisco: Harper & Row, 1979), 273–87.

special religious-ritual power runs the risk of revalorizing cultural feminine stereotypes.

In other words, to the extent that women's spirituality and Goddess movements invoke the ontology of the divine Woman and to the extent that their theology of woman's specific culture, religious intuition, special sphere, and feminine ontology shares in the patriarchal bourgeois articulation of "the eternal feminine," they cannot displace these values. Rather, by simply reversing feminine/masculine values they are in danger of reproducing them. For the patriarchal theologies of woman's essential difference from man and her identification with nature, body, sexual temptation, and sin legitimate women's subordination by granting her a complementary and compensatory role, thereby shoring up dominant male social and ecclesial structures. In such a cultural patriarchical context the divinization of woman and declaration of women's essential superiority does not overcome patriarchal gender stereotypes. Rather it reinscribes them as androcentric projections and idealizations stood on their head. While it is important to recover women's ritual powers and to rearticulate androcentric language about the Divine in the likeness of the Goddess, we must take care to disengage such a theological construction from the bourgeois metaphysics of the eternal feminine.

6. Rainbow Coalition: The essentialist Euro-American feminist discourse of universal generic woman is increasingly interrupted by the diverse resistant voices of women struggling for liberation from Western patriarchal colonialization and from their own indigenous patriarchal traditions. Since Simone de Beauvoir feminist theory has focused either on woman as the "other" of Western elite man, the subject of history, culture, and religion, or they have constructed an essentialist ideal concept of Woman that reproduces abstract universalist theories of gender dualism and gender complementarity.

In this attempt to construct an oppositional feminist discourse about woman or essential gender difference, feminist theory has kept in circulation the theories of Western philosophy and theology that seek to legitimate not only the exclusion of elite woman from cultural, religious, intellectual, and political power but also the exploitation of women and men of colonialized cultures, races, classes, and religions. Thus feminist theory has not always sufficiently attended to the fact that most women in the world are not just the others of elite white men but are also the others of elite white women and the others of the men of their own classes, cultures, races, and religions. In short, most women in the world are the "others of the others."

The voices of women around the globe therefore insist that patriarchy should no longer be theorized as universal, transcultural binary gender essentialism but as a complex, historically changing pyramidal system of dominations. The feminist movement requires a political-religious commitment not only to the struggle against sexism but also against racism, poverty, and militarist colonialism as multiplicative structures of women's oppression. Therefore, women from different cultures, races, and religions insist on the particularity of their experience and vision. To express such a particularity, African-American feminists have named their theology and movement "womanist," whereas Hispanic feminists speak of *mujerista* theology and the *mujerista* movement.

The African-American feminist theorist bell hooks has cautioned, however, that political solidarity among women must not be defined and limited by the terms and divisions engendered by patriarchal structures.[9] As long as we define our "particularity" in terms of patriarchal structural divisions, patriarchal politics will be able to divide us and to play us off against each other. To use a biblical image: Only when we speak in our own particular voice and still understand each other will we overcome the patriarchal divisions of Babel in the power of Pentecost. Rather than organizing along the lines of the patriarchal divisions of racism, sexism, classism, clericalism, homophobia, or religious sectarianism, feminists in religion need to develop theological visions that do not deny our particular differences but that nevertheless bring us together in political solidarity and ecclesial commitment to the struggle against patriarchal dehumanization.

7. *Base Community:* As the spelling that was adopted by the First Woman-Church Conference indicates, i.e., "woman" in the singular, the women-church movement in the United States vacillates between an essentialist understanding of woman-church and its conceptualization as an exodus-community or base community of liberated space. Mary Hunt, one of the theological shapers of the women-church movement in the United States, understands women-church to be the historical development of

---

9. bell hooks, *Feminist Theory: From Margin to Center* (Boston: South End Press, 1984), 43–65.

women's base communities, a network of feminist groups, who are "justice-seeking friends" and who share the same belief, vision, and religious agency. According to her the women-church movement sustains the tension between the radical critique of Christianity and the positive religious experiences of women. It provides "a religious safe place for women who have been spiritually abused in patriarchal churches."[10]

In her book *Sexism and God-Talk,* Rosemary Radford Ruether also called for "the creation of autonomous feminist base communities for developing a community of liberation from sexism." Such feminist base communities could take on a few or many functions of the institutional church. Their mission would be to create "liberated zones" in some sectors of the institutional churches. Radford Ruether is careful to insist that such an "exodus" from the institutional churches into the "freer" space of feminist base communities is not a sectarian movement. Rather, such "free zones" must remain related to the institutional historical churches in a "creative dialectic." In her understanding, feminist base communities are not restricted to women but are open to all who want to experience "liberating community" and "nurture liberated ways of living together" for transforming the historical church.[11] In line with the emerging women-church movement, in her book *Womanguides,* Radford Ruether renamed the feminist base community as woman-church, taking over the spelling of the First Woman-Church Conference. In a subsequent book she changed the spelling from *woman*-church to *women*-church because of the essentialist overtones of the singular, but she continues to understand women-church "as an exodus community from patriarchy."[12] She insists that the task of such feminist exodus-communities consists not only in liturgy and myth making but also in consciousness raising and political action. Nevertheless, in her two books the terms "Womanguides" and "Women-Church" focus on women-church as a liturgical exodus community of liberation.

---

10. See Mary Hunt, *Fierce Tenderness: A Feminist Theology of Friendship* (New York: Crossroad, 1991), 159–61. See also her article "The Challenge of Both/And Theology" in *Women and Church: The Challenge of Ecumenical Solidarity in an Age of Alienation,* ed. Melanie May (New York: Friendship Press, 1991), 28–33.

11. Rosemary Radford Ruether, *Sexism and God Talk: Toward a Feminist Theology* (Boston: Beacon Press, 1983), 206.

12. Rosemary Radford Ruether, *Womanguides: Readings Toward a Feminist Theology* (Boston: Beacon Press, 1985), 161; eadem, *Women-Church: Theology and Practice* (San Francisco: Harper & Row, 1988).

324 *Daughters of Vision and Struggle*

Whereas in *Beyond God the Father* Mary Daly had called for an exodus out of the institutional church and defined feminist sisterhood as "antichurch," Radford Ruether seeks to correlate the exodus base community of women-church in a creative dialectic with the institutional church. While Radford Ruether herself is careful not to reduce her "creative dialectic" to such a patriarchal complementarity, some women-church events seem not able to do so. Insofar as they extol women-church as an "exodus community from patriarchy" and as a "liberated zone" where women celebrate healing and feminist liberation, they are in danger of reinscribing the dialectic complementarity between "home" and state, between private and public, between religion and society, between feminine and masculine that typify Western patriarchy. If the "creative dialectic" between women-church as "exodus base community" and institutional patriarchal church is dissolved in favor of the institutional church, no transformation of church structures can take place. If this creative dialectic is resolved in favor of women-church understood as a "liberated zone," essentialism, sectarianism, and exclusivism loom large.

8. Feminist Parish: Whereas African-American feminists in general are skeptical toward the women-church movement since they fear it might be another ploy of white supremacy to undermine male-female solidarity in their struggle against racism and genocide, in an Asian context the Rev. Young Kim has built up Women Church of Korea and is its present pastor. Elga Sorge has started a similar project in Germany, but she seeks to replace rather than transform the institutional church.

Women Church of Korea, supported by the United Methodist Church World Division, is to my knowledge the first feminist parish. However, this "parish" is interdenominational and ecumenical; it works for justice for all, women, men, and children, in Korea. The founding committee states that the purpose of Women Church is to realize the call "to proclaim the good news of Jesus who liberates all women who have been oppressed, to transform the Korean churches and society, and to share with suffering women."[13] Women Church of Korea was founded in 1989 to model a different ministry especially to poor, lonely, and oppressed women. It seeks to develop a strong sense of community through creative

13. "Women Church of Korea: A Community with Suffering Women," *In God's Image* June 1990, 56–57.

ways of worship, Bible study groups from women's critical point of view, mission growth groups, and pastoral counselling. Their imaginative new style of worship has created a liturgy of light, a liturgy of salt, a liturgy of water and baptism, a table of holy communion, a Korean agape meal, a liturgy of perfume or healing service, evening services, and a visiting worship that can take place in various settings according to need and request.

In short, according to its own promotional material Women Church of Korea works for the liberation of women from domestic and social oppression and for the healing of their deep pains (*han* in Korean). It neither denies nor competes with the traditional church but transforms it by working to overcome mistrust and intolerance among the Korean churches. It receives women's life experiences as gifts, seeks to hear the voices of the least, especially of lowly women, and to awaken women to see the world and their role in it as prophetic in the global context. Women Church of Korea does all this and more because it sees the hope of the Korean church in women.

9. Synod: Since theological and spiritual discernment represents one of the powers of the oppressed, it is important to compare the vision of women-church as exodus base community, predominant in the United States, with the understanding of women-church as synod, which has been developed in Europe. Although the Dutch feminist movement in the churches was the first to hold such a synod, women-synods are taking place in several other middle European countries in preparation for a European Women-Church Synod. Here women-church is not understood primarily as a liturgical base community but as a gathering of women searching in their differences for a "common way" *(syn-hodos)* toward the *ekklēsia* of women.

According to a report by Lieve Troch, in the Netherlands the term "women-church" is very much controverted.[14] The notion of women-church stimulates debates, positive and negative reactions, and controversy. It helps women's groups to explore their identity and vision. In the Netherlands the feminist movement in the churches has gathered in the ecumenical Women and Faith Movement, which is supported by feminist theologians and sometimes receives financial and organizational support from Prot-

---

14. Lieve Troch, "The Feminist Movement in the Churches in the Netherlands," *Journal of Feminist Studies in Religion* 5 (1989): 113–28.

estant and Catholic church institutions. Its local, regional, and national gatherings are characterized by discussion and debate not only on theological issues but also on questions such as race, heterosexism, division of labor, unemployment, and political and economic power.

In August 1987 a three-day national conference was held that brought women together for discussions and workshops. This meeting not only introduced the term "women-church," for the first time, but the conference title also resembled that of the Second Women-Church Conference in Cincinnati: "Women and Power, Womenpower." Lieve Troch points to the differences between the Dutch and the American meetings. Whereas the meeting in the Netherlands was a fully ecumenical gathering that was defined by challenging debate and arguments, the meeting in Cincinnati was characterized by liturgy and ritual. The women at the Women-Church Conference in Cincinnati were mostly Roman Catholic, although leading Protestant feminists were present.

The conference in the Netherlands climaxed in a day-long Women-Synod, the first Women-Synod in the history of the church.[15] Seventy women from different churches and contexts were carefully chosen to move "from various backgrounds into an ongoing feminist process." The "delegates" represented the diversity of women and women's organizations in and outside the churches. They engaged in discussions of women's differences and commonalities in order to find out how much they can share a "common way." The recommendations of the synod were addressed to women in and outside the churches as well as to policy-making structures in the churches. They have engendered discussions on a wide range of women's issues all across the country.

TOWARD A COMMON VISION

The boundaries between the discrete movements of women in the churches cannot be drawn absolutely. Rather, like the strands of a rope these different movements are intertwined. This inter-

15. Before the First Woman-Church Conference I had suggested at a meeting in Washington that women-church should plan a women's synod as an alternative to the synod of bishops in Rome. However, my suggestion was not accepted because it was deemed to be too ecclesiastical.

twinement constitutes their strength but also generates certain weaknesses. Since the women's rights movements in biblical religion insist that the "daughters of the house" have full rights of citizenship in society and church with all freedoms and responsibilities, they oscillate between the assertion of women's rights and the attempt to incorporate women into the patriarchal system. In turn feminist movements gathering under the banner of the Divine Feminine find themselves negotiating the tension between a positive affirmation of their identity as women and the feminist critique of the social construct of woman and femininity. Finally, although the women-church movement has sought to articulate an ecclesial space for women in dialectic tension to patriarchal church, it also vacillates between women's base communities as "liberated space" and women-church as a "service station" for the liturgical needs and pastoral care of women.

By pointing to the differences and difficulties in the theological and organizational incarnations of the women's movement in the churches, I do not want to suggest that one form is "orthodox" and the others are not. I only mean to point out that different feminist frameworks engender different strategies. All forms must be positioned in relation to the growing patriarchal repression in society and church that seeks to co-opt or to "demonize" feminism as "radical" or "sectarian" in order to divide women against each other. Hence a "pulling together" of all of our feminist powers and spiritual resources becomes absolutely necessary if we are to be able to propel the women's movement into the future.

Such a pulling together of the different directions and strategies in feminist theology and the feminist movement requires that we combine the analysis of ideological androcentrism and gender dualism with one of systemic patriarchy. To do so, we must relinquish a dualistic oppositional stance that projects patriarchal evil onto others and claims liberation for itself. For positively articulating such a "common vision," I have coined the expression "*ekklēsia* of women" as a hermeneutical, re/constructive, and political term.[16] Thus my own work is positioned within the strands

---

16. Since the Greek terms *ekklēsia* and *synagogē* have very similar historical-theological connotations, I alternated between these two terms at first in order to indicate the significance of the ingathering of women as the biblical people of God. Thereby I sought to articulate an inclusive feminist vision for women in biblical religions. However, the inequalities of power and the brutal history of opposition between *ekklēsia* and *synagogē* are such that my speaking of the *synagogue of women* could

of the movement "rope" that seek to articulate the women's move-ment as an "imagined community"[17] which can foster solidarity and cooperation among diverse women in the liberation struggle.

This theoretical conceptualization of the *ekklēsia* of women starts with the recognition that no "exodus" from patriarchy and no "leap into freedom" is possible for anyone as long as we live in a world of patriarchal oppression. Unless every woman is free, no woman is free; until all nonpersons are liberated, no one is liber-ated; unless patriarchy comes to an end, all religious experiences and visions remain deformed and limited by patriarchal structures. This is true not only for traditional religions but also for feminist Goddess spirituality, which is also articulated and constructed by feminists socialized into patriarchal structures and mindsets. It also applies to women-church communities that do not represent a "liberated space."

In Pauline terms: Christians are not yet "saved" once and for all from the structural evils of this world. Rather they are energized to struggle against them in the power of the life-giving Great Spirit. A critical feminist theological vision does not allow us to be "at home" in a patriarchal world of oppression; nor does it enable us to leave it behind in a leap to the "Otherworld," nor can we withdraw from the "cigar-smoking idol" of patriarchy into the "liberated space" of women-church. Rather, such a vision calls us to daily struggle and responsibility as "inside-outsiders." Not "Exodus" but "Struggle Is a Name for Hope," to borrow the title of a collection of poetry by Renny Golden and Sheila Collins. The following three theological elements are constitutive for such a vision:

1. The expression "*ekklēsia* of women" is a *hermeneutical* way and a linguistic means to communicate that women are church. When Christian feminists speak of "the church," we of-ten tacitly assume that women are here and the church is there, an entity totally different from us. Since church has for so long been identified with the male hierarchy, church has become syn-onymous with patriarchal, hierarchical structures not only in the media but also in the minds of many Christians. Yet theologically the patriarchal hierarchy may not be identified with "institutional"

---

be construed as a sign of Christian supremacy and supersessionism. Therefore, I have not developed this aspect of a "common vision."

17. For this expression see Chandra Talpade Mohanty, "Introduction," in *Third World Women and the Politics of Feminism*, ed. Chandra Talpade Mohanty, Ann Russo, and Lourdes Torres (Bloomington: Indiana University Press, 1991), 4.

church – as though the church as an institution could only be patriarchal. Conversely, it is not just the male hierarchy that makes the church patriarchal. If this were the case we would only need to replace men with women. Rather, patriarchy affects every aspect of church. Thus if women insist that "we are church and always have been church," we must also recognize that women have been and still are "collaborators" of the patriarchal church. The expression "*ekklēsia* of women" is thus not a term exclusive of men but a linguistic means to lift into public consciousness that women are church.

In addition, the expression "*ekklēsia* of women" also seeks to envision and to create a theoretical and practical space where women can articulate a different vision of church, theology, and religion from a feminist vantage point – one that can replace the dominant androcentric "commonsense" mindset into which we all have been socialized. It seeks to create an intellectual, symbolic, and spiritual universe that is not just gynecentric, but feminist-centric. The vision of the *ekklēsia* of women focuses on the empowerment of women because women as church have been excluded from the interpretation of the world and of the divine. It seeks to enable women to find their own theological voices and to become visible as church.

2. Hence the expression "*ekklēsia* of women" has *constructive and reconstructive* aims. It seeks to recover women's heritage as church. If the oppression of a people is total because it has neither an oral nor a written history, then the reconstruction of such a history of suffering and resurrection, of struggle and survival, is an important means to empower women and other nonpersons. It can correct the deformation of our historical consciousness that has eliminated women's and other nonpersons' victimizations and struggles from our ecclesial memory. I have attempted to articulate such a feminist theological reconstruction of the discipleship of equals in the first centuries of the church as a heritage and memory for women-church. Other feminist historical and theological studies have done so for different periods of Christian history. However, the attempt to reconstruct the heritage of women-church must not succumb to apologetic patriarchal interests. Nor should it be done over and against its sociocultural political contexts. Rather its "dialogic imagination" (Pui Lan Kwok) must reconstruct women's history as church as one element of women's religious-cultural heritage.

3. The expression *"ekklēsia* of women" also seeks to name a *political* reality. The Greek word *ekklēsia* means the democratic decision-making assembly of free citizens. The *ekklēsia* of women seeks to create an alternative vision and reality of church that is not patriarchal. It does not position this vision and reality on the margins of the patriarchal church but in the center of it. Like ivy it seeks to envelop the patriarchal ecclesial weeds and to replace them one by one with a different praxis. Hence women-church is not an end in itself but has as its goal to make experientially available here and now the well-being and inclusivity of the *basileia*, of God's intended world. It is not dialectically related to the institutional church as exodus-liberation church; rather it seeks to replace patriarchal institutional ecclesial power with a practice of church that sustains the creative tension between leadership and community, local and national, regional and global, diverse particularity and "common ground." Women-church is constitutive of church, regenerating and transforming the patriarchal church into the discipleship of equals.

The *ekklēsia* of women is also not identical with the feminist movements in biblical religions. Rather, it becomes tangible reality in the feminist struggles to end religious and societal patriarchal relationships of domination and exclusion. It is not one feminist group within biblical religions but seeks to inspire them for concerted action. It seeks to articulate a "common ground" for the ingathering of the dispersed "powers of the weak" in divergent liberation struggles. These powers are embodied in different feminist strategies: in being at home and in rootedness, in ecclesial leadership, in intellectual, theological, and spiritual work, in the ritual power of naming the divine in women's image, in the power of interpretation, reconstruction, decision making, and transformation.

The *ekklēsia* of women does not delineate feminist movements in biblical religion as "liberated zones" but understands them to be deeply steeped in patriarchal relations of domination. Its spirituality and vision does not deny the entanglement of feminists in patriarchy but calls for constant *metanoia* – conversion. Its spirituality not only articulates visions of liberation but also names the "deadly" dangers and failures threatening feminist movements in religion. Such failures include: psychologism, which does not allow for any critical debate, but infantilizes women by "mothering" them; anti-intellectualism, which understands serious intellectual work as male and therefore unfeminine; collectivism, which neither recognizes nor respects creative leadership but usurps it by manipulating groups; horizontal violence, which thrashes strong women who refuse to remain feminine victims; guilt-tripping and confessionalism, which repeat the litany of patriarchy's sins without ever doing any thing about them; exclusivism, which insists on women-church as the gathering of the truly true feminists and which dehumanizes men as evil; dogmatism, which draws its boundaries in doctrinal terms instead of welcoming diversity of gifts and visions.

Facing increasing patriarchal repression in society and church, the *ekklēsia* of women must develop a politics and spirituality for survival and change. We need a spirituality that understands fear, co-optation, betrayal, male violence, and feminist burn-out in political-theological terms. Feminist retreats, liturgies, and rituals should not move us "beyond anger," encouraging us to deny our pain. Rather they should renew our vision, energy, and *exousia* (power). We must keep alive the burning indignation at the destructive powers of patriarchy in women's lives – an indignation that fuels the courage and faith necessary in the struggle for survival and liberation. Only if we keep this holy anger alive will we sustain the courage and love that is necessary to work for the conversion and transformation of the patriarchal church into the discipleship of equals.

The diverse women's movements in the churches must come together as the public forum and alliance of the *ekklēsia* of women. As a "rainbow" discipleship of equals we can voice and celebrate our differences because we have as a "common ground" our commitment to the liberation struggle and vision of God's *basileia*, God's intended world and community of well-being for all. We are not the first to engage in this struggle for ending societal and ecclesiastical patriarchy. Nor are we alone in it. A "great cloud of witnesses" surrounds us and has preceded us throughout the centuries in the *ekklēsia* of women. We derive hope and courage from the memory of our foremothers and their struggles for survival and dignity, from the remembrance of our foresisters who have resisted patriarchal dehumanization and violence in the power of the Spirit.

THE ETHICS AND POLITICS OF LIBERATION: THEORIZING THE *EKKLĒSIA* OF WOMEN

```
                        HEROINES
Exceptional
          even deviant
                      you draw your long skirts
across the nineteenth century
                        Your mind
burns long after death
· · · · · · · · · · · · · · · · · ·
You may inherit slaves
                  but have no power to free them
your skin is fair
              you have been taught that light
came
      to the Dark Continent
                        with white power
that the Indians
              live in filth
                      and occult animal rites
Your mother wore corsets
                  to choke her spirit
                              which if your refuse
you are jeered for refusing
                    you have heard many sermons
and have carried
              your own interpretations
                          locked in your heart
```

332

You are a woman
              strong in health
                            through a collection
of circumstances
              soon to be known
                            as class privilege
. . . .
Your mind burns
              not like the harbor beacon
                            but like a fire
of fiercer origin
              you begin speaking out
and a great gust of freedom
                            rushes in with your words
yet still you speak
              in the shattered language
                            of a partial vision
You draw your long skirts
              deviant
                            across the nineteenth century
registering injustice
              failing to make it whole
How can I fail to love
              your clarity and fury
how can I give you
              all your due
                            take courage from your courage
honor your exact
              legacy as it is
recognizing
       as well
              that it is not enough?[1]

CONTEXTUALIZATION

I am indebted to professors Lieve Troch and Hedwig Meyer-Wilmes, organizers of a feminist international conference on "Power and Difference in Women-Church." They suggested that I prepare a paper exploring a feminist ethics of liberation in light

1. Adrienne Rich, *A Wild Patience Has Taken Me This Far: Poems 1978–1981* (New York: Norton, 1981), 33–36.

of feminist theory. The language of the paper is conditioned by such an engagement with postmodern feminist theories.[2]

I also want to express my great appreciation and gratitude for the care and enthusiasm with which the Dutch women's movement in the churches has advanced, critiqued, and extended my theological approach and work.

FEMINIST THEORY has made us conscious that the way we frame our texts and choose our rhetorical strategies raises issues of power that need to be made explicit. Most of us who are able to engage in feminist discourses or attend feminist congresses are "infinitely privileged" — to use Gayatri Chakravorty Spivak's expression — *women.*[3] We have therefore to render theoretically explicit those institutional structures and academic or ecclesial patriarchal locations from which we speak, for feminists also are always implicated in structures of dominance and subordination.

The place from which I speak and where I begin my critical intervention is U.S. feminist/womanist[4]/mujerista[5] theology. I have therefore chosen to open this critical theoretical reflection with lines from a poem by Adrienne Rich that explore the contradictory position and heritage of nineteenth-century American feminism. And I will end my deliberations with an excerpt from an address that one of these feminists, Anna Julia Cooper, gave in 1893 at the World Congress of Representative Women in Chicago. By marking and framing my text in such a way, I explicitly intend to situate my discussion of an "Ethics and Politics of Liberation" within the discourse of the women's movement in the United States. By doing so I invite readers to adjudicate whether and in what ways my

---

2. The following chapter is a revised and shortened form of this paper.

3. Gayatri Chakravorty Spivak, *The Post-Colonial Critic: Interviews, Strategies, Dialogues,* ed. Sarah Harasym (New York: Routledge, 1990), 42f.

4. African-American feminists have derived the expression "womanist" from Alice Walker. See Katie G. Cannon, *Black Womanist Ethics* (Atlanta: Scholars Press, 1988) and the round-table discussion "Christian Ethics and Theology in Womanist Perspective," *Journal of Feminist Studies in Religion* 5, no. 2 (1989): 83–112.

5. To my knowledge this expression was first used by Ada Maria Isasi-Diaz. See her article "The Bible and Mujerista Theology," in *Lift Every Voice: Constructing Christian Theologies from the Underside,* ed. Susan Brooks Thistlethwaite and Mary Potter Engel (San Francisco: Harper & Row, 1990), 261–69, and the round-table discussion in *Journal of Feminist Studies in Religion* on *mujerista* theology.

theoretical reflections contribute to their own feminist discourses in different geopolitical locations.

Although I write from within the U.S feminist movements in theology and church, I do so from the sociopolitical location of a *resident alien*. The classification resident alien positions one as insider/outsider in a double fashion: In the United States I am an "insider" by virtue of my years of residence and professional position, and at the same time I am an "outsider" in terms of language, experience, and history. When visiting Germany, I am an "insider" in terms of citizenship, culture, and language, but an "outsider" in terms of professional status and reputation as an "American" feminist theologian. In similar fashion but on quite different grounds the sociologist Patricia Collins argues that black women citizens, especially womanist intellectuals, also occupy such a "doubled" insider/outsider position.[6]

I propose here that the metaphor of resident alien is an apt figure for a feminist movement and politics of liberation within the context of Western societies and churches. If the "White Lady"[7] has been the civilizing channel and feminine "glue" in Western patriarchal domination, then white women who are fairly recent "immigrants" in academy and ministry must resist the pressures to function as tokens who are "loyal to civilization." We must refuse to produce or disperse knowledge that legitimates intellectual and religious discourses that vilify, subordinate, and marginalize women. In order to enable such a practice of "disloyalty" to patriarchal authority, feminist theory and theology must preserve its "alien" character by constituting itself as a second order reflection on women's struggles for liberation, while remaining accountable to these struggles.

Academic "gender studies" or "women's studies" often seek to overcome women scholars' position as resident aliens by integrating them into the academic system and by making them the "same." Admittedly, it might sometimes be necessary for academic feminists to establish their discourses in terms of the standards of the academy. However, such a strategy for survival needs to be seen for what it is: a collaboration with androcentric academic

---

6. Patricia Hill Collins, "Learning from the Outsider Within: The Sociological Significance of Black Feminist Thought," *Social Problems* 33 (1986): 14–32.

7. H. V. Carby, "On the Threshold of Woman's Era: Lynching, Empire and Sexuality," in *Race, Writing, and Difference,* ed. Henry Louis Gates, Jr. (Chicago: University of Chicago Press, 1986), 301–28.

discourses that are either silent about women and nonprivileged men or marginalize us as "others." In a similar fashion ordained women might see themselves forced to perpetuate ecclesiastical discourses in order to exercise their ministry. Again, such institutional collaboration must be ethically justified and adopted as a *strategic choice* for subverting patriarchal systems. Unless the risk of such a collusion with the dominant systems is consciously acknowledged, feminist theological discourses and gender/women's studies in religion are in danger of simply reproducing knowledge about Woman within the patriarchal discursive frame that marginalizes and silences other women.

Positioning ourselves as resident aliens, as insiders/outsiders in the center of church and academy, calls for an ethos and ethics of patriarchal demystification, of common political struggles, and of multicultural visions for liberation. Such an ethos not only expresses who we are, but in so doing it also constitutes who we are. It requires a persistent critique of our own projects and their ideological implications as well as vigilance toward the historical and institutional structures from within which we speak.

To articulate feminist strategies for liberation as situated in the tension *between* center and margins does not mean to advocate fixed oppositional positions. Rather, it calls for strategic choices and situation-specific deliberations that could do justice to the shifting grounds of feminist struggles for ending systemic patriarchal oppressions. Focus on the theory and practice of struggle for transforming patriarchal relations of domination and subordination provides a descriptive as well as a normative principle for a feminist ethics of liberation.

When in the last century a slave by the name of Isabella was transformed by the experience of gaining her freedom as well as by her encounter with the abolitionist freedom movement, she articulated her religious interpretation of these experiences by choosing a new name: Sojourner Truth.[8] Although the relationship and interaction of *sojourn* and *truth* can be read and correlated in different ways, their dynamic tension nevertheless names, I suggest, a sustaining vision for the practice of an ethics of struggle and transformation. If in the words of Nelle Morton "the journey is

---

8. See Bert James Loewenberg and Ruth Bogin, eds., *Black Women in Nineteenth-Century American Life: Their Words, Their Thoughts, Their Feelings* (University Park: Pennsylvania State University Press, 1976), 234–42.

home,"[9] then it is important to create feminist "spaces in between" for solidarity, empowerment, and friendship in the struggle.

FEMINIST FRAMEWORKS

From its inception feminist discourse has sought to create woman-space not on the margins but in the center of academy and church. Therefore, feminist theory has analyzed and critiqued androcentric dualisms and asymmetric binary gender constructions. Nevertheless its own discourses have tended to reproduce dualistic taxonomies and to construe them as exclusive alternatives: either reformist or radical, socialist or liberal, private or public, equal rights or liberationist, insider or outsider, psychoanalytic or sociopolitical, essentialist or constructivist, European or American, First or Third World feminists.

The religious ethicist Carol Robb has convincingly argued that the differences in the theoretical constructions of feminist ethics are due to divergent theoretical analyses of the roots of oppression.[10] Rather than summarize the various, by now well-known and well-worn typologies of feminist theoretical constructions and engage in the ongoing debate between existentialism and feminist constructivism, I will attend to the notion of patriarchy,[11] a term that my narrative has frequently deployed but whose critical elaboration has been deferred.

While some feminist theorists reject patriarchy as an ahistorical, universalizing, and totalizing concept, most utilize it as a key theoretical notion for explaining the creation and maintenance of men's sexual, social, political, and ideological power over women. In feminist theory generally, the meaning of patriarchy is no longer restricted to the power of the father over his kinship group, as is the case in social theory. Rather, the concept is developed as a means for identifying and challenging the social structures and

---

9. See Nelle Morton, *The Journey Is Home* (Boston: Beacon Press, 1985).

10. Carol S. Robb, "A Framework for Feminist Ethics," in *Women's Consciousness, Women's Conscience: A Reader in Feminist Ethics,* ed. Barbara Hilkert Andolsen, Christine E. Gudorf, and Mary D. Pellauer (Minneapolis: Winston Press, 1985), 211–34.

11. For discussion and definition of the terms see Maggie Humm, *The Dictionary of Feminist Theory* (Columbus: Ohio State University Press, 1990), 159–61; Gerda Lerner, *The Creation of Patriarchy* (New York: Oxford University Press, 1986), 231–43. In distinction to Lerner, I am not interested in the *origins* of patriarchy but in its delineation as a heuristic *historical* category.

ideologies that have enabled men in general to dominate women in general throughout recorded history.

If the notion of patriarchy is defined in terms of male-female gender dualism, then gender dualism and hierarchy become the primary oppression. The difference between male and female is held to be the basic *essential* difference of humanity. Such an essentialist position can take a constructivist turn when it argues that the binary masculine/feminine social gender system is not biologically innate or divinely ordained but socially constructed. Such ideological gender constructs keep patriarchal domination in place and make it appear "common sense" and "natural" both to women and to men. Many feminists subscribe to such a social constructivist understanding of gender whereas others tend to reassert some form of female biological determinism or a philosophical essentialism of the feminine or both.[12] In short, these feminists insist that there are two sexes: Women are women and men are men.

Whereas feminists generally agree on the deconstructive move in sociocultural gender analysis, they part company in their articulation of a positive position from which to struggle. The feminist project, nevertheless, must search for such a positive theoretical space because only a critical conceptual standpoint different from the binary gender system allows one to demystify it as cultural ideology. Although the possibility for articulating such a theoretical space, I would argue, depends on the existence of a social movement for change, the articulation of such an alternative space in turn empowers the feminist movement.

The *theories of the feminine* seek to constitute such a positive theoretical space of "otherness" or "alterity" – which is both epistemological and social – by displacing and revalorizing female essence. The Italian feminist Adriana Cavarero expresses this theoretical position succinctly:

> ... by essential and originary difference I mean that, for women, being engendered in difference is something not negotiable; for each one who is born female, it is always already so and not otherwise, rooted in her being not as something superfluous or something more, but as that which she necessarily is: female.[13]

---

12. For a problematization and discussion of the essentialist/constructivist opposition see Diana Fuss, *Essentially Speaking: Feminism, Nature & Difference* (New York: Routledge, 1989).

13. Adriana Cavarero, "L'elaborazione filosofica della differenza sessuale," in *La ricerca delle donne: Studi femministi in Italia*, ed. Maria Cristina Marcuzzo and

Three basic strategic positions that seek to articulate the feminine as alternative theoretical space have been developed in the U.S. context: The first strategy consists in a feminist appropriation and critical reformulation of Jungian psychoanalytic theory that revalorizes the repressed feminine archetype.[14] The second position, most brilliantly articulated by Mary Daly, chooses an ontological-linguistic strategy for articulating such an alterity. It is a process of be-coming instantiated by the Wild, Original, Self-actualizing woman who has made the leap from phallocracy into freedom, into the Other-world of Be-ing. This strategy is actualized by metamorphosizing woman, by the Crone and the Original Witch, by the Archaic Elemental metapatriarchally moving Woman. She is the one who represents a new species, an Original Race.[15]

The third strategy for revalorizing Woman and the feminine has recently gained high currency in U.S. feminist academic discussions. The theory of the maternal-feminine is an import from what is usually called "French feminism," but generally refers only to the work of Kristeva, Cixous, and Irigaray.[16] Although American work on the "maternal" has generally concentrated on the sociohistorical critique of motherhood as an institution, more recent multidisciplinary studies on Maternal Thinking[17] "repeatedly extol

Anna Rossi-Doria (Turin: Rosenberg, 1987), 180. See also her "Die Perspektive der Geschlechterdifferenz," in *Differenz und Gleichheit: Menschenrechte haben [k]ein Geschlecht,* ed. Ute Gerhard, et al. (Frankfurt: Ulrike Helmer Verlag, 1990), 95–111.

14. In the United States see esp. the books of Anne Ulanov and in Germany the work of Christa Mulack and the discussion of her work by Cornelia Giese, *Gleichheit und Differenz: Vom dualistischen Denken zur polaren Weltsicht* (Munich: Verlag Frauenoffensive, 1990).

15. See Mary Daly, *GynEcology: The Metaethics of Radical Feminism* (Boston: Beacon Press, 1978); and her *Pure Lust: Elemental Feminist Philosophy* (Boston: Beacon Press, 1984). For a critical assessment of Daly's work see Hester Eisenstein, *Contemporary Feminist Thought* (Boston: G. K. Hall, 1983), esp. 107–15; Ruth Großmaß, "Von der Verführungskraft der Bilder: Mary Daly's elemental-feministische Philosophie," in *Feministischer Kompaß, patriarchales Gepäck: Kritik konservativer Anteile in neueren feministischen Theorien,* ed. R. Großmaß, C. Schmerl (Hgbinnen) (Frankfurt: Campus Verlag, 1989), 56–116.

16. For a critical discussion see Donna Stanton, "Language and Revolution: The Franco-American Dis-Connection," in *The Future of Difference,* ed. Hester Eisenstein and Alice Jardine (Boston: G. K. Hall, 1980), 73–87; Gayatri Chakravorty Spivak, "French Feminism in an International Frame," in her *In Other Worlds: Essays in Cultural Politics* (New York: Methuen, 1987), 134–53; Alexandra Busch, "Der metaphorische Schleier des ewig Weiblichen – Zu Luce Irigaray's Ethik der sexuellen Differenz," in *Feministischer Kompaß,* 117–71.

17. Sara Ruddick, "Maternal Thinking," *Feminist Studies* 6 (1980): 342–67. For a critical discussion see Anne Carr and Elisabeth Schüssler Fiorenza, eds., *Motherhood:*

preoedipal unboundedness, relatedness, plurality, fecundity, tenderness, and nurturance in the name of the difference of female identity."[18]

The American reception of so-called French feminist theory and its concern with the feminine as metaphor and construct tends to reinscribe the cultural feminine, especially in the popular receptions of religious feminists: fluidity, softness, plurality, sea, nature, peacefulness, nurturance, body, life, Mother-Goddess, as antithetical to solidity, hardness, rigidity, aggressivity, reason, control, death, Father-God. Thus the theory of the maternal-feminine sometimes comes dangerously close to reproducing in the language of deconstructivism the traditional cultural-religious ascriptions of femininity and motherhood — so familiar from papal pronouncements — that now have become feminist norms.

In the 1980s feminist theory — so the history is written — moved beyond the liberal feminist criticism of the sexism of knowledge and the structural critique of patriarchal theories to the critique of phallocentrism. Autonomous feminism moved from a theory that takes sexism and women as its objects of analysis toward a critical feminist investigation of theory as hiding its masculinity. An open recognition of "the masculinity of knowledge is necessary to clear a space within the 'universal' " for women *as* women, where women's "specificity" can be articulated — or so we are told. "In exploring the language of femininity and autonomy, feminist theory has introduced the possibility of a dialogue between knowledge now accepted as masculine and the 'alien' or 'other' voice of women."[19] Yet this historical narration of the rediscovery of the feminine fails to mention — and indeed represses — that the emergence of many different feminist voices around the globe, which deconstruct the unitary essentialist understanding of Woman, represents the major achievement of critical feminist theory during the 1980s.

It is very disturbing, to say the least, that white feminist theory

---

Experience, Institution, Theology (*Concilium* 206) (Edinburgh: T. & T. Clark, 1989); Ursula Pasero and Ursula Pfäfflin, eds., *Neue Mütterlichkeit: Ortsbestimmungen*, GTB Siebenstern 577 (Gütersloh: Mohn, 1986).

18. Donna C. Stanton, "Difference on Trial: A Critique of the Maternal Metaphor in Cixous, Irigaray, and Kristeva," in *The Poetics of Gender*, ed. Nancy K. Miller (New York: Columbia University Press, 1986), 176.

19. E. A. Grosz, "The In(ter)vention of Feminist Knowledge," in *Crossing Boundaries: Feminists and the Critique of Knowledge*, ed. Barbara Caine, E. A. Grosz, and Marie de Lepervanché (Sydney: Allen & Unwin, 1988), 97,103.

and theology have become fascinated with the revalorization of the feminine precisely at the moment when major theoretical work of so-called Third World feminists is emerging. For this work not only challenges the primacy of gender oppression but also theorizes it differently.[20] Feminists of color ask white feminists to join them in redefining feminism as a theory and practice that can conceptualize "the intermeshed oppression of class, race, ethnicity and gender as unacceptable," redefining "women's liberation as part of a struggle against all these forms of oppression."[21] Such a reconceptualization of feminist theory and practice seeks to make women's *differing* experiences of multiplicative oppressions central to all feminist discourses.

To approach such a recentering of feminist discourses, I argue that feminist theology should displace the primacy of the binary gender system as its frame of reference, in which "sexual difference constitutes the horizon" (Irigaray) of our theorizing. Instead, I seek to reconceptualize patriarchy as a key analytic category of feminist theory in such a way that it can articulate the interstructuring of the conflicting oppressions of different groups of women. Rather than posit a structure of binary male-female domination, one must theorize patriarchy as a shifting pyramidal political structure of dominance and subordination, stratified by gender, race, class, sexuality, religion, nation, culture, and other historical formations of domination.[22]

European-American feminist theory and theology that uni-

---

20. See, e.g., bell hooks, *Feminist Theory: From Margin to Center* (Boston: South End Press, 1984); her *Talking Back: Thinking Feminist/Thinking Black* (Boston: South End Press, 1989); and her *Yearning: Race, Gender, and Cultural Politics* (Boston: South End Press, 1990); Paula Giddings, *When and Where I Enter: The Impact of Black Women on Race and Sex in America* (New York: W. Morrow, 1984); Cheryl A. Wall, ed., *Changing Our Own Words: Essays on Criticism, Theory, and Writing by Black Women* (New Brunswick: Rutgers University Press, 1989); Henry Louis Gates, ed., *Reading Black, Reading Feminist* (New York: Meridian, 1990); Patricia Hill Collins, *Black Feminist Thought: Knowledge, Consciousness and the Politics of Empowerment* (Boston: Unwin Hyman, 1991); Joanne M. Braxton and Andree Nicola McLaughlin, eds., *Wild Women in the Whirlwind: Afro-American Culture and the Contemporary Literary Renaissance* (New Brunswick: Rutgers University Press, 1990).

21. Caroline Ramazanoglu, *Feminism and the Contradictions of Oppression* (New York: Routledge, 1989), 128.

22. Sylvia Walby, *Patriarchy at Work: Patriarchal and Capitalist Relations in Employment* (Minneapolis: University of Minnesota Press, 1986), 5–69, understands patriarchy in a similar fashion as a complex system of interrelated social structures. These different sets of patriarchal relations shift historically and produce a different constellation of patriarchy in different times and cultures.

versalize gender difference not only mask the complex inter-structuring of patriarchal dominations inscribed in the lives of individual women and in the relationships of dominance and subordination between women; but in doing so they also hide the implication of both elite white women and Christian religion in patriarchal oppression, insofar as both elite Euro-American women and Christian religion have been the civilizing conduits of patriarchal knowledge, values, religion, and culture.

This political, philosophical, and religious rhetoric of domination and "natural" differences serves to exclude the "others" of propertied, educated elite white Eurocentric Man from democratic government, citizenship, and individual rights. The Western "Man of Reason," who claims universality and truth for himself, is not only male but also white. He is European-American, educated, wealthy, and privileged. He has defined not only elite white woman but also subordinated peoples, classes, and races as his "others" in order to subordinate and exploit them under the guise of modern Western democracy and civilization.[23] Therefore, feminist discourses must recognize that the universalist androcentric rhetoric of elite Euro-American men does not simply elaborate the dominance of the male sex, but legitimates the "White Father" or, in black idiom, the "Boss-Man" as the universal subject.

It is precisely this interconnection between the exclusion of Euro-American women and all other "nonpersons" (Gustavo Gutiérrez) from citizenship and the ideological justification of this exclusion in terms of reified "natural" differences that is in danger of being overlooked. Such an oversight takes place when some feminists construe a contradiction between so-called equal rights feminists and those feminists of the 1980s who have critiqued phallocentrism and rediscovered the "feminine."[24] This periodization of recent feminist history misapprehends two vital issues:

First, emancipatory movements, including the women's liberation movement, do *not* struggle for equal rights in order to become masculine and equal to men, but in order to achieve the rights, ben-

---

23. In addition to the work of Chakravorty Spivak see also T. Minh-Ha Trinh, *Woman, Native, Other: Writing Postcoloniality and Feminism* (Bloomington: Indiana University Press, 1989).

24. Elizabeth Gross, "Conclusion: What Is Feminist Theory?" in *Feminist Challenges: Social and Political Theory,* ed. Carol Pateman and Elizabeth Gross (Boston: Northeastern University Press, 1986), 195.

efits, and privileges of equal citizenship that are legitimately theirs but that are denied to them by democratic patriarchy. Emancipatory movements create discursive communities based on shared assumptions and values that define boundaries and validate claims to authority. In the past two decades the feminist movement in society and church has offered one of the most dynamic examples of such a counterdiscourse. It has constituted an oppositional public arena for generating critical analysis of patriarchal oppression and the articulation of feminist interests and visions. However, insofar as the feminist movement has projected itself as a single oppositional front, generating a universalizing critique of sociopolitical structures from the standpoint of *woman,* it has been in danger of constituting its feminist counterpublic as a hegemonic sphere of privileged, white Euro-American women.

Second, oppositional discourses, such as feminist theory or theology, are never independent of the dominant discourses of their patriarchal societies or institutions. Rather, resisting discourses are inextricably intertwined with dominant ones insofar as they labor under the terms of those dominant discursive formations. The recuperative theory of the feminine, for instance, already participates in the patriarchal ideology that "naturalizes" biological sex-differences as having the same significance for all women.

In collusion with dominant patriarchal ideology, such oppositional discourses on the feminine make us think that just like race, sex/gender is a "natural category." It is this "naturalization" of gender and race differences that makes them "feel real" and seem like "common sense." This naturalization is achieved by taking "biological differences and infusing them with deep symbolic meanings that affect all our lives," rather than by seeking to "denaturalize" and demystify them as sociopolitical constructs. Instead of universalizing and essentializing elite white woman as a natural gender category, a feminist strategy for liberation, I argue, must seek to clear a discursive space where women as a political collectivity can define ourselves without needing to suppress patriarchal structural divisions among us. Through dialogue, debate, and deliberation in the *ekklēsia* of women feminist theological discourses can seek to transform unitary patriarchal identity formations into creative differences and political strategies for our multisided struggles.

THE *EKKLĒSIA* OF WOMEN

I have proposed the *ekklēsia* of women as such a discursive space and critical site. A democratic articulation of the *ekklēsia* of women must be aware of capitalist patriarchy's "troubled, even antithetical relationship with democracy." Such an awareness is necessary because only an appeal to political and ethical principles that are already inherent in a society can safeguard its pluralism and difference. Yet democratic principles of freedom and equality are not to be construed as foundational terms but must be seen as signifying practices within Western patriarchal society and Christian religion.

If feminist theology conceptualizes women-church in sociopolitical terms with radical democracy as its norm,[25] then it can conceptualize the *ekklēsia* of women as a positive theoretical site from which to think about feminist political strategies. Such a theoretical frame could displace the "otherness"-construct of woman with the democratic construct of the *ekklēsia* of women, which is at one and the same time an ideal vision and a historical reality. It is already present in society and church but not yet accomplished, real but in the process of realization. Historically and politically the image of the *ekklēsia* of women, in the sense of the democratic assembly, the synod or the congress of women is an oxymoron, i.e., a combination of contradictory terms. Its translation by "women-church" as antonym to patriarchal church identifies Christian community and theology as important sites of feminist political-religious struggles for transforming Western patriarchy.

Situating feminist theorizing and theologizing within the practice and vision of the *ekklēsia* of women allows one to contextualize so-called natural gender arrangements together with those of race, ethnicity, or class. Such a contextualization reveals them as sociopolitical ideological constructs of democratic patriarchy. Women live in societies that are not simply pluralist. Rather, society is "stratified, differentiated into social groups with unequal status, power, and access to resources, traversed by pervasive axes of inequality along lines of class, gender, race, ethnicity, and age."[26]

---

25. John McGowan, *Postmodernism and Its Critics* (Ithaca: Cornell University Press, 1981), 220–80.

26. Nancy Fraser, *Unruly Practices: Power, Discourse and Gender in Contemporary Social Theory* (Minneapolis: University of Minnesota Press, 1989), 165.

Feminist theory therefore must take care not to reinscribe such patriarchal status *divisions* as positive *diversity* and pluralistic *differences* among women. Rather, a critical feminist theory and theology of liberation must "denaturalize" patriarchal racial, gender, cultural, and other status inscriptions. It can relativize them by contextualizing sexual differences with a multiplicity of other biological, social, and cultural differences in and among women.

Therefore, it is possible to create the *ekklēsia* of women as a theoretical space where the meaning of women as a sociopolitical category and collectivity can be constructed in practice and theory. In this theoretical space feminist theory can "denaturalize" social assumptions about gender, sex, or femininity by politicizing them. Such a sociopolitical deconstruction of Woman and the feminine does not need to repress or deny gender differences. Rather it must first refuse to insert them into an essentializing frame of male-female dualism; then it must refrain from endowing them with ontological symbolic significance; and finally it must take care not to universalize their historically and culturally circumscribed gendered meanings and identity formations. "The very critique of an oppositional gendered identity simultaneously affirms its prior existence – not as an ontological given but as an actually existing discursive formation, which has generated a range of diverse and contradictory political and cultural activities."[27]

Moreover, the *ekklēsia* of women must not be defined in terms of the commonality of women *as woman.* Feminist political analyses have shown that assumptions concerning the just political order that surface in feminist texts operate within the parameters established by Plato and Aristotle. Plato's notion of a politically constructed commonality that can bring a heterogeneous population together in a hierarchically organized meritocracy is mirrored in the liberal feminist rhetoric concerning negative liberty, equal citizenship, and political participation. Aristotle's conflation of equality and uniformity as the precondition for political membership in an exclusionary *polis* reverberates in the "dream of separatist" feminist solutions.[28]

The *ekklēsia* of women as a feminist political collectivity must therefore avoid the exclusive alternative of classical philosophy:

---

27. Rita Felski, *Beyond Feminist Aesthetics: Feminist Literature and Social Change* (Cambridge: Harvard University Press, 1989), 170.

28. M. E. Hawkesworth, *Beyond Oppression: Feminist Theory and Political Strategy* (New York: Continuum, 1990), 156.

either formal equality among women that does not problematize
but reinscribes the patriarchal divisions of race, class, religion,
ethnicity, or sexuality among women; *or* essentialist equality that
constitutes women's space or feminist space by excluding theoretical and practical differences. In other words, the *ekklēsia*
of women must not constitute itself *either* in terms of formal
equality based on continuing patriarchal divisions *or* on equality premised on exclusionary homogeneity. Instead, its signifying
practices must create a feminist public that seeks equality and citizenship of women by articulating, confronting, and combatting
patriarchal divisions. It does so not by declaring itself to be a liberated space of sisterhood, but by engaging feminist theoretical and
practical differences as democratic discursive practices.

Hence the *ekklēsia* of women must avoid the pitfall of cod-
ing its relationships in familial, privatized metaphors. Whereas in
the 1970s sisterhood was the preferred metaphor for expressing
feminist collectivity and solidarity, in the past decade the mother-
daughter relationship or relationality as such has been valorized.
Insofar as the feminist understanding of sisterhood is based on
the shared victimization and collectivization of women's power,
it does not recognize the power-differentials among women. Nor
does it acknowledge the power and talents of individual strong
women. The rhetoric of noncompetitive structurelessness and
group collectivity allows those women who lack self-affirmation
and power to vent feelings of inadequacy on other women, to trash
women who stand out, and to exercise traditionally feminine indirect manipulative power. It makes critical dialogue taboo and
leads to "burnout," which is caused by the repression of anger at
the lack of recognition and respect.

This rhetoric engenders guilt-tripping and an arithmetic of oppressions. It fosters the kind of white feminist confessionalism
that admits collective guilt but does not take practical steps of responsibility and solidarity. To replace the metaphor of sisterhood
with Gyn/affection or female friendship[29] and to define "friend"
in the Aristotelian sense as "another Self" also tends to reinscribe
not only the privatization of sisterhood but also the Aristotelian

---

29. Janice Raymond, *A Passion for Friends: Toward a Philosophy of Female
Friendship* (Boston: Beacon Press, 1986); Mary E. Hunt, *Fierce Tenderness: A Feminist Theology of Friendship* (New York: Crossroad, 1991), seeks to go beyond the
Aristotelian notion of friendship but nevertheless codes women-church in terms of
friendship.

conflation of equality with *sameness.* To be sure, female friendship "gives depth and Spirit to a political vision,"[30] but it cannot be constitutive of the *ekklēsia* of women as a political movement and theoretical forum.

Recognizing the power differences between women, feminist theory in the past decade has problematized and revalorized the mother-daughter relationship. Although the construct of the "symbolic mother inscribed within the horizon of sexual difference" makes it possible to name inequalities among women and permits both the exchange between women across generations and the sharing of knowledge and desires across differences,"[31] it does so by reinscribing the totalizing notion of fundamental gender-difference developed by elite white women. Rather than remaining within the psychoanalytic story of gender system, whose core it is to promote masculinity as separation from the mother and femininity as continuity with the primary bond,"[32] women-church needs to look for an interpretive frame that neither reinscribes nor denies, but that undercuts the totalizing binary sex-gender system.

In *The Bonds of Love* Jessica Benjamin seeks to explain why we accept and perpetrate relationships of domination and submission in spite of our conscious commitment to equality and freedom. Having demonstrated the complex intertwinement of familial gender and social-political dominance that produces the psychological process of complicity, she proposes *intersubjective theory* as an interpretive frame rather than simply finding a female counterpart to the phallic symbolic mode of representing desire. Intersubjective theory situates gender identity in the relation between self and other with its tension between sameness and difference. It construes this relationship not as a linear movement from oneness to separateness but as mutual recognition sustaining the tensive, paradoxical balance between them. "Thus a person could alternately experience herself as 'I a woman'; 'I a genderless

---

30. Raymond, *A Passion for Friends,* 29.

31. See Teresa de Lauretis, "The Essence of the Triangle," 25, with respect to the Italian notion of *affidamento* as a social practice of entrustment and valorization between older and younger women. This is a very important concept insofar as younger feminists tend to valorize their academic or religious "fathers" but also tend to declare their originality and independence from their feminist "mothers" because of institutional pressures. This notion must therefore be reconceptualized in institutional political rather than in essentialist terms of gender difference.

32. Jessica Benjamin, *The Bonds of Love: Psychoanalysis, Feminism, and th* *Problem of Domination* (New York: Pantheon Books, 1988), 217.

subject'; 'I like-a-man.' A person who can maintain this flexibility can accept all parts of herself and the other."[33] However, I would insist that such an intersubjective frame must also be spelled out in terms of race, class, culture, and religion. Depending on what is given primacy in terms of identity, the interrelations of these patriarchal structures will define identity differently.

According to Benjamin such an intersubjective frame is best expressed with the metaphor of "open space." The notion of "open space" applies not just to the individual but also suggests a place from which to envision the *ekklēsia* of women as an open rhetorical space bounded by its struggles against multiform oppression. The *ekklēsia* of women metaphorized as "bounded open space," rather than as sisterhood or daughterhood, can engender historical community and continuity without denying existing differences of experience and power between women and between women and men. In contrast to a single, uniform, oppositional discursive community, it is to be envisioned as a coalition of overlapping subcommunities or semiautonomous sites that share a common interest in combatting patriarchal relations of oppression. As a feminist counterpublic open space the *ekklēsia* of women as the congress or synod of women is not to be envisioned as a coherent, consistent web but rather as a heterogeneous, polyglot arena of competing discourses. In order to "denaturalize" and to "deprivatize" the collectivity of sisterhood and the mother-daughter relationship, feminist theology needs to conceptualize the *ekklēsia* of women as such a political "open space" in which Divine Presence as mutual recognition and respect of self and others, of identity and difference, of oneness and separation can be experienced.

THE ETHICS AND POLITICS OF SOLIDARITY

As the intersection of a multiplicity of public feminist discourses and as a site of contested sociopolitical contradictions, feminist alternatives, and unrealized possibilities, the *ekklēsia* of women requires a rhetorical rather than a positivistic scientific conceptualization of feminist theory and theology.[34] In order to constitute

---

33. Ibid., 113.
34. See my book *But She Said: The Rhetoric of Feminist Interpretation for ~eration* (Boston: Beacon Press, 1992).

ekklēsia as a discursive feminist public and democratic polity that defines women as a political-historical category, feminist theological discourses at one and the same time need to engage and to move back and forth between different feminist rhetorical strategies, rather than to construct them as fixed oppositional positions that exclude each other. Such feminist theological strategies are: the rhetoric of liberation, the rhetoric of differences, not just of difference, the rhetoric of equality, and the rhetoric of vision.

Feminist theoretical discourses are then best understood in the classical sense of deliberative rhetoric that seeks to persuade the democratic assembly and to adjudicate arguments in order to make decisions for the sake of the "common good" of the *ekklēsia*. Feminist theology and strategy need to adjudicate, for instance, between appeals to the universal feminine or to unanimous sisterhood and those to women's historical-political specificity with respect to class, race, gender, ethnicity, sexual preference, and so on. Such a deliberation from within particular struggles and political coalitions acknowledges the multiple discourse locations of feminist voices manifesting themselves in a diversity of intellectual constructs and competing interest groups. If different feminist discursive publics articulate feminist analyses, proposals, and strategies differently, then it becomes necessary to adjudicate between competing feminist definitions of the world and alternative constructions of symbolic universes.

Moreover, such competing feminist analyses of patriarchal reality and divergent articulations of feminist visions are not simply right or wrong. They must not be construed as dogmatic positions but as strategic practices. Feminist theology as rhetorical intervention requires public debate and deliberation if it is not to deteriorate into dogmatic sectarianism. If there is not one "orthodox" feminist strategy or one single true feminist position, but a multiplicity of feminist positions and discursive practices, then a feminist praxis must be embodied in responsible debate and practical deliberation.

The *ekklēsia* of women can make available polyglot theological discourses through which individual women might shape their own stories in conversation with the stories of either contemporary, historical, or biblical women. Such discourses must render visible again those women who have remained invisible even in feminist discourses. By insisting in its own discourses on the *theoretical* visibility and difference, for instance, of black, poor, colonial, lesbian, or working women, feminist theory and theology make comprehensible that "women" do not have a unitary essence but represent a historical multiplicity. Many African-American women, e.g., have not just African, but also Native American, diverse European, and Asian ancestry. In addition, feminist discourses must also take care not to portray one group of women, e.g., lesbians, as a monolithic and undifferentiated sisterhood with no competing interests, values, and conflicts.[35]

Such a conceptualization of the *ekklēsia* of women as a democratic, public feminist arena for practical deliberation and responsible choice does not repress but invites debates about different theoretical proposals and practical strategies. Rather than simply silence differences as divisive to the movement, it can show that differing feminist positions are related to conflicting needs of different sections of the women's movement in society and church. By constantly engendering critique, dispute, and debate the *ekklēsia* of women must search for more adequate strategies and visions for constructing a different reality and for avoiding orthodox patriarchal divisions. Clarifying and adjudicating contested concepts and proposals, it seeks to engender a long process of moral deliberation and practical solidarity in diverse and often competing struggles for liberation.

The development of an ethics of solidarity is therefore crucial for the dialogic and strategic practices of the *ekklēsia* of women because its diverse subcommunities are differentiated and divided not only by class and race positions but also by institutional locations, professional allegiances, and ecclesial affiliations that draw on a wide range of discursive frameworks.[36] Yet if a feminist discursive rhetorical practice inviting theoretical and strategical differences is not to degenerate into a paralyzing pluralism in which even the most reactionary politics can be labelled "feminist," an ethics of solidarity must make explicit the patriarchal power relations inscribed in its own discourses and strategies. Moreover, it needs to articulate feminist criteria of assessment and evaluation that privilege the theories and strategies of feminists who speak from within the experience of multiplicative patriarchal oppressions.

---

35. E. Frances White, "Africa on My Mind: Gender, Counter Discourse and African-American Nationalism," *Journal of Women's History* 2, no. 1 (1990): 87.
36. Felski, *Beyond Feminist Aesthetics*, 171.

If there is not one orthodox feminist position, but a multiplicity of feminist discursive practices, then a feminist ethics of solidarity cannot consist in uncritical assent. Instead, it must be embodied in responsible debate and practical deliberation as a dialogic assessment of the moral significance of practices as it attempts to decide not only what to do next but also what is best in a particular situation and for a particular group of women.

A feminist ethics of solidarity therefore presupposes as sine qua non the democratic agency and self-determination of women. Women must claim the right and power for interpreting their own reality and for defining their own objectives. One group of women cannot speak for all women. Conflicting interests of women must be articulated and adjudicated in public debate so that strategies of solidarity can be forged. Moreover, the *ekklēsia* of women has critically to attend to its own discursive practices in order to enable such self-determination of individual women and subgroups. Which voices are allowed to speak, which are never heard, who is to say, and what stories are still to be told and proposals to be made? In short, the *ekklēsia* of women needs to model how people can work together in complex situations without exploiting one another.

A feminist ethics of solidarity seeks to develop a complex consciousness of liberation that can analyze and challenge the multiplicative interstructuring of patriarchal oppression both in the dominant society and within movements for liberation. It appreciates the ways in which women suffering from multiple oppression have not simply been victims but have also been agents in developing strategies of everyday resistance. At the same time it needs to avoid the glorifying "othering" and stereotyping of women of color or of poor women that is so typical of Euro-American middle-class romanticism. As the democratic *ekklēsia* women of diverse groups must be able to interact as individual citizens rather than as representatives of their race, class, or sex if they choose to do so. An ethical discourse of solidarity seeks to foster respect and "befriending" between women, but it does not presuppose the "naturalized" solidarity of "womanhood" or the intimate friendship of "sisterhood."

Last but not least: If not gender and biology but historical experiences and struggles against patriarchy are constitutive for a feminist identity formation in the *ekklēsia* of women, we must carefully attend to how we tell our stories and construct women' histories. I began this lecture with a poem by Adrienne Rich in praise of our nineteenth-century foremothers' and foresisters' struggles. Moving with me through the analysis and arguments of this lecture I hope that you have become painfully aware that this story of our heroines and heritage construes feminist struggle as the struggle of elite white Euro-American women in which Native American, African slave, and lower-class European immigrant women are present only as victims. Absent and silent from the record even of such a feminist poet as Adrienne Rich are those feminists who have fought for their equal rights both as women *and* as blacks, immigrants, poor, or indigenous Americans. Into this Euro-American feminist silence the recognition of their struggles and their visions needs to be spoken if feminism is to move out of its gender captivity and complicity. Anna Julia Cooper, I suggest, expresses such a vision that leads into the "bounded open space" of the *ekklēsia:*

> Now, I think if I could crystallize the sentiment of my constituency, and deliver it as a message to this congress of women, it would be something like this: Let woman's claim be as broad in the concrete as in the abstract. We take our stand on the solidarity of humanity, the oneness of life, and the unnaturalness and injustice of all special favoritisms, whether of sex, race, country, or condition. If one link of the chain is broken, the chain is broken. A bridge is no stronger than its weakest part and a cause is not worthier than its weakest element. . . . We want, then, as toilers for the universal triumph of justice and human rights, to go to our homes from this Congress, demanding an entrance not through a gateway for ourselves, our race, our sex, our sect, but a grand highway for humanity. The colored woman feels that woman's cause is one and universal; and not till the image of God, whether in parian or ebony, is sacred and inviolable; not till race, color, sex, and condition are seen as the accidents and not the substance of life, not till the universal title of humanity to life, liberty, and the pursuit of happiness is conceded to be inalienable to all; not till then is woman's lesson taught and woman's cause won — not the white woman's nor the black woman's, nor the red woman's. . . . The acquirements of her "rights" will mean the final triumph of all right over might, the supremacy of the moral forces of reason and justice, and love in the government of the nations of earth.[37]

---

37. Lowenberg and Bogin, eds., *Black Women in Nineteenth-Century America: Their Words,* 330ff.

24

A DEMOCRATIC FEMINIST VISION FOR A DIFFERENT SOCIETY AND CHURCH

I know that Spirituality when it comes together in all the Indigenous people... will make one big circle.... Spirituality is not just held by Indigenous people. I believe that Anglo people have that too.... If they could just find that – backtrack far enough to find out where the breakdown happened. Then I think, that they could join the Circle, if they wanted... if they wanted it enough. I think that's the only way we can seek justice and find justice. Through Spirituality.

—Geneva Platero, Diné Navajo[1]

CONTEXTUALIZATION

In September 1991 the theology department of the Jesuit Universidad Iberoamericana in Mexico City sponsored a symposium on "The Function of Theology in the Future of Latin America," for which this lecture was written.[2] Expanding some of the theological ideas presented at the international congress in Louvain, which

---

1. "To Tell the Truth: An Interview with Geneva Platero by Rosalinda Catitonauh Ramirez," *Common Ground* 6 (1992): 46.
2. An expanded form has appeared in Spanish as "Visión feminista para una sociedad o iglesia diferentes," in *La función de la teología en el futuro de América Latina: Simposio Internacional,* ed. Armando J. Bravo (Mexico: Universidad Iberoamericana, 1991), 216–37.

Concilium held in 1990 on the occasion of its twenty-fifth anniversary,[3] I sought to explore a feminist theological vision for the future by locating it within the context of two contemporary phenomena. First, such a vision must be seen in the context of the global democratic struggles to reclaim the "power of the people" in the face of torture, military dictatorships, political trials, and executions. Second, a feminist theological vision must be viewed in the context of the commemoration of the five hundredth anniversary of the occupation of the Americas. The failure of social democracy and ecclesial democracy, I argue, has not been a failure of the radical democratic dream, but a failure of spiritual vision and political realization that has not yet overcome its patriarchal limitations. Only when the Western notion of democracy becomes integrated with the Native American vision and praxis of the "Grandmothers' society" will a truly democratic world-vision emerge that can overcome patriarchal exclusions and oppressions.

In support of this democratic vision — which is endangered by capitalist takeovers in middle Europe, nationalist military explosions around the world, and the political repression of the "goddess of liberty" in the name of state communism or "free world" capitalism — theology must develop a vision for the future that can engage the church in these democratic struggles, sustaining the vision of justice, liberty, and well-being for all. The feminist notion of the *ekklēsia* of women, I suggest, can contribute to the fashioning of such a radical democratic vision and spiritual center of global dimensions.

———— ❖ ————

"THE GREAT NOBEL DEBATE," which was held in Stockholm this year, brought together recipients of the Nobel prize to debate the future of the world. Some members of the panel contended that humanity has the knowledge and the will to make the world's future possible. Another group of Nobel laureates argued to the contrary that modern knowledge and technology have brought our planet to the brink of destruction. Nadine Gordimer, the South African novelist, summed up the deadlock of the debate. In this debate, "knowledge" and "spiritual vision," she argued, are blindfolded

---

3. See my contribution "Justified by All Her Children: Struggle, Memory and Vision," in *On the Threshold of the Third Millennium*, ed. The Concilium Foundation (London: 'CM Press, 1990), 19–38.

and turned away from each other. Only when knowledge and spiritual vision embrace each other will we be able to create a humane future. However, Gordimer did not point to another grave impairment of knowledge and vision. Such an impairment was reflected in the very constituency of the audience gathered in the Swedish Academy of Arts and Sciences, namely, that the group consisted primarily of white elite men.

One hundred years earlier Anna Julia Cooper, an African-American feminist, made a similar appeal to restore the wholeness of vision and imagination. But in distinction to Gordimer, she insisted that those of us who until now have been excluded from knowledge and power must be allowed to participate in such a re-visioning:

> It is not the intelligent woman vs. the ignorant woman; nor the white woman vs. the black, the brown, and the red, – it is not even the cause of woman vs. man. Nay, it is woman's strongest vindication for speaking that *the world needs to hear her voice*. It would be subversive of every human interest that the cry of one half of the human family be stifled. Woman ... daring to think and move and speak, – to undertake to help shape, mold and direct the thought of her age, is merely completing the circle of the world's vision. Hers is every interest that has lacked an interpreter and a defender. Her cause is linked with that of every agony that has been dumb – every wrong that needs a voice.... The world has had to limp along with the wobbling gait and one-sided hesitancy of a man with one eye. Suddenly the bandage is removed from the other eye and the whole body is filled with light. It sees a circle where before it saw a segment. The darkened eye restored, every member rejoices with it.[4]

Like Anna Julia Cooper and Nadine Gordimer, Geneva Platero also speaks of the "circle" of the world's spiritual vision that can be completed only when women and Indigenous peoples participate fully in its articulation. Taking up their challenge, I would submit that feminist theory and theology must provide such a different ethical and religious imagination that can serve the present and the future. It should embrace knowledge and vision precisely in order to rectify our knowledge and vision of the world – a world that is still one-sided and one-eyed to the extent that it continues to be articulated and envisioned by elite white men.

---

4. Anna Julia Cooper, *A Voice from the South*, 1892; republished in the Schomburg Library of Nineteenth-Century Black Women Writers (New York: Oxford University Press, 1988).

In particular I would like to explore here how a critical feminist theology of liberation can contribute to an ethos and imagination that foster a radical democratic religious vision. Therefore, I seek to contextualize my feminist theological analysis within radical democratic movements around the globe, movements that struggle for the liberation and well-being of all. I argue that as long as these struggles are not consciously "feminist/womanist[5]/or mujerista,"[6] they will not be able to succeed in bringing about a different future for society and church.

Obviously my perspective is conditioned and limited by my sociotheological location in the North American and European academy. I speak from within the women's movement in the churches, especially in the Roman Catholic Church. Conscious of my particular and limited perspective, I dare not directly address the situation of Latin American women and the contributions they make to theology. Nonetheless, I do hope that some elements of my analysis will speak to your own experience and situation. Although I speak here *as a woman,* the only woman speaker in fact, I do not intend to speak *about* the *woman's question.* Instead, I will focus on what a feminist liberation theological analysis can contribute to the articulation of a Catholic theology that is able to participate in creating a "Spirit-Center" for the global village.

In her 1989 Harvard commencement address, the former prime minister of Pakistan Benazir Bhutto singled out "democracy" as "the most powerful political idea in the world today" and called for the creation of an Association of Democratic Nations that could "promote what is a universal value – democracy." Members of this democratic alliance would cooperate in the protection of human rights, principles of justice, and due process.

Acknowledging the influence of Western democratic institutions, Benazir Bhutto also asserted that in her country the love of freedom and human rights "arises fundamentally from the strong egalitarian spirit that pervades Islamic traditions." She pointed to herself, a Muslim woman and prime minister of a hundred million

---

5. For the expression "womanist" see Katie G. Cannon, *Black Womanist Ethics* (Atlanta: Scholars Press, 1988) and the round-table discussion introduced by C. J. Sanders, et al., "Christian Ethics and Theology in a Womanist Perspective," *Journal of Feminist Studies in Religion* 5, no. 2 (1989): 83–112.

6. To my knowledge this expression was introduced by Ada Maria Isasi-Diaz, "The Bible and Mujerista Theology," in *Lift Every Voice: Constructing Christian Theologies from the Underside,* ed. Susan Brooks Thistlethwaite and Mary Potter Engel (San ancisco: Harper & Row, 1990), 261–69.

Muslims, as the living refutation of the argument that a country cannot be democratic because it is Muslim. Islamic religion and its strong democratic ethos, she insisted, have inspired and provided sustenance to democratic struggles, faith in the righteousness of just causes, faith in the Islamic teaching "that tyranny cannot long endure." The maxim that the progress of a society can be judged by the progress of its women, she argued, must be applied also to religion. In other words, the criterion for measuring whether a religion is democratic and liberating consists in the practical test of whether it allows for the full participation and leadership of women.

If one accepts this pragmatic criterion of the degree of women's exercise of leadership for judging whether a religion can sustain and nurture a democratic society, then a theological conference like this gathering here must seriously attend to feminist questions and analyses. A theological dialogue that is not only positioned on the threshold of the "global village," but that also takes place on the eve of the five hundredth anniversary of the "discovery" of the Americas, of Abia Yala, must articulate its theological vision for the future in a feminist key. Whether and how much Catholic theology is able to engender liberating discourses and visions for the future must be judged in light of the exclusion of women not only from decision making and sacramental powers in the church but also from the teaching "authority" of theologians.[7]

Since the control of public discourse, according to Foucault, is a principal element of maintaining authority and power, the absence of central feminist questions from public theological discourse is an important form of women's ecclesial exclusion. In light of this, it seems no mere fluke that a foreigner is the only woman speaker to address this conference. True, like many other theological institutions this university admits women as students and even as professors. But theological schools and discourses admit women only as long as we accept the androcentric norms of scholarship while respecting the boundaries of patriarchal doctrine. Considered to be a "woman's issue," feminist theologies cannot have an impact on central theological discourses. However, insofar as feminist theology is often further isolated, stereotyped, and trivialized by some liberation theologians as a "white woman's" issue, lib-

---

7. See K. B. Jones, "On Authority: Or, Why Women are Not Entitled to Speak," in *Feminism & Foucault: Reflections on Resistance,* ed. Jane Diamond and Lee Quinby (Boston: Northeastern University Press, 1988), 119-33.

eration theologies remain captive to the hegemonic patriarchal theological regime. They are not able to spell out theologically that the option for the poor is first of all an option for women. Indeed, the poor have a particular face and body, for the majority of poor and illiterate people in the world today are women and children dependent on women. Therefore, the so-called woman question must also become the central theological issue for all forms of liberation theology.

Feminist theory has elaborated that Western thought is articulated by elite white men who define rationality as masculine and therefore exclusive of women.[8] This masculine intellectual framework is the structural reason why theological institutions cannot permit women to emerge as investigating subjects and shapers of theory in our own right.[9] Neither does such a framework allow feminist questions to become a central theoretical focus of theological disciplines. Feminist work must remain marginal (or absent altogether) in the master-discourses of academy and church.

Whether and how, in the face of the overwhelmingly patriarchal character of Western tradition, culture, and religion, Christian theology can articulate a "dangerous memory" (J. B. Metz) and a liberating vision for the future in "solidarity with the historical losers" and theological nonsubjects who are women remains to be seen. As long as this question remains a "woman's" question, androcentric theological scholarship will consider it a theological nonquestion. The fundamental theological questions that propel feminist theoretical, historical, and theological work will continue to be marginalized and robbed of its potential impact on "malestream" theology as long as its patriarchal structural and ideological underpinnings are not changed. While some feminist scholars in religion contend that we should affirm our position on the margins of the academy, I have argued that a critical feminist theology of liberation must move its work into the center of democratic struggles to transform patriarchal institutions.[10] Inso-

---

8. See Genevieve Lloyd, *The Man of Reason: "Male" and "Female" in Western Philosophy* (Minneapolis: University of Minnesota Press, 1984).

9. For the discussion of "women as subjects" see Linda Alcoff, "Cultural Feminism versus Post-Structuralism: The Identity Crisis in Feminist Theory," *Sign* 13 (1988): 405–36; Sandra Harding, "Rethinking Modernism: Minority vs. Majority Theories," *Cultural Critique* 7 (1987): 187–206.

10. See, e.g., my Society of Biblical Literature presidential address "The Ethics of Biblical Interpretation: Decentering Biblical Scholarship," *Journal of Biblical Literature* 107 (1988): 3–17, and my 1988 Harvard Divinity School convocation address, "Com-

far as theology as an intellectual and ecclesiastical discipline – be it
conservative, liberal, political, or liberationist theology – shares in
the patriarchal paradigm of church and academy, it constitutes an
important site not only of theological but also of cultural-political
struggles.

What do I mean by the labels "patriarchy and patriarchal?"
The first and predominant feminist definition of patriarchy understands it in terms of gender dualism as the domination of men over
women. Since Simone de Beauvoir Western feminist theory has
focused on woman as the "other" of man. White Euro-American
feminist theory has therefore tended to understand patriarchy
as gender dualism. Correspondingly, Euro-American feminist discourses have tended to take their measure either from an idealized
and abstract notion of universal humanity whose paradigm is
elite Western man, the subject of history, culture, and religion,
or they have constructed an essentialist ideal concept of woman
that does not take into account differences among women. They
have asserted on the one hand that women's oppression is the
most fundamental oppression. On the other hand they have postulated a sisterhood among women. Women are said to be in
solidarity with each other because, as women, they share the same
experience and female nature regardless of their ethnic, racial,
cultural, religious, or socioeconomic location. While liberation
theologians have not taken seriously enough that the option for
the poor must be spelled out as the option for poor women, feminist Euro-American theories have neglected the crucial impact of
ethnicity, culture, race, socioeconomic status, or religion on the
self-understandings and lives of women.

Since feminist theology has tended to position itself within the
theoretical framework of the Western gender system, it has not
sufficiently attended to the fact that most women in the world are
not just the others of white elite men. They are also the others of
white elite women, as well as the others of the men of their own
classes, cultures, races, and religions. In the attempt to construct
an oppositional feminist discourse about woman and essential gender differences, feminist theory has tended to keep in circulation
the theories of Western philosophy and theology of gender dualism. However, these theories not only understood woman but also

mitment and Critical Inquiry," *Harvard Theological Review* 82 (1989): 1–11 (included
as chapter 20 in the present volume).

colonialized peoples and races as the "others" both of elite white men and of elite white women. The Western philosophical and theological construction of the Other has legitimated both the exclusion of elite woman from cultural, religious, intellectual, and political power and the exploitation of women and men of colonialized cultures, races, classes, and religions at the hands of elite white women and men.

This essentialist Western feminist discourse of universal generic Woman as the other of universal generic Man is more and more interrupted by the diverse resistant voices of the two-thirds of the world's women struggling for liberation from Western patriarchal colonialization and from their own indigenous patriarchal traditions. Although the configurations of patriarchy vary in different cultural-historical formations, the voices of these liberation movements around the globe insist that feminism requires a political-religious commitment not only to the struggle against sexism but also to that against racism, poverty, and militarist colonialism – all of which are integral to the structures of women's oppression. These voices have therefore rejected liberal forms of humanism and democracy whose measure is elite white man. The grounds for such a rejection of anthropological essentialism are succinctly stated by Audre Lorde:

> I am a Black woman writing in a world that defines human as white and male for starters. Everything I do including survival is political.[11]

In short, so-called Third World feminist theorists have repudiated the liberal understanding of humanism that takes elite white men as the paradigm of being human.[12] Instead, they have articulated a "new humanism" that insists on the "solidarity of humanity" and that takes the humanity and dignity of women suffering from multiplicative oppression as the standard for being human. For instance, the African-American theorist Patricia Hill Collins defines Black feminism "as a process of self-conscious struggle that

---

11. Audre Lorde in *Women's Review of Books* 6, nos. 10–11 (1989): 27.
12. For Mexico see Jean Franco, *Plotting Women: Gender and Representation in Mexico* (New York: Columbia University Press, 1989), 187: "At a congress on women's writing, Elena Poniatowska declared that women's literature is part of the literature of the oppressed. Not all of those present agreed with her. Nevertheless, the tradition of women's movements in Latin America has always been to discuss feminism in relation to other social and political issues. It is not only a question of individual liberation but of social justice and democratization." See also the contributions regarding "Rassismus, Antisemitismus, Fremdenhass, Geteilter Feminismus," in *Beiträge zur feministischen Theorie und Praxis* 13, no. 27 (1990).

empowers women and men to actualize a humanist vision of community" because they are convinced that it is "only in terms of humanism" that a technological society can redeem itself.[13]

Women of color have consistently maintained that feminism defined in terms of a monistic gender theory must be transformed into a plurivocal movement and multifocal analysis that can get hold of the complex interstructuring of sexism, racism, class exploitation, and colonialism in routinized Western patriarchy. African, Asian, Latin American, Jewish, or Palestinian women therefore have rejected the universalizing tendencies in white Euro-American feminist theory and have insisted on doing theology from the particular experiences of their struggles.

However, this intervention of so-called Third World feminism has often led to an "adding on" method of listing oppression in feminist discourses, a method that conceptualizes the patriarchal oppression of women as parallel systems of domination that divide women against each other. To list parallel oppressions, or to speak of a "dual system oppression" (patriarchy and capitalism),[14] or even of the triple oppression of women in patriarchal societies, obscures the *multiplicative* interstructuring of the systems of oppression that affect women in different social locations differently. It neglects that systems of oppression criss-cross and feed on each other in women's lives.[15]

> Simultaneous oppressions are not just multiple but multiplicative: racism is multiplied by sexism multiplied by ageism, multiplied by classism multiplied by colonial exploitation.[16]

Women of color therefore have challenged white feminists to join them in redefining feminism as a theory and practice that can conceptualize "the intermeshed oppression of class, race, ethnic-

---

13. Patricia Hill Collins, *Black Feminist Thought: Knowledge, Consciousness, and the Politics of Empowerment* (Boston: Unwin Hyman, 1990), 39ff.

14. Iris Marion Young, *Throwing Like A Girl and Other Essays in Feminist Philosophy and Social Theory* (Bloomington: Indiana University Press, 1990), 21–35.

15. Hill Collins, *Black Feminist Thought,* 225–30, speaks of race, class, and gender as three distinctive but interlocking systems of oppression as part of one overarching structure of domination. What I have named as "patriarchy" she calls "matrix of domination." A better expression for either "patriarchy" or "matrix of domination" might be "patrix of domination."

16. Deborah K. King, "Multiple Jeopardy, Multiple Consciousness: The Context of Black Feminist Ideology," *Signs* 14, no. 1 (1988): 42–72; reprinted in *Black Women in America: Social Science Perspectives,* ed. Micheline R. Malson et al. (Chicago: University of Chicago Press, 1990), 270.

ity and gender as unacceptable," redefining "women's liberation as part of a struggle against all these forms of oppression."[17]

Such a reconceptualization of feminist theory and practice seeks to make women's *differing* experiences of patriarchal oppression central to all feminist discourses. Instead of essentializing elite white *femininity* as a natural, universal gender category, a critical feminist theology of liberation conceptualizes patriarchy as a key concept of feminist analysis in sociopolitical – rather than simply in anthropological – dualistic terms.

A second theoretical perspective of feminist theology no longer takes as its frame of reference a binary gender system. Rather, this approach seeks to reconceptualize patriarchy in such a way that it can articulate the interstructuring of the conflicting oppression of different groups of women. Instead of positing a structure of binary male-female domination, this feminist perspective conceptualizes patriarchy as a pyramidal political system of dominance and subordination, stratified by gender, race, class, religious, and cultural taxonomies and other historical formations of domination.[18] Western society and church are not just male; they are patriarchal because elite, propertied, educated men determine relations of power. Only if patriarchy is understood as a complex historically changing system of domination can it be transformed.

The articulation of patriarchy as an overarching system of domination, however, must not be construed as ahistorical since patriarchy changes by aligning itself with other social and political formations in different historical contexts. Rather than elaborate here the different historical formations of patriarchy in Western societies and biblical religions, I will focus on the classic and modern formations of Western democratic patriarchy which have decisively shaped Christian faith and community.

In ancient Greece the notion of democracy was not constructed in abstract and universal terms. Rather, it was seen as rooted in a concrete sociopolitical situation. Greek patriarchal democracy constituted itself by the exclusion of the "others" who did not have a share in the land, but whose labor sustained society. Freedom and citizenship were not only measured over and against slavery;

---

17. Caroline Ramazanoglu, *Feminism and the Contradictions of Oppression* (New York: Routledge, 1989), 128.

18. Sylvia Walby, *Patriarchy at Work: Patriarchal and Capitalist Relations in Employment* (Minneapolis: University of Minnesota Press, 1986), 5-69, understands patriarchy in a similar fashion as a complex system of interrelated social structures.

they were also restricted in terms of gender. Moreover, the socio-economic realities in the Greek city-state were such that only a few select freeborn, propertied, elite male heads of households could actually exercise democratic government. Indeed, even the attempt to equalize the situation by paying the male citizens who did not have sufficient wealth of their own to participate in government could not balance out the existing tension between equality and community.

Active participation in government was conditional not only upon citizenship, but also upon the combined privilege of property, education, and freeborn male family status. As Page Dubois has succinctly pointed out:

> The ancient democracy must be mapped as an absence. We have only aristocratic, hostile representations of it.... The *demos,* the people themselves, have no voice in history; they exist only figured by others.[19]

It is this tension between the ideal of democracy and its tension with the actual sociopolitical patriarchal structures that has produced the kyriocentric (master-centered)[20] ideology that naturalizes the social differences between elite men and women, between freeborn and slaves, between property owners and farmers or artisans, between Athenian-born citizens and other residents, between Greeks and Barbarians, between the civilized and the uncivilized world. Strictly speaking, slave women and alien resident women are not *woman.* They are "gendered" not with respect to slave men or alien resident men, but with respect to their masters. Slave women are not only subordinated to and therefore "different in nature" from elite men; but they are also both different and subordinate in relation to elite women. The patriarchal pyramid of dominance and subordination engenders the belief in the natural, divinely ordained differences not only between male and female, but also between male and male and female and female.[21]

---

19. Page Dubois, *Torture and Truth* (New York: Routledge, 1990), 123.

20. By the term "kyriocentric" I mean to indicate that not all men dominate and exploit all women without difference, but that elite, Western-educated, propertied, Euro-American men have articulated and benefited from women's and other "nonpersons'" exploitation. See my article "The Politics of Otherness: Biblical Interpretation as a Critical Praxis for Liberation," in *The Future of Liberation Theology: Essays in Honor of Gustavo Gutiérrez,* ed. Marc H. Ellis and Otto Maduro (New York: Orbis Books, 1989), 311–25.

21. Elizabeth V. Spelman, *Inessential Woman: Problems of Exclusion in Feminist Thought* (Boston: Beacon Press, 1988), 19–56.

Feminist theorists have shown that Plato and Aristotle, both of whom were critics of the democratic Athenian city-state, have nevertheless articulated a philosophy of patriarchal democracy.[22] Such a patriarchal theory cannot simply be blamed on their faulty biological knowledge; rather such a theory argues why certain groups of people, such as freeborn women or slave women and men, are not capable of participating in democratic government. These groups of people are not fit to rule or to govern, Plato and Aristotle insist, on the grounds of their deficient natural powers of reasoning.

The Roman imperial form of domination and subordination was legitimated by neo-Aristotelian philosophy. Such patriarchal legitimations found their way into Christian Scriptures in the form of patriarchal injunctions to obedience and submission. Whereas, for example, 1 Corinthians 11:2–16 argues for women's subordination in terms of the neo-Platonic chain of the hierarchy of being — God-Christ-Man-Woman — the First Epistle of Peter utilizes the neo-Aristotelian pattern of patriarchal submission. Indeed, 1 Peter admonishes Christians who are servants to be submissive even to brutal masters (2:18–25), and it instructs wives to subordinate themselves to their husbands, even to those who are not Christians (3:1–6). Simultaneously it also entreats Christians to be subject and to give honor to the supreme emperor and his governors (2:13–17). The paradigm of patriarchal submission that most closely resembles the Roman imperial pyramid in Christian terms developed institutional structures in the second and third centuries that largely determined the post-Constantinian Roman church.

A similar theoretical legitimation process becomes evident again with the emergence of modern Western democracy that has articulated itself as *fraternal* capitalist patriarchy. Since capitalist democracy is modeled on the classical ideal, it has inherited some of the same ideological contradictions in that it claims that its citizens "are created equal" and are entitled to "liberty and the pursuit of happiness," while retaining "natural" patriarchal, socio-

22. Susan Moller Okin, *Women in Western Political Thought* (Princeton: Princeton University Press, 1979); Page Dubois, *Centaurs & Amazons: Women and the Pre-History of the Great Chain of Being* (Ann Arbor: University of Michigan Press, 1982); and her *Torture and Truth*; M. E. Hawkesworth, *Beyond Oppression: Feminist Theory and Political Strategy* (New York: Continuum, 1990); Hannelore Schröder, "Feministische Gesellschaftstheorie," in *Feminismus: Inspektion der Herrenkultur,* ed. Luise F. Pusch, Edition Suhrkamp NF 192 (Frankfurt am Main: Suhrkamp, 1983), 449–78.

political stratifications. In short, it is "property" and elite male status of birth and education, not simply biological-cultural masculinity, that entitled one to participate in the government of the few over the many.

To be sure, the ideology of hierarchic dualism between human-animal, male-female, and free-slave, which was articulated in terms of "natural differences" in classical philosophy, is also inscribed in the discourses of modern Eurocentric political philosophy and theology. Pablo Richard has pointed, for instance, to the intrinsic correlation between colonial domination and racist, sexist, Eurocentric domination in the writings of the colonial theologian Sepúlveda:

> It is just and natural that prudent, honest, and humane men should rule over those who are not so.... [and therefore] the Spaniards rule with perfect right over these barbarians of the New World and the adjacent islands who in prudence, intellect, virtue and humanity are as much inferior to the Spaniards as children to adults and women to men, since there exists between them as great a difference as that between wild and cruel races and races of the greatest clemency, and between the most intemperate and the continent and temperate, and I would say between apes and men.[23]

This patriarchal Eurocentric theology is also reproduced in Western political science. It is apparent in the construction of the "Man of Reason"[24] by Enlightenment philosophy, in the ideology of "femininity" or the "White Lady" in Euro-American racist discourses, as well as in the Western colonialist depiction of "inferior races" and "uncivilized savages." Like the "White Lady," Christian religion has been believed to be a civilizing force among the savages. This political, philosophical, and religious rhetoric of domination and "natural" differences turns white privileged women into the agents and mediators of colonization. It not only serves to exclude the "others" of elite white propertied, Eurocentric Man from democratic government, citizenship, and individual rights, but in so doing it exploits their labor and natural resources.

In short, patriarchal power as the power of the master and lord operates not only along the axis of the gender system but also along

---

23. Quoted from Pablo Richard, "1492: The Violence of God and the Future of Christianity," in *1492–1992: The Voices of the Victims,* ed. Leonardo Boff and Virgil Elizondo, Concilium (Philadelphia: Trinity Press, 1990), 62.

24. For this expression see Lloyd, *The Man of Reason;* Robin May Schott, *Cognition and Eros: A Critique of the Kantian Paradigm* (Boston: Beacon Press, 1988); Linda J. Nicholson, *Feminism/Postmodernism* (New York: Routledge, 1990).

those of race, class, culture, and religion. These axes of power structure the more general, overarching system of domination in a matrix- (or better patrix-) like fashion. When one shifts the analysis for investigating the axes of power along which this patrix of domination is structured, one can see not only how these systems of oppression constitute the kyriarchal social pyramid, but also how they criss-cross the identity positions offered to individuals by the politics of domination.

In sum, the Western symbolic order not only defines woman as "the other" of the Western "Man of Reason," but such an order also maps the systems of oppression in opposition to the democratic logic of radical equality for *everyone*. Nevertheless, this institutionalized contradiction between the ideals of radical democracy and their shifting patriarchal actualizations has also engendered movements for emancipation seeking full self-determining citizenship. These emancipatory struggles for equal rights as citizens in the last centuries have gained national independence, voting rights, and civil rights for all adult citizens.

However, these movements have not been able to overcome the patriarchal stratifications that continue to determine modern constitutional democracies. Instead, they were only able to create liberal democratic formations that simply made the democratic circle coextensive with the patriarchal pyramid, thereby reinscribing the contradiction between democratic vision and political patriarchal practice. In turn, liberal theorists of democracy have sought to reconcile this contradiction through procedures such as periodic voting, majority rule, proportional representation, and procedural resolution of conflicts. In the process, democratic liberty is construed merely as the absence of coercion, and democratic process is reduced to the spectacle of election campaigns. To be sure, the inclusion of elite women, together with the functional equivalents of the slaves and aliens of the ancient world, into modern procedural democracies has deepened the contradictions inherent in patriarchal democracy. A critical feminist theological vision for a different church and society must consequently locate itself in a radical democratic imagination.

In an article entitled the "Red Roots of White Feminism," Paula Gunn Allen, one of the foremost Native American feminist critics in the United States, has argued that the roots for such a radical vision are not primarily found in the democratic traditions of Ancient Greece, which had no concept of a pluralistic democracy and which never allowed women to participate in decision-making government. Rather, she argues, the feminist vision of radical democracy must be derived from tribal governments in the Americas, such as the Iroquois confederacy, in which the Council of Matrons was the ceremonial, executive, and judicial center.

> The root of oppression is loss of memory. An odd thing occurs in the minds of Americans when Indian civilization is mentioned: little or nothing.... How odd then must my contention seem that the gynocratic tribes of the American continent provided the basis for all the dreams of liberation that characterize the modern world.... The vision that impels feminists to action is the vision of the Grandmothers' society, the society that was captured in the words of the sixteenth-century explorer Peter Martyr nearly five hundred years ago. It is the same vision repeated over and over by radical thinkers of Europe and America.... That vision, as Martyr told it, is of a country where there are "no soldiers, no gendarmes or police, no nobles, kings, regents, prefects, or judges, no prisons, no lawsuits.... All are equal and free."[25]

To European eyes, Native Americans seemed gloriously free. Their willingness to share their goods, their respect for the earth and all living beings, their preference for scant clothing, their derision of authoritarian structures, their permissive childrearing practices, their frequent bathing, their living in a classless and propertyless society led to the impression of a "humanity unrestrained." Iroquois observers who traveled to France in the colonial period in turn expressed shock at the great gap between the lifestyles of the wealthy and the poor and marveled that the poor endured such injustice without rebellion. In addition, Paula Gunn Allen argues that the contact of Columbus and other Europeans with the indigenous populations of the Americas and their reports about the natives' free and easy egalitarianism were in circulation by the time the Reformation took hold.

Although the system of American democracy in many ways resembles the nonfeudal Iroquois confederacy, it is also quite different from it. According to Gunn Allen, two of the major differences consist in the fact that the Iroquois system is Spirit-based and that the clan matrons performed the executive function, which was directly tied to the ritual nature of the Iroquois democracy. "Because

---

25. Paula Gunn Allen, "Who Is Your Mother? Red Roots of White Feminism," in *Multicultural Literacy, Gray Wolf Annual*, no. 5, ed. Rick Simonson Scott Walker, 18f.

the matrons were the ceremonial center of the system, they were also the prime policy makers."[26]

LIBERATION DISCOURSES AND
STRUGGLES FOR RADICAL EQUALITY

Taking my cue from Gunn Allen, I want to argue that only the "Indianization" of classical notions of democracy, a merging of the "Grandmothers' society" with Western visions of individual freedoms and equal rights, will result in a theological vision and practice of radical egalitarianism. To position a feminist theological discourse of possibility not only on the threshold of the global polis, but also to situate it in the "discovery" of the Americas, is to call for a multivoiced *ekklēsia* or "forum" of liberation theological reflection.

Only a critical liberation-theology "rainbow" alliance (à la Jesse Jackson), I argue, can engender a radical egalitarian vision for the future of church and society.[27] Such a feminist liberation theological *ekklēsia* or congress could begin to articulate a multicultural, multiecclesial, and multireligious catholic theology rooted in particular struggles for liberation and democracy around the globe. Satellite dishes, tele-communications, fax machines, and global travel have increased our awareness of cultural interdependence and have made us neighbors in the global village. Either this global village will realize the "Grandmothers' society" and become a worldwide democratic confederation governed by interest in the well-being of all its citizens, or it will turn further into a tightly controlled and manipulated patriarchal dictatorship that concentrates all economic and cultural resources in the hands of a few and consigns the majority to a permanent dehumanized "underclass." This contextualization compels theology to re-vision Christian church and faith as a radical egalitarian discourse and movement for the liberation and welfare of all without exception.

In the past two decades the feminist liberation movement in society in general and in biblical religions in particular has offered one of the most dynamic examples of such a discourse and move-

---

26. Ibid., 219.
27. For the beginning of such an articulation see Claude Geffré, Gustavo Gutiérrez, and Virgil Elizondo, eds., *Different Theologies, Common Responsibility: Babel or Pentecost? Concilium* 171 (Edinburgh: T. & T. Clark, 1984).

ment. It has constituted an oppositional public arena in which critical analyses of patriarchal oppression have been engendered and feminist interests and visions have been articulated. However, insofar as the feminist movement has projected itself as a single oppositional front in terms of the sex/gender system, generating a universalizing critique of sociopolitical structures from the standpoint of elite Euro-American woman, it has tended to constitute its feminist counterpublic sphere as a hegemonic circle of privileged white Euro-American women.

In response to such an essentialist feminist framing of Third World feminist struggles, Chandra Talpade Mohanty, among others, has suggested that the "imagined community" of Third World oppositional struggles can be the kind of space that provides

> political rather than biological or cultural bases for alliance. Thus it is not color or sex which constructs the ground for these struggles. Rather it is the way we think about race, class and gender, – the political links we choose to make among and between struggles. Thus, potentially, women of all colors (including white women) can align themselves and participate in these imagined communities.[28]

Within a theoretical feminist framework of radical equality, liberation theologies, I have argued, can envision the *ekklēsia* as a site of emancipatory struggles for transforming societal and religious institutions. In order to indicate that they envision the "Grandmothers' society" rather than patriarchal classical democracy as the future shape of the church and the world, these theologies must linguistically qualify *ekklēsia* with "women." A radical democratic conceptualization of the "*ekklēsia* of women" is at once a historically accomplished and an imagined future reality.

Historically and politically the image of the *ekklēsia* of women, in the sense of the democratic assembly or congress of women, is a combination of contradictory terms. Such an oxymoron serves to articulate a feminist political vision that identifies Christian community and biblical interpretation as important sites of emancipatory struggles for transforming Western patriarchy. As the intersection of a multiplicity of public emancipatory discourses and as a site of contested sociopolitical contradictions, feminist alternatives, and unrealized possibilities, the *ekklēsia* of women

---

28. Chandra Talpade Mohanty, "Introduction: Cartographies of Struggle," in *Third World Women and the Politics of Feminism*, ed. Chandra Talpade Mohanty, Ann Russo, and Lourdes Torres (Bloomington: Indiana University Press, 1991), 4.

requires a rhetorical rather than a scientific conceptualization of
theology.

Several crucial rhetorical strategies have been articulated by a
critical feminist theology of liberation. The first of such strategies
is a *rhetoric of liberation,* which cannot only make the oppressive structures and power relations inscribed in biblical texts and
Christian traditions visible, but can also question "commonsense"
assumptions in theological discourses – assumptions that natural-
ize, theologize, and mystify kyriarchal relations of subordination,
exploitation, and oppression. A second strategy is a *rhetoric of differences* (not just of difference), which reflects on biblical texts
and Christian traditions from different subject-locations, investigating not only gender strategies but also those elaborated on
the basis of race, culture, class, and religion. A third strategy –
a *rhetoric of equality* – does not understand Christian truth and
revelation as preordained and unchangeable doctrine. Instead, it
sees them as constituted in and through G–d's inspiring presence
in the liberation struggles that are engendered by the "democratic" vision. Its deliberative discourses of theological reflection
cannot assume a detached and abstracting posture; rather, these
discourses must engage the particular sociopolitical locations and
concrete desires of oppressed peoples. A fourth and final strategy is a liberation theological *rhetoric of vision,* which derives
its power from the hope for the *basileia,* the commonweal of
G–d. This vision of G–d's alternative world spells well-being for
everyone. However, a rhetoric of vision is not positioned within
postmodern theories that understand postindustrial capitalist society and culture as a "system without an author" or as a "subjectless,
self-transcending, economic mega-machine." It cannot afford to
relinquish truth claims for the discourses of human dignity, equal
rights, emancipation, equality, self-determination, and well-being
for everyone.[29] Instead, it must search through biblical texts, Christian traditions, and institutional practices for religious visions that
foster equality, justice, and the logic of the *ekklēsia* rather than
that of patriarchal domination.

Such a search for the radical egalitarianism of the "Grandmothers' society" brings liberation theological discourses in direct
conflict with theological assertions that the church is not a democ-

---

29. For a trenchant critique of postmodern theory and its sociopolitical implications
from a sociotheological point of view see Gregory Baum, "Theories of Post-Modernity,"
in *The Ecumenist* 29, no. 2 (1991): 4–11.

racy and therefore cannot be reconciled with the modern history of freedom and its processes of democratization. In the wake of the French Revolution, the Vatican became the resolute champion of antimodern feudal patriarchal ideas. According to Schillebeeckx it then began to maintain such patriarchal notions "almost as a truth of faith precisely at the point where positions were involved which ran directly counter to the basic bourgeois principles" of modernity. "According to all the popes who were against the Enlightenment, the rule of Christ over all the world is put in the hands of the church hierarchy to the exclusion of anyone else, even the people of G-d."[30] Although Vatican II was a gathering in which the male hierarchy broke with its feudal past and "caught up" on its social and cultural backwardness in terms of bourgeois freedom and democracy, it did not break with its patriarchal past.

Therefore, the "ordination of women" and the religious authority and self-determination of the people of G-d have become the focal point and litmus test in post–Vatican II struggles for a democratic practice of being church. However, since theology has not yet seriously begun to question the patriarchal character of theological discourses of exclusion inscribed in Christian Scriptures, traditions, and contemporary theological frameworks, it has not been able to recover the radical democratic religious roots of the Christian church and faith.

Utilizing a feminist approach and analysis, I have sought in *In Memory of Her* to reconstruct early Christian beginnings in terms of a democratic inclusive model as the practice of the discipleship of equals. Jesus and his first followers, I have argued, stood in a long line of Sophia's prophets and witnesses. They sought for the renewal and well-being of Israel as the people of G-d. Jesus and his movement sought to realize the Jewish vision of the *basileia*, of G-d's intended society and world that is free of domination and does not exclude anyone. This "envisioned" world is already initially present in the inclusive table community, in the healing and liberating practices, as well as in the domination-free kinship community of the Jesus movement, which found many followers among the poor, the despised, the ill, the possessed, the outcast, and women of all walks of life.

Moreover, such elements of the "Grandmothers' society" can

30. Edward Schillebeeckx, *Church: The Human Story of God* (New York: Crossroad, 1990), 200ff.

still be detected in the early Christian missionary movements, which rejected the religious and social status distinctions and privileges between Jews and Greeks, women and men, slave and free-women and free men, and which understood themselves to be called to freedom. Their equality in the Spirit is expressed in alternating leadership and partnership, in equal access for everyone, Greeks, Jews, Barbarians, slaves, free, rich, poor women and men. Therefore, the proper name for this movement is *ekklēsia*, the full decision-making assembly of free citizens who are alien residents in their patriarchal societies and who constitute a different third "race." The so-called household code injunctions to patriarchal submission can only be understood when they are seen as rhetorical statements seeking to adapt the egalitarian and therefore subversive Christian movement to its Greco-Roman patriarchal society and culture.

In short, a liberation theological integration of biblical roots both with Western notions of liberty and democracy and with the radical egalitarian vision of the "Grandmothers' society," I argue, can fashion theological discourses of possibility and vision for a different church and world within the "global village." The task of liberation theologies of all colors is, then, to envision a Spirit-center for a radical democratic confederacy of global dimensions. Affirming cultural and religious particularity and pluralism, such a "rainbow" theology of liberation can claim as its "common ground" the commitment to the struggles of all nonpersons[31] for dignity, freedom, and well-being. Liberation theologies can do so, however, only if they overcome their patriarchal frameworks and articulate instead a vision of faith and hope in a liberating G–d[32] – a G–d who is "justified (*edikaiothē*) by all Her children" (Luke 7:35 Q) who struggle against patriarchal oppression and dehumanization for a radical democratic church and society.

---

31. For this expression see Gustavo Gutiérrez, *The Power of the Poor in History* (Maryknoll, N.Y.: Orbis Books, 1984). It has the advantage that it overcomes the linguistic split between "women" and "the poor, black, Asian, etc." since this linguistic convention insinuates that women are not black, poor, etc., as well as that black, poor, African, or Asian people are not women. See also E. V. Spelman, *Inessential Woman*.

32. See Sharon Welch, *Communities of Resistance and Solidarity* (Maryknoll, N.Y.: Orbis Books, 1985), 7: "...the referent of the phrase 'liberating God' is not primarily God but liberation. That is, the language here is true not because it corresponds with something in the divine nature but because it leads to actual liberation in history. The truth of God-language and of all theological claims is measured...by the fulfillment of their claims in history."